Naval biography, or, The history and lives of distinguished characters in the British Navy, from the earliest period of history to the present time

Anonymous

THE HON.ᵇˡᵉ Sᴿ GEORGE BYNG

Publish'd 1 Jan.ʸ 1800 by Edw.ᵈ Harding 98 Pall Mall.

NAVAL BIOGRAPHY;

OR,

THE HISTORY AND LIVES

OF

DISTINGUISHED CHARACTERS

IN

THE BRITISH NAVY,

FROM THE EARLIEST PERIOD OF HISTORY
TO THE PRESENT TIME.

ILLUSTRATED WITH

ELEGANT PORTRAITS,

ENGRAVED BY EMINENT ARTISTS.

———

VOL. II.

———

LONDON:
PRINTED FOR JOHN SCOTT, NO. 442, STRAND.

1805.

S. Gosnell, Printer, Little Queen Street.

Pub. April 1802 by E.Harding 98 Pall Mall

SIR RICHARD HADDOCK Knight

NAVAL BIOGRAPHY.

SIR RICHARD HADDOCK,

THE defcendant of an Effex family, of fome antiquity and confequence, was born in the year 1630.
This gentleman poffeffed, as it were, an hereditary claim
to maritime publicity*; and after a proper initiation

in

* The Haddock family was fettled a great many years preceding the
birth of fir Richard, at Leigh, in that county. This being a feaport, it
appears highly probable, they were confidered among the moft eminent
people in the place; an opinion ftrongly confirmed by feveral monumental
ancient brafs plates, on which are engraved the effigies of the perfons whofe
memories they are intended to preferve, in habiliments which ftrongly denote
their confequence, in the abftract fphere they moved in. It appears from
heraldic records, that the grandfather of fir Richard was alfo Richard; he
alfo was a native of Leigh, was a feaman, and in the year 1652 received a
reward from parliament of forty pounds, no inconfiderable fum at that day,
on account of fome public fervice rendered by him, and moft probably in a
merchant-veffel hired by government. William, his fon, became captain
of a merchant-veffel, employed in the Spanifh trade, and was afterwards
appointed to the command of the America, a fhip of war, fitted out by
order of the then newly erected republican government. His commiffion,
figned by Popham, Blake, and Deane, is ftill preferved among the family
papers, and bears date March 14th, 1650. He behaved with fo much gal-

A 2

lantry

in the fervice, is fuppofed to have been appointed to
the Dragon of forty guns, about the time of the reftoration. Little or no fubfequent mention is made of
him after this time till the year 1666, when he was
appointed by the joint commanders in chief of the
fleet, prince Rupert and the duke of Albemarle, to
be captain of the Portland. In the attack made on the
iflands of Ulie and Schelling, he commanded one of
the companies of volunteer feamen and officers, picked
out from on board the fleet for that fervice. Peace
taking place with the Dutch prefently afterwards, he
appears to have retired into a private life, from which
he did not emerge till the recommencement of hoftilities with the ftates general. He was then appointed
captain of the Royal James, the flag-fhip of the brave
though unfortunate earl of Sandwich, at the battle
of Solebay, which took place on the 28th of May 1672.
The melancholy deftruction of this unfortunate fhip,
and the premature death of the noble lord, who fo
gallantly defended it, have been already particularly
related*; and no fmall degree of obloquy was thrown
upon fir Richard, as if the accident, particularly as
far as related to the death of the earl of Sandwich,
had been principally owing to the want of exertions
on the part of fir Richard. There exift, however, the

lantry during the Dutch war, which enfued prefently after, that he was fpecially rewarded by the parliament, Cromwell being at their head, with a
gold medal. In the early part of his life he refided principally at Deptford;
but having by his meritorious fervices and induftry acquired a comfortable
competency, he purchafed lands at the place of his birth; and having quitted
public life, died there in retirement.

* Vide volume 1ft, page 408, et feq.

ftrongeft

ſtrongeſt reaſons to believe, that the calumny was totally unfounded, and the charge no better capable of being eſtabliſhed, than thoſe which we may witneſs even in our own times, are daily brought forward on a baſeleſs foundation againſt the moſt meritorious characters.

No better proof can be adduced in juſtification of ſir Richard's honour, than the eſteem in which he continued to be held by his ſovereign, after his return to England ; and as the earl of Sandwich was known to have been among thoſe moſt highly eſteemed by his prince, it is natural to conclude he ſtood perfectly juſtified, and exculpated from all attachable blame.

The king; either from whim or caprice, or from ſome of thoſe lively ſallies of wit, with which his mind ſo copiouſly abounded, and which frequently cauſed him, though it muſt be confeſſed, rather in an un- princely manner, to turn the very honours he beſtowed into ridicule, preſented ſir Richard with a ſatin cap, which he took from his own head, and put on that of the knight with his own hand. It is ſtill preſerved in the family, with a manuſcript memorandum pinned on it to this effect: " This ſatin cap was given by king Charles II. in the year 1672, to ſir Richard Haddock, after the Engliſh battle with the Dutch, when he had been captain of the Royal-James, under the command of the earl of Sandwich, which ſhip was burnt, and ſir Richard had been wounded. Given him on his return to London."

Subſequent hiſtorians indeed have treated him with a tolerable degree of candour ; and ſpeaking of ſir

Richard's

Richard's conduct on that awfully melancholy occafion, relate, that when he found the flames had fo far
prevailed on board the Royal James, as to render the
deftruction of that fhip inevitable, he went down into
the earl's cabin, and with all the earneftnefs he was
capable of fhewing, preffed him to quit the fhip, and
preferve his own life ; but finding all his attempts
at perfuafion were in vain, and that it was impoffible
for him to render any further fervice by continuing
on board, he committed himfelf to the waves, and was
prefently afterwards taken up by one of the Englifh
boats.

In the month of July, fubfequent to the battle of
Solebay, captain Haddock was appointed to the Lion ;
and fo high was the eftimation in which his abilities
were held by prince Rupert, that in the enfuing
fpring, when that great perfonage refumed the command of the fleet, in confequence of the retirement of
the duke of York from public life, captain Haddock
was efpecially chofen by him, to command under him
the Royal Charles, his flag-fhip. Nor did the honour
fhewn him by the prince on this occafion, end here ;
for his highnefs, in confequence of the damage
received by the Royal Charles, in the action which
took place with the Dutch on the 29th of May 1673,
being obliged to abandon that fhip, and remove his flag
to the Royal Sovereign, he requefted captain Haddock to accompany him in his former capacity ; and
when in confequence of the peace all opportunity of
diftinguifhing himfelf as a naval commander appeared
fufpended, his auguft patron fo earneftly recommended
him

him to king Charles, that he was appointed commiſſioner of the navy, a ſtation he continued to fill without
incurring, even in thoſe troubleſome times, either cen-
ſure or reproach, till the revolution in 1688.

On the 3d of July 1675, captain Haddock having
attended the ſovereign on one of thoſe excurſions, which
he ſo frequently made to ſome of his naval ports,
received the honour of knighthood from him at Portſmouth. Though his civil appointment as commiſſioner, might be thought likely to have taken him out
of the line of actual ſervice, yet in the caſe of ſir Richard it proved otherwiſe. On the 1ſt of June 1682
he hoiſted his flag on board the Duke, a ſecond rate,
as commander in chief of all the ſhips and veſſels
ſtationed in the Medway, or employed in the narrow
ſeas ; and in the following year, was nominated firſt
commiſſioner of the victualling-office, an employment
he continued to hold till after the revolution, that is
to ſay, 1690. In the preceding year, a conſiderable
murmur aroſe, in conſequence of the badneſs of proviſions, with which the ſhips compoſing the royal navy
were ſupplied. Sir Richard was, as a natural conſequence, in company with the other commiſſioners,
very cloſely examined before the houſe of commons.
Not the ſmalleſt circumſtance, however, capable of
attaching to him the ſlighteſt blame, appeared in the
courſe of this inveſtigation. The new ſovereign himſelf, appeared ſo ſtrongly convinced of ſir Richard's
integrity and honour, that, as a public teſtimony of that
opinion, he appointed him comptroller of the navy,

a ſtation

a ſtation he from that time continued unremittingly to fill, till the day of his death.

If, at the hour of the revolution, no mention is made of the exertions of ſir Richard Haddock, it is to be imputed to the nature of the appointment he held, which prevented any conſpicuous diſplay of thoſe talents, and active ſervices, rendered to that great event by Ruſſel, and others, apparently more zealous, though not more honeſtly ſo in the ſame cauſe, than himſelf. Few men indeed, amidſt the jarring jealouſies of contending parties, ever preſerved their character more pure, or their honour leſs ſuſpected. Though his religious principles were known to be in direct oppoſition to thoſe of James his ſovereign, that ſovereign never regarded him with an eye of ſuſpicion or diſtruſt, becauſe he knew, however the heart of ſir Richard might diſapprove the conduct of his prince, it poſſeſſed ſufficient integrity, to wreſt the ſword of treaſon from his hand, and convert rebellion, into the patriotic oppoſition of an honeſt man.

The new ſovereign, for the very ſame reaſon, felt himſelf incapable of doing otherwiſe, than admire the virtues of a man, whom he knew to be from principle his friend, though his mind revolted at all meaſures, which ſeemed to threaten the imbruement of one Briton's ſword, in the blood of his fellow-countrymen. It is evident his ſovereign conſidered his ſervices highly valuable; for immediately on the very unmerited diſgrace of the unfortunate earl of Torrington, he was joined with ſir John Aſhby and admiral Killegrew

legrew in a commiffion, appointing them joint commanders in chief. The naval campaign paffed over
without any material occurrence. Afhby and Haddock formed a junction on the 29th of Auguft, with
the fquadron, which, till that time, had been under
the orders of Killegrew alone; but after having arrived from the Streights, and put into Plymouth,
were under the neceffity of continuing in port, owing
to the whole of the French fleet having made its appearance in the Britifh channel at a very early period,
and before it had been poffible to concentrate the fleet
of England. The junction, however, being effected,
the enemy was obliged to content himfelf with retiring
into Breft; and the united fquadrons, which amounted
to forty-three fail, exclufive of the Dutch, were
immediately prepared for an expedition to Ireland.
The feafon being too far advanced, to admit a probability of any naval action taking place, the firft and
fecond rates being confidered ill fuited to keep the fea
at fo boifterous a feafon of the year, were detached
to Chatham, to be laid up in the Medway during the
winter, as was then cuftomary, and the joint admirals
removed their flag into the Kent, a third rate.

The fleet having received on board the earl of
Marlborough, with a body of five thoufand troops,
with a requifite proportion of ftores and artillery,
proceeded to Cork, off which port it arrived on the
21ft of September. After a very trivial conteft between
fome of the light fhips detached for the purpofe, and
a battery erected at the entrance of the harbour, the
earl of Marlborough and his troops were put on fhore
in

in perfect fafety, and without experiencing the flighteft
further oppofition. So affiduous was the naval department in rendering every affiftance in its power,
to his lordfhip and his troops, by the fpeedy landing
of the ftores and artillery, that the fiege was immediately commenced, and preffed with fo much vigour,
as to caufe the furrender of the city on the 29th. No
further neceffity appearing for the continuance of fo
large an armament on that ftation, and the probable
feafon for all naval encounter with the enemy being
over, a fmall fquadron was felected, and left behind
under the orders of the duke of Grafton, to oppofe
any defultory attempts that might be made on the
part of the enemy, and to affift, if required, in any
further operations during the campaign ; the main
body of the fleet returned to England, and arrived in
the Downs the 8th of October. The foregoing fervice
being performed, the joint admirals refigned the command, in which they enjoyed, at leaft the fatisfaction
of having protected their country from the affaults of
its enemies, though the cautious conduct of the latter,
deprived them of the power of earning thofe verdant
laurels, which ever attend the pomp of victory. After
this time, fir Richard being now grown infirm, and
rather advanced in years, contented himfelf with filling
the lefs laborious duties of his civil appointment, as
comptroller of the navy ; and died full of years, and
with the univerfal lamentation of all who knew him,
in the month of January 1714-15.

SIR

SIR JOHN NARBOROUGH.

In the hiftory of naval charaēters, few perfons appear better entitled to gratitude and veneration, than
thofe great navigators, who, not content with confining themfelves to the fingle duty of oppofing the
enemies of their country, are bold and patriotic enough
to undertake the arduous tafk of exploring new feas,
in the hope their difcoveries may tend to promote the
comforts, or minifter to the wants of all the reft of
the world. The name of Drake will be recorded as
a feaman, when the fame of his viētories, perhaps, may
have funk into oblivion.

The family of Narborough is of ancient ftanding
in the county of Norfolk ; and Mr. Narborough
having very early in life attached himfelf to the fea
fervice, was appointed lieutenant in the navy early in
the year 1664. After continuing in that ftation, and
ferving in it on board divers fhips, under the moft
eminent officers, for the fpace of two years, during
which time, he gave conftant and repeated proofs of
thofe abilities, which, when better known, raifed him
fo high in the opinion of the world, he was promoted,
in confequence of his gallantry difplayed during the

long,

long, and defperate action, between the Englifh and
Dutch fleets in the month of June 1666, to be captain of the Affurance, a fourth rate. His appointment to this fhip, and the poft affigned to her in the
line of battle, fully evince the high opinion entertained of his courage and conduct, by the joint commanders in chief, prince Rupert, and the duke of Albemarle. So highly and rapidly did he rife in the
opinion of his fuperior officers, that in lefs than three
years from this time, he was fpecially felected from
among all the naval officers then exifting, to command
a projected voyage of difcovery into the South Seas.
This expedition had long been in contemplation, but
owing to the preceding war, and other ftate caufes,
had been deferred as to its execution till the year 1669.
The veffels felected on this occafion, confifted only of the
Speedwell frigate, commanded by captain Narborough,
himfelf, and the Batchelor, a fmall pink, mounting
four guns, and carrying a crew of twenty men ; but
where conqueft was not intended, or looked for, un-
needed ftrength and power becomes an inconvenience
and a burden.

The object, and intention of the voyage, was to
improve the general knowledge of navigation through
the ftreights of Magellan, to explore more fully the
fouth feas, and to endeavour, if poffible, to eftablifh
a friendly intercourfe with the inhabitants of all
thofe countries, which had come to the knowledge
of Europeans, but with whom very little material
intercourfe had hitherto taken place. - The little
armament reached cape St. Mary, at the entrance

of

of the ſtreights of Magellan; on the 22d of October 1670, without having experienced any incident whatever worthy of the ſmalleſt commemoration. At this place, one of the objeçts of the voyage commenced, and an intercourſe of the moſt friendly nature, was very judiciouſly eſtabliſhed between the wild inhabitants of that coaſt; and captain Narborough, having thus far fulfilled the tenor of his inſtruçtions in that reſpeçt, proceeded to Baldivia, which he reached without danger, or difficulty a ſhort time before the enſuing Chriſtmas. The Spaniards failed not to diſplay on this occaſion, all that narrow-minded policy, which never fails to pervade their conduçt towards all perſons who paſs into thoſe ſeas, and approach their territories. Captain Narborough found the European inhabitants of thoſe diſtant ſettlements, labouring under much want of many articles, which he poſſeſſed the power of furniſhing them with; and with that liberality natural to his country, and to his profeſſion, voluntarily offered to ſupply their neceſſities to the utmoſt of his power. His friendſhip was, however, rejeçted with the utmoſt hauteur; and captain Narborough was unable to procure any intercourſe further than a ſupply of proviſions abſolutely neceſſary for the exiſtence of himſelf and his people, but which were furniſhed with a very ſcanty hand, and at an expenſe enormous and oppreſſive.

The ill humour of the Spaniards reſted not here; for the new viſitants, unuſed to ſuſpicion, and inclined on all occaſions to repay it with frankneſs, having indulged themſelves in the hope that the diſplay of one would,

would, in the end, ferve as an antidote to the deleterious qualities of the other, were fo far thrown off their guard, as to ramble near one of their forts, the governor of which, indulging his national hatred to ftrangers, made four, two of whom were officers, prifoners. On a fpirited remonftrance being made by captain Narborough, the Spaniard defended his outrageous proceeding, under the plea of an order, fpecially fent him by the governor-general of Chili, to feize the perfon of every Englifhman, who through incaution, or accident, might fall within the reach of his fangs; at the fame time this account for fuch extraordinary conduct, was accompanied by a declaration, that the captives fhould not be releafed, unlefs the Englifh veffels would come to an anchor, under the guns of the fortrefs. This infolent demand, captain Narborough had too much fpirit to comply with; but not having a force under his orders fufficient to enforce the claims of national juftice, was under the neceffity of leaving them behind with their captors. Soon after his return to England, which happened in the year 1671, hoftilities recommenced with the ftates general of the United Provinces; and captain Narborough of courfe refumed his original ftation of officer, in the main fleet employed on that occafion. He was appointed fecond captain of the Prince, the flag-fhip of the lord high admiral the duke of York. In this ftation his exertions became particularly diftinguifhed at the memorable battle of Solebay; and on the death of fir John Cox, firft captain to the flag, was immediately appointed to fucceed him in that very arduous,

and

and highly refponfible poft of fervice. The duke of York, afterwards James II. appears to have regarded him with very partial attachment and love, having made his conduct a particular object for encomium. On the retirement of his royal patron, captain Narborough quitted the home fervice, and was in the enfuing autumn removed into the Fairfax, of fixty guns, and fent into the Streights, having a fmall frigate under his orders, for the purpofe of protecting thither a fleet of merchant-veffels. He returned to England the enfuing fpring; and after having paffed through a variety of uninterefting, though highly honourable commands *, was in the month of October 1674, appointed fenior or commanding officer of a fquadron, fent into the Streights, for the purpofe of checking the depredations committed by the ftates of Tripoli, and others in the fame quarter; on which occafion a variety of honourable and fpecial privileges were inferted in his commiffion. Remonftrance proving vain, hoftilities were, as a natural confequence, reforted to; and after a conteft of two years fuccefsfully carried on by the Englifh, the Dey was not only reduced to the neceffity, of agreeing to the releafe of all the Englifh captives in his poffeffion, but was compelled to pay the fum of fourfcore thoufand dollars, in reparation of the injuries committed by his corfairs; and was moreover content to grant the Englifh, as an implied remuneration for the loffes they had fuftained, a variety of very gratifying and very valuable privileges, which

---

* In the month of Auguft 1673, he received the honour of knighthood.

4

no nation before that time had ever boasted of, or
pretended to. The object of the expedition being
thus happily concluded, sir John returned to England
with his squadron in the early part of the year 1677;
but ere he had time to enjoy, or even retire into the
comforts of domestic society, he was reappointed to a
squadron ordered into the Streights, for the purpose of
remonstrating with, or bringing to reason the Algerines. The government of the latter state was not
sufficiently awed into obedience by the exertions of sir
John Narborough, against their neighbours; they had
committed a variety of depredations, and the almost
bloodless satisfaction obtained from the Tripolines,
was not sufficient, in its weight and consequences, to
influence the minds of their Algerine neighbours, so
that they should act with candour, with equity, and
with moderation. Repeated losses, however, compelled the stubborn spirit of the barbarians, to yield to
the force of necessity, and listen to the commands of
equity, and national justice; but, their implacable pro-
pensity to warfare and depredation, though strongly
curbed, was not effectually subdued; and sir John,
after a contest of two years continuance, returned to
England with such of his ships, as were in ill condition
for further service, leaving Mr. Herbert, afterwards
earl of Torrington, as chief in command, behind him,
to finish a train of warfare which sir John himself
had so spiritedly commenced, and so successfully pursued.

After the arrival of sir John in England in the month
of June 1679, he retired from the line of active ser-
vice

vice for fome years, and was on the 29th of April 1680, appointed one of the commiffioners of the navy. This ftation he continued to fill, not only during the remainder of the reign of king Charles II. but was alfo retained in the fame poft by king James, under the new arrangement made by him for the management of the navy after his acceffion to the throne. In the month of July 1687, he was appointed admiral and commander in chief of a fmall fquadron fent to the Weft Indies, on a fpeculating expedition, in the hope of recovering a quantity of plate and bullion, known to be funk there, in confequence of the lofs of feveral valuable Spanifh veffels. In this attempt, fir John, and thofe under his command, appear to have fucceeded by dragging, and other means, almoft beyond hope. Sir John having returned to England, and dying about the period of the revolution, was buried in Knowlton church, in the county of Kent; his fon, then an infant, was immediately, and almoft among the laft acts of royalty, exercifed by king James, created a baronet, an honourable though ufelefs token of regal gratitude, inafmuch as he was unfortunately drowned, together with his brother and their truly gallant father-in-law, fir Cloudfley Shovel, on the 22d of October 1707. The eftates of fir John Narborough paffed into the family of the D'Aeths, in confequence of a marriage between fir Thomas D'Aeth, and the daughter, the fole heirefs of fir John Narborough.

ARTHUR

ARTHUR HERBERT, EARL OF TORRINGTON.

THIS brave, honeſt, though unfortunate man, was the ſon of ſir Edward Herbert, attorney-general to king Charles I. and afterwards lord keeper of the great ſeal to king Charles II. while in exile. Having attached himſelf to the naval ſervice, he was appointed a lieutenant of the Defiance, early in the year 1666 ; and experiencing a very rapid promotion, was advanced on the 8th of November following to the command of the Pembroke frigate of thirty-two guns, and one hundred and thirty men. In the very commencement of his naval career, fortune furniſhed him with an occaſion of diſplaying that truly active ſpirit of gallantry which conſtantly manifeſted itſelf during the life of this noble perſon, on every occaſion where the ſmalleſt opportunity was allowed him to exhibit it. Having been ordered to the Mediterranean ſoon after his appointment to the Pembroke, he fell in with a frigate, belonging to the ſtates of Zealand, mounting thirty-four guns, and manned with a crew of one hundred and eighty men. An action took place, which continued from two o'clock in the afternoon,

afternoon, till night put an end to the conteſt. Captain Herbert, however, nothing diſmayed, and wiſhing to try his ſtrength with the enemy fairly, carried a light during the night, but his opponent little wiſhing a renewal of the conteſt, avoided his adverſary, and under the coverture of darkneſs, made good his retreat into Cadiz, a neutral port. Secure in the protection his retreat afforded him, the Zealander arrogantly aſſumed to himſelf the falſe repùtation of having re-pulſed an inferior foe. The Pembroke was foul, and it conſequently became neceſſary that captain Herbert ſhould cauſe the ſhip to be hove down, and refitted. The Dutchman ſeizing this occaſion, redoubled his vauntings; and conſidering the hour of retribution, and puniſhment, at ſome diſtance, vented all the arro-gant boaſtings an imbecile mind was capable of, by threatening nothing leſs than certain capture, ſhould he ever again meet the Pembroke at ſea.

The requiſite re-equipment being completed, captain Herbert, perfectly ready to convince both his adver-ſary, and the Spaniards themſelves, in how cheap a light he held his impotent threats, ſtood out to ſea, and offered him battle. The Dutchman, however, moſt ſtudiouſly ſhunned a repetition of the ſame hardy encounter which he had before experienced: nor was it in the power of captain Herbert to cloſe with him ſo effectually, as to diſable him ere he effected a re-treat a ſecond time into Cadiz, where, by the law of nations he ſtood protected, and unaſſailable. Captain Herbert returned to England ſhortly afterwards, the Pembroke forming one of a ſquadron, under the

orders

orders of rear-admiral Kempthorne; which came back to England as convoy to a fleet of merchant-veffels. His voyage, however, was unfortunate; the Pembroke having been fo unlucky as to fall on board the Fairfax, a fhip of the fame fleet, received fo much damage in the encounter, as to fink before the whole of her crew could be removed. Six or feven, who were in an helplefs ftate, having funk with her; captain Herbert was taken fafely on board another fhip, and was immediately on his arrival appointed captain of the Conftant Warwick. After a feries of highly honourable fervice, and a variety of encounters with the enemy, in which he conftantly difplayed the utmoft gallantry*, he was, on the 5th of November 1677, appointed

* While captain of the Dragon, he engaged, according to an official account, publifhed at the time, for the fpace of nearly three days together, two Turkifh men of war, and bearing up clofe with one of them, with the refolution of boarding him, the officer that commanded the fhip was unfortunately fhot, which caufing a miftake at the helm, the fhip caft a contrary way, and gave an opportunity to the Turks of getting the wind, and making feveral fhot at her; but as foon as fhe tacked about, they began to fly, and by this accident happened to efcape. Captain Herbert had ten of his men hurt, and himfelf wounded in the face with a mufket-ball. On his return from the Streights in 1672, he was appointed captain of the Dreadnought; from which fhip he was almoft immediately promoted to the Cambridge, on the death of fir Fretcheville Holles, killed at the battle of Solebay; and being detached by the duke of York, together with the Briftol, to watch the motions of the Dutch, they fell in on the 22d of Ju'y, with their Eaft India fleet, which they immediately attacked. Captain Herbert boarded the largeft fhip in the fleet, but was unable to carry her off, as well from her being extremely well feconded and fupported by her conforts, as, that in the midft of the action the Cambridge herfelf took fire. Captain Herbert commanded the Cambridge during the remainder of the fecond Dutch war; and

appointed captain of the Prince Rupert; and having been ordered to the Mediterranean, was, not long afterwards honoured with a special commiſſion, conſtituting him ſecond in command of the force employed on that ſtation, under the orders of ſir John Narborough. In the month of April 1678, he very particularly diſtinguiſhed himſelf in an action with one of the largeſt corſairs belonging to the Algerines. Her commander was eſteemed, the ableſt and braveſt in their navy; and defended himſelf with the utmoſt obſtinacy to the laſt extremity. On board the Rupert, nearly thirty officers and ſeamen were killed, and forty wounded, among whom was captain Herbert himſelf, who was grievouſly burnt in the face, by the exploſion of ſome bandaleers which took fire on the quarter-deck; and on board the corſair two hundred men were killed or diſabled, ere the piratical colours were ſtruck. In the month of May, in the enſuing year, on the return of ſir John Narborough to England, the chief command was left with Mr. Herbert, who on that occaſion, was officially called in the London

in the firſt action which took place the following year between prince Rupert and the Dutch fleet, behaved with wonderful bravery; a conduct leſs remarkable in him, as it was what every body expected. His ſhip was ſo much diſabled in the engagement, as to he ſent home, even when a renewal of it was hourly expected. He is ſaid by Campbell, to have been deſperately wounded in the action. This circumſtance may, in all probability, be ſtrictly true; and we are the more inclined to believe it, from finding no further mention made of him during the remainder of the Dutch war; but no notice is taken of it in the account given of the action by prince Rupert, who has been rather particular in mentioning the names of ſuch officers as were killed and wounded.

Gazette,

Gazette, vice-admiral Herbert.' The command, however, might be rather said to have devolved, than to have been conferred upon him, and a period of fifteen months elapsed, ere he received a special commission, appointing him regularly to exercise the functions of naval commander in chief in the Mediterranean. During this interval he rendered very considerable service to the city of Tangier, which, in addition to its having been menaced, and even blockaded, was now most unusually and formidably pressed by the Moors. Admiral Herbert arriving at a very critical period of the attack, landed in succour of the besieged, a battalion of three hundred and fifty picked men from the fleet, of which he himself assumed the command as colonel, and obtained no small addition to his honour, by rendering the most eminent services as a military officer. He afterwards very spiritedly renewed hostilities against the Algerines, who appeared to have been insufficiently chastized by the punishment they had already received. So prudent, however, were his dispositions, and so able his exertions, that the government of Algiers, the most formidable of any on the whole coast of Barbary, discovered to its cost the folly of any further resistance, and sued for peace, which, except in some few casual instances of petty depredation, has continued unbroken ever since.

No further necessity existing, for the maintenance of so formidable a force in so distant a quarter, admiral Herbert returned to England, and was not long afterwards created rear-admiral of England, in a manner too, which conferred additional lustre on the honour, as the notification

fication of it will evince. "Whitehall, Feb. 4, 1683.
His Majesty has been gracioufly pleafed to conftitute
Arthur Herbert, efq. rear-admiral of England, in confideration of the many good and acceptable fervices
performed by him, as well in the inferior commands
which he hath had in his Majefty's fleets, fo more efpecially of late years in the quality, firft of vice-admiral,
and then of admiral and commander in chief of his Majefty's fleet, employed in and about the Mediterranean,
againft the pirates of Algiers, and others his Majefty's
enemies of Barbary." The ftream of honour ftill continued to flow towards him ; and, on the acceffion of
James II. to the throne, Mr. Herbert was confidered
as one of the perfons ftanding higheft in favour with
the new fovereign. He was appointed mafter of the
robes; and additional honours might, not improbably,
have been heaped on him, had not the fteadinefs of his
principles, and the inflexibility of his political integrity, expofed him to the difapprobation of the court.
Having firmly oppofed the repeal of the teft-act, a
meafure which lay neareft to the heart of James, that
prince, in punifhment of his contumacy, caufed him
to feel the whole weight of his indignation. The lord
Thomas Howard, who was a ftrenuous fupporter of
the wifhes of the court, was appointed to fucceed him
as mafter of the robes ; and, as if princely indignation
was determined to demonftrate to the world its utmoft fury, he was almoft immediately afterwards removed from the honorary ftation of rear-admiral of
England, which had been beftowed on him merely as
a proof of the honour, in which his abilities were held,

B 4   and

and not as entitling him to any special command, in order to make room for sir Roger Strickland, who boasted not, like Mr. Herbert, any deeds justly entitling him to such an honour, and possessed no pretensions to royal favour, save that of most courtier-like, antici-pating, if possible, the very wishes of his sovereign, and most strenuously supporting them, even in cases which strongly militated against the interests of his country.

Herbert, though possessing as much loyalty as any honest subject need boast, regarded his sovereign as invested only with limited, not despotic powers. No sooner did he find the interests of his country were really at stake, and that he could no longer, consistent with his conscience, support the measures of that prince, whom in his heart he wished to regard in the two-fold capacity of friend and sovereign, than he openly avowed his dissent. He repaired to Holland, among the first of those who considered the interference of a protestant power necessary, ere the restoration of those rights which James had so violently invaded, could be obtained. His opposition, however, and the whole tenour of his conduct, was not that of a factious reformer, eagerly striving to new-model a system for the purpose of profiting by public confusion, but that of a man, who wished to set his sovereign right in points, where, to speak most mildly, he so manifestly erred, and to prevent his government falling either into decay, or into disrepute. It is not, perhaps, assuming too much to assert, that, at the time admiral Herbert first offered his service to the prince of Orange, nothing

was

was further from his thoughts than the idea of depofing James. He confidered the fituation of his country as dangerous, but not irremediable ; notwithftanding fubfequent events, and the folly of his infatuated prince, rendered an extenfion of his original views ab-folutely neceffary, it is certain, that in no inftance whatfoever, did the friends of the revolution acquire greater acceffion of ftrength, than by the declaration of admiral Herbert's political opinion, and the folidity his being united with them, gave their caufe.

He was known to be temperate, prudent, honeft in the extreme, brave, without rafhnefs, popular almoft beyond example among the feamen, and all ranks of perfons, over whom he had ever held any command. The States General were fenfible of his worth, and of his value ; they hefitated not a moment in conferring on him the chief command of their fleet, with the title of lieutenant-general-admiral. Through his exertions and his advice, repeated difficulties were overcome, and abfurd propofitions rejected ; to him, all perfons attribute the foutherly courfe which the fleet of the United States, with William and his army on board, held, inftead of fteering to the northward, which, moft probably, would have ended in their deftruction. To his mild remonftrance, his wife reprefentations to the officers and feamen on board the royal fleet, was principally, if not wholly, to be afcribed that quietude with which the revolution was accomplifhed. William, among the firft acts of royalty which he exercifed, appeared ready to do all poffible juftice to the exertions, and fervices of Mr. Herbert. He continued him in

the

the command of the fleet; and, on the 8th, of March
1688-9, nominated him firſt commiſſioner for executing the office of lord high admiral. In the enſuing
month, he was ſent admiral of a ſquadron, which,
though it conſiſted of no more than twelve ſhips of the
line, was ordered to Ireland to oppoſe that of France,
under Monſ. Chateau Renaud, which amounted to forty-
four ſail, no leſs than twenty-eight of which were of
the line. Unappalled by this ſuperiotity of force,
Mr. Herbert ſhrunk not from the truſt, and he fulfilled
every object of it, with the ſame intrepidity which induced him to accept it. Moſt providentially, on the
very eve of engaging the enemy, he received a reinforcement of ſix ſhips of the line, and two or three
ſmall veſſels; ſtill, however, the diſproportion of
eighteen to twenty-eight ſhips was tremendous. The
abilities of Mr. Herbert compenſated for the deficiency:
the enemy, purſuing that line of conduct which has almoſt generally been diſplayed by them in every ſubſequent action ſince that time, conſtantly ſtrove to prevent being cloſed with, and endeavoured by the thunder
of a diſtant cannonade only, to preſent to the world an
opinion of having actually engaged, and eſcaped from
the fury of their opponents, without defeat. To attain
this end appeared their ſole aim; and, after a very indeciſive conteſt, the ſuperior foe ſtood ſo far into
Bantry Bay, where the encounter took place, as to
render it inexpedient, if not impoſſible, for Mr. Herbert to follow them, with any proſpect of obtaining
further advantage. So valuable was the preceding ſervice, and ſo ſtrongly did the nation reſound with the
praiſes

praises of the admiral, and all who were engaged in the conteſt, that king William thought it expedient to repair to Portſmouth immediately on the return of the fleet thither. He was doubly induced, in deſpite of his own natural reſerve and hauteur, to adopt this mode of conduct: popularity, he prudently conſidered the moſt likely means of conciliating the affection of a brave and independent nation, who had juſt placed him at their head, not entirely as an act of choice, but of neceſſity, ſuperadded to it. During the ſhort period of his reign, his natural ſagacity, a qualification which he was by no means deficient in, led him ſtrongly to remark the difference between the phlegmatic Hollander, and the free-ſpirited Briton, as ſubjects. He ſaw, not perhaps without concern, that the eaſieſt, if not the ſole way of acquiring the love and veneration of his new people, was, by perſuading them firſt of the greatneſs, the liberality, and ſplendour of his own mental qualities, and give them at leaſt the appearance of reſembling their own. Thus far was he perſonally concerned ; but there was a ſecond, and, if poſſible, ſtill more imperative tie, that of juſtice. Engliſh ſovereigns had been in the conſtant habit of rewarding the bravery of their ſubjects, and the ſmalleſt deviation from this general line of conduct, would have been conſidered intolerable.

On the king's arrival at Portſmouth, pecuniary rewards were beſtowed on the ſeamen, and honours on the officers. Admiral Herbert, amidſt this general diſplay of royal munificence, was, on the 29th of May 1689, created a peer of England, by the titles of baron

Herbert

Herbert of Torbay, and earl of Torrington. An addition being made to the force which the noble admiral had before commanded, by the junction of a squadron under the orders of admiral Ruffel, and feveral Dutch fhips which had reached England in the interim, and all thofe fhips which had received any material damage in the preceding encounter, being refitted as expeditioufly as poffible, his lordfhip proceeded to fea early in the month of July. The enemy, having no further enterprife in view, of fufficient importance to render the hazard of a conteft neceffary, were content to confine themfelves within their own ports, and the remainder of the year confequently paffed on without encounter.

In the month of January of the enfuing year, the firft dawnings of that ill fortune, and fcandalous ill treatment he was foon afterwards deftined to experience, made their appearance. His paft fervices, his integrity, his conftant zeal in the fupport of every meafure that could poffibly tend to the furtherance of the public good, were, in an inftant, forgotten. Some very abfurd, and ill-founded clamours were raifed in the houfe of commons, relative to the quality of the provifions with which feveral fhips had been fupplied. Thefe acquired, in a fhort time, fuch a head, that the earl of Torrington, whofe character certainly rendered him as little liable as any man in the kingdom, to the fufpicion of having connived at any impofition, or impropriety, practifed by contractors, or other perfons connected with the navy, indignantly felt it an imperative duty impofed on him to withdraw himfelf

from

from the abuse of a faction whose contumely he despised. He accordingly resigned his office of first commissioner for executing the functions of lord high admiral, but retained that of commander in chief of the fleet.

The most indefatigable exertions had been constantly made by France, ever since the commencement of the war, and most particularly so during the preceding winter, in augmentation of her marine. On the contrary, the hands of the English admiralty board had been so cramped by parsimony, the idle slumber of security, or by a narrow-minded jealousy, that the same degree of activity, appeared by no means to prevail in the arsenals of England. The crime, in some measure, carried with it its own punishment; but that, unavoidably extended to the ruin of many innocent persons, but fell so strongly on no one, as on the earl of Torrington. The French fleet made its appearance early in the month of June, augmented to the almost incredible extent of seventy-seven sail of the line, attended by a proportional number of frigates, and smaller vessels. On the other hand, when reinforced by the Dutch auxiliaries, and by every ship the noble earl could collect, many of which joined him not, till, as at Bantry Bay, the encounter was on the very point of commencing, the combined fleet of England and of Holland exceeded not fifty-six sail. Great as the disparity was, his lordship, gallantly considering that it would tend more to the advantage of his country for him to put to sea, and, at least, watch the motions of the vaunting enemy, in the hope that fortune might

afford

afford him fome partial opportunity of attacking them
to advantage ; (rather than by confining himfelf ignominioufly within the covert of his own ports, allow
them to roam unmolefted through the extent of the
Britifh channel,) quitted his anchorage, almoft on the
inftant he heard of the arrival of the hoftile fleet.
The magnitude of the truft confided to him, caufed
him to act with extreme caution ; and, it is far from
improbable, that had he been permitted to follow the
dictates of his own opinion, the fleet of Louis XIV.
feeling itfelf incapable of effecting any advantageous fervice, would have retired, after having enjoyed the fhort and empty parade, of momentarily
alarming the timid part of the Englifh nation, back to
its own ports, fufficiently fatisfied with what it
would have confidered an affertion, of its national
fuperiority.

The ill fortune of Britain decreed the matter fhould
end otherwife. There have been, in all ages, particular periods, when the ruin and deftruction of an individual has been manifeftly preferred to the welfare
of the ftate ; fuch appeared to be the cafe on this occafion. The enemies of the earl of Torrington, by
unneceffarily alarming the fears of the queen, and
offering to her certain fallacious, though, apparently,
plaufible reafons for rifking an action, even againft
fuch fearful odds, induced her majefty to fend peremptory orders to him, for engaging the enemy
without further delay. The noble admiral inftantly
took every meafure in his power to render the event
of the expected conteft, if not fuccefsful, at leaft as

little

little difaftrous as poffible : he immediately convened
all the flag and principal officers of the fleet, and communicated to them his orders. It was for them, as
well as for himfelf, to obey, and not to remonftrate.
On the 30th of June the fignal for battle was difplayed
at the dawn of day, and, as foon as the line was
formed, which was not effected till near eight o'clock,
was followed by a fecond, for clofe action. The line
formed by the Englifh fleet was nearly ftraight ; the
van and rear extending almoft as far as that of their
opponents ; but there was fome diftance between the
red or centre fquadron, commanded by the earl in perfon, and the Dutch, who being in the van, contrary to
their ufual caution, preffed forward rather too rafhly,
to engage the van of the French fleet ; there was alfo a
fecond interval between the rear of the red fquadron
and the van of the blue, which cautioufly, and very
prudently, avoided clofing in with the centre, through
the fear of having their own rear completely deftroyed.
In few words, the whole of the fpace between the rear
of the Dutch divifion, and the van of the blue fquadron, was filled up in the beft manner circumftances
would admit, by the earl of Torrington and the red,
feparated into three fubdivifions, which, by neceffarily
narrowing the different openings in the line, rendered
it lefs eafy for the enemy to break through, or throw it
into any material confufion. Oppofed to the earl lay
the French centre, and, owing to the very fuperior
number of fhips which it contained, crowded in the
extreme ; in fo great a degree, indeed, were the fhips
of the enemy huddled together, that they were compelled,

pelled, in order to avoid falling on board each other, to form themselves into a kind of femicircle, of such depth, as caufed the centre of the French fleet to be confiderably diftant, from that of the earl of Torrington and the red fquadron. To have approached the enemy under thefe circumftances, would have betrayed the moft unpardonable rafhnefs in the earl's conduct, and have expofed the whole of his fleet to the dreadful difafter of the moft unqualified defeat; inftead of which, by adopting the fyftem of action which he difplayed through the whole unequal encounter, he completely kept at bay, with eighteen or twenty fhips, double that number, of which the French centre was compofed. But the very meafure which fo defervedly entitled him to public gratitude and applaufe, became inftantly the parent of invective, ingratitude, and perfecution. It was urged by his enemies, and implicitly believed by the ignorant, that he had traitoroufly and ignominioufly hung back from the conteft, and had thereby facrificed the firft interefts of his country. The trivial damage fuftained by the red fquadron, in confequence of its peculiar fituation during the action, afforded, to the clamorous, a fufficient proof of the delinquency and cowardice of the earl. To have faved the greater part of his fleet, was madly confidered inglorious; and the Dutch, who, fo far it muft in juftice be allowed them, fought with confummate, though illtimed gallantry, took every poffible means to augment the outcry, as fome fpecies of palliative to their own lofs.

Time,

Time, however, having foftened the afperities of public prejudice, there will, perhaps, very few perfons be found, who will be uncandid enough to infift that the battle off Beachy Head was not attended in its confequences, with the moft valuable advantages to Britain, and to the revolution. The whole of the lofs fuftained by the combined fleet on this momentous occafion, did not exceed feven fhips of the line, fix of which belonged to the Dutch, and the feventh, the Ann, of feventy guns, to the Englifh. It muft be obferved at the fame time, that none of thefe veffels actually fell into the hands of the enemy, and contributed, on that account, to augment their future force, but were deftroyed in action, or afterwards, in confequence of their difabled ftate; and the greater part of their crews were happily preferved. When it is confidered, in addition to this comparatively trivial lofs, that the fleet of the enemy, in confequence of the damages it fuftained in the action, was totally incapacitated from undertaking any further offenfive operation, though their opponents had been compelled to retire; perhaps, it is not unfair to infift, that the encounter off Beachy Head, though unattended with the brilliant honours of victory, was productive of many, and thofe, amongft the moft folid advantages, which could be expected to refult from it.

Such was the conduct of the great, the brave earl of Torrington; and fuch the virulence of his enemies, that his fervices were, from that time, loft to his country. He lived ever afterwards retired from public life, and died in a very advanced age, on the 13th day of April

1716. The principal part of his fortune he bequeathed to the earl of Lincoln; not fo much, as has been elfe-where obferved, on account of any private friendfhip, for relationfhip there was none, as in confequence of his uniform, honeft, and patriotic conduct on all pub-lic queftions, and his fteady fupport of that conftitution of which the earl of Torrington himfelf was fo enthu-fiaftic a friend and admirer. The remainder he be-queathed to captain, afterwards admiral Neville, who had been his captain. This noble earl was twice mar-ried; firft to Anne, daughter of ——— Hadley, efq. and widow of ——— Pheafant, efq.; and fecondly to Anne, daughter of Thomas, lord Crew, of Stene, but had no children by either. The earldom confequently became extinct. Sir George Byng was created a vif-count by the fame title, a few years afterwards.

SIR JOHN ASHBY

WAS the son of a merchant, whose ancestors had
long pursued the same line of business, at Loweftoffe,
in Suffolk. Maritime pursuits might, therefore, be
not unnaturally considered as particularly congenial to
his disposition. He preferred, however, the service of
the state to his own private advantage, and a continuance of the unwarlike occupation practised by his
ancestors. He was appointed a lieutenant in the royal
navy in 1665, and in 1668 was advanced to the rank
of captain. Few, and insignificant, therefore, were
the opportunities which he possessed of distinguishing
himself previous to the revolution; but, in 1689, being then captain of the Defiance, he signalized himself
extremely under the orders of admiral Herbert, at the
battle in Bantry Bay. He was among those who were
particularly honoured after the return of the fleet to
England, by king William, who conferred on him the
honour of knighthood, and presented him with a very
expensive watch, superbly set with diamonds. In the
month of July following, he was advanced to the rank
of rear-admiral of the blue; and, early in the ensuing
year, to that of vice of the red. In this latter station,

C 2

he

he commanded the van of the earl of Torrington's
division, at the battle off Beachy Head, and, though it
may appear somewhat singular, had the good fortune
to be totally exempt from those attacks of invective and
obloquy, which were so illiberally vented on the commander in chief and others.

On the retirement of the earl, the command of the
fleet was left with sir John, who had received previous
instructions how to act in the event of the enemies'
approach. Considering the importance of the charge,
and the very critical state in which public affairs were
at that time considered to be, such an appointment was
certainly to be ranked as the highest honour he could
possibly have received. When, as the season advanced,
it was deemed necessary again to send the fleet to sea,
and it was resolved, for some private political reasons,
to place it under the orders of three commissioners, who
were jointly to execute the office of commander in
chief, sir John Ashby was selected as one of them *.
The leading events of the expedition, undertaken by
the joint admirals, will be found on referring back to
the life of sir Richard Haddock. During the ensuing
year, which passed over without encounter, sir John
served as vice-admiral of the red, under Mr. Russel,
afterwards earl of Orford, who had been appointed to
the chief command of the main fleet. In 1692 he was
again employed under the same commander, having been
promoted to the rank of admiral of the blue squadron.
In this capacity he was present in the ever-memorable
encounter which took place with the French fleet on

* The others were sir Richard Haddock, and admiral Killegrew.

the

the 19th of May, and, although the dead calm which
then prevailed, prevented his getting up, and joining in
the action till six o'clock in the evening, an hour after
the French line was completely broken, and in confusion, yet the spirit with which he pursued, and drove
them through the Race of Alderney, was a sufficient proof
of the success which would have attended his exertions,
had fortune been more favourable to his endeavours:
nevertheless, as the want of success is very frequently
converted into a crime, so was it in the present instance.
Burnet, in the History of his own Times, has been bold,
and, as it appears, incorrect enough, to assert, that if
sir John had strenuously pursued the fugitives, who
made their retreat good into St. Maloes, he might,
from every appearance, have destroyed them all. Other
writers however, have done better justice to his memory; Gillingwater, in his History of Lowestoffe (the
native place of the admiral), observes, that " sir John
Ashby, with the blue squadron, and some Dutch ships,
pursued the rest of the French fleet, till they had run
through the Race of Alderney, among rocks and shoals,
where the English pilot refused to follow them. Sir
John has been much censured for his conduct in this
part of the transaction, though, probably, without any
reason, since some of the ablest seamen in England were
of opinion, that nothing could be more desperate than
the flight of the French through that dangerous passage;
and that, though despair might justify them in attempting it, yet the bare possibility of success attending the
pursuit, might not be equivalent to the danger of the
undertaking."

Sir

Sir John was afterwards detached, at two different periods, to fcour the French coaft; but his diligence and activity, which even his enemies prefumed not to queftion, failed meeting with that reward he unqueftionably merited. At the clofe of the year, the malevolence of his enemies ftill continuing to vent its impotent fury againft this perfecuted man, encouraged a parliamentary inquiry into the caufes which furthered the efcape of fo great a part of the French fleet, after the action of the 19th of May. The refult was both fortunate and honourable to fir John; for, inftead of falling under that cenfure, to which his antagonifts vainly flattered themfelves he would have ftood expofed, the houfe of commons was fo perfectly fatiffied of his good conduct, throughout the feveral tranfactions in which he was concerned, and, at the fame time, fo highly pleafed with the very ingenuous anfwers which he gave to the feveral queftions propofed to him, that he was complimented by order of the houfe, and thanked through the medium of the fpeaker, for the very great fatisfaction he had afforded them, upon the points in queftion.

The ftation of commander in chief being, as had been the cafe after the battle off Beachy Head, put into commiffion, fir John was not included therein, but returned to fill his former poft, that of admiral of the blue fquadron: this reappointment he did not long furvive; having died at Portfmouth, on the 12th of July 1693.

EDWARD

E Harding ex

THE RIGHT HON:ELE EDWARD EARL of ORFORD

Published 1. Nov.r 1799. by Edw.d Harding 98 Pall Mall

EDWARD RUSSEL, EARL OF ORFORD.

THIS celebrated character, far better known, however, to the world under the name of admiral Ruffel, than by the title which he acquired in the latter part of his life, was the fon of Edward Ruffel, fourth fon of Francis, earl of Bedford, by Penelope his wife, daughter of Mofes Hill, efq. of Ailefbury, in the kingdom of Ireland, and widow of fir William Brooke, knight. His own difpofition, and the wifhes of his father, leading him to make choice of the fea as a profeffion, he entered into the naval fervice as a volunteer, at a very early age; and, aided by the fplendour of his birth, and high rank of his family, was, when only nineteen years old, advanced to be a lieutenant. This promotion took place in the year 1671, and he remained without any further elevation for a period of nine years, a circumftance which, not improbably, contributed, in no flight degree, to the irreconcilable hatred he afterwards appeared to difplay towards the houfe of Stuart. At length, in the year 1680, he was raifed to the rank of captain in the navy, and appointed to the Newcaftle; but there is a complete chafm in his naval

C 4   life,

life, from this time till after the revolution had taken
place, when he was, in a very extraordinary manner, in reward for his political fervices, appointed by
king William to be admiral of the blue fquadron.
We are, probably, about to fay that, which may be
confidered by fome, a fpecies of literary treafon againft
the memory of a great man; and yet, a candid inveftigation of the leading events of this noble perfon's
life, will, probably, in a great meafure, exculpate us
from any charge of impropriety, when we affert, that
he appeared much better deftined by nature to manage
the political intrigues of a cabinet, than, (however fortunate he might prove in his latter occupation,) to
command a fleet. Poffeffed of the moft engaging and
polifhed manners, no man was ever better verfed in
the art of drawing over to his own party, not only
thofe whofe principles were wavering, and indetermi-
nate, but even all others who poffeffed not firmnefs
enough to adhere to one opinion unchangeably, and
who could hear, unmoved, the moft fpecious arguments, without being allured or fafcinated by them.

The oppofition of Mr. Ruffel to the meafures of
king James, was not merely that of a zealous defender
of the rights of his countrymen againft the affaults of
defpotifm, but it exceeded, in many inftances, thofe
limits which cuftom, and decency have generally prefcribed to what is called fair oppofition. As an inftance of this, forgetting his high rank, he condefcended
to become the mere meffenger between the various
parties and cabals, which were formed for a confiderable
time preparatory to the revolution. He was the confidential

fidential perfon, to whom the arrangement of all the
private negotiations, ftipulations, and intrigues between all thofe perfons who, on that occafion, affumed
the character of LEADERS, was intrufted; and, certainly,
no perfon could fill fo difficult a ftation with greater
addrefs and fuccefs. Many writers, whom prejudice
perhaps has irritated againft him, have been extremely
fond of affigning revenge as the caufe of his very early
diflike and oppofition to king James; but this affertion
is by no means fo fufficiently eftablifhed as to obtain
implicit credit. As the greateft men, in all ages, have
at different times poffeffed the greateft foibles, fo did
Mr. Ruffel, in many inftances, difplay a ficklenefs,
even in political concerns, connected with the revolution, which, it is impoffible any man, acting under
the impulfe of revenge only, could poffefs.

It was fingularly hard upon this noble perfon, that
after having condefcended to affume a character, which
men, lefs fanguine in the caufe than himfelf, would
have thought derogatory to their rank, and, after he
had by his own perfonal activity, contributed more to
overturn the defpotifm of the houfe of Stuart, than
any individual who then exifted, he fhould have been
fufpected, and moft ftrongly too, of wifhing to reftore
that ancient order of things, which he had before fo
ftrenuoufly laboured to overturn. Yet all thefe feeming
contradictions are very eafily reconcilable to one leading feature in the human mind, which it appears pretty
evident Mr. Ruffel poffeffed to a very eminent degree—
ambition. It were unfair to affign this as a caufe,
without producing reafons in fupport of doing fo.
The

The idea, his rank and profeſſional merit were ſlighted, was fully ſufficient to rouſe his anger againſt Charles, and his brother James, for the ſuppoſed neglect. The mal-adminiſtration from the latter, furniſhed him with the plauſible means of puniſhing it. He embraced the opportunity, and was ſuccefsful. Lofty in the appreciation of his own deſerts, it was by no means unnatural for him to think them inſufficiently rewarded by his new ſovereign ; he ſaw himſelf a plain commoner, acting in a ſubordinate naval command, while Mr. Herbert, who had been (certainly not injuriouſly, as he was his ſenior officer,) inveſted with the rank of admiral in chief, ſtood higheſt in the favour of the ſovereign, by whom he had been ennobled, for his meritorious ſervices againſt the natural enemies of his country. Hence aroſe jealouſy, and that vehemently rancorous ſpirit which cauſed him to exert every effort of his mind, in the hopes of cruſhing his rival : he was too ſuccefsful ; and after a very ſhort interval found his ambitious views in part gratified, on being raiſed to the rank of admiral of the fleet.

In the year 1692, fortune, and the ill ſtars of Louis XIV. aided by the indeciſive counſels which then prevailed in France, afforded him as eaſy an opportunity of acquiring fame by the exertions of others, as perhaps ever fell to the lot of any admiral or general in the univerſe. National pride, and poſitive vanity, for we know no better reaſons to aſſign for the extraordinary conduct of the count de Tourville, threw that admiral into nearly the ſame ſituation into which lord Torrington had been precipitated, immediately

immediately previous to the battle off Beachy Head.
The force of the enemy has been varioufly reprefented ;
fome afferting their number to have amounted to no more
than forty-four fail of the line, while others, in their
eagernefs to diminifh the difparity of ftrength, have aug-
mented them to fixty-three. The former, however, appears to have been the proper ftatement. The divifion from Toulon, which would have raifed the
fleet up to the higher number, certainly had not
joined. The combined fleets of England, and the
United States, fent forth to oppofe this armament,
amounted to no lefs than ninety-nine ships of the line.
Againft this mighty force the count de Tourville
having been hardy enough to make head, however rafh
the attempt might be, certainly difplayed every noble
trait of character that could adorn a great and able
commander. He contended the whole day, and at laft
made good his retreat, with the lofs of not more than
one fhip in the encounter itfelf, which blew up by
accident. In fhort, if the retreat had been managed
with as much dexterity as the action was fought with
gallantry, few nations have ever acquired greater naval
honour than might then, with juftice, have been boafted
of by France ; indeed we appear loft in amaze at a
conduct fo very extraordinary as that of the French
admiral. Several hiftorians have attempted to account
for it, but we know not on what good authority, in
the verfatility of Mr. Ruffel, and in the hope entertained as well by the French themfelves, as by the
exiled James, that the unfatisfied mind of the former
would, in conjunction with divers others, high in command

mand in the combined fleet, defert the standard of the
new fovereign, and again fupport the caufe of their
former mafter, whom misfortune, it was hoped, had
reclaimed, and whofe errors were confidered to have
been fufficiently punifhed. Whether fuch was the
real intention, or what folid grounds, thofe hiftorians,
who have been hardy enough to advance the fact, poffeffed in fupport of it, we know not. One point,
however, is certain; the execution of the project, if
fuch exifted, did not take place. Mr. Ruffel, in his
account of the engagement, declares the French fleet to
have been actually beaten by a lefs number of Britifh
fhips, than compofed the armament of the former, and
accounts for this circumftance by attributing it to the
calm, which then prevailed, and prevented a greater
number of the Britifh fhips from getting into action.
Admitting this, as it probably may be, to be the fact,
it does not however at all explain the reafon, why the
broken enemy was permitted to retreat, in the manner
they did, or refcue a fingle fhip of their whole fleet
from the fangs of the victors; but the fuccefs was
great; it was the firft action in which the French,
allies of James, had fuftained any lofs. The bravery
difplayed at Bantry, and the prudent firmnefs exhibited, in the greateft perfonal and national extremity
off Beachy, fhrunk diminifhed and abafhed before the
magnanimous fpirit of the almoft divine Ruffel. The
fhips deftroyed by Delaval, and by Rooke, after the
action, the number of which has been varioufly reprefented by hiftorians to have confifted of from
fixteen to twenty-four fail, were brought in, to fwell
the

the glories of the fortunate admiral, who on this occasion, certainly, had the happiness of being hailed as a conqueror by PROXY.

The English nation felt the pride of their foes humbled, and the paroxyfms of exultation probably, prevented in the extreme hurry of frantic joy, national gratitude from being properly apportioned, and divided among the feveral legitimate claimants of it.

Although the moſt fanguine hopes had prevailed throughout the kingdom, that the blow already given to the French marine was merely the prelude to its complete deſtruction, yet the remainder of the year paſſed on without any repetition of fuccefs, or victory. The French fecured themfelves within their own ports, and the Engliſh derived no fubfequent advantage, fave that of having confined their antagoniſts within them. On the approach of winter, fo capricious is popular opinion, that joy was converted into murmur, and public applaufe into public complaint. A parliamentary inveſtigation as to the conduct of Mr. Ruffel took place; and although, as it appears by the journals of the houfe of commons, that it was refolved that admiral Ruffel, in his command of the fleet during the laſt fummer's expedition, had behaved himfelf with courage, fidelity, and conduct; yet fo violent was the general clamour, that nothing lefs than the difmiffion of the noble admiral from his high office, appeared likely to appeafe it. The meafure was adopted, and Mr. Ruffel for a fhort time retired from the fervice.

The misfortune which, without any culpability
attachable

attachable to any party, befel the Smyrna fleet in the
enfuing year, and the total want of any fuccefs on
the part of England to counterbalance it, caufed a
fecond revolution in the minds of the people, and
ferved as an antidote, on this occafion, to heal Mr. Ruffel's late want of popularity. In 1694 he was again
placed at the head of the fleet; and as though it had
been intended by way of apology for his former removal, he was on the 2d of May, invefted with the
ftation of firft commiffioner for executing the office of
lord high admiral. The very commencement of naval
operations proved inaufpicious, but it were unfair to
attach to Mr. Ruffel the blame, naturally due fome-
where, in confequence of the failure of the attack on
Breft, and the almoft wanton facrifice of the brave
general Talmafh, with the troops under his command.
In his very oftenfible fituation of firft commiffioner
for executing the office of lord high admiral, he was
accountable only for the advice he gave on the occafion, the execution of the projeɛt having been confided to lord Berkeley, who certainly did every thing
in his power to procure fuccefs, that could be expected from an able and a gallant officer. How far
the advice of Mr. Ruffel was fuffered to have influence in the arrangement of the expedition, we know
not; and it would be extremely illiberal, even to
whifper blame, founded on the idle tales, perhaps
of rancorous enemies, or the lefs objectionable evidence
of common furmife.

France, feeling herfelf checked in the Atlantic, and
feeing little likelihood of her flag ever again reigning
triumphant

triumphant in the British channel, adopted a new measure, in the hope, that by transferring the seat of war to a more distant quarter, some opportunity might be offered for a desultory expedition, to be executed by an *escadre legere*, against some vulnerable or defenceless point on the shores of Great Britain, or Ireland. The count de Tourville, who, notwithstanding his discomfiture off La Hogue, still retained the command of the navy of France, was ordered to collect all the ships proper to be placed in a line of battle, at Toulon. It was consequently deemed necessary for Mr. Russel to proceed thither with a force, sufficient to counteract the operations of the enemy. He accordingly sailed at the head of an immense fleet, consisting of no less than one hundred and thirty-six sail, all of them vessels equipped for war, and eighty-eight of them of force sufficient to allow their being placed in a line of battle. The effect might easily have been foretold. The count, who, previous to the arrival of the combined fleet, had caused all the shores of the Mediterranean and of the Levant, to resound with his vain boastings concerning the power, and the prowess of France, was compelled to throw off the temporary disguise of heroism, which he had prematurely assumed; and to owe his safety to the batteries, which defended the dangerous entrance of the harbour of Toulon. The want of a military force prevented any operations on shore, and the remainder of the year, as well as all that part of the succeeding, during which any naval operation could take place, passed on in quietude and tranquillity. The combined fleet

during

during the winter of the year 1694, retired to Cadiz,
to avoid that inclemency of the weather, which ufually
prevails at fuch a feafon; and on this occafion,
Mr. Ruffel exhibited a generofity, which it confeffedly
muft be admitted has very rarely been equalled,
and never furpaffed. It was in thofe days, a matter
of no fmall difficulty, even in the beft inhabited and
cultivated countries, nay, in the ports of Britain itfelf,
to procure a fufficient fupply of provifions and ftores
requifite to the fupport of fo mighty a fleet. In Cadiz
it was a matter of threefold increafed difficulty. To
have tranfported from the fhores of Britain the various
articles which were neceffary, would have been an
attempt not merely extravagant, but impoffible. To
have procured them at Cadiz, or in the ports of the
Mediterranean, was a tafk, extremely arduous, but, as
it appeared by the fequel, not abfolutely unconquerable.
The zeal, and the liberality of Mr. Ruffel attempted
the latter meafure, and overcame every obftacle in its
way. He is even faid to have procured from the funds
of his own private fortune, and his perfonal credit, a
confiderable quantity of the neceffary fupplies, when the
influence of the Britifh government itfelf was, owing to
political caufes, infufficient for the purpofe. Yet even
this liberal and patriotic fpirit, inftead of purchafing him,
as it deferved, the general efteem of his countrymen,
expofed him to no fmall fhare of partial calumny and
abufe. He was charged with having wintered in
Cadiz, for the paltry purpofe of turning it to his
own pecuniary advantage, and with having degraded
the office of commander in chief of the Britifh navy,
into that of a purveyor, or contracter for provifions.
                                                    Similar

Similar misfortunes, if they can be confidered fo, for they certainly merit the contempt only of a great mind, have in almoft every age of the world, fallen upon the nobleft characters.

Nor was it in the inftance already ftated, that the liberality, and if we may be allowed the term, the grandeur of Mr. Ruffel's character, was confpicuous ; a fplendid fête, or entertainment given to the Spaniards, during the ftay of the combined fleet in the harbour of Cadiz; was regarded, even by that expenfive and profufe nation; with the higheft admiration. The magnificence of it, and the elegant tafte, which pervaded all the arrangements connected with it, created aftonifhment by their production, pleafure by the long remembrance of them, and were; for a feries of years; not obliterated from the minds of the gay votaries of luxury, with which Spain has always abounded. Towards the clofe of the year 1695, Mr. Ruffel and the fleet returned to England, nor did he ever afterwards refume the ftation of a naval commander.

In 1697, king William being then about to embark for Holland, he was appointed one of the lords juftices for conducting the affairs of government, during his abfence, and was at the fame time raifed to the peerage by the titles of baron Shingey, vifcount Barfleur, and earl of Orford. His increafed rank did not, however, fhield him from a variety of popular attacks, which it is of little confequence to particularize. Suffice it to fay, they were repelled with the higheft honour and credit to the party accufed. The noble earl contented himfelf, from this time, with acting in

VOL. II. D a private

a private station, so far as was compatible with a person of his rank, influence, and fortune; that is to say, he took no part in the administration of public affairs, till the 8th of November 1709, when he accepted the station of first commissioner for executing the office of lord high admiral, which latter post itself indeed, was offered him, but which he very modestly declined, in consequence of the too heavy responsibility attachable to it, and which he did not think proper to expose himself to. On the removal of the earl of Godolphin, about eleven months afterwards, his lordship again quitted the admiralty board, but on the decease of the queen, became one of the lords justices for managing public affairs, till the arrival of king George I. The new sovereign received him into the highest favour, appointed him one of his privy council, and in a short time after his arrival, reinstated him in his former honourable post at the admiralty board. On the 16th of April 1717, he finally quitted that situation, and also all further concern with public affairs. He died on the 26th of November 1727, being then in the 75th year of his age; and leaving no issue by his countess, Mary, third daughter to William duke of Bedford, the title became extinct.

THE RIGHT HON^e GEORGE ROOKE

Pub^d Novr 1,1799 by Edwd Harding 98 Pall Mall.

SIR GEORGE ROOKE,

Son to fir William Rooke, knight, the descendant of a very ancient Kentish family, after serving for nearly twenty years in the royal navy, as lieutenant and captain of divers ships of war, and during the whole time displaying every species of qualification that can render valuable the character of an officer and of a man, was, at the epoch of the revolution captain of the Deptford. From his rank, as well in life as in service, and from that natural modesty which uniformly pervaded every action of his life, he bore no ostensible part in driving one prince from the throne, or in placing a successor on it; yet his totally unoffending manners, have not been sufficient to exempt him from the charge of having been more zealously attached to the cause of the first, than became a proper friend of his country. On what chimerical basis such an idea may be founded, we will not pretend to say, but certainly no person by his actions ever shewed stronger attachment to the welfare of his country, or warmer fidelity to the reigning prince, who claimed his allegiance, than himself.

The

The firſt enterpriſe in which we find him engaged, was the relief of Londonderry, a city moſt cloſely beſieged, and ſeverely preſſed by the Catholic army, and the French allies of James; the eagerneſs, and the ability which he diſplayed on this occaſion, intereſted the earl of Torrington ſo much in his favour, that he was, as it is ſaid, in conſequence of the expreſs recommendation of that noble lord, advanced to the rank of rear-admiral of the red. In this ſtation he ſerved under his unfortunate patron, and friend, at the battle off Beachy Head. The evidence which he gave upon the trial, in defiance of the outrageous clamour of party, reflected on him the higheſt honour; it was firm, candid, and impreſſive; and ſhewed that he was as little ſubject to the odium of being a Jacobite, as he was to that of being a noiſy partizan, in the hour of public tumult, and commotion. In the month of May 1692, a very few days only previous to the memorable encounter off cape La Hogue, he was ſpecially choſen by his colleagues, to tranſmit to the admiralty board, a loyal addreſs from the flag-officers and captains of the fleet, profeſſing, in the warmeſt terms, their attachment to their majeſties, and their government. He was, but whether on account of this circumſtance, we will not pretend to ſay, promoted to be vice-admiral of the blue, and bore a very conſpicuous part in the immediately ſucceeding engagement with the French fleet; a fuller, and more ſatisfactory account of it, cannot probably be given than in the words of ſir George's own journal, the original of which is ſtill in exiſtence. " May 19th, 1692. At

nine

nine o'clock this morning weighed, and with little
wind at W. S. W. ſtood over for the coaſt of France
in a line of battle all day, and in as good order as
poſſible all night, the Dutch leading the van. At daybreak this morning, having little wind weſterly, we
ſaw the enemies' fleet about four leagues to windward
of us, on which we both drew into a line of battle. At
ſeven, the enemy, not above ſixty ſail, bore down upon
us, but there being very little wind, it was near eleven
o'clock before they began to engage the admiral's
ſquadron and the Dutch. The enemies' number not
permitting them to cover the blue, we had the opportunity of gathering to windward of them, and were
bearing down upon the rear of their fleet ; but it fell
quite calm, with a very thick fog, ſo that we could
not ſee a ſhip's length. It continued ſo till about ſix
in the evening, and then cleared, with very little wind
eaſterly. Seeing a cloud of ſmoke riſe to the eaſtward of us, I tacked towards it, with the Windſor
Caſtle, and the Expedition, and found ſir Cloudeſley
Shovell, the Kent, and another frigate at an anchor,
firing their ſtern chaſes at monſieur Tourville, his
vice-admiral, and one of their ſeconds, whom they engaged ſharply for about an hour, when they cut from
their anchors, and ſtood away to the weſtward. We
followed them all night. At noon cape Barfleur bore
S. W. about twelve leagues.

" 20th. This morning, at four o'clock the wind
ſprung up pretty freſh at E. and E. S. E. with foggy
weather. We ſteered away to the weſtward, with a
preſſed ſail. About ten o'clock it cleared up, and we

ſaw

saw the enemy to leeward of us. At noon it fell little wind, and shifted westerly, with which we plied after the enemy till five o'clock in the afternoon. The tide being done, we came to anchor in forty fathom water, cape La Hogue bearing W. S. W. five leagues, as the enemy did to windward.

"21st. At one o'clock this morning weighed, and with the wind fresh at S. W. plied to windward till seven. We came to anchor in forty fathom water, the isle of Alderney bearing S. S. W. four leagues off. The enemy came to in the Race, but fifteen of them could not ride, but drove away to leeward of us. At ten, the admiral made the signal to cut, which we did, and gave chace to them. We drove a vice-admiral and two other ships into Cherburg bay ; twelve more got into the Hogue, of which one overset ; at ten at night we came to an anchor before the place in twelve fathom water.

"22d. The admiral, who came to an anchor last night in the offing, weighed this morning, and turned into the bay. We looked in upon the enemy, but the tide and day being too far spent to make any attempt upon them, we came to an anchor again before the place, the admiral ordering sir Cloudesley Shovell, in the Kent, with a squadron of third rates, small frigates, and fire-ships, to try if he could burn them. The next day we had the wind at N. W. and N. by W. Sir Cloudesley Shovell being ill, I asked the admiral leave to go upon the service of burning the ships, which he granted me. I immediately went on board the Eagle, hoisted my flag, and, after giving the necessary orders

to the captains of the ships, and the officers of the
boats, I weighed, and run into the Hogue, and anchored in fix fathom water. After battering the ships
and the forts about an hour, I fent the boats and a fire-
ship on board them, and burnt fix capital ships, with
their ftores and provifions ; the tide being too far fpent,
I did not think it neceffary to attempt any thing more
that night.

" 24th. This morning I ordered a fquadron of fmall
frigates to work up and batter the inner fort, clofe
under which lay five capital ships and a frigate ; after
which I ordered two fire-ships in, but before they got
to them, our boats got on board them, and fet them
on fire ; and, as the water arofe, the wind being at
E. S. E. and S. E. I thought it feafible to put the fire-
ships into the harbour, with the tranfport ships, and
accordingly ordered it, but they being long coming in,
the water pinched, and they ran aground, where I
directed them to be burnt ; but we went in with our
boats, and burnt fome of the tranfport ships, and brought
others out, after which we weighed, and plied out to
the fleet. I returned on board the Neptune, and
hoifted my flag again."

It has been afferted by fome writers, that Mr. Rooke,
on account of his great gallantry difplayed on the foregoing occafion, was rewarded by his fovereign with a
penfion of one thoufand pounds per annum ; but,
though it is highly probable fuch mark of royal favour
was beftowed on him, it does not appear fufficiently
eftablifhed, to warrant our afferting it as a pofitive fact.
Admiral Rooke was, during the remainder of the year,

employed

employed in reiterated attempts to deftroy the fhattered remains of the French fleet,. which had taken refuge within their. ports.- That conqueft did not crown his fpirited endeavours was a misfortune, but not a crime. Even popular opinion appeared fatisfied with this fact, for although in that outrageous hour, the want of fuc-cefs was. fo conftantly converted, into treafon, or neg-lect, Mr. Rooke feems, on this occafion, to have ftood as an exception to the general rule.

In the enfuing fpring he received the honour of knighthood, and was promoted to be vice-admiral of the white fquadron; almoft. immediately afterwards, he was ordered to the Streights, for the purpofe of convoying thither a very numerous fleet of merchant-fhips, amounting to no lefs than four hundred fail. The force put under his command confifted of twenty-one fhips of two decks, Englifh and Dutch, two fri-gates, and five fmaller veffels. The grand fleet, under the orders of the joint admirals, Shovell, Delaval, and Killegrew, for the better protection of fo valuable a ftake, faw fir George Rooke in fafety, fo far as the dif-tance of fifty leagues to the fouth-weft of Ufhant. Such, however, was the addrefs of the enemy, the cor-rectnefs of their information, and the total want of it on the part of Britain, that the armaments of Breft and Toulon formed a junction in Lagos bay, where they continued quiet, in expectation of their glorious prize, without any of the commanders in the combined fquadrons, being in the flighteft degree aware of the circumftance, or of the danger that awaited, them. The misfortune, though great, was alleviated in a

confiderable

confiderable degree, by the ability and activity of fir George; more than three fourths of the fleet were preferved, and, of the fhips fent for its protection, three only, and thofe belonging to the Dutch, who behaved with the moft confpicuous gallantry on the occafion, fell into the hands of the count de Tourville.

Grievoufly as the reflection muft have preffed on the mind of the admiral, it muft have received confiderable alleviation, from the foothing attention beftowed on him by the public, and the total abfence of all murmur that could either irritate his mind, or increafe his diftrefs. The flames of war, after this time, fubfided merely into the embers, ferving rather to point out the extent of the conflagration, than the fury with which it had raged; fo that, although fir George continued in conftant employment, and, after the retirement of Mr. Ruffel, was invefted with the dignified and weighty truft of admiral in chief of the combined fleet, the occurrences which took place were few in number, and uninterefting in their confequence. The moft material circumftance we find recorded, is, the complete ftop which he put to the illegal and contraband trade carried on with the enemy, in defiance of all treaties, under the fanction of a neutral flag. The occurrence is thus related: " He fell in with a fleet of Swedifh merchantmen, on the coaft of France, and, rightly judging them loaded with French property, captured the whole. The nation difapproved, and the Swedes bluftered; but the admiral was firm, and through his penetration, the whole of this iniquitous fcheme was laid open. The property proved to be totally French, and that this

this contraband trade, fo injurious to the faith of
nations and the intereſt of Britain, had been long
carried on under the covert of Swediſh paſſes, and a
nominal foreign commander. In time they were all
condemned as lawful prizes. May other neutral nations read this event, and profit by the misfortunes of
their neighbours."

In 1698 ſir George was choſen repreſentative in
parliament for the town of Portſmouth, and he ſoon
afterwards had an opportunity of diſplaying the qualities of his mind, as ably as a ſtateſman (though ab-
ſtraĉted from parliamentary conduĉt), as he had before
done in what may be called his natural capacity of a
naval commander. A formidable confederacy had
been entered into, between the northern powers of
Ruſſia, Denmark, and Poland, the avowed objeĉt of
which was the deſtruĉtion (for no leſs harſh term could
be given to the projeĉt) of the young king of Sweden.
Britain poſſeſſed too much magnanimity patiently to
look on, and permit ſo dreadful an invaſion of the rights
of nations; and ſir George was accordingly ſent into the
Sound with a fleet, fitted out with the intention of
aĉting in conjunĉtion with the Dutch, not only for the
purpoſe of freeing Sweden from the terrors of annihi-
lation, but compelling her confederated foes to agree
to an equitable peace. The moderation, and the firm-
neſs of the Britiſh admiral on this occaſion, refleĉted
the higheſt honour on his judgment as an officer, and
his integrity as a man : while he, on the one hand,
declared himſelf to the Danes and their allies, fully
determined to cruſh their injurious projeĉt, ſo on the

other

other did he moft peremptorily refift every folicitation made to him by the youthful fovereign of Sweden (who, with all that enthufiafm and ardour fo natural to his character, confidered the then exifting moment, as that of retribution and punifhment of his enemies), to continue the war, even for an inftant longer, than was abfolutely neceffary for the acquifition of a fair and honourable peace. His anfwer to the king himfelf was too great, and too memorable for us to omit it: " I was," faid fir George, in reply to him, " fent hither to ferve your majefty, but not to ruin the king of Denmark." The treaty of Travendahl was accordingly concluded, in defpite of every remonftrance the impetuous Charles could make, and every objection which his heated imagination could propofe. On the profpect of a war with France in 1701, fir George was again invefted with the chief command; but that power confidering the hour of hoftility not yet arrived, peace remained unbroken till after the acceffion of queen Anne. Among the very firft acts of her majefty's reign, are to be reckoned the appointment of fir George to be vice-admiral of England, and commander in chief of the Britifh fleet. The firft enterprife refolved on by government, was the attack of Cadiz; and the failure of it, though not in the flighteft degree imputable to fir George, was moft uncandidly attempted to be attributed to him, by fome of the virulent party writers of the time, and by Burnet in particular.

Fortune, however, feemed ready to afford him fome recompenfe for his recent difappointment; for, he had

scarcely

scarcely left Cadiz, on his return home, when he received intelligence that a moſt valuable fleet of Spaniſh
galleons had put into Vigo, together with their eſcort,
a ſtrong ſquadron of French ſhips of war, commanded
by that well-known officer. Monſ. Chateau Renaud.
Notwithſtanding, ſir George received information, at
the ſame time, that every means which art and profeſſional knowledge could contrive, had been planned
and executed by the enemy to produce their ſecurity,
the gallant admiral, conſidering all artificial impediments as trivial, when oppoſed by true valour, and the
ardent ſpirit of enterpriſe, he reſolved on the immediate
attack. The great and fortunate reſult was modeſtly
entered by ſir George in his journal, in the following
terms :

" Oct. 12. Anno 1702. At break of day this morning, I removed and hoiſted my flag on board the So-
merſet. The wind being at W. S. W. promiſed a
favourable opportunity of attempting the enemy, according to the reſolutions of yeſterday. His grace the duke
of Ormond uſed great diligence in diſembarking the
troops, and landing them in a bay on the ſouth ſhore,
about four miles to the eaſtward of Vigo ; he ordered
the grenadiers to march under the command of my
lord Shannon, towards the fort, on the ſouth ſide of
Ronondello. At nine o'clock I made the ſignal to
weigh, which was accordingly done, the line of battle
formed, and the ſhips went in upon the enemy ; but
falling calm, the van of our line was forced to anchor
within ſhot of the enemy's batteries, as the reſt of the
ſhips did in their order. At one o'clock captain

Jennings

Jennings came on board, from vice-admiral Hopfon, to inform me that the paffage at the boom was extremely narrow, that both fides were well fortified, and that, in all probability, the firft fhip that attempted the paffage would be loft, and defired I would come on board him, and view the place; upon which I immediately went on board him, and the more I looked, the more I liked it; for I faw the paffage was half a mile wide, fo that it was impoffible a boom of that length could be of any ftrength.

" I faw the batteries on the larboard fide were open, and not fo many guns mounted on the ftarboard fide as was reported. I faw the enemy had not made a difpofition of their fhips for a vigorous defence, but that they were in a confternation and confufion, fo that I ordered Mr. Hopfon, and the reft of the officers, to execute their orders, and do their duty. At two o'clock in the afternoon, vice-admiral Hopfon, with the fhips next the enemy, flipped their cables, and ran in upon them. Mr. Hopfon, being the headmoft fhip, run through without a ftop; but the reft of the fhips in his divifion ftopped, and hung in till they cut their way through, and, as foon as they got through, the enemy deferted their fhips, fetting fome on fire, and running others on fhore.

" The Torbay was very near being burnt by a fire-fhip of the enemy, which would have certainly done the execution, had fhe not blown up. This accident happened by the Torbay's going too far in before fhe anchored. My orders were that none of our fhips fhould go within the enemy to board them, as they
might

might then get the opportunity of burning ship for
ship; which would have been a better bargain, than I
intended them; but the fire-ship blowing up, the fire
was extinguished by the exemplary bravery and diligence of captain Leake, his officers and men, and the
ship wonderfully preserved. The attack was made
with as much spirit and resolution as ever I saw, and
the enemy's defence was as mean, except two or three
of their ships, who acquitted themselves honourably.
Monf. Chateau Renaud did not behave very well, for
he hardly fired his guns once, before he set his ship on
fire, and ran away as fast as he could.--What facilitated the reducing the fort on the starboard side, was
the good conduct of our forces, who contrived to attack it by land at the same time that our ships poured
in their broadsides upon it, between which the enemy
was in such a consternation, that they surrendered at
discretion in less than a quarter of an hour. I sent a
message to his grace the duke of Ormond, with my
humble opinion, that if he would please to march the
forces on to Ronondello, he might probably find a
considerable quantity of plate and other rich goods;
upon which his grace continued his march thither.
Thus ends this glorious day to the eternal honour of
her majesty and our country, and with very little loss
sustained, though some of our ships had like to have
come to a misfortune by the enemy's burning ships
driving with the tide of ebb, and an off-shore wind,
upon ours, so that some of them were forced to cut
two or three times from their anchors to save themselves. Had I, therefore, as I was advised, run into
                                                    the

the Ronondello with the whole squadron, we muſt
have been in a huddle, and, in all probability, ſhould
have burned all together, by which we would have paid
too dear for our victory ; therefore I do ſet it down for
a maxim and rule without exception in our ſea ſervice, that a huddle is a thing moſt to be apprehended
and avoided.

" Oct. 13th. At break of day this morning, I went
up to Ronondello, and gave the neceſſary order for
ſecuring the ſhips of war and prizes that were afloat,
and their ſtores, as well as for getting off thoſe that lay
on ſhore with any hopes of their being ſaved ; to get out
the braſs guns of thoſe that were loſt, and to preſerve
the goods of the galleons, as well of thoſe that were
on ſhore, as thoſe afloat, from any kind of embezzle-
ment ; and that all the plate that could be found in
the bottoms of the burnt galleons, might be preſerved
for the uſe and ſervice of her majeſty. I was all the
day on this buſineſs, and returned late at night aboard,
being very much indiſpoſed with ſharp ſymptoms of a
fit of the gout."

Spain had never before, in reſpect to pecuniary loſs,
experienced ſo dreadful a blow. The treaſure and articles of merchandiſe taken and deſtroyed on the occaſion, amounted to between four and five millions
ſterling ; while the injury ſuſtained in reſpect to ſhips
of war, had never before been exceeded, except in the
inſtances of the deſtruction of the Armada, and the
battle off cape La Hogue. Twenty ſhips and veſſels
of war, fifteen of which were of two decks, together
with thirteen galleons, were included in the deſtruction
and

and capture, made, and effected on this occafion. . Severe as. was the. lofs fuftained by the enemy, and confequently advantageous to the interefts of the combined powers, as the termination of this expedition proved, ftill, was it not fufficient to filence the difaffected clamours of the factious, in refpect to the failure againft Cadiz ; but the impotent fhafts of malice can only excite mental contempt, they inflict not the flighteft injury. againft the ftamina of character, or political conftitution.

The war with France was, throughout its whole extent, conducted in a manner totally varying from every one that had preceded. Except in one folitary inftance, that country never ventured to fend an armament to fea, that could be faid to merit the name of a fleet. Yet even during the time when enterprife neceffarily flumbered, the abilities of fir George by no means funk into a dormant ftate. He projected expeditions which the contradiction of party deprived him of the glory of carrying into execution ; and the vifitation of natural difeafe, was ingenioufly converted by his enemies, into the ftrongeft proofs of difaffection, and neglect of his country's fervice. But thefe are attacks to which the beft and the braveft men are continually fubject.

The year 1704 formed a very diftinguifhed epoch in the life of fir George. In the month of January the very honourable truft of convoying king Charles III. to Spain, was confided to him : by his firmnefs, added to the greateft complacency of manners, he got over a variety of delicate punctilios on this occafion, particularly

larly one where the honour of the British flag was concerned, with the highest credit to himself, and to the maintenance of his country's dignity. In respect to more active service, the capture of Gibraltar still stands with undiminished lustre, one of the brightest gems that ever ornamented British valour or British conduct: that is to say, as well in respect to the execution, as to the plan of the enterprise; while the battle off Malaga convinced the enemy of the danger they incurred by meeting a British fleet, except under circumstances most particularly advantageous to them, and a superiority of force, which would almost draw on resistance, the imputation of madness. "This morning," says sir George, in his own manuscript remarks on the action, "we were within three leagues of the enemy, who brought to, with their heads to the southward, and formed their line, the wind still continuing easterly. We steered down upon them until ten o'clock, or half an hour past, when being a little more than a musket shot distance, I was forced to make the signal, and begin the battle: the enemy setting their sails, and seeming to intend to crowd ahead of our van. The fight was maintained on both sides with great fury, for three hours: their van then began to give way to ours, as their rear did afterwards. But several of our ships, as well of mine as the rear-admiral of the red and white divisions, were forced to go out of the line, some being disabled, but most for want of shot, so that the body of their fleet fell very heavy upon my ship, the St. George, Shrewsbury, and Eagle, the last of which towed out of the line also for want of shot, two hours

before

before night, fo that we were much fhattered and difabled. The enemies' line confifted of fifty-two fhips
and twenty-four gallies; their fhips, moft of them,
were large. Their line was formed very ftrong in
their centre; and weaker in their front and rear: this
defeét they endeavoured to fupply by their gallies,
which were moft of them pofted in thofe quarters.

"It had been the fharpeft day's fervice I ever faw;
and what was moft extraordinary, every officer in the
fleet performed their duty without the leaft umbrage or
reflection ; and I never obferved the true Englifh fpirit
more apparent in our feamen than on this occafion.
The engagement lafted till about feven o'clock, when
the enemy bore away and left us. Moft of the mafts
and yards in the fleet were wounded to an irreparable
degree. The captains flain were fir Andrew Lake and
——— Low. Thofe wounded, viz. captains Baker,
Myngs, Jumper, Mighells, and Kirkton. Many lieutenants and warrant-officers flain and wounded, of
whom I have not yet got a particular account. Sir
Cloudefly Shovell, and the other flag-officers, of our
front and rear, fay the enemy did not behave themfelves
well in thofe quarters. I am fure thofe in the centre
did their duty very gallantly and heartily. We lay by
all night repairing our defeéts. At noon cape Malaga N. by E. feven leagues.

"Auguft 14, 1713. This morning the wind
backed northerly, and fo to the weftward. We lay by
all night repairing our defeéts, as did the enemy till
the evening, and then they filled and plied away to
the weftward. In the evening I called a council of flag-
officers ;

officers: I ordered, as equal a diſtribution of ſhot as I could, to fit the fleet for another day's engagement. At noon cape Malaga N. by E. nine leagues.

"15th. This morning about ten o'clock, we had a ſmall breeze, eaſterly, with which we bore upon the enemy till four o'clock in the afternoon: being within four leagues of them, and being too late to engage before night, I did, by the advice of the Engliſh flag-officers, bring to with our head to the northward, and lay by all night, and wait a freſh levant. At noon Targa Head S. W. by S. ſix leagues.

"16th. This morning, not ſeeing the enemy, or any of their ſcouts to leeward of us, we concluded that they were put away to the Streights mouth, ſo that we bore away W. and W. by N. till ſix in the evening. Being hazy weather, and we not ſure of our diſtance from the land, we brought to with our heads to the northward, and lay by with a little wind and a great eaſtern ſea all night. This afternoon the Albemarle, a Dutch ſhip of ſixty-four guns, blew up, and loſt all her men except nine or ten."

The force of the combined fleet amounted to no more than fifty ſail, two thirds of which number were ſmall ſhips, particularly the whole of the Dutch diviſion, though it muſt be allowed they fought with great ſpirit. The enemy's ſhips, on the other hand, were much heavier, and the advantage which they derived from the aſſiſtance of their gallies, was almoſt incalculable. Upon the whole, if the arbitrament of national diſputes, could have been ſubmitted to the eſtabliſhed proofs of the ſuperior valour evinced on board the combined fleets

E 2

over

over their enemies, and if, as in the days of chivalry, the conteſt was to end, with the acknowledgment of ſuperior prowefs, the diſpute between France, Spain, and the powers of Britain and the United Provinces, all further warfare would have ceaſed with the ſetting ſun, which cloſed the conflict.

The enemy, by their retreat, confeſſed their inferiority. Except in reſpect to the loſs actually incurred by them, the injury they ſuſtained, in its conſequences, proved equally oppreſſive with that, which they experienced on their former chaſtiſement off cape La Hogue. They were under the neceſſity of leaving to ſir George the unreſtrained dominion of their own ſeas; and after every poſſible exertion to bring them to a further action had proved ineffectual, in conſequence of their flight, ſir George had the ſatisfaction of returning to England with the loſs of only a ſingle ſhip (the Albemarle, one of the Dutch ſquadron), which was deſtroyed, not by the efforts of the enemy, but by mere accident. The honeſt applauſe of the candid part of the community, and the juſtly merited approbation of the ſovereign herſelf, were not ſufficient to ſhield this great and highly injured man, from the aſſaults of public clamour. It can be a matter of little wonder then, that under ſuch reiterated and ill-founded perſecution, his mind became, in a conſiderable degree, alienated from public life. It has been remarked of him elſewhere, that few men ever ſtood better entitled to the general love and approbation of mankind, whether conſidered as a commander, a private gentleman, or a ſtateſman. As the

lines.

lines of conduct, fufficient to mark the great, and good man, in both of the former ftations, are extremely clear, and eafy to be comprehended, it becomes materially lefs wonderful that the enemies of fir George, viewing him completely impregnable in thofe fituations, fhould refort to the third, where character neceffarily becomes lefs clearly definable to the human mind. But his carriage and behaviour in political concerns was not of that impetuous nature likely to betray him into violence, nor were his principles fuch, as to induce him to engage in any of thofe intrigues with the adherents of the exiled part of the houfe of Stuart, with which treafonable practices feveral among his cotemporaries were, with no fmall fhare of juftice, charged. His great crime, among the patriots of that day, was his being, according to a quaint and well-known term, a tory; the true definition of which character is not a little curious; it was a perfon zealoufly attached to that mode of worfhip eftablifhed, in what is called the church of England, and to thofe principles of government, under which the proper and legal authority of princes, has ever been maintained in the greateft fplendour, and with the moft perfect happinefs to the people. Continued feuds, diffenfions, and tumults, have invariably grown out of thofe tenets, which have inculcated a contrary opinion. Pretended patriotifm, republicanifm, treafon, and rebellion, uniformly follow each other, like caufe and effect.

It is allowed, that in refpect to his character as a naval officer, no perfon has ever prefumed to caft the fmalleft afperfion on it; that he poffeffed the moft

E 3 wonderful

wonderful coolnefs, which enabled him, even in the
heat of action, to counteract the moft fubtle attempts
of a wary enemy ; and if he difplayed to the world tho
fire of Alexander, he took fufficient care to temper it
with the prudence of Fabius. In his political capacity,
he ftood as a beacon to future ftatefmen, firmly fixed
to teach them to avoid thofe quickfands of corruption,
in which the fame of fo many great men, has been
fwallowed up, and loft for ever ; for he is truly reported
to have difplayed an honefty in every public capacity,
incorruptible by avarice, or thofe opportunities of
fecret gain, which few perfons boaft the firmnefs of re-
fifting. He is faid, when on his death-bed, to have
made the following impreffive anfwer to fome perfons prefent at the execution of his will, and who
could not refrain from making fome remarks on the
narrownefs of his circumftances. " What I leave,"
faid he, " 'tis true is not much, but what I do leave
has been honeftly acquired. It never coft a feaman a
tear, or the nation a farthing." As the earlier part of
his life had been embittered by faction, fo was the
latter by difeafe. From the time he quitted the line
of active fervice, he was intolerably afflicted with the
gout, which put a period to his life at a very premature
age. This event took place on the 24th of January
1708-9, fir George being then in his fifty-eighth year.
His executors, with the moft liberal and commendable
attention to the memory of this good man, caufed a
magnificent monument to be erected to him in Canterbury cathedral ; fuch being the tribute of friendfhip, it therefore deferves to be revered : but no re-
                                                    mark

mark was certainly ever made with more propriety, than
that, which declares the fame of this great man, will add
to the fplendour of the hiftoric page, when the marble
record is crumbled in the duft. The heraldic particulars of fir George Rooke are: He was thrice-married,
firft to Mrs. Howe, daughter of fir Thomas Howe,
of Cold Berwick in the county of Wilts, baronet;
fecondly, to Mrs. Mary Luttrell, daughter of colonel
Luttrell, of Dunfter caftle in the county of Somerfet;
this lady died in childbed of her firft child, in the month
of July 1702-3, and the letter of condolence written to
fir George by queen Anne, with her own hand, certainly
deferves to be recorded: " I am fo concerned for the
great affliction which hath befallen you, that I cannot
forbear letting you know the compaffion I have for
you. I think you are of fo great importance to my
fervice, that if any affurance of my favour can help to
fupport you under it, you may depend upon me.
ANNE R." He was laftly married to Mifs Catharine
Knatchbull, daughter to fir Thomas Knatchbull, of
Merfham Hatch in the county of Kent, baronet: he
left one fon, George, born of his fecond wife, who
became fole heir to his fortune.

SIR RALPH DELAVAL

WAS the third fon of fir Ralph Delaval, of Seaton Delaval in the county of Northumberland, baronet, fo created by king Charles the fecond, on the 29th of June 1660. The family of Delaval is among the moft ancient in the kingdom, as appears by a pedigree drawn by Thomas Challock, bifhop of the Orcades, fteward to Margaret princefs of Denmark, confort to James II. king of Scotland, entitled, " An exact and true Genealogy of the moft noble and ancient Lords of Gouldbranfal, in the Kingdom of Norway, from the Heathens' Time, Progenitors of the moft noble and ancient Name of Delaval." The pedigree commences with Harold, furnamed Hairfauger, faid to have been crowned king of Norway in the year 858, and who married Offa, or Offa, third daughter of Goulbrand, or Colbrand, king of Dall, and Signielda, daughter of Sigefrid, or Sigrichm, otherwife Sichtrig, with the filken beard, king of Sogan in Norway. The pedigree is carried on lineally from Goulbrand, whofe grandfon appears to have been the celebrated champion who attended St. Olanus to England, and was killed by the well-known Guy, or rather Hugh,

earl

ſ

earl of Warwick, through fourteen defcents to fir
Guido Delaval, knight, in the reign of king John.
The great-grandfather of Guido, Henry, was the firft
who is faid to have refided at Seaton, which appears
to have been, ever fince that time, the family feat ; and
the father of .Henry, fir Henrick, was one of the
knights appointed to carry the chief banners at the
time William duke of Normandy, his kinfman, invaded England.

Concerning fir Ralph, of whom we are about
to fpeak, the early events have very little, or nothing
in them fufficiently interefting, either to engage
our attention and notice, or to promife that difplay of ability for which, in later days, the name of
Delaval became fo well known. He received a commiffion as a lieutenant in the navy in 1666, and eight
years afterwards, that is to fay, in 1674, was advanced
to the rank of captain ; but his commands were few,
and totally deftitute of affording the means of rendering
either his gallantry, or his abilities in any degree confpicuous. It is evident, however, that he ftood extremely high in the opinion of his countrymen, as
well as in that of king William, for immediately after
the revolution had taken place, he was appointed
rear-admiral of the blue : thus advanced, the rapid
tide of promotion appeared to pafs all former bounds,
for, in the month of May or June 1690, he was ftill
further promoted to be vice-admiral of the blue, and
received the honour of knighthood at the fame time,
in confequence of his having been deputed to prefent a
loyal addrefs to his majefty, from the officers of the
fleet. As vice-admiral of the blue, he hoifted his flag

on

on board the Coronation, and quickly after his being
elevated to that rank, was prefent at the unfortunate
encounter off Beachy Head. The hurricane of clamour, if. the term be allowed, which arofe in confequence of that difafter, attempted to vent its rage,
though impotently, on the vice-admiral, as well as
many others, who fought moft bravely. The illiberal
rancour of the Dutch writers, and the malevolence of
Evertzen himfelf, endeavoured moft weakly and wic-
kedly to throw the odium of that lofs, which their part
of the combined fleet fuftained, on the mifbehaviour of
many among the Britifh commanders. Evertzen himfelf, was fcandalous enough to affert, that none of the
Britifh fhips fought properly, except two or three of
the van fhips of the red fquadron, who engaged, contrary to the earl of Torrington's command. Fortunately, however, for the reputation of this gentleman,
there are official documents ftill exifting, fufficient to
refute this abfurd charge in the completeft manner.
The evidence would be fully fatisfactory, if it refted
merely on that part of the account, tranfmitted by the
lords commiffioners of the admiralty to the queen,
which refers to the immediate conduct of fir Ralph, in
which it is ftated, " that the vice-admiral of the blue,
being about nine, in the line with the admiral, finding
he brought to at the diftance of twice gun-fhot, he,
with his divifion, edged nearer to the enemy till he
came within mufket-fhot, and then began to fire ; and
fo continued, the enemy ftill edging from him, and he
preffing forward, till he came, at laft, almoft into their
line ; thofe he engaged with, fetting up their top-gal-
, lant

lant fails, fprit-fails, and main-fails for their getting away; and when there was but little wind, they towed from them with their boats ahead."

As an additional proof to this teftimony, it appears from the moft indifputable evidence, that the whole of the blue fquadron engaged that of France, which was oppofed to it, quite as near, as the Dutch themfelves did the French van; and that if the latter had to boaft their having contended with twenty-two fhips only, againft the whole of the French van, fir Ralph Delaval, with no more than twelve fhips, fought their rear, which was very nearly as ftrong as the divifion oppofed to the fhips of the States General, for the fpace of five hours; that he fuftained no lofs, that he compelled his opponents to retreat before him, and that he vented no complaints whatever, of his having been unprotected and facrificed. The Dutch themfelves indeed, do not appear to have been exempt from blame, many of the Britifh commanders, and among the reft, fir Ralph Delaval himfelf, having declared in evidence on oath, that it was his opinion, the lofs fuftained by the Dutch, was principally attributable to their having gone into action, in a very irregular, and confufed manner.

Sir Ralph Delaval was foon afterwards appointed prefident of the court-martial, convened for the trial of the earl of Torrington; and, however indelicate, or improper it may be confidered at the prefent day, that an officer, in a fubordinate ftation, fhould be appointed the chief among the judges, affembled to decide on the conduct of a fuperior officer, under whom

he

he had himfelf ferved, when the caufe of complaint
arofe, yet it certainly flood as no fmall proof of the
opinion entertained of his integrity, while his conduct
during the court-martial, more ftrongly confirmed it.

No appointment could, in its event, difplay the in-
genuoufnefs and candour of Delaval, in more brilliant
colours, than that of which we are treating. He was
known to have lived widely diftant from the habits of
friendfhip, though on what account does not appear,
with the noble earl: he even publicly expreffed his
difapprobation as to feveral points in his conduct, before he was appointed prefident ; and the declaration of
the earl's innocence, from the very mouth of a man,
thus fituated, certainly reflected no lefs honour on the
character of the judge, than it did on that of the accufed.

To remedy as much as poffible the extent of
that misfortune, which the fuccefs of the enemy had
threatened, a light fquadron was formed, and put
under the orders of fir Ralph, for the purpofe of checking any petty attack, that might be made by fmall armaments fitted out from the minor ports of France :
this object was not only effected, but the commerce of
the enemy was very materially interrupted. During
the year 1691, he was invefted with various commands,
which it is needlefs to recite, for they were, owing to
the quiefcent ftate of the enemy, in refpect to naval
operations, not graced with any ftriking or interefting
occurrence. Immediately after his return from the
Streights, in the month of March 1692, he was promoted to the rank of vice-admiral of the red, and in
that capacity held a very confpicuous fhare in the defeat

of

of the French fleet off La Hogue. An attempt towards the deſtruction indeed of a ſmall ſquadron, with
which he had been ſent over to the coaſt of France,
upon a cruiſe, was one of the leading events, preparatory as it were, to that great encounter; for, the
pride of France, taking the alarm, and feeling its
greatneſs debaſed by the inſult of ſo inferior an armament, hovering unmoleſted, on their ſhore, drove out
the count de Tourville, who, owing to a variety of
cauſes, fell a ſacrifice, with a conſiderable part of his
force, to the temerity of the meaſure. The whole
ſtreſs of the action lay on the red diviſion, where ſir
Ralph commanded; and he rendered himſelf moſt
conſpicuous, even amongſt the moſt active.

When the flight of the enemy had enſured the
honour of victory, his diligence in reaping the more
ſolid advantages of it were no leſs honourable and
prominent. The Soleil Royal, which had borne the
flag of the count de Tourville himſelf, the Admirable,
and the Conquerant, were driven on ſhore and burnt,
by a detachment of the red ſquadron, with ſir Ralph
at their head; who, deſpiſing the empty parade of
continuing on board his own ſhip, ſhifted his flag on
board a fourth rate, a cuſtom, at that time, little uſed,
though, by ſubſequent commanders, frequently brought
into practice, under circumſtances moſt honourable to
themſelves, and advantageous to their country. The
lightneſs of the ſhip which then bore his flag, permitting
him to approach the ſhore much cloſer than he could
have done in one having three decks; he perſonally
directed every meaſure, and with the utmoſt magnanimity,

nimity, detracted rather from that share of applause
which he himself had justly acquired, by attributing
the glorious success entirely to those, whose exertions he
had superintended.

Party intrigues having driven Mr. Russel from the
command, it was resolved by the king and his ministers,
that the high office should be confided to three commissioners: sir Ralph had the misfortune to be one;
we say misfortune, for, owing to the disaster which
fell on the Smyrna fleet, through the want of intelligence respecting the enemy's measures, so dreadful a
popular outcry was raised against the commanders in
chief, that sir Ralph Delaval determined never more
to accept of a naval command. This resolution he
strictly complied with, and the remainder of his life
was accordingly spent principally in retirement, at his
estate in Northumberland, where his extensive possessions furnished him with the means of the most
liberal charity, benevolence, and munificence, while
the openness of his heart daily prompted him to the
exertion of all those noble qualities. He died in the
month of January 1707, and was buried with great
solemnity in Westminster Abbey, on the 27th of that
month.

SIR

SIR CLOUDESLY SHOVELL.

THE hiftory of this brave man affords an irrefragable proof that greatnefs of mind is not confined to noblenefs of birth, but that from the humbleft origin, may fpring a mind capable of difplaying all the talents that can adorn a hero. According to the beft authorities, he was defcended from parents fo extremely poor, that they were incapable of making any better provifion for him in life, than that of binding him as an apprentice to a fhoemaker. His native fpirit, ill brooking fuch an occupation, and difplaying itfelf even in the moft early periods of his life, he was recommended by fir Chriftopher Mingh*, who had cafually noticed his conduct, to fir John Narborough. He received him, and appointed him one of his cabin-boys, when no more than nine years old. The recommendation very foon proved to have been moft meritoriously beftowed. The difcerning eye of his commander, found him to poffefs a mind capable of forming the moft extenfive projects, aided by an heart ever prompt to carry them into execution. It is re-

* See vol. 1. page 451.

lated

lated of him as a fact, and though, perhaps, generally
known, muft not be omitted in this place, that while
yet a boy, in refpect to years, he undertook to fwim
through the line of the enemy's fire, in one of the
piratical ports on the coaft of Barbary, and convey
fome difpatches to the commander of a diftant fhip,
which it would have been extremely inconvenient for
the commander in chief, to have tranfmitted thither by
any other, lefs concealed, means. This, joined to other
proofs, perhaps of lefs fingularity though not lefs
merit, impreffed fo high an opinion of him on the
mind of his patron fir John Narborough, that almoft
ere he reached manhood, he was intrufted with mif-
fions, that required all the fubtlety of a ftatefman, and
all the firmnefs of a veteran commander. He was fent,
more than once, to the dey of Tripoli, to make remonftrances againft the piratical conduct of his corfairs : though his arguments proved infufficient to bend
the haughty mind of the prefumptuous chief, yet, the
obfervations made by him, when attempting to perform the objects of his miffion, were fuch as enabled
him to form a plan for the demolition of the enemy's
fquadron, notwithftanding it lay at anchor under the
very guns of the town. The project having been
communicated to the admiral, fir John, without hefitation, thought it moft prudent to appoint this young
hero to fuperintend, and conduct the execution of his
own plan. The moft complete fuccefs crowned the attempt, and Mr. Shovell was honoured with the command of the Sapphire frigate, as the moft proper reward that could have been beftowed upon him, for

performing

performing that fervice which he had been the fole caufe of rendering to his country.

From the month of March 1674-5, the period when the occurrence juft mentioned took place, to the year 1686, he remained conftantly employed as captain in divers fhips ftationed in the Mediterranean. The catalogue of his fucceffes againft the ftates of Barbary, would be tedious in the very recital. Their moft formidable corfairs fell a prey to his gallantry, and the little commerce which the enemy poffeffed, was completely annihilated by his activity. On his return to England, James II. in the midft of that ferment which preceded the revolution, entertained fo high an opinion of Shovell's honour, as to appoint him, at that critical period, captain of the Dover, although his political principles were known to be inimical to the wifhes of the tottering fovereign. But his integrity was too fteady to be bent to the fmalleft breach of the truft confided to him, for his nature fhrunk back with all the indignation poffible to be poffeffed, by an honeft and loyal fubject, at the bare idea of qualifying the term treafon, by fubftituting that of revolt. Acting under thefe impreffions, he remained a perfectly tranquil and inoffenfive fpectator, of the great event which was then carrying into execution. The recognition of the prince of Orange, by the people of Britain, as their fovereign, under the title of William III. left Mr. Shovell perfectly at liberty to obey the dictates of his confcience, without reducing him to the neceffity of facrificing, even in the fmalleft particle, his honour or his reputation.

VOL. II. F Among

Among the firft naval appointments of the new
reign, was that of Mr. Shovell to be captain of the
Edgar, on board which fhip he led the van of admiral
Herbert's fquadron, at the battle in Bantry Bay, where
he diftinguifhed himfelf fo remarkably, that king
William conferred on him the honour of knighthood,
at the fame time when the earl of Torrington was
raifed to the peerage. His alertnefs had been fo repeatedly proved, that he was chofen as the fitteft perfon
to command, with the rank of commodore, a fmall
armament confifting of light fhips, equipped for the purpofe of intercepting any fupplies fent from France, for
the fervice of king James and the Irifh army. In this
occupation, he did not derogate from his former conduct, and the caufe of the exiled monarch was very
materially diftreffed, by his unremitted activity. In
the enfuing year, he commanded the fquadron which
covered the paffage of king William and his army to
the north part of Ireland; and fo attentive was he to
the fafety of this important charge, that his fovereign
confidered it a reward juftly due to his merit, to advance him to the rank of rear-admiral of the blue.
At the time the French fleet made its fudden and unexpected appearance in the Britifh Channel, in the year
1690, fir Cloudefly commanded a light detached fquadron, owing to which circumftance he was prevented
from fharing in the unmerited obloquy, fo generally caft
on the many brave men who commanded under the earl
of Torrington. He remained in conftant employ, and
having been in the interim promoted to be rear-admiral of the red, bore a diftinguifhed fhare in the de-

feat

feat of the count de Tourville. A sudden illness, with
which he was attacked, prevented his being engaged
in the same service which was confided to the care of
sir George Rooke, and executed by him with so much
adroitness and success. The misfortune of having
been named one of the commissioners for executing
the office of commander in chief of the fleet, in the ensuing year, necessarily involved him, for a moment, in
the general obloquy, so copiously vented against himself and his colleagues, in consequence of the disaster
which attended the naval campaign of that year. But
this frequently noxious popular rage, effected no injury, nor left the smallest stain. It was the breath of
impotent calumny, puffed on the face of a mirrour,
the high polish of which rendered it impervious, and
which instantly passed from the surface, without leaving
behind it the smallest vestige of its effect.

In 1694, sir Cloudesly, who had been advanced to
the rank of vice-admiral of the red, was appointed second in command, under lord Berkeley, of the fleet
sent into Camaret bay; and, when that noble lord
struck his flag for a time, which he did on the return
of the armament to England, sir Cloudesly succeeded
him in his command, and, by the express order of king
William, proceeded against Dunkirk. Successless as
that expedition proved, not the slightest complaint was
ever made, in respect to the conduct of the admiral:
indeed, it would have been singularly unjust if there
had; for, impelled, on one hand, by the truest zeal for
the public service, and warned, on the other, as to the
extreme caution it was highly incumbent on every

commander

commander in chief to ufe, provided he wifhed to avoid popular cenfure, in cafe of failure, he reconnoitred the fituation of the enemy fo completely, as to enable him to demonftrate moft clearly, the abfolute impracticability of carrying the plan into effect, according to the method propofed by the projectors, and fully to expofe their inexperience, their abfurdity, and folly. He was employed in the fame line of fervice, during the whole remainder of the war: St. Maloes, Calais, and others among the minor French ports, felt the dreadful effect of his artificial thunder, fo that it might be truly faid, where the completeft fuccefs was wanting, the fault refted not with fir Cloudefly Shovell. His naval employment ceafed for a time, with his having commanded the efcort which attended king William to Holland, immediately previous to the peace of Ryfwic. When the turbulent temper of Louis XIV. began again to manifeft itfelf in 1699, the abilities of fir Cloudefly were immediately called for to fill an active ftation. He accordingly affumed the command of a ftrong fleet, fent into the Channel, as he afterwards did during the two fucceeding years: a cautionary fhow of refiftance, which, in all probability, tended to render the actual difplay of it unneceffary, till after the acceffion of queen Anne. The firft important fervice on which he was employed after the recommencement of the war, was not more difficult and dangerous, than the more active and brilliant occupation of performing that which preceded, had proved; the triumphant fleet of fir George Rooke, in which were comprifed feveral large heavy fhips,

as

as it was confidered dangerous that they fhould remain out of their own ports, during the winter, was ordered to return to England, and fir Cloudefly was in confequence difpatched to Vigo, with a fleet, amounting to nearly twenty fail, for the purpofe of efcorting from thence, the captured fhips of the enemy, with the treafure, and valuable commodities they contained. In the execution of this fervice, the exertion of the moft confummate prudence, as well as of activity, became neceffary. The feafon of the year was peculiarly unfavourable, the difabled ftate of a confiderable part of the fleet, particularly of the prizes, was alarming; the weight of the truft, with refpect to pecuniary value, immenfe; but the genius of fir Cloudefly obviated the two firft difficulties, and the reward of his diligence was found in the enrichment of the happy captors, together with the delivery of their well-earned fortunes in the ports of Britain, with lefs diminution from accident, than could poffibly have been expected.

In 1703, he commanded the fleet of Britain, ftationed in the Mediterranean, and in the enfuing year, commanded the van of the combined fleet, in the battle off Malaga. The gallantry which he difplayed on this occafion, had nearly proved fatal to him. The French, who were fuperior, particularly in that part of their line, attempted to furround him, and the execution of the project feemed on the point of being effected. The commander in chief, however, fir George Rooke, perceiving the danger, with which he was threatened, preffed forwards to his refcue, and

effected

effected it without difficulty. Historians correctly observe, that the chance of war, immediately afterwards, afforded sir Cloudesly an opportunity of repaying the assistance rendered him by sir George, the centre division being severely pressed by the enemy, in consequence of several of the ships which composed it, being obliged to quit the line, through the want of shot, and fixed ammunition, an inconvenience, occasioned by the long continuance of the action. In the month of January 1704-5, sir Cloudesly received the honorary appointment of rear-admiral of England, and in the month of May following, was sent to the Mediterranean, commander in chief of a noble armament, ordered thither for the purpose of co-operating with king Charles III. and his generals, in the reduction of Spain to his dominion. The capture of Barcelona, one of the most important services performed during the war, has been with justice, attributed principally to the assistance afforded by the admiral.

It was determined in the British cabinet, to renew the operations in the same quarter, during the ensuing year ; but the extremely reprehensible, though customary tardiness of the Dutch, prevented the combined fleet from quitting Torbay, till the 1st day of October; a period when reason and common sense, must have impressed it, most forcibly on the meanest capacity, that no naval operations could possibly be entered into, during the then current year. Nor was this the whole of the inconvenience to be complained of ; subject to the assaults of adverse winds, and the tempestuous weather, which rarely fails to prevail at that season of

the

the year, the fleet received fo much damage on its paſ-
fage to the fouthward, and fo completely was it difperfed, that its rendezvous at Liſbon, and the refitment it was neceſſary it fhould undergo, confumed
a very confiderable portion of the fhort remainder
of it.

During the continuance of fir Cloudefly at Liſbon,
the whim, caprice, and ill temper of the Portugueſe,
inflamed by the improper conduct of one of the princes
of the royal family, created much anxiety in the mind
of the admiral, and might, under men lefs firm and
prudent than himfelf, have been attended with very difagreeable confequences. The bufineſs ended, however,
with the greateſt eclat and credit, both to the admiral
himfelf, and the whole Britiſh nation. In the enfuing
year, he was engaged in co-operating with the duke
of Savoy, who undertook the fiege of Toulon, the
failure of which expedition was certainly by no means
afcribable, to any want of exertion on the part of the
fleet. After having feen the military force, which he
had in vain attempted to lead to victory, in fafety back
to Italy, from whence it had proceeded, he prepared
to return to his own native country, a fpot, which fate
had deftined him never to reach; the Affociation, alas!
which bore the admiral's flag, having, together with two
other ſhips of war, one carrying feventy, the other fifty
guns, been unfortunately thrown on the rocks of
Scilly, on the evening of the 22d of October 1707.
Such was the melancholy fate of the brave fir Cloudefly
Shovell, who fell a prey to the element, on which he

F 4   had

had acquired fo much honour, in the fifty-feventh year
of his age. As a well-merited tribute of national gratitude, his body, which was taken up on the Scilly
iflands, was conveyed to England, and buried with the
greateft funeral pomp in Weftminfter Abbey, at the
public expence, as appears by the following notification, in the London Gazette. "Whitehall, December 31ft. On the 22d inftant was performed the interment of fir Cloudefly Shovell, who was unfortunately loft in the Affociation, on the rocks called the
Bifhop and Clerks, off Scilly, on the 22d of October
laft, and his body taken up under the rocks of St.
Mary's. He was, at the time of his death, rear-admiral of Great Britain, and admiral and commander
in chief of her majefty's fleet, one of the council to
his royal highnefs prince George of Denmark, an
appointment with which he was honoured on the 28th
of June, preceding his death; one of the elder bro-
thers of the Trinity Houfe; of Deptford Strond, and
one of the governors of the royal hofpital for the
maintenance of aged and difabled feamen at Greenwich. He acquitted himfelf in thefe ftations with an
univerfal reputation; and through the whole conduct
of his life was honoured for a certain peculiar frank-
nefs and honefty of behaviour. The body, after having
lain in ftate for many days, was conveyed, at the
queen's expence, from his late dwelling-houfe in Soho
Square, to the Abbey of Weftminfter, where it was
interred with all the pomp and magnificence fuitable
to fo mournful an occafion, and her majefty's high
regard

regard to the remains of fo brave and faithful an officer."

A particular circumftance attending his death has been preferved in the family of the earl of Romney, and is too interefting to be omitted: " The admiral was not drowned ; but, after having reached the fhore in fafety, was, according to the confeffion of an ancient woman, by her,, treacheroufly, and inhumanly murdered. This atrocious act, fhe, many years afterwards, when on her deathbed, revealed to the minifter of the parifh who attended her ; declaring fhe could not die in peace, till fhe had made this confeffion. She acknowledged, having been led to commit this horrid deed, for the fake of plunder ; and that fhe then had in her poffeffion, among other things, an emerald ring, which fhe had been afraid to fell, left it fhould lead to a difcovery. This ring, which was then delivered to the minifter, was by him given to James, earl of Berkeley (in poffeffion of whofe family it now remains), at his particular requeft, fir Cloudefly Shovell and himfelf having lived on terms of the moft intimate friendfhip. The manner of his death, as well as the difcovery of the ring, is related differently by Campbell, and others ; but from the channel through which the communication was made, we have every reafon to conclude this account is undoubtedly moft authentic."

He married the widow of his patron, fir John Narborough. The arms he bore were granted to him by order of queen Anne, in commemoration and honour of his well-known gallantry at Tripoli, and his

repeated

repeated fucceffes againft the French. He left two
daughters, Elizabeth, firft married to Robert, lord
Romney ; and fecondly, to John, earl of Hyndford ;
and 'Anne, firft married to the honourable Thomas
Manfel, eldeft fon to lord Manfel ; and fecondly, to
John Blackwood, efq.

JOHN LORD BERKELEY OF STRATTON.

WAS the second son of fir John Berkeley, and Chriftian, daughter of fir Andrew Piccard, prefident of the East India company. This lady was the widow of Henry, lord Kenfington, fon of Henry, earl of Holland. Sir John had ever fhewn himfelf the conftant, and loyal adherent to that unfortunate prince, king Charles I. ; and afterwards became the no lefs faithful follower of the apparently ruined fortunes of his fon, king Charles II. when in exile. The latter prince, in grateful confideration of the many eminent fervices, rendered to himfelf and his father, by this noble, and truly faithful perfon, raifed him to the peerage with the title of lord Berkeley of Stratton, by letters patent, dated at Bruffels on the 19th of May 1658. The family was of the greateft antiquity, being a branch from the ancient barons of Berkeley, of Berkeley Caftle, who were defcended from Robert Fitzharding, a perfonage of confiderable note at the time of the conqueft. The loyalty and attachment of the father to the caufe of his fovereign, and the fervice of his country,

try, appears to have defcended without the fmalleft
diminution, to his fons. Charles, the eldeft, having
entered into the fea-fervice, fell an unfortunate victim
to the fmall-pox ; and on his deceafe, the title devolved
on the fubject of the prefent memoirs. After having
been appointed a lieutenant in the navy on the 14th
of April 1685, he was rapidly promoted from thence,
to be captain of the Charles galley, a frigate, on the
9th of July in the enfuing year. He proceeded
immediately afterwards to the Mediterranean, and returned not until the month of May preceding the revolution, when he received two commiffions for different
fhips fucceffively, the Montague, and the Edgar ; the
latter being one of the fleet, put under the orders of lord
Dartmouth, in confequence, of the impending cloud
which then hung over the affairs of king James II.
It has been remarked of this nobleman, that he poffeffed the uncommon faculty, of rendering himfelf
loved and refpected by all parties, even when men
were moft fufpicious of each other, and the jarring
conflict of oppofite opinions, threatened the fubverfion
of all confidence whatever.

So high a rank did he hold in public eftimation, that
although he had himfelf, as well as his noble anceftor
and relative, ever fhewn the ftrongeft attachment to
the male branch of the houfe of Stuart, yet in the hour
of general ferment, when it might naturally have been
expected, that thofe who had openly declared themfelves inimical to the meafures of the fovereign, who
had abdicated, would have poffeffed a preference of
appointment, lord Berkeley was raifed to the rank of
a flag-

a flag-officer, though extremely young in the service, and appointed to act as rear-admiral of the fleet, under the orders of lord Dartmouth.

The honourable manner in which he filled the station, last mentioned, raised him as high in the estimation of his new sovereign, as he had been in that of his former master. He was established in the rank of rear-admiral of the red, and not only served in that capacity, under admiral Herbert, afterwards earl of Torrington, but was held in such high estimation as an officer, that when that noble lord, together with the larger ships, retired into port, at the approach of winter, lord Berkeley was left to cruise with the remaining ships to the westward, for the purpose of checking any attempt that might be made by France, in favour of the deposed James. After his return into port, about the middle of the month of January, he struck his flag, and did not accept of any subsequent command till the year 1693, when, having in the interim, been progressively promoted to the ranks of vice-admiral of the blue and of the red squadrons, in the month of July 1693, on the decease of sir John Ashby, his lordship was appointed to succeed him, and hoisted his flag accordingly on board the Victory, a first rate.

Though the naval operations of this summer were extremely unfortunate, no particle of blame was attached to lord Berkeley; nor was he less happy in the succeeding year, when the total failure of the expedition, sent out under his orders, for the attack of Brest took place. The public, nevertheless, pitied him, and instead of reproach,

reproach, endeavoured to heal and footh his anxiety; by
beftowing on him all the confolatory, compaffion they
poffeffed ; for, in this inftance, all Europe faw the
uncommon transfer of public fury, from the fhoulders
of the man who had been intrufted with the execution
of the projeçt, and who is moft generally, though erro-
neoufly held, firft in refponfibility as to the fuccefs of
it, to the characters of thofe, who had fo impotently
and unadvifedly contrived it. During the remainder
of the life of this noble perfon, he continued to be
employed in the attack of the different French ports,
immediately oppofite to the fhores of England ; and
notwithftanding thefe defultory attempts were very
rarely, if ever, attended with the fuccefs which was
expected from them, and fometimes might be faid to
be repelled with complete difcomfiture, the noble commander ftill continued to retain as high a place in popular efteem as ever. In fhort, his countrymen were convinced his lordfhip had on all occafions, literally fulfilled
the words of the poet ; and fhewn, that though it was
not in mortals to command fuccefs, he had done more,
he had deferved it.

Having been unfortunately attacked by a pleurify
and fever in the month of February 1696-7, medical
aid proved ineffectual to the prefervation of a life, which
during its fhort continuance had been exerted in a manner
fo highly honourable to the country which gave it birth.
He died on the 27th of February, being then only in
his thirty-fourth year. At the time of his deceafe, he
was admiral of the fleet, having never refigned that
appointment ; colonel of the regiment of marines ;
groom

groom of the stole to his royal highnefs prince George, and firft gentleman of his bedchamber. He married Jane, daughter of fir John Temple, of Eaft Sheen, in the county of Surrey, by whom he left one daughter, who died an infant.

It has been obferved, with juftice, that we have fcarcely an inftance in the annals of naval hiftory, of any officer's attaining fo high a rank, at fo early an age ; a rank he maintained for a feries of years, with a moft unblemifhed reputation, at a time when mif-carriages were frequent, and the undeferved reproach often attached to them, exceffive. Though no more than thirty-four years old at the time of his deceafe, yet he had borne the office of an admiral during eight. The fervices in which he was chiefly employed, were of a particular nature, new almoft in practice ; and previous to this time, little underftood. The firft in which he was engaged, was the moft unfortunate ; yet the ill fuccefs damped not his ardour, nor made him diffident of future victories. Nothing is more common than to charge a want of fuccefs to an impropriety in the orders received from the commander in chief, becaufe nothing more alleviates that particular weaknefs, and diftrefs of the human mind induced by defeat ; yet the marquis of Carmarthen, who was ordered upon the attack of Camaret fort, paid him, in his account of the expedition, the higheft compliments in the arrange-ments he made, and the great ability with which he conducted the fervice. Although it is not at all to the purpofe to inquire whether the fuccefs attending expe-ditions of that clafs in which he was engaged, was equi-valent to the expence of fitting them out, yet we can-

not

not help obferving, the advantages accruing from them were certainly of much greater national moment than the enemy would admit, or the opponents of adminiſtration were willing to believe. Among the foremoſt in the hour of danger, he encouraged thoſe whom he was ſent to command, by his perſonal example; he had, on every occaſion, the happineſs of effecting, all that fortitude, joined to prudence and ability, could poſſibly hope for, and died with the juſt reputation of a brave, experienced, and great commander, at an age when few have had ſufficient opportunity to acquire the ſmalleſt reputation or celebrity.

SIR JOHN LEAKE

From an Original Picture in the Trinity House.

Published June 1 1809, by J. Wilkie & Co. Paul Mall.

SIR JOHN LEAKE.

―――――

He was the second son of captain Richard Leake, the master-gunner of England, an appointment considered at that day of no mean consequence, which he is said to have obtained from no other recommendation than that of his own personal merit. Sir John was born at Rotherhithe, in the year 1666; and having entered into the navy at an early age, served as a midshipman on board the Royal Prince, in the ever-memorable sea-fight, which took place between the English and Dutch fleets on the 10th of October 1673. The reconciliation which was effected between the contending powers, almost immediately after the engagement, just mentioned, necessarily placing a temporary bar between Mr. Leake, and any hope for promotion, till some succeeding hostilities, or the expectation of them, should once more call him into notice, he engaged in the service of the merchants; but being not long afterwards appointed to succeed his father as gunner of the Neptune, he again returned into his original line of service. We find him present at the battle in Bantry Bay, as commander of the Firedrake, fire-ship, to which he had been appointed on the 24th of September, in

Vol. II.　　　　G　　　　the

the preceding year. As this was the firſt opportunity, which, owing to his former ſubordinate ſtation, fortune had favoured him with, of diſtinguiſhing himſelf, ſo did he not · fail to improve it, to the beſt advantage of his own charaȼter, and to the injury of the foe, oppoſed to him. His father, who appears to have been a man, poſſeſſing conſiderable ſcience in his profeſſion, had invented a particular ſpecies of ordnance, which threw a ſmall ſhell, or carcaſe, like the more modern invention of the cohorn, or howitzer. Mr. Leake having, under his inſtruȻtion, acquired conſiderable adroitneſs, in the management of this, at that time, extraordinary piece of artillery, threw ſeveral carcaſes, with ſuch effeȻt, as to ſet on fire one of the enemies' line of battle ſhips, commanded by the chevalier Coetlogon. Admiral Herbert particularly noticed his merit on this occaſion ; and rewarded it by promoting him, in two days after the aȻtion, to be captain of the Dartmouth, a ſhip of forty guns.

  Few men, perhaps, ever obtained promotion, more fairly earned, than was that of this gentleman, from the hour of his firſt appointment as an officer, to that of the concluſion of his life. In proof of this, he was not advanced from the rank of captain, which he obtained, as juſt mentioned, in 1689, to that of a flag-officer, till the month of December 1702 ; notwithſtanding he was, during the whole of the war, always aȻtively employed, and had on very many occaſions, moſt conſpicuouſly diſtinguiſhed himſelf. Among the ſervices which he had the fortune to perform, was that of the relief

of

of Londonderry, in the month of July, fubfequent to the battle of Bantry ; and the very remarkable, not to fay defperate, though fuccefsful manner, in which he fought the Eagle, off cape La Hogue, to the deftruction of the enemy, and the high advancement of his own reputation.

In general encounters it rarely happens, except in cafes where a fhip has been completely difmafted, and left to the mercy of the enemy, that the lofs of any one in particular, fhall exceed at leaft fourfold, that, of any other in the fleet ; yet fuch was the cafe in the inftance we now allude to ; and the recital of the cafualties fuftained, might, in days more remote, be confidered as exaggerated, or fabulous ; did not the fact reft on the proud bafis of official, and indifputable proof. Seventeen of the Eagle's guns were difmounted in the action, feventy of her crew killed, and one hundred and fifty wounded ; yet damaged as this unfortunate veffel, if fhe could be confidered fo, muft inevitably have been, fir George Rooke, when ordered to the attack of the fhips which had efcaped, removed his flag on board her, well knowing, and appreciating the value of Mr. Leake's abilities, together with the affiftance he would certainly receive from the exertion of them, in the particular enterprife on which he was then fent. During the remainder of the war, he conftantly was retained in commiffion ; having, after quitting the Eagle, been appointed to the Plymouth, a third rate, and fecondly, to the Offory, of ninety guns. Soon after the conclufion of the peace at Ryfwic, on the 20th of September 1697, the Offory was ordered to

G 2 be

be difmantled, and Mr. Leake was of courfe out of commiffion, though for the firft time, fince he had been promoted captain in the navy, previous to the revolution.

The death of his father taking place in the month of July 1696, the friends of Mr. Leake, in their honeft, well-meant zeal to ferve him, exerted their endeavours to procure him the appointment, as fucceffor to his parent, of mafter-gunner of England. Admiral Ruffel, in particular, interefted himfelf ftrongly on the occafion, with the earl of Romney, who was at that time mafter-general of the ordnance. All thefe exertions, however, as they had been made without the knowledge or privity, fo were they, without the approbation of captain Leake; who confidering his acceptance of fuch a poft, as a probable preclufion from obtaining any higher rank in the navy, than that which he then held, wifely, but in the handfomeft manner, declined availing himfelf of their recommendation; and, tired with a life of inactivity, requefted fome re-appointment, as a captain in the navy. His defire was complied with, and he was fucceffively commiffioned to the Kent, and Berwick, both of them third rates; but the fluctuating ftate of politics which then prevailed, and the alternate hefitation between peace, or war, fo manifeft in all the proceedings of the French court at that time, prevented both thefe commands, from being of any duration.

At length, when the intentions of Louis XIV. began to wear a ftill more ferious afpect than before, as was the cafe immediately preceding the death of

king

king William III., and it was determined on, that a
powerful armament fhould be fent to fea, under the
command of the earl of Pembroke and Montgomery,
then lord high admiral of England, who had never
been bred to the fervice ; captain Leake was ftrongly
recommended by his friend, Mr. Churchill, to his
lordfhip, who refolved to appoint him his captain, as
needing the fcientific abilities of the former, in aid of
his own natural zeal for the fervice of his country.

The death of the king, caufed the removal of the
earl of Pembroke from the admiralty board, for the purpofe of making room for prince George of Denmark,
hufband to the queen; which alfo, as a natural confequence, cancelled the appointment, as well of the
earl, as commander of the fleet, as of Mr. Leake, his
intended captain. As a recompenfe, however, for this
difappointment, he was made captain of the Affociation, a fecond rate, but in lefs than three weeks
removed from that fhip into the Exeter, of fixty guns,
on being ordered to Newfoundland, on an expedition
againft the fifhery, and colony eftablifhed there by
France. The moft complete fuccefs attended this
little defultory attempt ; upwards of fifty fail of the
fhips, and enemies' veffels, being taken or deftroyed,
together with the whole of their fettlements, and
buildings on fhore, that were of any confequence.
Soon after his return, that is to fay, in the month of
December 1702, he was advanced to the rank of rear-
admiral of the blue, and commander of the fhips at
Spithead. In the month of March following; as if as
a recompenfe for the dilatorinefs of his advancement

from

from the rank of captain, while he himfelf had beheld many younger, though not more meritorious officers than himfelf, placed over his head, he was appointed vice-admiral of the blue fquadron.

During the year 1703, no naval occurrence took place worthy of being commemorated; and early in the enfuing year, the vice-admiral was appointed to command the convoy ordered to Lifbon, for the protection of the immenfe fleet of tranfports and ftorefhips, fent thither for the fervice of king Charles III. Immediately previous to this, he received the honour of knighthood, and having reached the Tagus, with his important charge, in perfect fafety, put himfelf in the month of March under the orders of fir George Rooke; and in April following accompanied that gallant admiral, on his very fuccefsful cruife, into the Mediterranean. The fleet was on its return from thence back, as it is reported, to Lifbon; but this refolution was changed, while on their paffage thither, by the recommendation, and as many people, with apparent truth infift, by the exprefs advice of fir John Leake, who propofed to attempt Gibraltar by a coup de main. The fuccefs which attended the execution of this fpirited project, is well known.

In the battle off Malaga, which took place in the month of Auguft following, fir John, who had his flag flying on board the St. Gecrge, a fecond rate, commanded the leading divifion of the blue, which was the van fquadron, and fo warmly attacked the French flag-officer oppofed to him, Monf. D'Imfreville, vice-admiral of the French white and blue, as to

compel

compel him, after a very warm conteſt of four hours
continuance, to ſeek his ſaſety in retreat ; a conduct,
which appeared almoſt as the immediate prelude, to
the retirement and flight, of the enemies' whole van diviſion. On the return of the combined fleet to England, ſir John was ordered to remain at Gibraltar and
Liſbon, for the protection of the former place, from
any attempt that might be made by France to recover
it. He diſplayed, while thus employed, the greateſt
activity and diligence ; for having received intelligence,
while the ſquadron was in a ſtate of reſitment at Liſbon, of the arrival of a French force, he haſtened back
to the Mediterranean with ſuch expedition, as to
ſurpriſe, and either capture, or deſtroy all the light
veſſels attached to the armament of the enemy, the
line of battle ſhips, having unfortunately quitted Gibraltar bay a few days before. In the check given
to them on this occaſion, two large frigates, of thirty-
ſix guns each, a corvette, a fire-ſhip, and ſeveral
veſſels of inferior note, were driven on ſhore, and deſtroyed.

In the month of January 1705, he was joined at
Liſbon by ſir Thomas Dilkes, who reinforced him
with a ſquadron of five ſhips of war, carrying him at
the ſame time a commiſſion, appointing him vice-
admiral of the white ſquadron, and commander in chief
of her majeſty's ſhips and veſſels employed in the Mediterranean. Having on the 6th of March collected
his whole force, he proceeded from the Tagus, at the
head of a noble fleet, conſiſting of no leſs than thirty-
five ſhips of the line ; twenty-three of which were

G 4 Engliſh,

Englifh, and the remainder either Dutch or Portûguefe.
His arrival in the bay of Gibraltar, was a fecond time
fo fudden, and fo totally unexpeâed by the enemy,
that he had the good fortune completely to furprife the
baron de Pointi, together with the whole of his fquadron, confifting of five fhips of the line; which had in
vain attempted to co-operate with the army that befieged it. The following fuccinâ account was officially given of this little fuccefs : " About half an
hour paft five in the morning, the fquadron got within
two miles of cape Cabarita, and difcovered only five
fail making out of the bay, at whom a gun was fired
from Europa point ; whereupon, concluding that the
garrifon was fafe, we gave chafe to thofe five fhips,
which proved to be the Magnanimous, a French fhip
of war of feventy-four guns; the Vaiffeau, of eighty-
fix (this fhip is generally called the Fleur-de-lis) ;
the Ardent of fixty-fix ; the Arrogant of fixty ; and the
Marquis of fifty-fix. At firft they made for the Barbary fhore, but feeing our fleet gained upon them, they
ftood for the Spanifh fhore. At nine o'clock, fir
Thomas Dilkes, on board her majefty's fhip the Revenge, together with the Newcaftle, and a Dutch man
of war, got within gun-fhot of the Arrogant ; and,
after a very little refiftance, fhe ftruck, the Newcaftle's
boat firft getting on board her. Before one o'clock,
the Ardent and the Marquis were taken by two Dutch
men of war ; and the Magnanimous, with the Vaiffeau,
driven on fhore a little to weftward of Marbella ;
the former, which the baron de Pointi was on board
of, run afhore with fo much force, that all her mafts

came

came by the board as soon as she struck upon the ground, and only her hull, from the taffril to the midships, remained above water, which the enemy set fire to in the night, as they did to the Vaisseau the next morning."

The consequence, as might have been foreseen from this smoke, was the immediate retirement of the besieging army, and the complete termination of the siege, for that time. Although persons unacquainted with the nature of the sea service, may, on a comparison of the superiority of the victors, with the diminutive force of the enemy, be inclined to think more lightly of the merit, truly due to this advantage, than it very fairly deserves; yet others, better informed, will know well how to appreciate the talents of the commander, who could, joined to such secrecy, exert so much activity, and effect the surprise of an exceedingly wary and alert enemy. The prince of Hesse, at that time governor of the relieved fortress, bore the highest testimony to the admiral's worth, and in grateful proof of the honourable estimation in which he held his service, presented him with a very valuable gold cup, expressly provided on the occasion. Having returned back to Lisbon, he put himself under the orders of sir Cloudesly Shovell, who arrived there with a formidable reinforcement. The Mediterranean was chosen, as the destined sea of marine enterprise for the year; and after the reduction of Barcelona, that admiral, with the larger ships, having returned to England for the winter, sir John resumed the chief command of the naval force

in

in that quarter, and in the enfuing fpring rendered
the common caufe of the allies the moft fignal fervice, by raifing the fiege of Barcelona, in which
city king Charles III. was then reduced to the
greateft extremity, by the preffure of the duke of
Anjou, with his army on the land fide, and that
of the count de Touloufe, with a powerful French
fleet from the feaward.

He was not, however, fortunate enough, as on the
foregoing occafion, to furprife the French naval armament, which, having unfortunately received timely
intelligence of his approach, fought its fafety in flight
to the harbour of Toulon, but the confequence was,
in a different line of fuccefs, productive of equal advantage with the former; the duke of Anjou having
precipitately raifed the fiege, and abandoned to his
rival, the whole of his cannon, camp-equipage, and
military ftores.   The reduction of Carthagena, of
Alicant, of the iflands of Yvica, and Majorca, added
to the catalogue of meritorious fervices, performed by
fir John Leake during the fame naval campaign.   On
the approach of winter, he returned to England, where
the honeft applaufe of his countrymen, and the complete approbation of his conduct, on the part of prince,
George of Denmark, and the queen, fatisfied his higheft
ambition, without augmenting his vanity.   The latter,
as a more fubftantial proof of her efteem, ordered
him a thoufand pounds from her privy purfe, and her
royal confort prefented him, as a token of his regard,
and as a more appropriate gift from himfelf, with a
gold-hilted fword, and a valuable diamond ring.   During

ring the fummer of the year 1706, fir John Leake commanded in chief, in the Britifh channel, but no enemy
appeared for him to encounter.   In the enfuing year,
having been appointed admiral of the white, and com-
-mander in chief of the fleet, he was fent again into
the Mediterranean ; while on his paffage thither, having had the good fortune to fall in with a numerous
fleet of victuallers, belonging to the enemy, he captured no lefs than feventy-five fail, which he carried with
him to Barcelona ; and, as in the former inftance, he
had enjoyed the good fortune of preferving his majefty,
king Charles III. and his army, from the fwords of
their enemies, fo had he, in the prefent, the happinefs
of preventing their perifhing by famine, with which
they were then grievoufly threatened, in confequence
of the fuperiority derived by the duke of Anjou, from
his victory at Almanza.

After having relieved Barcelona, and convoyed thither the confort of king Charles, with a confiderable
reinforcement of troops, which accompanied her from
Italy, he proceeded to Sardinia, which ifland he fpeedily
reduced, as he immediately afterwards did Minorca ; fervices fo highly advantageous to the common caufe, that
medals were ftruck, for the purpofe of perpetuating
the memory of them.   He returned to England, in
the month of October, having been appointed, during
his abfence in the Mediterranean, one of the council
to prince George of Denmark, the lord high admiral.
Sir John, however, fcarcely reached England in time
to take his feat at the board, the prince dying on the

28th

28th of October, only fix days fubfequent to his arrival. The earl of Pembroke, who fucceeded the prince.
in his office, again appointed fir John admiral of the
home, or channel fleet, for the enfuing year; and on
the 24th of May, he was created by letters patent rear-
admiral of Great Britain. It is properly remarked
in his life, publifhed by Stephen Martin Leake, efq.
of the college of arms, that this appointment, highly
honourable in itfelf, was rendered ftill more fo, by the
very marked manner in which it was given on the
prefent occafion. Queen Anne had purpofely kept
it vacant ever fince the death of fir Cloudefly Shovell,
and now conferred it on fir John Leake, without the
fmalleft interpofition on the part of her minifters, or
application from his friends. In beftowing it on him,
fhe ufed, as is reported by Campbell, the following
high compliment, " that fhe was put in mind of it by
the voice of the whole people."

The remainder of the war paffed on without any
occurrence, that in the fmalleft degree difturbed the naval
tranquillity of the contending powers; and on the 8th
of November following, fir John, having been appointed
one of the commiffioners for executing the office of
lord high admiral, relinquifhed his naval command
for a time, and remained on fhore during the enfuing year. He, however, re-hoifted his flag in the
following fpring, but the fame inactivity continuing
to prevail on the part of the enemy, the naval occurrences of the time, were ftill reftricted to harmlefs
cruifes, and the inoffenfive operations of putting to

fea,

fea, and returning back into port: When the preliminaries of peace were figned, in the year 1712, fir John was fent, with general Hill, in the month of July, to take poffeffion of Dunkirk, according to the treaty; and having on his return from thence ftruck his flag, never again accepted of any naval command.

Owing to fome court cabal, and the perfonal diflike to fir John, entertained by fome individuals, who poffeffed irrefiftible influence in the councils of king George I., the admiral, although it was impoffible for the moft inveterate malice, to affix the flighteft ftigma, or flur on his character, was moft unjuftly and fcandaloufly difmiffed, not only from the admiralty board, but from every appointment he then held. Future ages may read the fact in the page of political hiftory, but it is to be hoped, for the honour of nature, many of thofe, who do read it, will be fceptical enough to doubt it. To crown at once, obferves his biographer, the ill ufage he met with from thofe perfons, who, at that day, called themfelves friends to their country, this man, who had fpent the whole of his life, honeftly, and with unblemifhed reputation in its fervice, who had procured it at leaft as folid, if not as brilliant advantages, as any, either of his cotemporaries, or predeceffors had done, was obliged to retire, on a munificent penfion of 600*l.* a year, a fum barely equivalent to his half-pay; yet this he accepted without a murmur; without the fmalleft attempt, by painting the hardfhips of his cafe, to render odious, the government

vernment of that nation, to which he had ever
proved himfelf a fteady friend, a zealous defender,
and an able minifter. Retiring to a country villa,
erected by himfelf, near Greenwich, he continued
ever afterwards to live a private life, and died on
the 21ft of August 1720, in the fixty-fifth year of
his age.

GEORGE BYNG, LORD VISCOUNT TORRINGTON.

This noblemen was the eldeſt ſon of John Byng, eſq. of Wrotham in the county of Kent, of whoſe family the following heraldic particulars are given by Collins. "Robert Byng, of Wrotham, the direct anceſtor of the lord viſcount Torrington,- ſerved for the borough of Abingdon, in the firſt parliament of queen Elizabeth, in the year 1559, and in the thirty-fourth year of her reign was ſheriff for the county of Kent. He married to his firſt wife, Frances, daughter and heireſs of Richard Hill, eſq. by whom he had iſſue, three ſons, George, John, and Francis, the two latter of whom died without iſſue. The ſaid Robert dying the 2d of September 1595, left George, above-mentioned, his ſon and heir, then thirty-nine years old. This George was choſen member of parliament for Rocheſter in the county of Kent, in the 27th of Elizabeth, and for the port of Dover in the firſt of James I. He married Jane, daughter of William Cromer, of Tunſtall, in Kent, eſq. and by her had iſſue, three ſons and four daughters. Dying in 1616, he was ſucceeded

ceeded by George his eldeft fon and heir, born at
Wrotham 1594. He married in 1617, Catharine,
daughter of John Hewet, of Headly Hall; in the
county of York, efq.. John Byng, his fon and heir,
conveying away the eftate of Wrotham, was the laft
of this family which was fettled there. He married
Philadelphia, daughter of ———— Johnfon, of Loans in
the county of Surry ; and by her had feveral children,
of which the eldeft was George Byng, the firft lord
vifcount Torrington, born at Wrotham on the 27th
of January 1663." Having imbibed, according to report, a very early attachment to the naval fervice, he
procured, in the year 1678, through the intereft of his
royal highnefs·James, duke of York, what was then
called the king's letter; a neceffary fpecies·of warrant
or permiffion for entering into the fervice, in the line
of an officer, of late years almoft totally forgotten :
but when granted, conferring on the perfon who
poffeffed it, the fame rank and character, with that of
the midfhipman of the prefent day ; from this circumftance, young officers in that clafs, continued to be
called king's letter boys, long after the cuftom of iffuing
fuch warrants fell into difufe. In 1681, he quitted
the fea-fervice for a time, and, entering into the army,
through the perfuafion of general Kirk, at that time
governor of Tangier, became a cadet. He was quickly
afterwards·progreffively advanced by the fame friend
and patron, to be an enfign, and afterwards lieutenant
in the general's own company.. In the year 1683-4,
it having been determined by the Englifh government
to evacuate Tangier, Mr. Byng was advifed, employ-

ment

ment as a military officer being, at that time, extremely circumfcribed, to return again to his original
line of fervice. The lord Dartmouth, from whom,
as it is faid, this counfel proceeded, appointed him, on
the 23d of February 1683-4, lieutenant of the Oxford; but, notwithftanding; he had thus quitted the
army, he is faid to have retained his rank therein, for
feveral years afterwards.

Having proceeded to the Eaft Indies, in the courfe
of the enfuing fummer, as lieutenant of the Phœnix,
he there was favoured by fortune with a fignal opportunity of difplaying that intrepidity and total contempt of danger, which, even his bittereft enemies have
not been hardy enough to deny him, the credit of having poffeffed. The opportunity alluded to, was an
action with a Cinganian pirate, in the courfe of which
encounter, Mr. Byng having boarded the enemy, by
order of his captain, fucceeded, after a moft defperate
refiftance, in compelling the foe to fubmit, though
not till a confiderable part of his people were killed,
and himfelf dangeroufly wounded. The hour of péril,
however, did not ceafe with the capture itfelf, for the
pirate veffel had received fo much injury in the encounter, that it funk almoft in the fame inftant, and
Mr. Byng was refcued from the waves with the utmoft difficulty, when nearly deprived of every appearance of life.

Although he held no higher ftation than that of lieutenant in the navy, at the time of the revolution; yet, having returned to England fome months before the event
juft mentioned took place, he foon difplayed all the propenfity to political intrigue, which renders the fervice of a

man fo gifted peculiarly valuable in the hour of popular tumult, and commotion. His abilities in this abftract line of fervice naturally caufed him to be fpecially recommended, to the prince of Orange, who,
finding both his temper and qualifications remarkably
well adapted to the then exifting exigencies of his fervice,
employed him as a confidential perfon to found the difpofitions of, and tamper* with fuch officers as it was
thought could be ufeful, and attach them, if poffible, to
the caufe of the revolution. It is invariably to be expected, that a man who really acts from principle, will
always act well, even though he may act illegally. Mr.
Byng being, from the ftrong bias of his political prejudices, a vehement enemy to the government, and perhaps
to the perfon of king James II. executed his function
with all the diligence, and zeal of a Machiavel. He
ftrengthened the minds of the timid, he fixed thofe of
the wavering, he converted vehement oppofition, he
inflamed the minds of friends, and endeavoured to in-
timidate thofe of foes ; in fhort, he neutralized the
alkali of loyalty with the acid of republicanifm.
He confidered the prince of Orange as ufeful to his
purpofe ; a fpecies of ftalking-horfe that it was neceffary for him to conceal himfelf behind, in order
to procure the permiffion of promulgating even thofe
qualified political tenets, within the bounds of which,
the moderation and good fenfe of certain perfons, to
whom Mr. Byng condefcended, on this occafion, to
become the creature and the agent, compelled him to
reftrain the fiery qualities of his own mind.

* In the lower fphere of political intrigue ; while Ruffel, afterwards earl
of Orford, was engaged in the higher circle. See vol. ii. page 41.

The activity, which, as has been before obſerved, he diſplayed throughout the whole of this buſineſs, neceſſarily procured him conſtant employment in the ſame ſpecies of ſervice. He was ſelected by the lord Dartmouth from among all the officers, even thoſe of the higheſt rank in the fleet, to convey to the prince of Orange his ſubmiſſion to the voice of his country, and his obedience to any future commands his ſerene high-neſs might pleaſe to honour him with. Mr. Byng was attended on this occaſion, by the captains Haſtings and Aylmer, both of them his ſuperiors in command and even in rank. But, however ſingular the choice may appear, to thoſe who are unacquainted with the cauſe of it, they, certainly, when poſſeſſed of the de-velopement, will not refuſe their aſſent, that the rea-ſon was one of the moſt politic that ever exiſted. It was extremely natural for the noble admiral to conſider no perſon ſo proper to make his peace with the new ſovereign, as the man whoſe intrigues had ſo ably aſſiſted, in raiſing the prince to that ſituation. How far the lord Dartmouth was juſtified in his expectation, the cool reflection of future ages will be beſt able to determine : ſuffice it on the preſent occaſion, to ſay, that the noble lord died a ſhort time afterwards, a priſoner in the Tower.

Immediately after the acknowledged acceſſion of king William to the Britiſh throne, Mr. Byng was appointed to the Dover, and quickly afterwards ad-vanced to be captain of a third rate, the Hope, of ſeventy guns, in which ſhip he very conſpicuouſly diſplayed that bravery which was naturally inherent in

H 2   him,

him, at the battle off Beachy Head, as one of the feconds to fir George Rooke. He afterwards removed into the Royal Oak, and fignalized himfelf as much as on the occafion juft mentioned, in the battle off La Hogue. About this time a very cordial intimacy is faid to have taken place between Mr. Byng, and admiral Ruffel; but writers have been divided in their opinions, whether this mutual attachment originated in the fimilarity of their political fentiments, or in that admiration which frequently attracts the attention and love of one brave man, towards the actions of another, whofe conduct as an officer, promifes to be no lefs brilliant than his own. The remainder of Mr. Byng's appointments during the war, were extremely honourable to himfelf *, though they would prove uninterefting in the detail; his naval and civil life having, during the period to which we allude, been unmarked by any occurrence, or anecdote, worthy to be related.

Mr. Byng held no naval commiffion fubfequent to the peace of Ryfwic, till after the acceffion of queen Anne; he was then appointed captain of the Naffau, one of the fquadron fent under the orders of fir Cloudefly Shovell, to Vigo, in the month of October 1702; and, foon after his return to England, that is to fay, in the month of March 1702-3, was advanced to the rank of rear-admiral of the red fquadron. Hav-

---

* In the year 1694, he was appointed firft captain, or, in other words, captain of the fleet to his friend admiral Ruffel, who hoifted his flag on board the Britannia, and with whom he remained fo long as he continued in command.

ing

ing hoifted his flag on board the Ranelagh of eighty guns, he proceeded to the Mediterranean almoft immediately, under the orders of fir Cloudefly Shovell, his former commander. Towards the clofe of the year, he was fent to Algiers, by his commander in chief, to renew a treaty of peace which then fubfifted between Great Britain and that regency. Having arranged the bufinefs, perfectly to his fatisfaction, and to his credit alfo, he proceeded to return to England; and, when arrived in the Britifh channel, very narrowly efcaped deftruction in that hurricane, by way of pre-eminence, called the great ftorm, which took place in the month of November 1703. In the enfuing year he was fent, for the third time, under the orders of fir Cloudefly Shovell, to join fir George Rooke, who had failed thither before them, at Lifbon. In the brilliant operations which took place during the naval campaign of this year, admiral Byng bore a very pre-eminent fhare. The attack on Gibraltar was folely confided to his command by the admiral in chief; and, at the battle off Malaga, his divifion fuffered more than any in the fleet, that of fir George Rooke only excepted. The fhips which he more immediately commanded unfortunately laboured under the fevereft difqualification during the action: the greater part of their fhot had been expended againft Gibraltar, and nothing but the moft fcientific exertions, in point of feamanfhip as well as gallantry, could have enabled them to counteract this difadvantage, or prevent the line from being forced in that part of the fleet, feveral of the fhips in the divifion having been obliged to quit

it,

it, through the abfolute want of ammunition to annoy the enemy.

His merit neither paffed unnoticed, nor unrewarded, though it has been believed; the reward was confidered by the admiral, not adequate to the fervice for which it was beftowed. On his return to England, he was received at court with the moft flattering approbation by the queen, who took the opportunity of declaring on the occafion, that fhe conferred on him the honour of knighthood, which fhe then beftowed, as a teftimony of the regard fhe entertained for his fervice, rendered in the preceding battle. In the enfuing year, having, at the very commencement of it, been advanced to the rank of vice-admiral of the blue, he was appointed to command a ftout fquadron, compofed of fmaller fhips of the line and frigates, fitted out to cruife in the Britifh channel, for the purpofe of preventing the dreadful depredations which were perpetually committed by the large privateers, and frigates of the enemy, as well as to confine, within the narroweft bounds poffible, the commerce, which ftill continued to be carried on from the ports of France, in defiance, as it wer, of the acknowledged fuperiority of the Britifh and Dutch navies.

The activity of fir George was crowned with confiderable fuccefs: among the prizes taken by him during the fummer, were reckoned, one French fhip of war, mounting forty-four guns, twelve privateers, mounting from twelve to thirty-fix, together with fix merchant-veffels, and many others of inferior note. During the year 1706, he commanded in the Mediterranean,

terranean, under fir John Leake, and very gallantly contributed to the manifold fucceffes, with which the operations of that powerful armament were crowned. On the return of fir John to England, the chief command of the remaining fhips refted with fir George, till the arrival of fir Cloudefly Shovell; and, on his return homeward with that brave but unfortunate admiral, very narrowly and almoft miraculoufly efcaped being fhipwrecked,[1] as well as himfelf. " At fix at night," fays the London Gazette, " the admiral hoifted the fignal to make fail; foon after feveral fhips made fignal of danger, as did alfo fir Cloudefly himfelf. The Royal Anne, the flag-fhip of fir George Byng, that was not then half a mile to windward of him, faw feveral breakers, and, foon after, the rocks above water; upon one of which fhe faw the Affociation ftrike, and, in lefs than two minutes, difappear. The Royal Anne was faved by great prefence of mind, both in officers and men, who, in a minute's time, fet her top-fails, one of the rocks not being a fhip's length to leeward of her."

[1] On the 26th of January 1707-8, fir George was advanced to be rear-admiral of the blue, and was appointed to command a fquadron fent into the North Sea, in order to oppofe a French armament, commanded by the chevalier de Forbin, one of the ableft officers in the French navy, equipped for the purpofe of covering the invafion of Scotland. The activity difplayed by fir George, and the furprife occafioned by his fudden appearance off the coaft of Flanders, produced, as it were, the inftantaneous effect of paralyzing the fur-

ther

ther profecution of the plan. Expreffes were difpatched to Paris, with an account of the combined armament, which had been fo unexpectedly, and, according to the enemy's opinion, almoft miraculoufly collected. The chevalier de Forbin, the French naval commander in chief, himfelf, remonftrated againft the further profecution of the attempt, at that time, and, confequently, advifed its poftponement.

The imagination of Louis had, however, become fo heated, and confident of fuccefs, that he immediately fent orders for the armament to fail; at all hazards. A violent gale of wind having, in the beginning of March, blown the Englifh fquadron off the coaft, and compelled it to take fhelter in the Downs, Forbin feized the opportunity, and pufhed out to fea. Such had been the vigilance of fir George, in ftationing his light veffels to watch any movements that might take place from Dunkirk, that the rear of the enemy's fleet had fcarcely quitted the harbour, ere fir George was apprifed of the event. An immediate and moft active purfuit took place, and, notwithftanding Forbin difplayed the moft confummate abilities, in parrying and avoiding the attempts made by the armament under fir George, to bring him to action, or otherwife defeat the intended project, the threatened invafion terminated in the capture of one of the enemy's fhips (the Salifbury, of fifty guns, which had been taken from the Englifh fome time before), and the return of the remainder back to the port from whence it proceeded, without having fulfilled the fmalleft object to attain which it had been equipped.

Although

Although the fuccefs which attended the conduct of
the British admiral was as complete as it poſſibly could
have been, except in the event of actually deſtroying
or capturing Forbin, and his whole fleet; although
the expedition had been totally fruſtrated, the vain-
preſumptuous hopes of Louis entirely blaſted, and a
probable check given to all repetitions of a ſimilar attempt in future : although theſe advantages had been
acquired to England, without difficulty, and without
loſs, there were, nevertheleſs, many perſons who
affected to depreciate the character of the British admiral, and even to condemn him for not abſolutely
preventing that, which was totally out of his power,
the return of Forbin back to France. Had any other
officer, perhaps, than Forbin been ſelected to command
the expedition, it might not have eſcaped ſo well;
but, under the management it was placed, the retreat
was too carefully and ably conducted, to have been
poſſibly attended with greater ruin, than that which
actually befel it.

These partial clamours were ſoon, however, ſtifled
by the general approbation expreſſed of his conduct by
all ranks of people. Corporate bodies preſented him
with their thanks, and the freedom of their towns.
The legiſlature declared its complete ſatisfaction for the
happy diſcomfiture of an expedition, which, in its outſet, had threatened ſo much ; and the queen herſelf
finiſhed the climax of general applauſe, by declaring
her acquieſcence in the propriety of it. From this
time ſir George continued to be employed in the two-
fold capacity of one of the council to the lord high
admiral,

admiral, and, after his deceafe, of one of the commiffioners for executing the office, added to that of a
naval commander, as long as it was neceffary to keep
a fleet at fea. Some political, difagreement caufed him
to refign the poft of commiffioner of the admiralty, in
the year 1713; and, during the very fhort remainder
of the queen's reign, he retired into private life. The
acceffion of king George I. reinftated him in his civil
appointment; and, in the year 1715, he was again
made commander in chief of a fleet fent into the North
Sea, for the purpofe of preventing the introduction of
any fupplies from France into Scotland, for the ufe of
the Pretender, who had arrived there in perfon a fhort
time before. The activity which he difplayed on this
occafion, and the political addrefs with which he, in a
great meafure, neutralized the fupport of France, fo
far as it extended to the caufe of the houfe of Stuart,
was fo extremely fatisfactory and grateful to the king,
that he created him a baronet, and prefented him with
a very valuable diamond ring, as an efpecial mark of
his own perfonal efteem for him. In 1717, a repetition of a fimilar attempt being threatened, under the
aufpices of that ever-reftlefs prince, Charles XII. of
Sweden, fir George Byng was fent into the Baltic,
with a ftrong fquadron, and his appearance there put
an end to the bufinefs at once, for it prevented the
Swedifh fleet from ever getting out to fea.

In the following year, Spain having manifefted the
ftrongeft inclination to difturb the public quietude, by
equipping a very formidable fleet in the Mediterranean,
deftined, as it was fuppofed, for the attack of Naples,

fir George was fent thither with an armament, confifting of twenty fhips of the line, and fix fmaller veffels. The Britifh fleet was, on its arrival, hailed by
the Neapolitans with a joy, almoft bordering on
frenzy; they relied with the firmeft confidence on its
protection, and felt their minds relieved from all the
expected horrors of a fiege and bombardment. ʃ   ᴜ

A body of German troops having been received on
board the fhips, for the purpofe of being conveyed to
Sicily, where the Spaniards had actually begun hoftilities
by land, and were then befieging Meffina, with an army
of thirty thoufand men, the admiral refolved to proceed thither; and, that nothing might be wanting on
his part, to avert, if poffible, the horrors of war, he
made every mild reprefentation to the Spanifh general,
the marquis de Lede, that was likely to produce fo
defirable an effect. Thefe were; however, ineffectual:
finding, therefore, there was no alternative, and having received intelligence, on his arrival off Meffina,
that the Spanifh fleet had quitted the road of Paradis, he
put to fea in fearch of the enemy. His endeavours to
meet them, were immediately accomplifhed; for, having fallen in with two Spanifh light veffels, that were
on the look-out, thefe, on being purfued, immediately
led him into the midft of their fleet. An active purfuit inftantly commenced, and fir George, after having detached captain Walton, one of the officers under
him, with fix fhips, to follow a divifion of the Spanifh armament, which feparated itfelf during the chafe
from the main body, under the command of a rear-
admiral, continued to prefs, with all the fail he could
carry,

carry, on the Spanish admiral in chief, who was equally active in flight, but still kept the remainder of his force with him. After a long, though flying contest, the enemy were completely overcome; thirteen of their ships, which had compofed the main body, including three of their flags, having fallen into the hands of the Britifh admiral, exclufive of the whole of that division, againft which captain Walton had been detached; and which he completely annihilated or captured.

Thus, were any further naval operations on the part of Spain, completely put an end to, at one ftroke.

But though a conclufive ftroke was given to all maritime conteft, no relaxation took place in the profecution of hoftilities on fhore; during the remainder of the current year, and the whole of the enfuing, the admiral continued in the Mediterranean, and, by the fuccour and affiftance of different kinds which he unremittingly afforded to the imperialifts, he enabled them to maintain their ground fo fuccefsfully againft the fuperior army of Spain, that the court of Madrid at length condefcended to accede to the quadruple alliance, in the month of February 1719-20, and to the ceffation of hoftilities in the month of May following. "Thus," as is remarked by Mr. Corbett, in his account of the expedition to Sicily, "ended this war, wherein the fleet of Great Britain bore fo illuftrious a part, that the fate of the ifland was wholly governed by its operations; both competitors agreeing that the one could not have conquered, nor the other have been fubdued without it. Never was any fervice conducted

in

in all its parts with greater zeal, activity, and judgment; nor was ever the British flag in so high reputation and respect in those distant parts of Europe."

The eminent services rendered by the admiral, could
not fail of placing him extremely high in the esteem
of his sovereign; indeed, we believe, there are, few
persons who ever possessed a greater share of royal
favour than himself. The honorary appointment of
rear-admiral of Great Britain, with that more pecu-
niarily advantageous one, of treasurership to the navy,
were among the first marks of his sovereign's munificence; but they appeared only as the forerunners or
earnest of his future honours. In the month of January 1720-21, he was sworn in a member of his
majesty's privy council; and, in the month of September following, was raised to the peerage, by the
titles of baron of Southhill, and viscount Torrington.
In the year 1725, on the revival of the order of the
Bath, his lordship was elected and installed as one of
the knights companions; and, during the whole continuance of the same reign, possessed, not merely, the
favour, but the personal friendship of his sovereign.
On the accession of king George II. he was appointed
first lord commissioner of the admiralty, which high
office he continued to hold during the remainder of his
life. He died on the 17th of January 1732-3, being
then in the 70th year of age.

It would be no easy task to attempt a delineation of
this nobleman's character: to speak with candour and
with truth, would inevitably lead to a discussion of
some points in it, which are better glossed over by his

victories

victories and his fuccefs, than they poffibly could be by the pen of a difinterefted biographer. Thus far it may certainly be urged, in his excufe for condefcending to hold, in fome particular inftances, fituations fomewhat fubordinate, and, perhaps, derogatory to the character of a man, who afterwards attained fo high a rank as his lordfhip, as well as for having fhewn himfelf fo completely fubfervient to the purpofes of political chicane and intrigue, that he was compelled thereunto by the neceffities of the times, and, what he confidered, the actual fafety of his country.

VICE-

VICE-ADMIRAL JOHN BENBOW

WAS one of the braveſt and moſt ſingular characters that, perhaps, ever filled the ſtation of a naval
officer. Many perſons have taken no inconſiderable
degree of pains, to prove him to have been of a very
humble, not to ſay low, origin. In this attempt they
have rendered, themſelves extremely ridiculous, for,
even admitting it to be a fact (which really was not the
caſe), ſuch a circumſtance, never ſhould be permitted to
militate againſt the well-earned reputation, of a brave
and gallant man. The truth, however, is, that he
was the deſcendant of an ancient and very honourable
family, long ſettled in the county of Salop: a family
brought to decay by the noble fidelity, and loyalty to the
ſovereign, diſplayed by the anceſtor and uncle of the
admiral. Theſe gentlemen were both of them colonels
in the ſervice of king Charles I. and, after the death of
that monarch, continued to live in privacy, till the
time when the Scottiſh army marched into England,
with king Charles II. at its head. Having immediately joined his ſtandard, they became captives
to the uſurper Cromwell, at the unfortunate battle of
Worceſter,

Worcefter, and were both condemned to be fhot, by the fentence of a court-martial. This was carried into execution, fo far as it refpeded Thomas the uncle; but John, the father, having contrived to make his efcape, lived in obfcurity, and want, till the reftoration, when he obtained a very fmall appointment in the Tower, which afforded him a fcanty pittance, barely fufficient to preferve him from ftarving; but which, we are forry to add, was the only remuneration the royal munificence of king Charles II. ever thought proper to give, to the fervices and the fufferings, of this gentleman and his relative.

Under the circumftances juft mentioned, it is not to be expeded that the education of Mr. Benbow, could have exceeded that ufually received, by boys intended for the fea, in the fervice of the merchants. At the fame time, however, fuch education was neither mean, nor defpicable; and it certainly cannot be thought as depreciating the greateft charaders in the Britifh navy, to fay, that many of them, in their outfet in life, have poffeffed no better advantages. Mr. Benbow exerted thofe talents and abilities, which nature had endued him with fo confpicuoufly, that he acquired, at an early age, the command of a veffel employed in the Streights trade. Even the fervice of the merchants, when their commerce was direded to that quarter of the world, was at that time replete with danger. The piratical ftates on the coaft of Barbary, carried on an almoft uninterrupted courfe of warfare and depredation againft all veffels belonging to the Englifh nation, which they thought themfelves ca-

pable

pable of maſtering; and Mr. Benbow had, in conſequence of his gallant and ſucceſsful defence on repeated occaſions, acquired ſo much reputation and profit, that, in the year 1686, he became commander of a veſſel, his own property, called the Benbow frigate. While thus occupied, a ſingular anecdote is related of him, which at once diſplays, in the moſt forcible colours, his gallantry, and his very whimſical turn of mind. He was attacked, ſay hiſtorians, in his paſſage to Cadiz, by a Sallee rover, againſt whom he defended himſelf; though his crew was very inferior in point of numbers, with the utmoſt bravery; till at laſt the Moors boarded him; but were quickly beaten out of his ſhip again, with the loſs of thirteen men, whoſe heads captain Benbow ordered to be cut off, and thrown into a tub of pork pickle. When he arrived at Cadiz, he went on ſhore, and ordered a negro ſervant to follow him; with the Moors' heads in a ſack: He had ſcarcely landed before the officers of the revenue inquired of his ſervant, what he had in his ſack: the captain anſwered, Salt-proviſions for his own uſe; "That may be," anſwered the officers; "but we muſt inſiſt upon ſeeing them." Captain Benbow alleged, that he was no ſtranger there, that he did not uſe to run goods, and pretended to be much offended that he was ſuſpected. The officers told him, that the magiſtrates were ſitting not far off, and that if they were ſatisfied with his word, his ſervant might carry the proviſions where he pleaſed; but that, as for themſelves, it was not in their power to grant any ſuch diſpenſation.

The captain confented to the propofal, and away
they marched to the cuftom-houfe, Mr. Benbow in
the front, his men in the centre, and the officers in
the rear. The magiftrates, when he came before
them, treated captain Benbow with great civility, told
him they were forry to make a point of fuch a trifle,
but that, fince he had refufed to fhew the contents of
his fack to their officers, the nature of their employment obliged them to demand a fight of them ; and
that, as they doubted not they were falt provifions, the
act of fhewing them could be of no confequence, one
way or the other. "I told you," fays the captain,
fternly, "they were falt provifions for my own ufe ;
Cæfar, throw them down on the table; and, gentlemen, if you like them, they are at your fervice."
The Spaniards were exceedingly ftruck at the fight
of the Moors' heads, and no lefs aftonifhed at the account of the captain's adventure, who, with fo fmall
a force, had been able to defeat fuch a number of
barbarians.

Owing to the repeated inftances * in which he diftinguifhed himfelf againft the enemies of his country,
he became fo much noticed by thofe perfons who were

* In the month of May 1687, he commanded a veffel called the Malaga
Merchant, and was attacked, near the mouth of the Streights, when on his
return to England, by a Salletine cruifer, of confiderable force. The pirate,
after difcharging his broadfide, accompanied by a volley of fmall fhot, rigged
his fpritfail-yard fore and aft, and attempted to board captain Benbow's
fhip, but met with fo warm and fteady a reception, that he was quickly
glad to fheer off. and betake himfelf to flight, having loft many men in the
attempt. It was now captain Benbow's turn to attack ; but the corfair,
being by far the fafteft failor, foon got clear out of reach.

officially

officially intrufted with the management of the royal
navy; that without previoufly paffing through the
fubordinate ranks, he was at once advanced to that of
captain, and appointed to the York, a fourth rate, of
fixty guns, by commiffion bearing date September the
3d, 1689. Captain Benbow did not long retain the
fame commiffion which he had firft received : in the
following year, the earl of Torrington, to whom it is
believed he was indebted for his firft introduction
into the royal navy, invited him to take upon him
the office of mafter of the Sovereign, the fhip on
board which, his flag was hoifted as commander in
chief of the fleet. No greater compliment could
poffibly have been paid him ; for, to that gallantry
which he had before rendered fo eminently confpicuous, as not to be doubted, was now added the moft
honourable and public teftimony, that his nautical knowledge and profeffional fkill were thought by no means
inferior. It is not improbable, that the misfortunes
and totally unmerited difgrace of the earl, had a
temporary influence on the employments of captain
Benbow, for no fubfequent mention is made even of
his commanding a fhip of war, till the latter end of
the year 1693, when he was appointed to the Norwich, and intrufted with the very honourable command of a fquadron of frigates, and bomb-ketches,
fitted out to bombard St. Maloes ; and the very great
fkill, as well as fpirit, which he difplayed on that occafion, appear to have marked him in the eyes of the
fovereign, and the admiralty board, as one of the propereft men in the kingdom, to whom all operations of

a fimilar

a similar nature could be intrusted; few, or none,
ever having been undertaken during the remainder of
the war, without his being invested with the chief, or
second command in them. In 1694, he covered the
attack made on Dunkirk, the failure of which, nothing diminished his reputation, the whole of the miscarriage having been, very properly, attributed, by
the popular opinion, to its true cause, the incapacity
of Meesteers, who projected it. Of this circumstance,
sir Cloudesly Shoveli, who commanded the squadron
in chief, bore the most ample testimony. The public
sympathized with captain Benbow, in lamenting his
disappointment, and suffered all that popular anger
which usually attends the want of success, to be
drowned, in the more amiable display of compassion.
In 1695, he commanded the Northumberland, of seventy guns, and was employed, on different occasions,
in the same line of service as before, under the orders
of lord Berkley. The size of this ship being extremely
inconvenient, and ill adapted to many of the little
desultory expeditions on which he was, from time to
time, engaged, caused him to remove on board divers
smaller vessels, that he might be enabled to approach
the shore with greater facility, and direct, in person,
the operations of the force intrusted to his command.

Early in the year 1696, he covered, under the direction of sir Cloudesly Shovell, the bombardment of
Calais, and seems to have acquired so much reputation on this, as well as the preceding services, that
he most particularly attracted the notice of king
William, at whose special instance he is said to have

been

been promoted to the rank of rear-admiral of the blue. This singular elevation of a very private man, unsupported by wealth or rank, to so high a station, after having been only seven years in the navy, computing from his first entrance into it, was unprecedented, but not obnoxious; many of the most distinguished captains comprised in the list, continuing to serve under him without murmur, or conceiving themselves disgraced, notwithstanding they were considerably his seniors in rank, previous to his promotion. In the month of May 1697, he was sent with a small squadron to block up the port of Dunkirk, where that well-known partizan Du Bart, then lay, with several ships ready for sea; this service he probably would have executed with his usual adroitness, had he been properly seconded by the Dutch, under vice-admiral Vandergoes, or had the British admiralty board followed the advice which he gave them. But the want of proper co-operation on the part of the Hollanders, and the neglect of sending him a constant supply of clean ships, to replace those which were becoming foul, proved an insurmountable obstacle to his preventing the escape of the enemy, whose vessels were all clean, and in the most perfect condition for service, as well as flight. He afterwards commanded a squadron, stationed in the channel, and was employed on various immaterial services, during the languishing state in which the war was permitted to linger; some time previous to the conclusion of the treaty at Ryswic.

The

The return of peace produced; however, but little cessation, in the employment of Mr. Benbow; the conduct of Louis XIV. and his ministers, appeared extremely suspicious; and some apprehensions being entertained that they were meditating a blow against the British colonies in the West-Indies, it was deemed expedient to send a squadron thither, for the purpose of counteracting any sudden attack that might be attempted, by an insidious enemy. He accordingly hoisted his flag on board the Gloucester, and sailed from St. Helen's with all the ships that were put under his orders, but which amounted only to three fourth rates, and a small sloop of war. The force of this armament, could scarcely be considered as capable of protecting the colonies from any attack, beyond that of a few privateers; and actuated, probably, by this consideration, many historians have insisted, that the suspicion of any attempt made by France, was a mere pretext; and that the real object of Mr. Benbow's mission to that quarter of the world, was to sound the temper of the Spaniards, and discover, if possible, what their conduct would be, in the event of his catholic majesty's death, which was then daily expected, and the commencement of a rupture between France, and Great Britain. State secrets, however, are not easily to be developed, without some of those fortuitous aids, or the casual production, either of letters, or written evidence, by which the greatest seeming mysteries have sometimes been explained.

But

But to return to the fact; Mr. Benbow having diftributed the troops which he carried out with him, among
the different iflands, in the proper proportion to each,
as his inftructions directed him, proceeded to Carthagena, where his fpirited remonftrances to the Spanifh
governor, procured the releafe of feveral Englifh merchant veffels which had been detained by the Spaniards,
under the pretence of procuring fatisfaction, for fome
fettlements made by the Scotch, on the ifthmus of Darien, contrary to the treaty then exifting, between the
Britifh, and Spanifh nations. He afterwards proceeded on a miffion of nearly a fimilar nature to Porto
Bello ; and his inability on this occafion to procure
more ample fatisfaction, than a mere promife of reparation (which was never fulfilled), produced much
lamentation among the perfons interefted, that the
force under the gallant admiral, had not been adequate
to the tafk of compelling compliance. His return to
England in the month of June 1700, was marked by
the moft cordial reception from his fovereign, and the
moft unqualified affent on the part of the public, to
his having, in their opinion, executed every thing that
could be effected by fo fmall a force, as that, which he
had been intrufted with the command of. He was
promoted, almoft immediately after his arrival, to be
vice-admiral of the blue fquadron ; and the conduct
of the French court continuing, or to fpeak probably
nearer the truth, becoming now in reality fufpicious,
Mr. Benbow was fent to cruife off Dunkirk, in order
to block up a ftrong fquadron, faid to be fitting out
in that port, for the puipofe of covering a defcent on

the

the coaſt of England. This apprehenſion continued but for a ſhort time ; but it became quickly afterwards revived, and much more ſtrongly than it had been on the former occaſion, in reſpect to the Weſt Indies. The armament, deſtined for that quarter of the world, amounted to no leſs than ten ſhips of the line, beſides ſmaller veſſels ; the command was an important one ; and it was conſidered, that ſome caution was neceſſary in the appointment of the officer, who was to be employed on that occaſion. It was offered, however, to two or three different perſons, who ſtood rather high in public opinion, but who, either diffident of their own abilities, or fearing ſome unpleaſant conſequences might occur, during the time they held ſuch command, thought proper to decline it.

In conſequence of the diſappointment, juſt mentioned, all thoſe perſons who then poſſeſſed his majeſty's confidence, united in adviſing him to ſend Benbow to the Weſt Indies a ſecond time. King William objected to it; not on account of any diſlike to the vice-admiral, or doubt of his abilities, but becauſe he thought, it extremely hard, that a man who had ſo recently returned from ſuch a diſagreeable ſervice, ſhould be ſo ſoon ſent back to a ſtation, where there was leſs probability of his acquiring either honour, or any other advantage to himſelf, than he would, if he remained in Europe. At length, however, his majeſty, finding the difficulty which occurred in procuring an officer, to accept of the command, who was thought capable of executing the functions of it properly, is ſaid to have uttered the following bon mot:

" *Well*

"*Well then, as I find I must spare our beaux, I will send Benbow,*" and immediately offered it to the vice-admiral. The latter, who was perfectly well acquainted with all the circumstances that had taken place, previous to his appointment, told the king, in his usual blunt manner, that "he knew no difference of climates; for his part, he thought no officer, had a right to choose his station, and that he himself should be, at all times, ready to go to any part of the world, whither his majesty thought proper to send him."

The whole of this important business being thus adjusted, Mr. Benbow hoisted his flag on board the Breda, of seventy guns, and proceeded to the West Indies, towards the latter end of August. He was accompanied, by the main fleet, under the orders of fir George Rooke, who saw him fifty leagues to the westward of Scilly, and then detached fir John Munden, with a strong squadron, to proceed with him as far as the Western Islands, at which distance, it was supposed, he would be perfectly safe from the attack of any superior force, that might have slipped out of Brest, or others of the French ports, in the hope of intercepting him. The vice-admiral reached the Leeward Islands, early in the month of November, and finding them in so good a state of defence, as to render any immediate assistance from him, unnecessary, proceeded almost immediately to Jamaica, where he arrived on the 5th of the ensuing month. Circumstances demanded his instant, and most energetic exertions; he had scarcely cast anchor, ere he received advice, that monsieur Chateau Renaud, well known as one of the

ablest

ableſt officers in the French ſervice, had reached Martinique, with a ſquadron ſuperior to his own; that De Coetlogon, who had juſt before taken upon himſelf the command of the Spaniſh armament in that quarter, was lying at the Havannah, waiting for the French ſhips to come down from Martinique, to form a junction with it; moreover, that the French admiral Du Caſſe, was daily expected with a conſiderable reinforcement. If,

Such, however, were the prudent, and ſpirited meaſures taken by the vice-admiral, that the projects formed by this combined hoſt of foes, againſt Jamaica, and the reſt of the Britiſh poſſeſſions in that quarter of the world, were all of them fruſtrated. A ſmall reinforcement joined him from England, two veſſels were fitted out as fire-ſhips by the governor and council of Jamaica, and put under his orders; ſuperadded to theſe, rear-admiral Whetſtone joined him not long afterwards with a ſmall ſquadron: but notwithſtanding theſe aids, the force of the enemy continued infinitely ſuperior; Chateau Renaud, however, being under the neceſſity of convoying to Europe that valuable fleet of Spaniſh galleons, which, together with the ſhips of war under his command, fell into the hands of ſir George Rooke, at Vigo, and deeming it neceſſary for that ſervice to take with him ten of the largeſt ſhips of the line, the danger and diſparity became infinitely leſſened, though the force of Mr. Benbow ſtill remained manifeſtly inferior, to that of his opponents. He accordingly took care to keep his principal ſhips always collected, ſo as to be ready for any ſudden emergency the ſervice might require; and by ſending out ſmall detachments, formed of his

lighter

lighter fhips, he not only kept the enemy in a continual alarm, and thereby diftracted their attention, fo
far as to prevent their undertaking any thing material
againft him, but diftreffed their commerce extremely, by
making many valuable prizes. From the moment he
received official information of the rupture between
Great Britain and France, he redoubled his activity ;
and having put his fhips in the beft condition for
fervice, his circumftances would permit, put to fea
from Port Royal on the 11th of July, having with
him eight fhips of the line, a fire-fhip, a bomb-ketch,
and a floop. His intention was, to form a junction
with rear-admiral Whetftone, whom he had detached
a few days before; but having received advice on the 14th,
by the Colchefter, and Pendennis, which both joined
him that day, that Du Caffe was expected at Leogane,
in Hifpaniola, he directed his courfe thither, and
though he was not fortunate enough to meet with Du
Caffe there, his difappointment found fome palliative,
in the deftruction of a French fhip, capable of carrying
fifty guns, but having thirty mounted, whofe captain
thought proper to run her on fhore, and burn her, to
prevent her falling into the hands of the Britifh fquadron. He afterwards took, and deftroyed five other fhips,
one of which mounted eighteen, and the other fixteen
guns. Having thus effected all the mifchief he was
capable of doing the enemy, without the affiftance of
a military force, he put to fea on the 2d of Auguft,
in purfuit of Du Caffe; of whofe route, having
received correct intelligence, he refolved to follow,
and either bring him to action, or drive him out of
thofe

thofe feas. On the 19th of the fame month, he fell
in with ten fail, to the eaftward of St. Martha, which
he very foon difcovered to be French. Their force
confifted of four fhips of from feventy to fixty-fix
guns each, a large Dutch-built frigate, mounting nearly
forty guns, a tranfport with troops, and four fmall
veffels. The vice-admiral, immediately made the
fignal for his fquadron to form, he himfelf being, as
is cuftomary, in the centre ; but the dilatorinefs in
many of the captains, prevented the line from being
properly arranged, till the day was too far advanced
for him to expect any material advantage, ere night
would put an end to the encounter. 'He refolved
however, to make the attempt, but the abfolute flight
of captain Kirkby, who commanded the Defiance, of
fixty-four guns, and the mifbehaviour of captain Con-
ftable, in the Windfor, of fixty, contributed to render
the fhort action much lefs decifive, than it might have
proved, had their conduct been otherwife. Indeed,
the whole weight of the engagement lay upon the
Breda, the vice-admiral's fhip, and in all probability,
he might have fallen a facrifice to his own gallantry,
had he not been moft ably fupported by captain George
Walton, in the Ruby, of forty-eight guns. Mr. Benbow, in the hope of reclaiming the recreant difpofition
fhewn by many of the officers under his command, made
an alteration in his line of battle, and thinking that his
example might poffibly ftimulate, even the moft backward, to do their duty, led the van himfelf, on both
tacks, in the Breda. In this expectation he was unfortunately difappointed, for at break of day, on the
morning of the 20th, he found himfelf clofe to the
enemy,

enemy, without a single ship near him, except the Ruby. The remainder of the squadron were three, four, and five miles astern; but though the admiral appeared to be so deserted, the enemy seemed irresolute, and afraid of making the best use of that advantage, which fortune had thrown in their way. Although the Breda was within gun-shot of them, they suffered her to remain unmolested, and a breeze springing up about three o'clock, crowded all the sail they could to avoid any further encounter. It was in vain; the vice-admiral and captain Walton made the best attack they were capable of doing, on the enemy, with their chase-guns. The night came on, and the French ships continued their retreat, without having suffered any material damage. On the 21st, the engagement was renewed at break of day, for the admiral, with his gallant second, had succeeded in keeping close to their antagonists, during the whole of the night. The Breda had the good fortune to drive one of the largest of the enemies' ships out of the line; but the Ruby, being small, and ill adapted to contend against such powerful ships as Du Casse had with him, the vice-admiral was obliged to send his own boats to tow her out of reach. No other ship of the British squadron came up during the whole of this day's encounter, and the contest consequently remained undecided; the enemy using every effort to escape, while Mr. Benbow was equally strenuous on his part to prevent their flight.

On the 22d, the Greenwich, of fifty-four guns, commanded by captain Wade, was near three leagues astern, although the signal for the line of battle had

never

never been ſtruck, from the hour it was firſt hoiſted
on the 19th. The reſt of the ſquadron however, the
Ruby excepted, which was in a very wretched and
diſabled ſtate, were pretty well up with the Breda;
but the whole of the day paſſed on, without its being
poſſible for the vice-admiral to effect any thing
deciſive. Appearances, on the morning of the 23d,
were ſtill more inauſpicious; the enemy were ſix
or ſeven miles ahead, and the Engliſh ſquadron
very much ſcattered, ſeveral of the ſhips being four
or five miles aſtern. The exertions of the admiral
were ſuch, that in ſpite of every impediment, he
nearly cloſed with the French by ten o'clock, and after
exchanging ſeveral ſhot with two of the ſhips that
compoſed it, captured the Anne galley, an Engliſh veſſel, which Du Caſſe had made prize of, on his paſſage
to the Weſt Indies. The Ruby, being found too
much diſabled, to be capable of rendering any further
aſſiſtance, was ordered to Port Royal. The enſuing
night put an end to the conteſt, which, though it terminated unfortunately, ended moſt glorioufly for the
reputation of Mr. Benbow. "On the 24th," ſays
the journal of the encounter, " at two in the morning,
we came up within hail of the ſternmoſt. It being
very little wind, the admiral fired a broadſide, with
double and round below, and round and partridge aloft,
which ſhe returned. At three o'clock the admiral's
right leg was ſhattered to pieces by a chain-ſhot, and
he was carried down; but preſently ordered his cradle
on the quarter-deck, and continued the fight till day,
when appeared the ruins of a ſhip of about ſeventy
guns; her main-yard down, and ſhot to pieces; her
fore-

fore-topsail yard, shot away, her mizen-mast shot by
the board, all her rigging gone, and her sides bored
through and through, with our double-headed shot.
The Falmouth assisted in this matter very much, and·
no other ship.   Soon after day, the admiral saw the
other ships of the enemy coming towards him with
a strong gale of wind easterly ; at the same time the
Windsor, Pendennis, and Greenwich, ahead of the
enemy, ran to leeward of the disabled ship, fired their
broadsides, passed her, and stood to the southward;
then, the Defiance followed them, passed also to
leeward of the disabled ship, and fired part of her
broadside.   The disabled ship did not fire above
twenty guns at the Defiance, before she put her
helm a-weather, and ran away right before the wind ;
lowered both her topsails, and ran to leeward of the
Falmouth (which was then a gun-shot to leeward of
the admiral, knotting her rigging, without any regard
to the signal for battle).   The enemy seeing our other
two ships stand to the southward, expected they would
have tacked and stood with them.   They brought to
with their heads to the northward ; but seeing those
three ships did not tack, bore down upon the admiral,
and ran between the disabled ship and him, firing all
their guns ; in which they shot away his main-topsail
yard, and shattered his rigging much.   None of the
other ships being near him, nor taking any notice of
the battle signal, the captain of the Breda hereupon
fired two guns at those ships ahead, in order to put them
in mind of their duty.   The French, seeing this great
disorder, brought to and lay by their own disabled ship,
remanned, and took her in tow.   The Breda's rigging
being

being much shattered, she lay by till ten o'clock; and being then refitted, the admiral ordered the captain to pursue the enemy, who was then about three miles distant, and to leeward, having the disabled ship in tow, steering N. E. the wind at S. S. W. The admiral, in the mean time, made all the sail after them he could; and the battle signal was always out. But the enemy, taking encouragement from the behaviour of some of our captains, the admiral ordered captain Fogg to send to the captains to keep their line, and to behave themselves like men, which he did. Upon this captain Kirkby came on board the admiral, and pressed him very earnestly to desist from any further engagement, which made the admiral desirous to know the opinion of the other captains. Accordingly he ordered captain Fogg to make the signal for all the other captains to come on board, which they did; and most of them concurred with captain Kirkby in his opinion; whereupon the admiral perceiving they had no mind to fight, and being not able to prevail with them to come to any other resolution, though all they said was erroneous, he thought it not fit to venture any further. At this time the admiral was abreast of the enemy, and had a fair opportunity of fighting them; the masts and yards in a good condition, and few men killed, except those on board the Breda."

Du Casse himself is said, although a foe, to have most grievously condemned that cowardice and misconduct which saved him from destruction; and he is even reported to have written Mr. Benbow a letter with his own hand, couched in the following terms: "Sir! I had little hopes on Monday last; but to have

supped

fupped in your cabin; but it pleafed God to order it otherwife; I am thankful for it. As for thofe cowardly captains who deferted you, hang them up, for by ——— they deferve it. Yours, Ducaffe." The vice-admiral, finding it impoffible to effect any thing decifive againft the enemy, till the fhips under his orders were commanded by officers otherwife affected, than thofe to whom their command was then intrufted, returned to Jamaica, and it being found neceffary to amputate his fhattered limb, for the purpofe of preventing a mortification, a fever enfued, which, though his robuft conftitution enabled him for a long time to contend againft, at length put a period to his life, on the fourth day of November.

It is truly faid of him, that as to his character, his bittereft enemy cannot deny him, the honeft reputation of a brave, active, and able commander; while on the other, his warmeft friends and admirers muft allow, he wanted thofe conciliating manners, which were neceffary, to fecure the perfonal attachment, and regard of the officers he commanded. Honefty, integrity, and blunt fincerity, were the prominent features of his private character; and we can only lament the depravity of human nature, when we find ourfelves obliged to confefs, thefe truly valuable qualifications are not fufficient, to acquire the love of our cotemporaries, though they can fcarcely fail of engaging the warmeft efteem of every fucceeding generation. It has been a generally received opinion, that the admiral's body was buried at Jamaica, but Campbell, and many other writers, deny the fact, and affert, it was fent home

for

for the purpofe of being interred at Deptford. This circumftance appears ftrongly confirmed by the tefti-mony of feveral very ancient people, living at that place a few years fince; who, though they did not remember the funeral itfelf, declared they had fre-quently heard it fpoken of in their youthful days, as an event then recent. Some perfons have been par-ticular enough to point out the very fpot of his inter-ment, and affert, they remember to have feen a part of the flat ftone laid over his remains, with the name of Benbow at that time legible on it. This, however, to the difgrace of national gratitude, and the inattention of his fucceeding pofterity, has fince become totally loft. He left behind him a numerous race of both fexes; his fons dying without iffue, two daughters, who then furvived, confequently became coheireffes. The eldeft married Paul Calton, of Milton, near Abingdon, in the county of Berks, efq. Of the youngeft daughter there is no account.

SIR

JOHN JENNINGS

Publſhd 1 Mar. 1800, by Edwᵈ Harding 98 Pall Mall.

SIR JOHN JENNINGS.

THIS gentleman having attained the rank of lieutenant in the navy, in the month of May 1687, and
continued in the fame station for two years and a
half, was, on the 16th of November 1689, promoted
to be commander of the St. Paul fire-ship. In 1690,
he became captain of the Experiment, a cruifing frigate, mounting thirty-two guns, stationed off the coaft
of Ireland, for the purpofe of intercepting any fupplies
or reinforcements, deftined for the fupport, or fuccour
of the Irifh adherents to the exiled James. In this
employment he was extremely active and fuccefsful,
having captured a number of veffels, which, though
infignificant in themfelves, would, in confequence of
their fafe arrival, have proved of material differvice to
the caufe of king William. In 1693, he was appointed
captain of the Victory, the flag-fhip of fir John Afhby,
but was quickly removed from thence into a private
fhip, the Winchefter, of fixty guns. He continued
employed during the whole remainder of the war, and
in the year 1697, commanded the Plymouth, a cruifer,
in which he had the good fortune to capture three
privateer frigates belonging to the enemy, one of which

K 2   had

had the temerity to engage him a confiderable time. He afterwards fell in with a French convoy, having the Rye and Severn in company with him. Out of twelve fail, he captured three, one of which formed a part of the efcort to the remainder. The peace at Ryfwic prefently fucceeding, no occurrence, worth recording, took place in the occupations of this gentleman till after the acceffion of queen Anne, notwithftanding he appears to have been in conftant employment during the whole of the intervening period. In 1702 he was appointed to the Kent of feventy guns, one of the fhips compofing the armament fent under fir George Rooke, on the ill-concerted expedition againft Cadiz. In the fubfequent and more fuccefsful part of the operations, which took place on the return of the fleet towards England, the attack on Vigo, the Kent was ftationed, as one of the feconds, to vice-admiral Hopfon, whofe divifion led, and fuftained the greateft weight of the attack made on that place. Soon after his return to England, he was promoted to the St. George, a fecond rate of ninety-fix guns, and continued to retain the fame command, till he was advanced to the rank of a flag-officer. During the naval operations of the fleet in 1703, the St. George formed one of the fleet fent under the orders of fir Cloudefly Shovell, on the fruitlefs expedition into the Mediterranean, for the relief of the Cevenois; and in the enfuing year, was ftationed as one of the feconds to fir George Rooke, during the attack on Gibraltar, and the battle off Malaga, which prefently fucceeded to it; on the latter occafion, captain Jennings diftinguifhed himfelf fo

confpicuoufly,

conſpicuouſly, that, immediately on his return to England, he received from her majeſty the honour of
knighthood.

In the month of January 1704-5, he was promoted to be rear-admiral of the blue ſquadron, and
from this time, till the year 1713, during which period
he had been regularly advanced through the different
ranks, till he had attained that of admiral of the white
ſquadron, he was uninterruptedly employed as a flag-
officer. France never having ventured to ſend forth
a fleet from her ports, after the chaſtiſement ſhe experienced off Malaga, no encounter took place by ſea,
in which ſir John was, or could be engaged. His ſervices, however, were of the moſt active kind : among
theſe are to be reckoned the relief of Barcelona in
1706 ; on which occaſion, the activity of ſir George
Byng and himſelf, in carrying an extraordinary preſs
of ſail, had very nearly proved fatal to the whole of the
French force, which had previouſly formed the blockade
of that city by ſea ; the enemy, who fled with the
greateſt expedition, having, with the utmoſt difficulty,
ſaved their rear from falling a ſacrifice. The capture
of the two very important poſts, the cities of Carthagena and Alicant, added to the honour before gained by
this gentleman ; nor were his abilities as an officer, inferior to thoſe which he diſplayed in the civil appointment, of regulating the government of the former place,
after it had ſurrendered, and in conciliating the minds
of the inhabitants towards king Charles III.

: At the cloſe of the year, he was ordered to the Weſt
Indies, with a ſquadron of nine or ten ſhips of the
line, beſides ſmaller veſſels. The object of his miſ-

ſion

fion was rather of a political than of an hoftile nature.
It had been confidered probable, by the Britifh cabinet
at home, that the Spanifh colonies in that quarter of
the world, might, on the appearance of a ftrong naval
force, under the orders of a man of known probity,
gallantry, and prudence, be induced to declare in favour of king Charles III. to whofe intereft, they had
appeared to be inclined a year or two before, when
his arms in the mother-country had acquired a manifeft
afcendancy. Experience proved, however, the opinion
ill-founded; for king Philip having, by the capture of
Madrid, and a variety of other fuccefles, eftablifhed a
decided fuperiority in Europe, the governor of Carthagena, in very civil and refpectful, though peremptory terms, refifted the entrance of the Britifh fquadron into that port, and refufed to confide to its charge
and protection, the galleons which were lying there,
ready to fail for Spain. Compulfion being confidered
impolitic, fir John forbore to act as an enemy, where
he had profeffed himfelf a friend; and returned to
Europe in the month of April 1708.

. He enjoyed a ceffation, of a few months continuance,
after his arrival, from the fatigues of active fervice; but
at the clofe of the year, was advanced to be rear-admiral
of the white, and in lefs than a month afterwards, to the
fame rank in the red fquadron. In regard to the rapidity
of his promotions, which might otherwife be confidered
wonderful, were they to pafs without remark, it has
been elfewhere obferved, with truth, " that he had
ferved fome years as rear-admiral of the blue; and, at
that day, it was rather extraordinary for fo active and
well-

well-efteemed a commander, to remain in the fame
ftation fo long without experiencing promotion; but
now the current had once found its channel, it appeared to rufh on him like a torrent;" for after the
fhort interval of eighteen days, from the time of his
appointment to be rear-admiral of the red, he was
moft rapidly promoted, to be vice-admiral of the fame
fquadron.

In a few weeks fubfequent to his laft advancement,
the activity of the French, in the ports of Dunkirk, and other places conveniently fituated for the
purpofe, added to very correct fecret information
received by the Britifh miniftry of their intentions,
caufed the appointment of fir John Jennings to be
commander in chief of all her majefty's fhips and
veffels in the rivers Thames and Medway, as well as
that of fuperintendant of all the naval equipments in
the fame quarter, for the purpofe of repelling the meditated invafion of Scotland by the enemy, in favour
of the pretended fon of the exiled, and then deceafed
James. His activity, on this preffing emergency,
acquired him the higheft credit; and, as foon as the
cloud of apprehenfion had paffed over, he was ordered
to the Mediterranean, as fecond in command of the
fleet under fir George Byng. He continued to be employed in the fame ftation, during that and the fucceeding year, but without meeting with any occurrence
worth our relating, except his promotion, on the 9th
of November 1709, to be admiral of the blue. At
the commencement of the year 1711, he was raifed to
the rank of admiral of the white fquadron, and invefted with the command in chief on the Mediterra-

nean

nean ftation: but the fame caufes, which have been already noticed, continued to produce the inactivity of the Britifh naval force, fo far as fleets were concerned. The operations of war now languifhed towards a clofe; and it has been remarked, that after the arrangements of the articles of the peace concluded at Utrecht, it might naturally have been fuppofed, a life of eafe and inactivity would have fucceeded to thofe fatigues of watchful fervice, in which he had for fo many years been engaged; and in which, care and diligence, being the only exertions that were, on his part, neceffary, coldly fupplied, in the opinion of the people, the more attractive, though not more valuable purfuits, of enterprife and glory. The admiral, however, cannot be faid to have remained in a ftate of ufelefs inactivity, notwithftanding hoftilities had ceafed between the allied powers. The Salletine corfairs had of late committed fome acts of violence; thefe, fir John, during the enfuing winter, not only took care properly to reprefs, but alfo to prevent the repetition of. He refigned his Mediterranean command towards the latter end of the year 1713, after he had convoyed back to Italy, the troops which had been employed in Spain, to the amount of thirty thoufand men, and had conducted the duke and dutchefs of Savoy, from Villa Franca to Sicily, their new kingdom.

During the fhort remainder of queen Anne's reign, fir John appears to have fought, in retirement, fome reft and refrefhment, after thofe fatigues of mind, as well as body, he had fo lately endured. The convulfions of the domeftic government of the country,

and

and the rancour of party, which probably never were carried to a greater height than at this period, in all likelihood contributed not a little to his having, in some degree, quitted the service for a short time, for at the accession of George I. he was not upon the list of admirals. The new sovereign had, however, scarcely taken possession of his throne, ere a complete revolution took place, in the appointment of persons chosen to superintend, and direct the naval department. Sir John was nominated a commissioner of the admiralty, and almost immediately afterwards, invested with the chief command of an armament sent into the North Sea, to prevent the introduction of any reinforcement of troops, or supply of stores into Scotland, for the use of the adherents to the Pretender, who had a short time before, landed in that kingdom. The activity which he displayed on this occasion, stands declared by the public record of an official account *. Nevertheless, it did not prove sufficient to shield him from the shafts of obloquy, and unmerited calumny. The escape of the Pretender, was urged as an incontrovertible proof of neglect, though the circumstance was most fairly accounted for, by the extreme darkness of the night when it took place, notwithstanding every precaution had been taken to prevent it, by stationing

---

* In the Gazette published at this time, is the following remarkable sentence ; " All the ships kept the sea diligently, when wind and weather would permit, and observed the motions of his majesty's army so carefully, that the duke of Argyle did not pass through any port town, without finding some ship ready, to carry into execution any service he might have to propose."

a number

a number of veffels, more than adequate to the purpofe, except in the cafe of an event intervening, as it
did, which certainly was extraordinary, and among
bigots was confidered almoft fupernatural. The fituation of the kingdom, rendered it unneceffary to call
forth the zeal and abilities of the worthy admiral, for
fome years, after the commotion in the North had
ceafed; and the only interruption to his retirement
from active fervice *, during the eleven years next enfuing, appears to have been his appointment in the
month of November 1720, to command the convoy
which protected the paffage of his majefty to Holland.
In 1726, the conduct of the Spanifh court, appearing
to manifeft ftronger difpofitions towards a difturbance
of the public peace, than it was deemed proper fhould
be permitted to pafs unnoticed, fir John was ordered
to the Mediterranean, with a fquadron of nine fhips
of the line. His appearance produced the utmoft
terror, a terror which, however, proved temporary
only, and which ceafed almoft immediately after the

* On the 28th of Auguft 1720, fir John was appointed ranger of Greenwich park, and governor of the hofpital, of which noble inftitution he
proved a moft worthy ruler and protector. A marble ftatue of George I.
cut out of a block of white marble, taken in a French fhip by fir George
Rooke, was prefented by fir John Jennings, and is erected in the centre of
the great fquare of the hofpital. An exceedingly good portrait of him, at
full length, painted by Richardfon, is preferved in the council-room there.
We know not, however, fo well to affociate our ideas, at the prefent day, as
to perfuade ourfelves of its being a reprefentation of the admiral and commander in chief of the Britifh fleet. This is occafioned by his being painted
in the whimfical habit of the times; a full-drefs fuit of brown velvet, rolled-
up ftockings, and immenfe fquare-toed fhoes.

object

object of it was removed, by the return of the British force to England. Quietude was, nevertheless, preferved for, a time, and the flames of war were, fmothered till the enfuing year. Thefe were the only effects his voyage from England was likely, or indeed able to produce ; and, with this fervice, his naval life clofed. He continued, fay writers, to live ever afterwards in peaceable and honourable retirement, quitting the office of commiffioner of the admiralty, on the acceffion of king George II. and refigning alfo his rank as an admiral, which he had till then retained, in the year 1734. The honorary civil appointment of rear-admiral of England, was given him in the month of January 1732-3 ; but that appears to have been beftowed, only as a refpectable mark of the fovereign's hearty approbation and efteem for his former fervices, inafmuch, as being a mere finecure, it interfered not with that repofe from the fatigues of duty, which he continued to enjoy happily, unenvied, and uninterrupted, till the time of his death, which happened on the 23d of December 1745, at which period he had attained a very advanced age.

It is truly obferved by writers, that few men, through fo long a period of active fervice, ever enjoyed lefs opportunity of diftinguifhing themfelves; yet, what did fall within his power, fir John improved to the utmoft advantage, and, on fuch occafions, afforded the world as ftrong a proof of his bravery, and contempt of danger, as he did, at all other times, of his prudence and ability, as a great commander. Campbell very juftly pays him the compliment, of having been one of the greateft

feamen

feamen of the age; and his political integrity none have, we believe, ever dared to queſtion. Without entering into the factious views of party, or ſupporting the ambition of a corrupt adminiſtration, he always proved himſelf the honeſt faithful ſubject of his ſovereign, and the ſincere friend of his native country. In ſhort, he was as an officer, brave, cool, diligent and determined; as a ſtateſman, honeſt, and unſuſpected; and, as a private gentleman, friendly, generous, and humane.

THOMAS,

Pub May 1 1805 by E. Harding 98 Pall Mall

THOˢ EARL of PEMBROKE

THOMAS, EARL OF PEMBROKE AND MONTGOMERY.

THE British genealogists, and a pedigree, drawn by Thomas Jones, of Tregaron, in the year 1582, deduce this family from Herbert, a natural son of king Henry I.; but it seems more evident, that Henry Fitz-Herbert, chamberlain to the said king, was the ancestor to all of the name of Herbert; it being certain, from our records, that Henry Fitz-Herbert married Julian, concubine to king Henry I. and daughter of sir Robert Corbet, of Alencester (now called Alcester) in Warwickshire, whereby he became possessed of the lordship of Alcester, bestowed on the said sir Robert Corbet, by that king. His son, Herbert Fitz-Herbert, was also lord chamberlain to king Stephen, in the fifth year of his reign, when he gave three hundred and fifty-three pounds (an immense sum in those days) for livery of his father's lands. William Herbert, a descendant from the above-mentioned stock, was created earl of Pembroke, by king Edward VI. which title, after having been held by six inter-

mediate

mediate poſſeſſors *, deſcended to Thomas, the noble
perſonage of whom we are about to ſpeak ; who ſucceeded to the title on the 29th of Auguſt 1683, on the
death of Philip his brother, without male iſſue.
In the year 1689, ſoon after the acceſſion of king
William III. he was ſent ambaſſador to the States-
General of the United Provinces, and ſworn one of
the members of his majeſty's moſt honourable privy
council; being among thoſe perſonages who baſked in
the brighteſt ſunſhine of court favour, he was honoured,
at different periods, with the multifarious appointments
and honours of colonel of a regiment of marines, firſt
commiſſioner of the admiralty, lord privy ſeal, firſt
plenipotentiary at the treaty of Ryſwic, knight of the
garter, lord high admiral † of England and Ireland,
preſident of the council, and ſeven times one of the
lords juſtices, whilſt his majeſty went to Holland.
In 1702, immediately after the acceſſion of queen
Anne, he was again nominated lord preſident of the
council ; and in the ſixth year of the ſame reign, was
appointed one of the commiſſioners to treat of an
union between England and Scotland ; after which he
was made lord lieutenant of Ireland, and, in a month
after the death of his royal highneſs prince George of
Denmark, was honoured with the very high office of lord

* Philip, the fourth of this family, who bore the title of earl of Pembroke, was created earl of Montgomery alſo, by patent, bearing date.
June 4th, 1605.

† From the 26th of January 1701-2, to the 20th of May 1702, when
he was ſucceeded by prince George of Denmark, conſort to queen Anne.

high

high admiral of Great Britain. To this latter promotion he owes the place he holds in the collection of memoirs here given. Though not educated in the line of naval fervice, he refolved, neverthelefs, to take upon himfelf the command of the fleet, a determination which he, however, did not carry into execution, having, on the 8th of November 1709, refigned the important truft repofed in him, which was immediately afterwards put into commiffion.

His lordfhip does not appear to have held any other ftate office, during the remainder of the reign, but on the demife of the queen, was appointed by his majefty king George I. one of the lords juftices of Great Britain, till his arrival from Hanover; and, on the 20th of October, at the ceremony of his majefty's coronation, carried the fword called Courtana. He was likewife, in that reign, lord lieutenant of the counties of Wilts, Monmouth, and the fouthern diftrict of the principality of Wales, and one of the privy council. At the coronation of his late majefty, the 11th of October 1727, he again carried the fword called Courtana; and, on the 10th of November following, was once more made lord lieutenant of the county of Wilts.

His lordfhip appears to have been a man of very enlightened tafte in the polite arts, as the admirable collection of antiquities, which he formed at Wilton houfe, in the county of Wilts, fufficiently proves; it contained no lefs than one hundred and thirty-three bufts, thirty-fix ftatues, fifteen bas-reliefs, and ten mifcellanies. He alfo made a very curious and chargeable collection of medals and coins. His lordfhip

died,

died, full of honours, on the 22d of January 1732-3.
He married firſt, Margaret, ſole daughter and heir to
ſir Robert Sawyer; and by her (who died November
17th, 1706), had ſeven ſons and five daughters. By
his ſecond wife, Barbara, daughter of ſir Henry
Slingſby, baronet, and widow of John lord Arundel,
of Trerice, who died in 1721, he had a daughter of
her name, who, October the 3d, 1730, married Dudley North, of Glenham Hall, in Suffolk, eſq. His
lordſhip married, for his third wife, Mary, ſiſter to
Scrope viſcount Howe, but by her he had no iſſue.

SIR

SIR JOHN NORRIS.

THIS gentleman, who was the descendant of a respectable family in the kingdom of Ireland, having received the king's letter at an early age, and passed, with a considerable degree of credit, through the stations of midshipman and lieutenant, was, on account of his very meritorious conduct at the battle off Beachy Head, promoted, on the 6th of July 1690, to be commander of the Pelican fire-ship. He owed every subsequent advancement entirely to his own merit; and is known to have experienced, in the course of his life and service, many of those checks, or retrograde motions, to which divers of the bravest, and best men have been oftentimes subjected.

In the year 1693, he was captain of the Sheerness, a frigate mounting twenty-eight guns, one of the unfortunate squadron under sir George Rooke, to whose protection the ill-fated Smyrna fleet, was in that year confided. Captain Norris acquired, nevertheless, on that occasion, the highest credit; for his diligence, adroitness, and activity in executing the commands of his Admiral, were considered among the most efficient

means that leffened the weight of the difafter, by preven!-
ing many of the merchant-fhips from falling into the
hands of the enemy, as in all probability they otherwife
inevitably would have done. In reward for his conduct,
he was, after his return into England, promoted to the
command of the Carlifle, a fourth rate; and, having
diftinguifhed himfelf very highly, in the month of
January 1694-5, he being then in company with, and
under the command of captain James Killegrew, in
the attack of two French men of war, the Content
and Trident, both of which were captured, after a
fevere action, was, as a very proper compliment, recommended by Mr. Ruffel to the admiralty board, to
command the Content. This fhip was confidered one
of the fineft of her clafs then exifting; for, though
mounting only fixty guns when captured, fhe was, after
being refitted, and taken into the Britifh navy, claffed
as a third rate, of feventy guns. Though attached
to the main fleet, a line of fervice in which he could
naturally expect very little opportunity of diftinguifhing himfelf, except in the event of a general encounter; yet fortune appeared preeminently to favour him,
by throwing in his way, one of the fineft frigates in
the French fervice, which he made prize of without
difficulty. In 1696, he was appointed commodore of
a fmall fquadron, confifting of four fourth rates, an
equal number of frigates, two bomb-ketches, and as
many fire-fhips, ordered to Hudfon's Bay, for the recovery of the Britifh fettlements in that quarter, which
had furrendered a fhort time before to an armament
purpofely fent out from France. On his arrival at
Newfoundland,

Newfoundland, he very unfortunately received intelligence that a fquadron, confifting of five large French fhips, had been feen in the bay of Conception ; and it being fpecially enjoined him by his inftructions, that, in the cafe of any fuch event, he fhould immediately call a council of war, in which the officers of the land-forces on board, down to a certain rank, as well as the captains of the navy, were to be included, it was accordingly convened ; and, as generally proves the cafe in fuch fpecies of deliberation, the refult completely overturned that fuccefs, which, in all human probability, would have attended his exertions, had no fuch meeting taken place. It was a prevailing, and indeed unanimous opinion, that the fquadron which had been feen, was a part of that commanded by the marquis de Nefmond, which was known to be infinitely fuperior to the force under Mr. Norris. The land-officers confidered it extremely imprudent that the fhips fhould venture to fea, but infifted they fhould wait the approach of their antagonifts, under the protection of the batteries raifed on fhore. A few of the naval officers were unhappily of the fame opinion, and the queftion of putting to fea was accordingly carried againft Mr. Norris, and thofe who entertained the fame fentiments with him, by a great majority. Mr. Norris himfelf had indeed the fagacity to fuggeft, that it was probable the enemy's veffels were not any of thofe under the orders of the marquis de Nefmond, but fome which had cafually put into the bay, for the fupply of wood, water, or other refrefhments; he accordingly difpatched a frigate to reconnoitre, and received, on her

return,

return, the truly mortifying intelligence that his own
fuggeftions were true, and that the fhips difcovered,
were thofe returning to Europe under the command of
Monf. Pointi, laden with the plunder of all the Spanifh
Weft Indies, and which, from the inferiority of their
force, would undoubtedly have fallen an eafy prey to
the Britifh armament.

Reftricted, however, as the commodore was by his
orders, he was a fecond time under the neceffity of
calling a council of war, and requefting its advice in refpect to his ulterior proceedings: when he found himfelf
again, as before, baffled in his own views. The report which had been received was difcredited, and even
confidered as fabricated, for the purpofe of betraying
them into the hands of a fuperior antagonift. Ill
fuited as this pufillanimous idea was, to the known
fpirit and gallantry of Mr. Norris, his rage had no
other means of venting itfelf, than in vain complaints
and reproaches, and he was compelled to remain in a
ftate of inactivity, waiting the approach of a foe, who,
as it indeed would have been madnefs in them to have
done, never made their appearance.

The cautious conduct juft mentioned, though apparently reproachable, proved, in the event, not fo
replete with blame, as the natural fpirit of a brave man
would certainly have pronounced it; for, in about a
month after the firft alarm, the marquis de Nefmond
in reality arrived, at the head of a fquadron, confifting
of fixteen fhips of war, ten of which were of the line,
and fome of them very large. The French chef d'efcadre,
on his approach, difcovering the difpofition made
by

by Mr. Norris, prudently defifted from all attack, and the ifland of Newfoundland remained, for that time, unmolefted. The difappointment, however, in the capture of Pointi, roufed a confiderable degree of indignation among the people at home, but it proved of no long duration, particularly, in refpect to captain Norris, who, after all the proceedings which had taken place under his command, had paffed the ordeal of parliamentary inveftigation, was immediately reinftated in the good opinion of all ranks of men.

During the peace, which prefently afterwards took place, captain Norris was conftantly employed as captain of the Winchefter, firft on the Mediterranean, and afterwards on the Newfoundland ftation. Immediately after the acceffion of queen Anne, he was appointed to the Orford, of feventy guns, one of the fleet fent on the expedition againft Cadiz. On his paffage thither, he had the good fortune to make no lefs than five, or fix prizes ; but, during the continuance of the fleet before that place, he became unfortunately involved in a difpute, that threatened to terminate his naval life. He was naturally of a very warm, not to fay violent temper ; extremely irritable, and highly difficult to be appeafed. A difference having arifen between captain Ley, who then commanded the Sovereign, as captain to fir George Rooke, the commander in chief, he was fo outrageous as not only to ftrike, but alfo to draw his fword on that gentleman. The infult was rendered ftill more heinous, from the circumftance of its having taken place on the quarter-deck of captain Ley's own fhip, who was

L 3   alfo

also a much older officer in the fervice than captain Norris. The confequence might eafily have been forefeen ; fir George Rooke felt himfelf reduced to the neceffity of putting the latter under an arreft ; but this very difagreeable bufinefs was fpeedily compromifed, by the interference and interceffion of the duke of Ormond, the general in chief ; and the whole affair was quickly afterwards terminated by the death of captain Ley.

In the following year, captain Norris ftill continuing in the Orford, had the good fortune, when on his paffage to join the fleet under fir Cloudefly Shovell, deftined at that time for the Mediterranean, to fall in with a very large privateer, called the Philippeaux, carrying thirty-fix carriage-guns, together with twelve patararoes. The enemy's fhip being very bravely commanded, and manned with a chofen crew of two hundred and forty men, did not furrender till after a moft obftinate difpute, in the courfe of which fhe had fifty of her crew killed or wounded, and the Orford herfelf received no inconfiderable damage, although trivial when compared with that of her antagonift. The fuccefs of captain Norris by no means ended with this capture ; he having in three or four days afterwards, made prize of a fecond armed fhip belonging to the enemy, carrying fixteen guns, and one hundred and ten men. When the fleet was on its return from the Streights, in the month of November following, the Orford, being ordered ahead, in company with the Warfpite and Litchfield, when they were at the entrance of the Britifh Channel, captain

Norris

Norris had the additional good fortune to fall in with the Hazard, a French fourth rate, carrying fifty-two guns, and four hundred men, which he compelled to fubmit to him, though not till after a very gallant defence on the part of the foe. In 1704 he acted as one of the feconds to fir Cloudefly Shovell, in the battle off Malaga, and his gallantry on that very interefting occafion, may be faid to have raifed his character higher, than all his preceding fervices had done. So ftrongly did it recommend him to the notice of the admiral, by whofe fide he fought, and who, confequently, was rendered a competent, and accurate judge of his conduct, that in the enfuing year captain Norris was felected by him to command the Britannia, a firft rate, on board which himfelf and the earl of Peterborough hoifted their flag, as joint commanders in chief. His behaviour was fo confpicuous in the attack of Fort Montjuic, that the arch-duke Charles, better known, perhaps, by the appellation of king Charles III. wrote a letter to queen Anne with his own hand, for the exprefs purpofe of announcing the efteem he had for this gentleman, and foliciting the queen's favour and protection to him. Being fent home fhortly afterwards, on board the Canterbury, as the bearer of the happy news that the city of Barcelona had furrendered, he received the honour of knighthood, and was prefented with a purfe of one thoufand guineas. He is not known ever to have been fubfequently employed as a private captain; but, having been, on the 10th of March 1706-7, advanced to the rank of rear-admiral of the blue, he was ap-

.L 4   pointed

pointed to ferve under his former friend and patron, fir Cloudefly Shovell, who was once more invefted with the Mediterranean command. The admiral in chief, who knew well his gallantry and ability, feleƐted him to lead the detachment, employed on the very arduous and important fervice of forcing the paffage of the Var. The fhips put under his orders on this occafion, amounted to four Britifh and one Dutch, all of the line, and a detachment of fix hundred chofen men were alfo embarked on board the boats of the fleet, fo as to be ready to land, and ftorm the entrenchments of the enemy, fo foon as it fhould be vifible that the fire of the fhips had effeƐted any impreffion.

Sir Cloudefly himfelf accompanied fir John, that he might be a nearer witnefs of the operations, and be the better able to direƐt any immediate motions that he fhould confider neceffary. The effeƐt of the cannonade becoming apparent, very foon after its commencement, fir John was ordered to land, and affault the flank of the lines; this fervice he performed with fo much fpirit and aƐtivity, that the enemy almoft inftantly gave way, and the paffage of the river was effeƐted with a lofs fo trivial, as to be nearly incredible; for it amounted to no more than ten perfons, who were unfortunately drowned through their over-eagernefs and precipitancy. At the fiege of Toulon, which prefently afterwards fucceeded, his counfel and advice, was, on all occafions, fought by the commander in chief, as a perfon in whofe judgment the moft implicit confidence might be placed. On his return to England, he efcaped, though not without con-

fummate

fummate difficulty, the melancholy fate which befel his
friend and patron, the admiral in chief.

Early in the enfuing winter, he was one of the fix
flag-officers felected to affift his royal highnefs prince
George of Denmark, to whofe opinion the decifion of
the court-martial on fir Thomas Hardy had been referred; an honour which, though apparently trivial in
itfelf, conferred no fmall luftre on the abilities of fir
John; for, from the circumftance of the decifion of
this court of reference, which was completely in favour of fir Thomas Hardy, and produced the effect of
removing from him the ftigma of popular odium, under
which he then lay, it becomes indubitably eftablifhed,
that the refolutions of fir John and his colleagues were
held in public opinion to be perfectly exculpatory.
The fubfequent occupations of fir John Norris during the remainder of the war, were rendered, by the
laffitude of the enemy, extremely uninterefting. In
the year 1708, he was employed under fir John Leake
in the Mediterranean *, and the only fervice of moment, that it was poffible to effect in that quarter, was
executed by him : this was the capture, near Barcelona, of a very numerous fleet of tartans and barks,
bound for Penifcola, near the mouth of the Ebro, all
laden with provifions for the duke of Anjou's army;
of which, through the great activity of this admiral,
fixty-nine, or, as fome fay, a greater number, fell into
the hands of the Englifh.

* On the 8th of January he was appointed rear-admiral of the white;
and, on the 26th of the fame month, vice-admiral of the fame fquadron.

On his return from the Streights, he was, on the 21ſt of December, promoted to be vice-admiral of the red ſquadron, and is ſaid by Burchett to have commanded in the enſuing year an armament ſent into the Baltic. There appears ſome doubt whether this information is correct, but it is known that in 1710, having on the 26th of November preceding, been raiſed to the rank of admiral of the blue, he was ſent into the Mediterranean, as commander in chief on that ſtation, where he unfortunately met with no material opportunity of effecting any ſervice againſt the enemy, except that, of repulſing a deſcent, made by them on the iſland of Sardinia. Sir John did not return to England till the month of October 1711, and the peace at Utrecht almoſt immediately ſucceeding to his arrival, an unavoidable ſtop was put to his further naval exertions, till after the acceſſion of king George I.

In 1716, the reſtleſs temper of Charles XII. of Sweden, and the depredations committed by the privateers of that nation, under his ſanction, rendered it highly expedient to the preſervation of the Britiſh commerce, together with the due maintenance of the kingdom's dignity and honour, that an armament ſhould be ſent into the Baltic; ſir John was choſen to command it: and, having in conſequence hoiſted his flag on board the Cumberland of eighty guns, he ſailed from the Nore on the 18th of May, having with him eighteen ſhips of the line, a frigate, and a ſloop of war, together with a very numerous fleet of merchant-veſſels, which he was ordered to protect on their voyage to the northward. On the arrival of this force in the Sound,

an

an event which took place on the 10th of June, fir
John hoped that the very appearance of his ships
would ftrike fufficient terror into the Swedes, to induce their making the fatisfaction that was required,
without compelling him to have recourfe to hoftile
meafures. The manifeft prevarication, however, of
his opponents, and the evident intentions they difplayed
of ufing every poffible political chicane, for the purpofe of gaining time, till the feafon was fufficiently
advanced to prevent their being molefted during the
current year, compelled the admiral to purfue his ulterior inftructions, and join the fquadrons of Ruffia,
Denmark, and Holland. That of Ruffia was commanded by the czar in perfon, well known in Europe
by the diftinguifhing appellation of Peter the Great.
In compliment to his high dignity, it was agreed,
that he fhould have the chief command of the whole ;
that fir John, with the Englifh fquadron, fhould lead
the van ; the Danes, under count Gueldenlew, the
rear ; and that the Dutch, joined by five Englifh
fhips of war, fhould take the charge of efcorting, to
their feveral places of deftination, the trade of all the
allied powers.

This decided conduct produced the continuance of
public quietude, during the remainder of the year ;
for the Swedes were not fo rafh, as to venture forth
beyond the protection of their forts and batteries ; and
on the approach of winter, fir John, with the main
body of the fleet, returned to England, having, as directed by his orders, adopted the prudent precaution
of leaving commodore Cleland behind him, with a

fquadron

squadron of seven ships of war, and inſtructions to act in conjunction with the other allied powers, as cir-cumſtances·might ariſe. Matters not being ſufficiently accommodated, it was deemed proper to ſend a fleet into the ſame quarter the following ſpring. Sir John. was again ſelected to direct its operations; and to his former character of admiral· in chief, was added that of ambaſſador and miniſter plenipotentiary to the czar, Peter *. Nothing, it has been obſerved, could poſſibly have been more agreeable, than this appointment to the emperor, who always preferred the character of a naval commander, particularly of ſo brave a one as ſir John, to that of the moſt conſummate politician in the univerſe. From this trait, might be expected, as a natural conſequence, that cordial intercourſe to enſue, which never fails to take place between two perſons influenced by the ſame turn of mind. That conſideration, probably directed the choice; and the perſonal friend-ſhip which ever afterwards ſubſiſted between the par-ties, ſufficiently proved the wiſdom of it. The ſame ſyſtem was purſued for the third time, in 1718, and was productive of the ſame effects as before. The death of Charles at the ſiege of Fredericſhall, in the month of November following, put a period to theſe northern expeditions, which from long uſe might be conſidered an annual practice. In the year 1719, the very extraordinary conduct of the court of Spain, and

* After the return of ſir John from this miſſion, he was, on the 19th of March 1717-18, appointed one of the commiſſioners for executing the office of lord high admiral, a ſtation he continued to fill with the higheſt reputation, till the 19th of May 1730.

its

its avowed intentions of making a defcent on Great Britain, in favour of the pretender; caufed the equipment of two fquadrons, which were fent out for the purpofe of intercepting the Spanifh armament, confifting of five fhips of war, having under its protection a fleet of forty tranfports, filled with ftores, troops, and fpare arms, together with one million of dollars in fpecie. The abfence of fir John, however, on this fervice was but of fhort duration, for in lefs than three weeks from the time of his failing, he received authentic information, that the Spanifh fleet had not only been totally difperfed, in a violent gale of wind, off Cape Finifterre, but that the greater part of the fhips had put back, and had, with the utmoft difficulty, reached their own ports, on account of the damage they had fuftained in the tempeftuous weather. Scarcely had the clouds of war been difperfed in one quarter, ere they began to collect and affume a much more threatening afpect in another, far diftant, and totally unexpected. The animofity of Peter, or rather his anxiety to add the realm of Sweden to his own dominions, caufed his troublefome fpirit to relax in no degree from that fury, with which he had acted during the courfe of fo many years pending the life of Charles XII. The court of Great Britain, equitably viewing the project, as one of the moft unjuftifiable infringements of the law of nations, determined to check the ambition of this outrageous prince, and fir John was accordingly chofen to chaftife his former friend and pupil. Such an event was fingular, but not unprecedented in the annals of national warfare; and perhaps it contributed not a

little

little to the reftoration of public tranquillity, that the czar had, on a former occafion, been accidentally fur-nifhed with fo good an opportunity of difcovering the genius, and temper of his antagonift.

The Englifh fleet reached Copenhagen in the month of June, and after fome time, fruitlefsly fpent, in nego-tiation, proceeded to Carlfcroon for the purpofe of forming a junction with the Swedes. This, however, not being effected till the 10th of September, the feafon became too far advanced to permit any naval opera-tions of moment. But the appearance of the Britifh armament in the Baltic had neverthelefs the good effect of preferving the fhores of Sweden from ravage ; for the czar, who, during the early part of the year, had fed his own fpleen by carrying the war into thofe territories, attended with all that dreadful devaftation, which he was fo well accuftomed to authorize, no fooner heard of his preceptor's approach, than he, with the utmoft expedition retired to Revel, and confidered him-felf happy, that his navy could find an afylum in that port, from the thunder of the Britifh cannon. The fer-vices of fir John did not, however, end, for this feafon, with the protection afforded to the Swedes againft Ruffia. When on his return to England he exerted his beft powers, to effect a reconciliation between Sweden, and the king of Denmark ; but though the latter did not entirely accede to the propofals made by the admiral, yet he contributed very materially to foften his afperities, and render him lefs hoftile to the queen of Sweden, than, in all probability, he otherwife would have been.

The

The enfuing fpring produced a repetition of the fame ferio-comic fcene; the czar, who during the winter, had ufed very imperative language to the Swedifh fenate, and infifted they fhould reverfe their own act, by which they had placed the prince of Heffe, the confort to the queen, on the throne, in exclufion of the duke of Holftein, who was the legal heir; no fooner found fir John a fecond time, approaching to oppofe his officious, and impertinent interference, than he withdrew, as before, to his own ports, and once more fuffered the defencelefs coafts of Sweden, to remain unmolefted. The negotiation which fir John had entered into the preceding winter at Copenhagen, with the king of Denmark, was in the courfe of the prefent year, happily terminated; the two monarchs became perfectly reconciled to each other, and Sweden had the happinefs of feeing the number of her enemies leffened, under the mediation of the Britifh admiral. Peter ftill remained obftinate, and Britain found herfelf under the difagreeable neceffity, of fending fir John into the Baltic for the third time, in the following fpring. The armament was more formidable than it had been on either of the preceding occafions, for it confifted of no lefs than twenty-one fhips of the line, with feven frigates, or fmaller veffels. The rage of Peter, which by this time was grown fomewhat cool, became foftened into the reflection, that all refiftance or oppofition would be in vain, though exerted to the utmoft of his powers, againft fo formidable an opponent as Britain. The peace figned at Nieftadt clofed the fcene; much to the fatisfaction of Sweden,

and

and highly to the honour of the country which had espoufed her caufe.

From this time, fir John enjoyed a temporary relaxation from the fatigues of public fervice; for except that in the year 1723, when he was appointed to command the fquadron which convoyed king George I. from Helvoetfluys to England, he held no naval command till the year 1727, when the apprehenfion of an attack meditated on Sweden by the czarina, rendered the equipment of a fleet of twelve fhips of the line, befides five frigates and fmaller veffels, abfolutely neceffary. Its appearance in the Baltic, produced the fame inftantaneous effect which it always had, on every preceding occafion; and Sweden remained unattacked, becaufe fhe was protected by Britain. From this time, till the year 1735, fir John Norris held no command; but a difpute having then arifen between the crowns of Spain and Portugal, the latter applied to Britain, as her ancient ally, for protection. The command of the fleet fitted out on this occafion was given to fir John, who had, during his retirement from public fervice, been advanced in the year 1732, to the rank of admiral of the white. His arrival at Lifbon was regarded by the Portuguefe as a certain deliverance, and the terror excited by the interference of Britain, now produced in a fouthern clime, the fame effect which we have already feen it did in the north; the ftorm of war inftantly breaking away, the fleet returned, and was difmantled. On this occafion the Britifh admiral might, with fome truth, vie with the Roman general, who is faid to have

have finifhed a war in feventeen days after he had taken upon him the command. In after-ages, many truly brilliant exploits of the prefent day, may, probably, eclipfe in fame, thofe of antiquity, which are now moft celebrated.

The conduct of the court of Spain had, for a feries of years, been extremely infulting to Great Britain. The numerous depredations committed by the guarda-coftas of the former, together with the infults, the injuries, and the barbarities, which they were in the conftant habit of exercifing towards all thofe, who were unfortunate enough to fall in their way, and were not fufficiently powerful to refift their attack, roufed at length the fleeping vengeance of Britain, and the pacific temper of her minifter fir Robert Walpole. Among other preparations for hoftility, a formidable fleet was equipped for home fervice, and placed under the orders of fir John. The collection of fuch an armament, and the opinion univerfally entertained of the commander, under whofe orders it was placed, caufed the higheft exultation in the public mind, throughout the whole Britifh nation. The people fancied they beheld half the Spanifh navy, at leaft, brought in triumph into their ports, and anticipated the deftruction of almoft every arfenal, or fortrefs their enemy poffeffed, near the fea coafts. In both, however, they were difappointed. The Spaniards were too wife to venture fending any armament to fea, all their harbours of any note, were too well defended by batteries, to render fuccefs probable, unlefs the efforts of the navy had been feconded by a fufficient body of land

forces, embarked on board the fleet, which was not
the cafe ; and thofe ports, where injury might have
been effected, without danger of difcomfiture, were too
contemptible, to render their deftruction otherwife than
ridiculous, fince it would have been productive of mifchief
and ruin to a few private individuals only. Neverthelefs,
hiftorians, and others, have thought proper to caft no
fmall fhare of obloquy on the conduct of the admiral, for
not doing that, which it was either actually impoffible for
him to do, or not engaging in frivolous enterprifes, the
very fuccefs of which ought, in the eye of candour, to
have expofed him to cenfure. In 1744, France, ever
folicitous to meddle, and become a partner in political
mifchief, attached herfelf to the caufe of Spain, and
among other of her cuftomary fchemes, to diftract
the attention of the Britifh councils, projected the
invafion of Scotland, in favour of the pretender. A
very formidable force was collected at Breft, for this
purpofe ; it confifted of no lefs than twenty-three fhips
of war, the chief command of which was beftowed on
monf. De Rouquefeuille; an officer of eminence and
reputation ; but though thefe meafures had been concerted with the utmoft fecrecy, the Britifh miniftry
had the good fortune to procure information of them ;
and ere it reached the Britifh channel, a fleet confifting of twenty-nine fhips of the line, was collected in
the Downs under the orders of fir John Norris. This
unforefeen circumftance broke at once all the meafures
of the enemy ; they beheld with aftonifhment the fuperiority of their opponents, and at the very inftant,
when they confidered themfelves abfolutely certain of
fuccefs,

Tuccefs, found they were obliged to owe·their fafety to their fpeedy flight back to their own ports, and regard the winds, the fogs, and the ftate of the weather unfavourable in all refpects, except that of being propitious to their flight, as the friends which preferved them from deftruction. With this laft fervice, the naval life of fir John Norris ceafed. He had been in conftant employment for the fpace of nearly fixty years, fo that his age, and his infirmities, rendered his retirement a matter of neceffity. This relaxation from fatigue, however, he did not long enjoy, having died in an advanced age on the 19th of July 1749.

In refpect to his character, it may be truly remarked, that although many may have had the good fortune to acquire a greater fhare of popular applaufe, none have had a nobler, and jufter claim to public gratitude, than this brave and able commander; or have been more truly entitled to the compaffion of thofe, who are capable of feeling for that degree of misfortune, which rarely failed to attend him through life. Seamen, who are, as a body of people, in all probability, the moft fuperftitious in the world, conftantly foretold a ftorm, whenever fir John put to fea. The frequent accidents which befel the fhips, and fquadrons under his command, the misfortunes which attended him, and which, being inflicted merely by the hand of Heaven, could not be warded off by any prudence, or fagacity, procured him the whimfical appellation of *foul weather Jack*; by which fofter name he was, perhaps, better known in the fervice, than by his own proper ftyle and title. In reviewing his *public* life and conduct, we

cannot

cannot find a single point * in which he appears liable
to cenfure ; and were we to fay no more, this would,
perhaps, be a fufficient degree of applaufe, to acquire
him the admiration cf all confiderate men.   Let thofe,
if any, who think otherwife, reflect, for a moment,
on the difficulties which muft have furrounded a man,
acting in a public capacity for fixty-years: let them
recollect thofe accidents, which daily baffle the moft prudential, and beft founded fyftems.   Let them not forget
that public envy, and perfonal malice, are perpetually
on the watch to depreciate renown, and victory itfelf ;
and let them then decide, whether to die unaccufed,
is not to have always lived, worthy of applaufe.

The incidents of war for the fpace of forty years
fucceeding the battle off Malaga, in 1704, were totally
uninterefting in the fcale of grand operation ; in fuch
alone are we to look for thofe brilliant achievements
which high-founding fame delights in publifhing to
the world, and preferving to our memories.   Thefe
having failed, the voice of envy never ceafing to demand what could not exift, impofes herfelf, at laft,
on the world, for that candour and juftice, which
forbid us to beftow honours, which have not been
truly earned.   That courage and fpirit of enterprife,
which fir John fo frequently and happily difplayed, when
in the ftation of a private commander, would certainly
have borne him through the moft arduous and difficult
undertakings, when moving in the moft elevated
fphere ; and no reafonable man can doubt, but that

* His difpute with captain Ley could not be confidered a breach of
public conduct.

the

the fame glory which is fo juftly attached to the characters of Ruffel, or Rooke, would have been acquired
by Norris, had he been fortunate enough to have experienced the fame opportunity.

In the lefs dazzling duties of his profeffion, which
were all that fortune put it in his power to exercife, no
man could be more affiduous.   When commander in
chief in the Baltic, he ufed every poffible means to
procure to his country, a complete knowledge of that
dangerous and intricate navigation, which was, till
his time, much feared, as being little underftood.   For
this purpofe he took uncommon pains to compile an
accurate draught of that fea, by caufing all officers
under him to make every remark, and obfervation in
their power.   This conduct laid the foundation of
that more enlarged and general knowledge, which has
at laft rendered the navigation of it lefs difficult
than that of the Thames.   His abilities as a nego-
tiator were never difputed, becaufe in that line of
fervice he was always moft fuccefsful.   His temper,
as a commander, armed with powers either to enforce
obedience, or accept fubmiffion, were fuch as entitled
him to the praife, even of thofe againft whom he ferved;
fo that among all his enemies, he had at leaft the fatiffaction of knowing there were none who could, with
propriety, openly rank themfelves under fo defpicable
a banner.

SIR WILLIAM JUMPER.

───────

Of the many perfons, who have at different periods contributed to raife the fplendour of the Britifh name, and render its maritime greatnefs refpected in every quarter of the globe, few, or none perhaps, have been, better entitled to popular applaufe, and public veneration, than the gentleman of whom we are now about to fpeak. The early part of his fervice, as it has been frequently the lot of the braveft men, contains no intereft fufficiently material, to recommend it to particular notice. He was appointed a lieutenant juft at the epoch of the revolution, and after having continued in that rank, for four years, during which period he ferved on board divers fhips, with the higheft reputation, was, on the 17th of February 1692, promoted to be commander of the Hopewell fire-fhip. After having been advanced to two or three different commands, each progreffively rifing above the other, he was, in 1694, made captain of the Weymouth, a fourth rate, in which fhip he continued during the remainder of the war ; and no man, perhaps, was ever more fortunate in a command of fo little importance.

In

In the course of his first cruise, having the Medway in company, he fell in with a very large private ship of war, carrying fifty-four guns, and three-hundred and forty men. The Weymouth far outstripping her companion in speed, brought the enemy to action, about two o'clock in the morning, but the Invincible, her opponent, being as well as herself, a prime sailer, and making every possible effort to escape, captain Jumper was prevented from closing, till after a running fight of eighteen hours continuance. The enemy having immediately afterwards lost her main-topmast, as well as being otherwise materially damaged, and the Medway being enabled to draw up, in consequence of the two combatants having brought to, for action, thought proper to prevent further bloodshed, by surrendering to captain Jumper.

In fourteen days afterwards, he had the additional good fortune, to capture a privateer of twenty-four guns, which was considered at that time, one of the best sailing vessels that ever had put to sea, and had done incredible mischief to the commerce of the allied powers. On the 31st of August ensuing, he captured a third private frigate of war, mounting twenty-eight guns, and notwithstanding the force of this vessel, was so much inferior to his own, he experienced a more material resistance, than on either of the preceding occasions. The commander of the enemy's vessel possessed a courage, bordering on frenzy, and was supported by a chosen crew, each individual of which was no less hardy, and daring than himself; the consequences were accordingly fatal to the lives of many

M 4 brave

brave men, who fruitlefsly fell during a refiftance,
which at the very commencement of it, muft have
been confidered by all cool perfons, rafh, and of no avail.
Thirty of the enemy's crew were killed, and twenty-
five wounded, the greater part of them mortally.

In the month of September he engaged a large private fhip of war, called the Count de Thouloufe, mounting forty-four guns, but having had the misfortune to
carry away his fore-topmaft, while in chafe, his
opponent, deriving courage from this difafter, and
confidering the Weymouth fo difabled as to be almoft
entirely at his mercy, tacked and ftood to meet captain
Jumper, who received him with the very rough falu-
tation of a broadfide, fired with fuch exact precifion,
as compelled him to confult his future fafety, by immediate flight, nor was it poffible, on account of the
difabled ftate of the Weymouth, to prevent his efcape.
In the month of May 1695, being ftill employed in
the fame line of fervice, he made prizes of two privateers, one mounting fourteen, the other fixteen guns ;
and on the 19th of July following, had the good fortune to fall in with a very large private fhip of war,
belonging to St. Maloes, called the Count de Revelle,
pierced for forty-eight guns, but having on board,
when taken, only thirty-fix ; the extra ports, being
intended to be fupplied, as is even at the prefent day,
very frequently the cafe in French fhips, from the
oppofite fide. The enemy's veffel, being of much
larger fcantline than the Weymouth, and her commander, a man poffeffed of great judgment and intrepidity, a long and fpirited encounter enfued ; but the

Frenchman

Frenchman having loft all his mafts, and the greater part of his crew, was under the neceffity of furrendering; and captain Jumper had, in a very few days afterwards, the happinefs of receiving fome folid fatiffaction for his trouble, on the preceding occafion, by the capture of three valuable merchant-veffels bound to different ports of France. In the month of November, he captured a large fhip of war, built for the king's fervice, and while fo employed, carrying forty guns; but when taken, lent to the merchants, and in confequence of her having on board a valuable and weighty cargo, mounting only twenty-four.

This ftream of public good fortune, was unhappily interrupted in the courfe of the following month, by a very melancholy private difafter. Having returned to Plymouth, to recruit his ftock of water and provifions, as he was coming on fhore in his pinnace, accompanied by his wife, and a captain Smith, who commanded the Portland, the boat overfet, and captain Smith, as well as Mrs. Jumper, unhappily loft their lives. What rendered this accident, if poffible, ftill more afflicting was, that Mrs. Jumper was actually alive when taken up, but expired almoft immediately afterwards. Captain Jumper having, in fome degree, recovered from this fhock, again put to fea, and in the month of February, captured another French privateer, of twenty guns, and feveral other prizes of inferior confequence. In the beginning of December, he attacked a very large French fhip of war called the Fougeux, pierced for fixty, and actually

mounting,

mounting, when taken, forty-eight guns ; but misfortune deprived him of that reward, his gallantry demanded ; for the enemy's ſhip having unhappily ſtruck
on a rock during the encounter, ſunk, almoſt immediately after ſhe had ſurrendered. In a very few days
afterwards, as a ſort of douceur given by fortune for
this diſappointment, he made prizes of ſeveral merchant-veſſels, and on the 22d of the ſame month, attacked a French ſhip of war, mounting fifty guns, off
Cape Clear ; but almoſt immediately after the action
had commenced, and which, owing to the ſpirit with
which the Weymouth fought, did not threaten to be
of any long continuance, a quantity of cartridges unfortunately took fire on the Weymouth's quarter-deck,
blew up the round-houſe, and diſabled a conſiderable
number of men, who were ſtationed in that part of
the ſhip. The enemy ſeizing inſtant advantage of
this unforeſeen accident, ſet all their ſails that were
manageable, in the hope of eſcaping.

Captain Jumper, however, and his people, having
ſpeedily extinguiſhed the fire, and in ſome meaſure
recovered from the ſurpriſe into which they had been
thrown, crowded all the ſail they could in the purſuit,
and were ſo far ſuccefsful as to bring their opponent
for the ſecond time to cloſe action. Misfortune, however, ſeemed to attend the whole of captain Jumper's very gallant exertions on this occaſion ; for
the French ſhip endeavouring to paſs a-head of the
Weymouth, they both fell on board each other, and
the main-maſt of the former carried away the latter's
bowſprit ; the loſs of which was immediately followed
by

by that of all the mafts. The natural confequence was the efcape of the enemy, and the privation of that reward, which the bravery of captain Jumper and his crew moft juftly merited. The war now drew near a clofe, but the activity of this gentleman, in no degree relaxed from what it had been, when French cruifers more abounded, and contefts were confequently more frequent. In the month of April 1697, he captured a privateer belonging to Granville, mounting eighteen guns; and in that of July following, difplayed the greateft adroitnefs, in the attack of a French fhip of war, built on a new conftruction, of which tranfaction he has left us an account, written by himfelf, which will probably not prove unacceptable.

"From on board his Majefty's fhip the Weymouth, Auguft 19th, 1697:

"The 19th, in the afternoon, I faw a fail to leeward, between the land of Olonne, and St. Martin's ifland, and underftood by a Bifcay privateer, of fix guns, whom I fpoke with, that it was a French man of war; and that there were feveral others cruifing along the fhore, between Belle-ifle, and Bourdeaux; whereupon I crowded fail to leeward to him, trimming my fails on a wind, though I went before it, that he fhould not difcover my fquare yards, keeping my head to him, and making a little yaw fometimes to fhew my French enfign. He kept his wind to me, and braced to. I faw feveral fifher-boats, and to leeward of them a fleet of about forty fail, ftanding into the land. Another frigate that was at anchor under a caftle, weighed, and ftood off to us; and be-
lieving

lieving I could beat them both, I brought all the
ftrength I could, on one fide, for difpatch. The man
of war firft mentioned, coming near, fufpected me,
and made fail off fhore; but I outfailed him, and went
clofe, under his lee fide. My main-yard brufhing his
main-fhrouds, we afked him whence he came, and
told him we were from Breft, and he anfwered, from
Rochfort. I kept my French enfign flying to prevent
his firing at my mafts till I was near enough; then
put up the Englifh enfign, and poured a broadfide in
him. Moft of the fhot went out on the other fide,
killed one lieutenant, and eleven men. We wounded
defperately as many more, the captain himfelf being
fhot in the belly. I braced my main-topfail aback,
and before half the other round was fired, the French
ftruck, being called L'Aurore, of Rochfort, the king's
fhip, one year old; in the nature of our galleys, carrying twenty guns on the upper deck; none on the
lower deck, but four on the quarter deck, and between
decks fmall ports for oars, being the beft failer I ever
met with by a wind. Having fecured the prize, I
made ready for the other, but he tacked about a mile
and a half from me, and ran to the fleet before mentioned. I then made a fignal for the prize to follow
me; and we chafed the fleet, which ftood in, and got
into St. Martin's before we could reach them. I took
this fhip four leagues S. W. from the headland of
Olonne, where fhe had been watering two days before.
The other was a fhip of twenty guns likewife; and
the fleet I underftood came from Bourdeaux with a
convoy of forty-fix guns. I lay there three days
                                        afterwards,

afterwards, but could fee nothing, except a row-boat in a calm, who was fent to know what we were, but would not come near."

During the peace, which took place not long after the event juft mentioned, he was appointed to fome fhip of the line, the name of which is not known, nor indeed is it of any confequence if it were, and he continued in the fame command till after the rupture with France had taken place, fubfequent to the acceffion of queen Anne. He was then appointed to the Lenox, one of the fleet, fent on the expedition under fir George Rooke, againft Cadiz; on which occafion it fo happened, that he was more actively employed than perhaps any commander in the fleet, having been ordered to filence the caftle of St. Catharine's, and cover the landing of the troops, a fervice which he completely executed, and, with the utmoft promptitude. In 1703, he ferved on the Mediterranean ftation under fir Cloudefly Shovell, and having been detached foon after the fleet paffed the Streights, with a convoy to Scanderoon, did not return to England till the month of December. Early in the following fpring, he again failed under the orders of fir George Rooke to the Mediterranean, and the very confpicuous fervice which he rendered, while thus employed, will ftand for ever recorded in the page of Britifh hiftory. The capture of Gibraltar was, in a great meafure, owing to his own perfonal exertions, feconded by thofe of captain Hicks. "The admiral," fay hiftorians, "confidering that by gaining the fortifications at the South Mole Head, he fhould of confequence reduce the town, ordered

4   captain

captain Whitaker, with all the boats armed, to endeavour to poſſeſs himſelf of it, which was performed
with great vigour and ſucceſs by captain Hicks, and
captain Jumper, with their pinnaces and other boats;
and with the loſs only of two lieutenants and forty,
men killed, and about ſixty wounded, by the ſpringing
of a mine, that blew up the fortifications upon the
Mole.   However, the confederates kept poſſeſſion of
the platform, which they had made themſelves maſters
of.   The fact was, that the order was no ſooner iſſued
for captain Whitaker to arm the boats, than captain
Hicks and captain Jumper, who were neareſt the
Mole, puſhed on ſhore with their pinnaces, and actually ſeized the fortifications, before the reſt could
come up."

The conduct of captain Jumper, in the battle off
Malaga, which took place preſently after the ſucceſs
juſt mentioned, was no leſs worthy of the moſt exalted
praiſe, he having perſonally engaged no leſs than three
of the enemies' ſhips, and driven them out of the line.
He was ſeverely wounded on this occaſion, but does
not appear to have ever quitted his ſhip on that account ; and it is noted, as a ſingular circumſtance, that
no one of his cotemporaries (or perhaps his ſucceſſors)
ever ſhifted his command ſo unfrequently.   He was
captain of the Weymouth, as has been already ſeen,
during the greater part of the preceding war, and after
the acceſſion of queen Anne, never again changed his
ſhip while he continued in ſervice, a period of many
years duration.

Immediately after his return to England, the well-earned honour of knighthood was moft defervedly beftowed upon him. He continued to command the Lenox till the year 1707, being always employed under the different admirals, who were annually fent to the Streights, and to the Mediterranean, and to fay more, would only afford a dull and uninterefting account, of departures and returns from a quarter of the world, where the flames of war might be faid to lie nearly dormant. After his arrival from the Streights, whither he had accompanied fir Cloudefly Shovell, and by whom he was difpatched to England, on the very morning of the day when that admiral was loft on the rocks of Scilly, he never again went to fea, but is faid to have been immediately made fuperintendant of the fhips at Chatham, an office fince fuppreffed, and rendered totally unneceffary, by the modern appointment of port admiral. He had a handfome penfion granted him on his retirement from fervice ; and no perfon appears to have thought this mark of royal munificence, or public gratitude, improperly, or extravagantly beftowed. In the year 1714, he was appointed commiffioner of the navy, refident at Plymouth, but did not long enjoy his new office, dying on the 12th of March in the following year.

SIR CHARLES WAGER

Is, very defervedly, faid to have been one of thofe truly amiable, and praifeworthy perfons, who by dint of their own proper merit, unaffifted by friends, relatives, or influence, have attained the higheft reputation in their profeffion; and, in a civil line, have executed the moft important offices of the ftate, not only without incurring cenfure and reproach; but having alfo, in the moft momentous concerns, and arduous undertakings, acquitted themfelves to the admiration of all, have at laft died, when full of years and glory, as univerfally regretted, and lamented, as they lived beloved. Of the earlier part of this gentleman's naval life, there is no account; not the flighteft mention being made of him till he was appointed captain of the Ruzee fire-fhip, by commiffion, bearing date June 7th, 1692. His time during the whole of the war, then exifting, was conftantly occupied in the fervice of his country; but from the nature of his employments, appears to have paffed extremely barren of incidents; for the only occafions on which his name occurs, previous to the acceffion of queen Anne, are, that

Harding sc

S.^R CHA.^S WAGER KN.^T

Publish'd July 1,1800 by Edw. Harding 98 Pall Mall.

that in the year 1695, he commanded the Woolwich, of
fifty-four guns, one of the ships employed under the orders of fir Cloudefly Shovell on the Channel ftation, and
in 1699, was captain of one of the ships of the line,
kept in commiffion for fervice, in cafe of any fudden
emergency. In 1703, he was captain of the Hampton-
court of feventy guns, and invefted with the temporary
rank of commodore, as being the fenior officer of a
fmall fquadron, fent to cruife off the coaft of France.
He does not appear however, to have had the good
fortune of meeting with any fuccefs, either while thus
occupied, or on any fubfequent occafion ; fo that his
appointment in 1707 to the chief command of a fquadron, fitted for the Weft India ftation, was certainly
one of the moft honourable proofs of the high eftimation in which his talents were held, notwithftanding
the nature of his employments had not afforded him any
opportunity, of raifing himfelf into that public notice,
and notoriety, fufficient to render him what is called
a popular character. He failed from Plymouth on the
10th of April ; the force under his command amounting to nine ships of war, to the protection of which was
intrufted a fleet confifting of forty-five fail of merchant-veffels. His rank, according to his commiffion,
was, when he failed, merely that of captain of the
Expedition, but he was fpecially empowered to hoift a
broad pendant, fo foon as he fhould be clear of the
Britifh channel, and appoint a captain to command
the ship under himfelf.

. He arrived in the Weft Indies, after a fpeedy and
profperous voyage, and applied himfelf on his arrival,

fo attentively to the interefts, and protection of thofe
colonies, that it was univerfally admitted, the trade of
that quarter had never been in a more flourifhing ftate,
than while commodore Wager continued to command
on that ftation. During the enfuing winter, a report
prevailed that the well-known French chef d'efcadre
Du Caffe, was hourly expected to arrive with a fquadron of confiderable force, having for its object the
attack of the ifland of Jamaica. A different deftination quickly fucceeded (in report) to the former; it
being ftated that the real caufe of his errand, was that
of protecting home to Spain, an exceedingly valuable
fleet of galleons, which were to rendezvous at the Havannah, and which the whole national marine of that
country, was in itfelf unequal to the tafk of convoying,
to fo low, and diftreffed a ftate was it then reduced.
Mr. Wager, with all that ftrength of mental faculty,
which a great man, when fairly entitled to that appellation, invariably poffeffes, formed a plan of making
himfelf mafter of this valuable charge, ere the arrival of
thofe, who were expected to be its guardians. The
proper feizure of this interval was the only circumftance that could in any degree, even forebode fuccefs.
On the arrival of Du Caffe, the great fuperiority of
his force would have rendered it abfolutely imprac-
ticable. Mr. Wager was perfectly well acquainted with
the courfe and route of the galleons; he knew they were
to proceed from Porto-Bello to Carthagena, and from
thence to the Havannah, where he expected Mr. Du
Caffe would wait for them, and he refolved, if poffible,
to intercept them while on their paffage thither.

He

He accordingly divided his force into two parts, and after retaining with himself such ships as he deemed sufficient to master the galleons, which he knew to be stout vessels, and well armed, he dispatched the remainder to watch the motions of the enemy, and if possible, to procure some intimation of their intentions. He proceeded to carry this plan into execution, about the middle of the month of January, when he sailed from Port Royal; but, after a successless cruise of two months continuance, he received intelligence, that the galleons were not to quit Porto-Bello till the first day of May; he accordingly resolved to return immediately to Jamaica, in the hope that the Spaniards might, by such a measure, be lulled into a belief, that, finding himself baffled in his expectations, he had given up all hope of success, and had sunk into the same state of inactivity, which had marked the conduct of many of his predecessors. All the ships that could be got ready for sea, and which consisted of no more than the Expedition, the Portland, and the Kingston, with an attendant fire-ship, being equipped, as well as circumstances would permit, the commodore sailed from Port Royal on the 14th of April; and early in the ensuing month, had the misfortune to encounter a dreadful storm, in which the ships under his orders, and more particularly his own, the Expedition, received much damage. He resolved, however, to repair it as well as he could, at sea, fearing the enemy might escape, if he ventured to return back to port. After a long and tedious interval of suspense, Mr. Wager's anxiety was relieved on the 28th of May, by his discovering,

at

at daybreak, two ſhips ſtanding in ſor Carthagena,
which were by noon, increaſed to ſeventeen. The
following particulars of the ſubſequent encounter may
be conſidered authentic.

" The enemy, confident in their ſuperior numbers,
and, in ſome degree, even contemning the ſmall force
of the Engliſh, ſeemed rather careleſs and indifferent
whether to fight or endeavour to eſcape. They
held on their courſe, but without crowding ſail, ima-
gining their numbers would deter the Engliſh commodore from following them. In this they were miſ-
taken. Finding themſelves purſued, and that towards
evening, they could not weather Baru, a ſmall iſland
in their track to their deſtined port, they formed
a kind of line, and reſolutely determined to conteſt and
end the matter at once. The three moſt valuable
ſhips, that is to ſay, thoſe which had the ſpecie on
board, were diſtinguiſhed as admirals', or commanders'
ſhips. The largeſt, carrying a white pendant, was in
the centre. She was in force not at all inferior to the
Expedition. She mounted indeed, only ſixty-four
guns, which were all braſs, but was very ſuperior, as
to the numbers of her crew, having on board near ſeven
hundred men.

" The van was led by a ſhip, mounting forty-four
guns, and carrying a ſimilar pendant, at her mizen-
topmaſt head. The rear was cloſed by a very fine
ſhip, mounting fifty braſs guns, with a pendant at her
fore-topmaſt head, and acting as vice-admiral, or
commander, in the ſecond poſt. Theſe three ſhips
were at the diſtance of about half a mile from each
other,

other, the interval being filled up with other vessels, many of which are said to have been of good force. Boyer afferts, that one of them, a French ship, carrying thirty-six guns, was engaged with the Expedition, and fupported her Spanifh companions a confiderable time; while on the other hand Lediard, and after him Campbell inform us, there were only two French fhips in company, that one mounted thirty, the other twenty-four guns, and that they both ran away, immediately on the commencement of the action. Of the remainder, two were floops, and one a brigantine, which ftood in for the land, and made their efcape, but after thefe various detachments were made, the commodore, and his two feconds, had twelve fhips to contend with. Mr. Wager got along-fide of the centre or largeft fhip, juft at fun-fet, and immediately began to engage. He is faid by Boyer, to have had, at one time, both the vice, and rear admiral upon him, as well as the large French fhip juft mentioned. No notice, however, is taken of this circumftance by any other hiftorian, but thus far, all agree, that neither the Kingfton nor Portland did their duty, or fulfilled the commodore's orders, notwithftanding he purpofely hailed the former, and having ordered her to engage the rear-admiral, and fent his boat to the Portland, with inftruction for him to engage the vice-admiral. Finding thefe directions were neither of them likely to be complied with, he made the fignal for a line of battle, as both the fhips kept to windward out of their ftations; but of this they were as regardlefs as they had been of his former orders.

N 3   " The

"The Expedition, and the Spanish admiral had been engaged about an hour and a half, when by some accident the latter blew up, eleven only of her crew being saved, which were picked up floating on some part of the wreck the next day. This melancholy disaster not only deprived the commodore of his best, and nearly acquired prize, but was attended with the greatest danger, to the Expedition herself, as well from the intense heat of the blast, together with the flaming plank and timbers which were carried on board her, as from the violent shock and concussion, which forced a considerable quantity of water into the commodore's lower deck ports. These inconveniences being got rid of without further damage, Mr. Wager made sail for a large ship ahead of him, which was the only one he could keep sight of, as it was now become extremely dark; and the enemy immediately on the blowing up of their commander's ship, began to separate, so that each might shift for himself in the best manner he could. About ten o'clock, however, he came up with the ship he was in pursuit of, which afterwards proved to be the rear-admiral. It was then so extremely dark that it was impossible to discover which way the enemy's head lay; so that, firing at a venture, he had the good fortune to pour his whole broadside into the Spaniard's stern, which did him so much damage as to disable him from making sail. The commodore being then to leeward, tacked, and after a short stretch, put about, and weathered his antagonist, whom he immediately re-engaged. The Kingston and Portland being directed by the flashes of his guns, soon after came up,

and

and affifted in the capture of the enemy, who furrendered about two o'clock in the morning.".

The commodore having in the foregoing actions not
only received very confiderable damage, both in his
mafts and rigging, infomuch, that he was under the
neceffity of bringing to with his prize, but being,
moreover, much encumbered with the prifoners he
had on board, ordered, at daybreak, the Kingfton and
Portland to chafe a large fhip, feen on the weather-
bow, which he very properly fuppofed to be the Spanifh vice-admiral of the galleons. In confequence
of the inactivity, or the neglect of the officers *, who
commanded thofe fhips, the enemy nevertheless effected his efcape. The Expedition, and her prize,
being put in as good a condition as circumftances
would permit, he refolved to proceed to Jamaica, with
all poffible fpeed ; but being much diftreffed for pro-

* At a court-martial held on board her majefty's fhip Expedition, at Port
Royal, in Jamaica, the 23d of July 1708, captain Simon Bridges, commander of her majefty's fhip the Kingfton, was tried for not having performed his duty in a late action with the Spanifh galleons, on the coaft of
Carthagena, in New Spain, on the 28th, 29th, and 30th of May laft ; and
it did appear by evidence, upon oath, that the faid captain Simon Bridges,
through mifconduct, did not ufe his utmoft endeavour to engage, and take
the enemy, on the 28th of May laft, at night, and that he did too negligently
purfue the chafe of the Spanifh vice-admiral, on the 29th, and 30th, and
that he left off chafe when within fhot of the f id fhip, doubting the pilot's
knowledge, and being near the fhoal, called the Salmadinas, though the pilot
offered to carry the fhip within the faid fhoal, after the faid vice-admiral, but
no want of perfonal courage being alledged againft him, this court does only find
him guilty of the breach of part of the twelfth, and part of the fourteenth
articles of war, and for the faid offence do difmifs him, the faid captain Simon
Bridges, from being captain of her majefty's fhip Kingfton.

N 4   vifions

vifions and water, he yielded to the folicitations of
his prifoners, and fet them on fhore on the ifland of
Baru. Having been rejoined by the fhips he had detached, which had returned fuccefslefs, he refolved
to fend them to deftroy a galleon, mounting forty
guns, which had taken fhelter under the ifland juft
mentioned. His own fhip, being found in a very
ill condition for fervice, he fhifted his broad pendant
immediately afterwards to the Portland, and ordered
the Expedition and Kingfton, together with his
prize, to make the beft of their way to Port
Royal. Reflecting, however, that it could not
poffibly be in his power to effect any material fervice with a fingle fhip, he refolved to return thither
himfelf alfo, and, on his arrival in port, in the beginning of July, had the fatisfaction of finding the
veffels in queftion had got in five days before
him. Almoft immediately after this time, he
received advice from England of his promotion to
the rank of rear-admiral of the blue fquadron, an
advancement which he was till then ignorant of,
notwithftanding it had been conferred on him on the
19th of November in the preceding year.

The moft honourable teftimony is borne to his private conduct in the management and diftribution,
among the captors, of the treafure which had fallen
into their hands. He exhibited, fays the reporter,
on his arrival at Jamaica, a fingular proof of honefty,
integrity, and benevolence. Previous to this year,
there was no regular and eftablifhed mode of dividing,
according to a fixed fyftem, the property taken from
                                                    the

the enemy among the captors ; each individual plundering, and feizing to his own particular ufe, as much as could be found, out of the hold. There were, indeed, fome ill-defined regulations, which cuftom had, in fome degree, erected into a law ; but thefe were, according to circumftances, as often broken through, as obferved ; and even were they to have been maintained in their ftricteft fenfe, were, to the major part of the crew, inequitable and unjuft. To remedy this defect, and animate the feamen, on fuch occafions, to more fpirited exertions, an act of parliament was paffed, fettling the future diftribution. This arrived at Jamaica, a fhort time before the commodore's return from his cruife ; and, though he had, according to the ufual cuftom, permitted the people to plunder at the time of taking the prize, he now appointed regular agents for the captors, in compliance with the law. He, moreover, ordered Mr. Long, his captain, to deliver up the filver, and other valuable effects, which, according to the old cuftom, he had feized between decks, for the commodore's ufe, as well as his own. This moft honourable inftance of felf-denial, wrought that impreffion on the minds of the feamen under him, that his praifes, traditionally handed down through that extenfive clafs of people, rendered him, ever afterwards, the conftant idol of their affection.

Campbell, with the moft laudable intention, and in order to refcue the character of this great and good officer, from having been actuated by avaricious motives in the enterprife juft mentioned, very judicioufly obferves,

that

that the idea which gave birth to the bold attempt, did
not originate with Mr. Wager, in the hope of enriching himfelf, but merely in a defire of doing his
duty, and effecting every thing that was in his power
againft the common enemy. It is reported of him,
that he was accuftomed to fay, " A man who would
not fight for a galleon, would not fight for any thing ;"
but, fay hiftorians, this declaration by no means proceeded from the defire of accumulating wealth to
himfelf, but from that more honourable affection of
the mind, the recollection of the fervice he rendered
his country, by depriving its enemies of the finews of
war. Confidering it, indeed, on a national ground,
it certainly was of a much more important nature, than
the world might in general be led to think it, at the
firft fight. It appears from the collateral teftimony of
all writers, who have treated of the events which took
place at this period, that the difficulties and rifk of
fending home treafure to Europe, in time of war, had
caufed the Spaniards to defer the return of this fleet
feveral years, fo that its accumulated riches were now
become almoft incredible ; amounting, according to
fome, to little lefs than fifty million pieces of eight.
Nothing but a want of credit, almoft productive of
general bankruptcy, would have induced the enemy to
venture it, even at this time ; and they relied entirely
on the protection to be afforded it by the French fquadron under Monf. Du Caffe, who was not only efteemed
one of the beft officers in the French fervice, but was
alfo the beft acquainted with the navigation of thofe feas.

Mr.

Mr. Wager was, on the 2d of December 1708, promoted to be rear-admiral of the white ; but, though he continued to command on the Weſt India ſtation, till the enſuing autumn, the enemy allowed him no ſecond opportunity of making them feel that chaſtiſement, which he ſo well knew how to inflict, on every occaſion that fortune thought proper to furniſh him with. Indeed, towards the concluſion of this year, a report was ſtrongly in circulation and belief, that the celebrated officer Du Guay Trouin, was hourly expected in thoſe ſeas, at the head of a powerful force, deſtined according to public opinion, for the attack of Jamaica; Mr. Wager, therefore, knowing the great inferiority of his own numbers, in compariſon of thoſe of his predicted opponents, took every means that prudence could ſuggeſt to a brave and good officer, to prevent their aſſault, whenever it might take place, from proving ſuccefsful. His ſhips were moored acrofs the harbour of Port Royal, in a line ſo ſituated, as to be flanked completely by the fort. This, with other precautions that were uſed, appeared rather to render an attack a wiſhed-for, than a feared event, as not the ſmalleſt doubt was entertained, but that the total diſcomfiture of the foe would be the natural conſequence of their proud attempt. No enemy, however, appeared; and, after continuing inactive till all idea of their ever approaching had entirely vaniſhed, the ſhips were again unmoored, and reſumed their former occupations. So ſuccefsful were the different cruiſers under the rear-admiral's command, that it was remarked, four times the number of prizes were

made

made·from the enemy, while he continued on the·
Jamaica ftation, than had been, during any preceding
period of,the fame duration.

On his return to England, he was received with the
ftrongeft teftimony of regard, not only by the queen
and her minifters, but by all ranks of people ; repeated
addreffes, votes of thanks, and other incontrovertible
proofs of the fatisfaction of the public mind, were received from the Weft Indies, each exceeding the other
in the warmth of their expreffions of refpect, and unit-
ing only in one point, their general applaufe of the
vigilance, the integrity, and the fpirit which Mr.
Wager had uniformly difplayed, while he continued in
that quarter of the world. This,·fay authors, is a
clear refutation of the generally-received principle,
that it is impoffible for any commander in chief to
pleafe all parties and ranks of men. Immediately
after his return to England, he was advanced to be
rear-admiral of the red, and received from the queen
the honour of knighthood; but he did·not take on
himfelf any fubfequent command, till after the acceffion of king George I. Immediately after that event,
he was appointed commander in chief in the Mediterranean *, as fucceffor to fir James Wifhart, and
the very appearance of the naval force which he commanded in thofe feas, obviating the rupture which it
had been juft before apprehended would take place,

---

* Nearly about the fame time he was appointed comptroller of the navy,
but quitted this office in the year 1718, on being appointed commiffioner
of the admiralty.

he

he returned to England, and did not again go to fea till the year 1722, fo that nothing occurs for us to record during this interval, except his promotions, which took place in the following progreffion : on the 16th of June 1716, he was advanced to be vice-admiral of the blue ; on the 1ft of February 1717, to be vice-admiral of the white ; and on the 15th of March following to be vice-admiral of the red.

At the period already mentioned (1722), the infolent conduct of the Portuguefe, who had confifcated the effects, imprifoned, and abfolutely condemned to death two Englifh gentlemen, for offending againft an obfolete law, forbidding the exportation of any coin whatever out of the kingdom, but which had never been put in force for a long feries of years, induced the Britifh government to order the equipment of a fquadron, confifting of nine fmall fhips of the line, with four frigates and bomb-veffels, for the purpofe of chaftifing the infult offered to the Britifh nation, by the act of violence juft ftated. The mere fhow of inflicting punifhment was fufficient, without the fmalleft attempt of carrying the threat into execution. The Portuguefe fubmitted to the terms which were prefcribed to them. Sir Charles therefore ftruck his flag, and the fquadron was ordered to be difmantled, without its ever having quitted Spithead. From this time the vice-admiral experienced a fecond relaxation from the fatigues of public fervice, for the fpace of four years ; when certain intrigues, which were difcovered to be carrying on between the courts of Madrid and Peterfburgh, rendered it neceffary to equip three powerful fquadrons,

fquadrons, which, from their force, rather merited
the name of fleets, in order to crufh this political con-
fpiracy, ere it had acquired fufficient head to render
it dangerous. The armament, which was deftined
for the Baltic, was configned to the charge of fir
Charles Wager, who was accompanied by that celebrated naval character fir George Walton, as fecond
in command. It amounted to no lefs than twenty
fhips of the line, and its very appearance at the entrance of the Sound, produced the fame effect which it
had done on all former occafions, that of confining the
Ruffian fleet to its own port. The feafon for naval
operations confequently paffed on without the commiffion of hoftility, and fir Charles returned to England when the winter approached, with the fatisfaction
of leaving the exifting differences in a fair way of
accommodation, though he had not been fortunate
enough completely to arrange the terms, on which tranquillity was to be reftored.

Spain, notwithftanding the reconciliation of her ally,
and her confequent feceffion from the confederacy,
began without referve to avow her hoftile intentions.
Gibraltar was openly threatened ; and fir Charles was
ordered thither with a fquadron, confifting of fix fhips
of the line and two frigates, having on board feventeen companies of foot, intended to reinforce the
garrifon; after which he was, taking under his
orders Mr. Hopfon, who had commanded on the
fame ftation during the preceding winter, with a
fquadron nearly equal in force to his own, to protect the place from any naval attack. The
arrival of the vice-admiral was extremely critical;

the conde de las Torres having encamped a few days before, within a league of the place, for the purpose of forming the siege, at the head of an army consisting of fifteen thousand men. The Spaniards felt disheartened, but they did not actually abandon the attack: the attack commenced; but the exertions of the garrison, aided by the assistance afforded to it from the British fleet, prevented the progress of it so effectually, that it soon became apparent, its termination must be unfavourable to the assailants. A negotiation, the last resource of an impotent enemy, accordingly commenced, and, after the fruitless exertion of every political chicane that could be contrived by a wily foe, a cessation of hostilities was agreed to about the middle of the month of June.

Notwithstanding this appearance of public tranquillity being restored, it was considered improper to order the return of sir Charles to England, till the month of March in the following year, and, during this interval, he had to combat every species of torment that a disingenuous foe could invent, to prolong the conclusion of a treaty which they wished, if possible, to avoid perfecting. The firmness of the vice-admiral parried every difficulty, and it is elsewhere properly remarked, that a commander employed at so critical a period, ought to possess a species of judgment far superior to that, which is necessary to conduct the most arduous and desperate undertakings of declared war. A brave man, who carries himself with temper on such an occasion, demands the highest applause a

nation

nation can beſtow ; becauſe he is frequently, through
political reaſons, compelled to embrace meaſures totally oppoſite to his feelings ; meaſures which his
heart would diſdain to ſubmit to, were not his country's welfare involved in his temperance.

Although the haughty temper of the court of Spain
had felt itſelf compelled to affect a ſubmiſſion, it was
merely temporary ; and the thorough conviction entertained of this fact by the Britiſh miniſtry, cauſed
rather an increaſed activity in the preparation for war,
than a relaxation of it. During the greater part of
the year 1729, it was judged prudent to keep a fleet,
conſiſting of twenty ſhips of the line, and a proper
number of frigates at Spithead, in conſtant readineſs
for actual ſervice. This important charge was confided to ſir Charles ; and although thoſe perſons, who
are to be continually met with in every reign, and whoſe
ſole delight appears to conſiſt in depreciating the meaſures of men who are intruſted with the management of
public affairs, affected to complain of the inactivity of
this force, together with the uſeleſs expenſe, in which
the nation was involved by its equipment, yet it was
evident to all, who did not view the public conduct of
miniſters through the jaundiced medium of an oppoſition atmoſphere, that no other meaſures than thoſe
which actually were purſued, could have prevented the
flames of war from furiouſly burſting forth. Towards the concluſion of the year, the terms of pacification were arranged, and the return of public tranquillity was made known by the order to diſmantle
                                                  and

and put out of commission the different ships, which had been ordered to be fitted out on the preceding occasion.

Early in the year 1731, in consequence of an apprehended intention in the court of France to invade Great Britain, and the supposed collection of a formidable flotilla, applicable to that purpose, in the ports of Dunkirk and Calais, sir Charles again received orders to hoist his flag, for the last time. The appearance, however, of an attack, vanished as suddenly as the report of it had been raised; but sir Charles, who was, in the month of July, advanced to the rank of admiral of the blue, was ordered to proceed to Cadiz, with a fleet, consisting of twenty ships of the line, under his command, for the purpose of seeing the articles of the treaty, concluded between the emperor of Germany and the king of Spain, under the mediation of Great Britain, properly carried into effect. After his return to England, in the month of December following, he never again went to sea. His abilities, however, lay not dormant, and it would, perhaps, be a difficult matter to decide, whether they had appeared most transcendant in his character of a naval officer, or in the exalted civil stations he was, at different times, intrusted to fill. On the 21st of June 1733 *, he was appointed first commissioner for executing the office of lord high admiral; of this post he continued to fulfil

---

* In the month of January 1744, on the apprehension of a general war, he was raised to the rank of admiral of the white squadron.

the duties with the higheft integrity and reputation, till the 19th of March 1742, when, on refigning it, he was appointed treafurer of the navy. The latter lefs fatiguing fituation, than that which he before poffeffed, his advanced age did not long permit him to enjoy, he having died on the 24th of May 1743, in the 77th year of his age.

SIR FRANCIS HOSIER

BECAME a lieutenant in the navy, in the year 1692, when, after serving in that station on board different ships for the space of four years, he was raised to the rank of captain, and appointed to the Winchelsea, a new frigate, mounting thirty-two guns. Though the service never boasted a more gallant, or able officer than this gentleman, yet misfortune, or, at least, the absence of good fortune, appears to have attended him, on most occasions, throughout life. His advancement in the navy was flow, but not, on that account, less merited; his opportunities of distinguishing himself few, yet no person ever doubted either his gallantry, or his promptitude in improving every possible occasion he could meet with, of being serviceable to his country. After a variety of uninteresting commands, he was, about the year 1710, appointed captain of the Salisbury; and, being sent on a cruise off Cape Clear, in company with the St. Albans, there experienced, for the first time, a gleam of success, by falling in with a French ship of war, mount-

O 2   ing

ing fixty guns, which ſtruck to the Saliſbury, after a
very ſmart action, of which that ſhip bore the principal weight.　In compliment to Mr. Hoſier, the
captured veſſel was taken into the ſervice, and named
the Saliſbury's Prize.　Here we cannot omit pauſing
for a moment, on the remarkable coincidence of circumſtances, which ſeemed to oppoſe the elevation of
this gentleman to the public notice.　No hiſtorian
whatever has taken notice of this impoitant capture,
and it is only from a private, though authentic memorandum, that the fact has been tranſmitted to poſterity.　The Saliſbury, together with her prize, were
ordered to be refitted, immediately after their arrival in
port, and when ready for ſea, were ſent to the Weſt
Indies, to reinforce the ſquadron already ſtationed in that
quarter, under the command of commodore Littleton.
In the month of July 1711, the Britiſh ſhips, being on
a cruiſe, in the hope of falling in with the French admiral Du Caſſe, who was ſaid to have ſailed with a fleet
of Spaniſh galleons under his protection for Europe, fell
in with four large veſſels, which were immediately
chaſed.　The Saliſbury, with her former prize, which
was then commanded by captain Harland, conſiderably
outſtripped their companions, but ſo trivial was the
advantage they poſſeſſed, in point of ſailing, over thoſe
they were in purſuit of, that the Saliſbury's Prize,
which was the beſt ſailer, and, conſequently, the
headmoſt, was not able to get up, and cloſe with the
ſternmoſt of the enemy, till near ſix o'clock in the
evening ; but captain Hoſier, joining him ſoon afterwards, their united aſſaults compelled their antagoniſts

to

to furrender, before any other fhip could get within gun-fhot. : The prize proved to be the vice-admiral of the Spanifh galleons, mounting fixty brafs guns. Although captain Hofier continued feveral years in commiffion, fubfequent to this time, yet no particular mention is made of him till 1719, when he was appointed fecond captain of the Dorfetfhire, the fhip on board which the earl of Berkley hoifted his flag, in virtue of a fpecial commiffion; under which he poffeffed authority and powers, little inferior to thofe of a lord high admiral; vice-admiral Littleton commanding under him as firft captain, and Mr. Hofier as fecond, with the honorary rank of rear-admiral of the blue. On the 8th of May 1720, he was advanced to be rear-admiral of the white, and ferved during the current year, as well as the fucceeding, as fecond in command of the fleet fent under the orders of fir John Norris into the Baltic: and, in 1722, was appointed to act in the fame capacity, under fir Charles Wager, on board the fquadron ordered to be equipped for the chaftifement of the Portuguefe. Mr. Hofier was, on this occafion, promoted to be vice-admiral of the blue, but the fleet being ordered to be difmantled, without ever having put to fea, the above promotion was the only advantage he derived from his appointment.

Public tranquillity remaining, in a great meafure, undifturbed, for the fpace of four years, after this cloud had paffed over, Mr. Hofier, confequently, held no command: but the confederacy, which in 1726 was fuppofed, and indeed avowed to have been entered into, between the Spanifh and Ruffian courts, render-

ing

ing it prudent, in the eyes of the Britifh miniftry, to difpatch fquadrons into different parts of the world, that deftined for the Weft Indies, with the intention of overawing the Spaniards in that quarter, was put under the orders of Mr. Hofier, which, when joined by the fhips that had been previoufly fent thither, would, it was calculated, ftrike terror and amazement throughout the whole of that quarter of the world.

The vice-admiral, having hoifted his flag on board the Breda, of feventy guns, failed from Plymouth on the 9th of April, and, after a very tedious paffage of nearly two months continuance, arrived off the Baftimentos, near Porto-Bello : the very fight of this armament produced all the effect which it had been expected it would do. The Spaniards, in the utmoft difmay, requefted, with all civility, to know the caufe of this extraordinary vifit. The vice-admiral, who had no inftructions to act with hoftility, except in the event of certain circumftances taking place, replied mildly, that he had been fent thither to efcort the Royal George, a large fhip belonging to the South-Sea company, which was then in the harbour of Porto-Bello, difpofing of her very valuable cargo for fpecie. The governor, after receiving this information, ufed every effort in his power to expedite the bufinefs; and, in order to rid himfelf as fpeedily as poffible from fuch troublefome intruders as Mr. Hofier and his fleet were confidered, enforced, with the whole weight of his authority, the immediate payment of the fums due from the Spanifh merchants to the vendors, on account of the different parts of the cargo which

they

they had feverally purchafed. As foon as this neceffary preliminary was completed, the fhip was hurried out of the harbour with all poffible expedition, and a meffage, at the fame time, was fent to the vice-admiral, requeft-ing him, that as the object which he had himfelf de-clared to have in view, had been fulfilled, he would no longer remain where he was, but return to the British fettlements. To this Mr. Hofier coolly and firmly-anfwered, that he fhould continue in the fame fituation fo long as he thought proper; or until he had received further orders from England. The better to convince the governor he was ferious, he ordered one of the fhips of his fquadron to anchor within gun-fhot of the fortrefs, and examine every veffel that at-tempted to pafs into, or out of the harbour; this mea-fure was certainly an incontrovertible proof of the fu-periority of the Britifh arms; but it is, at the fame time, fagacioufly remarked, that in no other way did it render any fervice to its country: that if its prin-cipal object of being fent to block up the harbour of Porto-Bello, was the prevention of the Spanifh gal-leons, from returning to fea during that feafon, fuch fer-vice, would have been as well effected by anchoring off the port, for the fpace of three weeks only, inftead of its being ftationary, as it continued for fix months. In time that armament, which had at firft, as both po-litical and hiftorical writers obferve, been an object of univerfal terror to the Spaniards, became, ere it withdrew, a theme of univerfal ridicule and contempt. The naturally unwholefome climate, and the dreadful effects of that deftructive malady the fcurvy, at length

O 4 compelled

compelled the vice-admiral to return to Jamaica, and
fo miferably had the foregoing caufes reduced the
ftrength of the people, on board the different fhips,
that there were fcarcely men enough left alive to navigate the fquadron back into port.

Fortunately there chanced to be a confiderable number
of feamen at Jamaica, who were out of employ, and,
when added to thofe, who, by the care and attention paid
them by Mr. Hofier, and the people under his orders,
had been reftored to health, the vice-admiral was enabled to put to fea, at the expiration of little more than
two months, during which the fhips of the fquadron
were as well refitted as circumftances would permit.
From the time of his having quitted port, the latter
end of February, till the month of Auguft enfuing,
the Britifh fquadron, with the moft undaunted perfeverance, kept the fea. The conduct, however, which
Mr. Hofier was compelled to obferve towards the
enemy, began to have a vifible effect on his mind and
health ; he was reftrained, by his orders, from acting
offenfively towards thofe who daily infulted him, by
the outrages they committed againft his countrymen,
and his pride felt itfelf wounded irrecoverably, by that
enjoined apathy, with which he was compelled to behold
the infolent conduct of an arrogant, and prefuming
enemy. In the ports of the Havannah and Vera Cruz
alone, the Prince Frederick, a valuable fhip belonging to the South-Sea company, a frigate, and three or
four veffels of inferior confequence, were detained on
the hacknied, but cuftomary pretence of reprifals.
Mr. Hofier, whofe gallant fpirit could ill brook fub-

miffion

miſſion to ſuch repeated injuries, proceeded to Vera Cruz, with four of his ſhips, and demanded ſatiſfaction in the peremptory, deciſive tone of a Britiſh officer. But the Spaniards had recovered from their panic, and being aware, perhaps, that from the tenor of his orders, and the timidity of thoſe from whom he received his inſtructions, he was reſtrained from chaſtiſing them, they repaid his threats with ſcoffing anſwers, which he could no otherwiſe puniſh than by the ſeizure of ſome of their veſſels, the greater part of which were afterwards reſtored.

These accumulated misfortunes, added to the reflection, that though intruſted with ſo important a command, he had been totally incapable of rendering his country that ſervice, which he knew muſt naturally be expected from the force confided to his direction, at length overcame him, for he died at ſea, as is moſt confidently reported, of mere chagrin, on the 23d of Auguſt 1727. He was, a few days before his death, advanced to be vice-admiral of the white ſquadron, but he died ere the news of his promotion reached the Weſt Indies. A commiſſion was alſo ſent out, empowering the governor of Jamaica to confer on him the honour of knighthood; this, it is believed, he received, although ſome have doubted the fact: but whether it be true, or falſe, it was a miſerable douceur, and ſtands as an irrefragable proof, how perſons, intruſted with the higheſt offices, will have recourſe to the moſt wretched expedients, for covering their own neglect, or concealing their own want of ſpirit, by attempting, through a paltry bribe, to quiet the feelings of a man,

whoſe

whofe fpirit they have broken, and whofe character
they have irreparably injured. The body of this brave
and unfortunate officer, after being embalmed, and
buried in the ballaft of the fhip he commanded, was
afterwards brought to England for interment. His
misfortunes and merit have furvived him longer than is
ufually the cafe, either with the greateft, or the moft
unhappy of mankind; and it is no flender teftimony
of worth, when the abfence of panegyric is feelingly
fupplied by compaffion.

SIR JOHN BALCHEN.

THIS brave, though unfortunate officer, was born on the 2d of February 1669, and, after entering into the royal navy at a very early age, paffed regularly and progreffively through every rank, till he, at laft, reached the higheft in the fervice. The firft particular mention fpecifically made of the commiffion he held, was in 1697, when he was about twenty-eight years old; and was then appointed to a fmall frigate, called the Virgin, but fo unintereftingly was he employed, for ten years after this period, that no mention is made of any fubfequent commiffions he held till the year 1707, at which time he was captain of the Chefter, a fifty-gun fhip. The circumftance which attends this notice was a difaftrous one, for it appears, that having been ordered, in conjunction with the Ruby of equal force, to convoy to Lifbon a fleet bound thither, he had the misfortune to be captured by a ftrong French fquadron, under the orders of the count de Forbin, the particulars of which difafter are thus related: " As the fleet was not only of a very confiderable intrinfic value, but of the higheft confequence and importance, confidered in a national light, for all

the

the provisions, stores, and upwards of one thousand
horses for the service of the ensuing campaign in Spain,
were embarked on board it, it was thought proper to
strengthen the convoy by the addition of two ships of
eighty guns, and one of seventy-six, all under the
command of commodore Edwards, who was to see
them fifty leagues to the south-west of Scilly, where it
was presumed they would be perfectly out of danger
from the Dunkirk squadron, which was the only quarter from whence any attack was apprehended. The
fleet was not completely collected and ready to sail till
the 9th of October; and, on the 10th, having then
proceeded on their voyage no farther than the Lizard,
they fell in with the united squadrons of Forbin and
Du Guai Trouin. Reinforced as the escort was, it
was unable to contend against an enemy so wonderfully
superior. The commodore's ship, the Cumberland,
as well as the Ruby and Chester, after having sepa-
rately made a most gallant, and, indeed, desperate defence, fell into the hands of the enemy. The Chester
became the prize of the count de Forbin himself,
who, notwithstanding the disparity of force, which
totally annihilated every thing like glory in his conduct, was wonderfully elated at the success, which
was most romantically magnified on the part of the
French. He not having been exchanged till the conclusion of the ensuing year, the investigation of captain Balchen's conduct on this occasion, was neceffarily deferred, and it may, perhaps, be considered a
needless redundancy of words to say, he was most
honourably acquitted. The commands he held after

this

this time, for the space of nine years, are not noticed; but in the year 1717, he is found to have been captain of the Orford, of seventy guns, one of the fleet ordered into the Baltic, under the command of fir George Byng; from this time, he continued to be conftantly employed till he became promoted to the rank of a flag-officer; but the fervices which neceffarily occur during peace, cannot be expected to abound with incidents fufficient, to render the detail of them in any degree interefting.

On the 19th of July 1728, he was promoted to be rear-admiral of the blue, after having continued in the ftation of a private captain for no lefs a period than nearly thirty-two years. On the 4th of March following, he was advanced to be rear-admiral of the white, but did not take upon himself any command till the year 1731-2, when he proceeded to Cadiz and the Mediterranean, as fecond under fir Charles Wager, who was ordered thither for the purpose of caufing the treaty of Vienna to be duly carried into execution. On the 16th of February 1733, he was promoted to be vice-admiral of the white, and in the enfuing year was invefted with the command of a fquadron collected at Plymouth, and intended to be fent to Lifbon, for the purpose of reinforcing fir John Norris, who had already proceeded thither, in confequence of a difpute then exifting between the courts of Portugal and Spain. The bufinefs, however, was amicably terminated, and, notwithftanding the repeated infults offered to Great Britain, by the Spanifh cruifers, the Britifh councils, then under the influence of fir Robert Walpole,

pole, were fo pacifically inclined, that no active fteps were taken to chaftife them, nor any fleet fitted out in the command of which it was found neceffary to call forth the abilities of Mr. Balchen, till the year 1739 *. It was then confidered neceffary to increafe the force already ftationed in the Mediterranean, under Mr. Haddock ; and the chief command of the whole was beftowed on this gentleman. The firft object intended to be effected by the armament, was the interception of a valuable fleet expected to arrive at Cadiz, from Vera Cruz, laden with a confiderable treafure, the annual tribute paid by the Spanifh fettlements in the weftern world, to the mother-country. Accident prevented this important prize from falling into the hands of the Englifh : admiral Pizzaro, who commanded it, having cafually received information of the alarming fituation of public affairs in Europe, fteered to the northward, inftead of making for Madeira, which was the ufual route, and, after having actually paffed the mouth of the Britifh channel, fortunately reached St. Andero without being molefted.

Towards the latter end of the year 1740, Mr. Balchen was appointed to the command of the home, or Channel fleet, which it was deemed prudent to keep in a ftate of equipment, againft any fudden emergency, notwithftanding the Spaniards never ventured to fit out any armament for the Atlantic, or to act offenfively to the weftward of the Streights in Europe, during the whole continuance of the war. On the 9th of Auguft 1743,

---

* On the 2d of March 1735-6 preceding, he was promoted to be vice-admiral of the red.

he

he was promoted to be admiral of the white, and, immediately, after the ensuing Christmas, was most deservedly appointed governor of Greenwich hospital, as successor to sir John Jennings; the honour of knighthood being also conferred upon him about the same time. It might now, say authors, have been naturally expected that he would, in this honourable retirement, have been permitted to pass the remainder of his days in that enviable tranquillity, which a noble and good mind must naturally enjoy, from a reflection of having been uniformly employed in the constant pursuit of public virtue, untainted, uncontaminated by the private vices of avarice, or oppression. Such, however, were the necessities of his country, and such the spirit of this gallant man, that even at the very advanced age he had then reached, an age felt more severely in consequence of infirmities naturally brought on by so long and active a service; that, in the year 1744, he accepted the command of a fleet, equipped and drawn together with all possible expedition, for the purpose of relieving the squadron under sir Charles Hardy, who was at that time blocked up in the Tagus, by a very superior force, under the orders of the count de Rochambault. The force of this armament amounted to twenty-one ships of the line, seven of which belonged to the states of Holland, and were furnished according to treaty. Sir John Balchen hoisted his flag on this occasion, as commander in chief of the whole, on board the Victory, a first rate, of one hundred and ten guns, a ship universally reputed, at that time, to have been the finest ever built.

Her

Her crew, amounting to eleven hundred men, contained a much greater proportion of prime feamen,
fpecially felected for the purpofe, than had ever been
before cuftomary in the Britifh, or any other fervice.
There were, moreover, upwards of fifty young gentlemen on board, ferving as naval cadets, many
of them belonging to families of the firft diftinction
in the kingdom, who entered as volunteers, being
ambitious to enrol themfelves, and learn the firft rudiments of naval tactics under fo worthy, fo experienced, and fo able a commander. The fleet failed
from Spithead on the 7th of Auguft, having upwards
of two hundred merchant-veffels under its convoy.
Owing to this (as it proved in the event) fatal incum-
brance, and the contrary winds that prevailed, the
paffage to Lifbon was extremely tedious, the admiral
not having arrived off the Tagus till the 9th of September. The French fled at his approach, and took
refuge in Cadiz. Sir Charles Hardy being thus freed
from his confinement, immediately put to fea, and,
having joined the main fleet, proceeded with it to
Gibraltar; the reinforcement of which garrifon was
among the principal objects confided to the direction
of fir John Balchen.

The latter fervice being effected, the fleet, after a fhort
and fruitlefs cruife off the coaft of Portugal, made, in
the hope of falling in with the count de Rochambault,
on his return back from Cadiz to Breft, prepared to
bend its courfe back to England; when, having entered
the Bay of Bifcay on the 30th, it was completely difperfed
by a violent ftorm on the 3d of October following.
                                        Many

Many of the ships were, with the utmost difficulty, preserved from foundering ; they all of them, however, reached England in perfect safety, the Victory excepted: This noble veffel, feparating from all her companions, was fuppofed to have ftruck on the Cafkets, a ridge of rocks near Alderney, on the 4th. Fate thus, in one Inftant, overwhelmed a moft worthy and able commander, with nearly twelve hundred of his brave affociates, and deftroyed a fhip which was juftly, at that time, confidered the pride of Britain, and was confeffedly the terror of her enemies. The inhabitants of Alderney are faid to have heard many fignals of diftrefs made during the night, but, from the darknefs, added to the violence of the tempeft, they were totally unable, even to attempt affording the fufferers any affiftance. The whole nation was filled with the trueft grief, at this dreadful and accumulated misfortune. The merits of the admiral himfelf, the diffufed lamentation of relatives, and the lofs of fuch a number of brave men, all tended to increafe the public anxiety; to a poignancy that had fcarcely been ever felt fince the lofs of the brave Shovell. Sorrow, on fuch an occafion, is the only tribute gratitude can pay to deceafed merit ; and the generous mind finds fome relief, in beftowing it worthily. On a fmall but elegant monument, erected to his memory in Weftminfter Abbey, is the following epitaph, which, in addition to fome of the leading particulars of his life, contains feveral remarks fo juft, in refpect to the tranfactions of it, and his general character, that it would be an injuftice to the memory of a great, and good man to

omit

omit it. "Sir John Balchen, knight, admiral of the white squadron of his majesty's fleet, who, in the year 1744, being sent out commander in chief of the combined fleets of England and Holland, to cruise on the enemy, was, on his return home, in his majesty's ship the Victory, lost in the channel by a violent storm; from which sad circumstance of his death we may learn, that neither the greatest skill, judgment, or experience, joined to the most unshaken resolution, can resist the fury of the winds and waves; and we are taught from the passages of his life, which were filled with great and gallant actions, but accompanied with adverse gales of fortune, that the brave, the worthy, and the good man, meets not always his reward in this world. Fifty-eight years of faithful and painful service he had passed, when, being just retired to the government of Greenwich Hospital, to wear out the remainder of his days, he was once more, and for the last time, called out by his king and country, whose interest he ever preferred to his own; and his unwearied zeal for their service ended only with his life, which weighty misfortune to his afflicted family, became heightened by many aggravating circumstances attending it. Yet, amidst their grief, they had the mournful consolation, to find his gracious and royal master mixing his concern with the general lamentations of the public, for the calamitous fate of so zealous, so valiant, and so able a commander; and, as a lasting memorial of sincere love and affection borne by his widow, to a most affectionate and worthy husband, this honorary monument was erected by her.

"He

"He was born February 2d, 1669; married Su-
fannah, the daughter of colonel Apreece, of Wafh-
ingly, in the county of Huntingdon: died October
7th, 1744, leaving one fon and one daughter; the
former of whom, George Balchen, furvived him but
a fhort time; for, being fent to the Weft Indies in
1745, commander of his majefty's fhip the Pembroke,
he died at Barbadoes, in December the fame year,
aged twenty-eight, having walked in the fteps, and
imitated the virtues and bravery of his good, but unfortunate father."

CAPTAIN

CAPTAIN WILLIAM DAMPIER.

THE obfervation already made, in the inftance of
fir John Narborough, will apply, with the ftricteft
propriety, to this gentleman ; he was the defcendant
of a very refpectable family in the county of Somerfet,
and was not originally intended for an officer in the royal
navy, his entrance into which, did not take place till he
was fomewhat advanced in life, and till he had acquired,
like that more recent and able navigator captain James
Cook, the higheft celebrity, on account of his nautical purfuits and knowledge. Having, at a very early
age, difplayed a character moft ftrongly impreffed with
the fpirit of adventure, but more particularly with that
immediate fpecies of it, connected with a maritime
life, he was, on the death of his father and mother,
taken by his guardians from the fchool where he had
been placed by his parents, and, after having been properly inftructed in the firft rudiments of navigation,
was bound apprentice to the mafter of a trading veffel
belonging to Weymouth. In the account and memoirs he has given of himfelf, he very fairly exonerates
thofe who had the care of him, from any blame that
might

might be thrown out against them, for this apparent defeat
of his parent's intentions, by confessing, that in adopting the above measure, they only complied with a very
early inclination he had, of seeing the world. He first
began by making a short voyage to France, and afterwards one to Newfoundland, at which time he was
only eighteen years old. He tells us, that he suffered
so much from the severity of the cold, at the last place,
that he, for a time, gave up all thoughts of pursuing
a naval life: nevertheless, as if fate had preordained
his celebrity as a navigator, he relaxed from this resolution, on hearing of an East India ship that was then
ready to sail. He entered on board her as a foremast-man,
and continued in that station during the whole voyage.
He was not absent from England much longer than
twelve months; and the second Dutch war breaking
out soon after his return, he continued at home during the remainder of that year, living with his brother, who appears to have been a man of some property and estate, in the county of Somerset.

In the ensuing spring, he grew weary of so indolent a
life, and entered on board the Royal Prince, the ship
which carried the flag of sir Edward Spragge. He was
present at both the first and second actions, which took
place with the Dutch fleet in this year; but being
taken very suddenly ill only a day or two before the
third happened, was put on board an hospital-ship,
in which he was conveyed to Harwich, with a number of other sick and wounded men. The war nearly
concluding with the battle above alluded to, and having continued some time in the hospital in a very weak

and

and languishing condition, he went home to his brother, where, owing to better care and attention being
paid him, he quickly recovered. The nation being at
peace, and his health perfectly reestablished, he agreed
to go to Jamaica, on an offer made him by a colonel
Hillier, of East Coker, in Somersetshire, his native
parish, to be his agent or steward in that island, under
a Mr. Whalley. He continued with that gentleman for
six months, and then entered into an employ, in the
same line, under a captain Hemmings. This, however, ill suiting his genius, and perhaps ability, he
shipped himself with a captain Hudsel, who was
bound to the bay of Campeachy, to load logwood.

. They sailed from Port Royal, about the beginning
of August 1675, and met with no very extraordinary
occurrence during the voyage. This ship returning
to Jamaica, and the crew being discharged, Mr.
Dampier engaged, in the month of February 1675-6,
with a Mr. Johnson, of New England, who was
bound to the bay on an errand similar to the former.
This voyage was much longer than the preceding, and
he did not return to Jamaica till the month of April
1678. He sailed from thence for England, from
whence he again prepared to return to the bay of
Campeachy, having embarked, early in the year 1679,
as a passenger on board the Loyal Merchant, a trading
ship bound to Jamaica. When he reached that island,
he changed his former resolution, and, having disposed
of such commodities as he had brought with him from
England, for the purpose of trade, was about to return to his native country, when he was prevailed upon

                                              to

to alter his plan a fecond time; and accompany a Mr.
Hobby to the Mufquito fhore. They had proceeded
no farther on their voyage than the weft end of Jamaica, when all the men, himfelf excepted, deferted
his patron, to go on a buccaneering expedition to the
Spanifh main. After a few days, Mr. Dampier, who
was thus left alone with Mr. Hobby, was prevailed
on to accompany them alfo. Their firft expedition
was againft Porto Bello, which having fucceeded in,
they fet forth, on the 5th of April 1680, to march
acrofs the ifthmus of Darien, and when they reached
the South Seas, embarked in fuch canoes and veffels
as the Indians furnifhed them with. By the 23d of
April, they reached Panama, and, after having in vain
attacked Puebla-Nova, in which affault they loft captain Sawkins, who, till then, acted as their commander, they fteered their courfe to the fouthward for
Peru. They continued in the South Seas, varioufly
occupied in cruifing, though with indifferent fuccefs,
againft the enemy, and quarrelling amongft themfelves,
till the month of April 1681. A feparation then took
place between the two contending parties; the moft
formidable of thefe continued with a captain Sharp,
who had been chofen commander, though not unanimoufly; being thought, by Mr. Dampier and others, ill
qualified for fuch a ftation; while the latter gentleman,
with the remainder, amounting to about fifty perfons,
embarked to feek their fortune, furnifhed only with a
large boat, or launch, and one or two canoes; thefe
being far inadequate to the purpofe, they took the firft

P 4　　　　　　　　opportunity

opportunity of bettering their condition, by seizing a
bark, laden with timber for Guiaquil.

After escaping a multitude of dangers from the
Spanish, guarda-costas, Mr. Dampier and his people
agreed at last, to run their vessel on shore, and return
back over the isthmus, to the gulf of Mexico. They
began their march on the 1st of May 1681, and, after
a tedious and dangerous journey of twenty-three days,
got on board a buccaneer, lying near the mouth of
the river Conception, commanded by captain Tristram,
a Frenchman. This vessel, with several others,
manned with crews of the same profession, continued
cruising, with moderate success, till the month of
July 1682, when they put into Virginia. A new
band of adventurers was here formed in the following
year, consisting of several from among those who
came from the South Seas, with Mr. Dampier, re-
cruited by some newly-entered men, so as to make up
a crew of seventy persons. Their vessel, which was
called the Cygnet, was well equipped for the intended
service, mounting eighteen guns, and well stored with
every thing necessary for a cruise in the South Seas,
whither it was determined to proceed. They sailed
from Virginia, on their intended voyage, on the 23d
of April 1683, having chosen a Mr. Cook, who had
come with them from the South Seas, as their commander. They passed through the streights Le
Maire, and round Terra del Fuego, so that they did
not reach the island of Juan Fernandez, in the above-
mentioned quarter, till March 22, 1684; but, during

ring their whole voyage they met with no occurrence worth relating, except falling in with a ſhip during their paſſage to that iſland, ſent from London on the ſame errand with themſelves, and commanded by a captain Eaton, with whom they all agreed to aſſociate, and join company.

Having refreſhed their people, they ſailed from Juan Fernandez, after a ſtay of ſixteen days, and cruiſed in the South Seas with very good ſucceſs, being afterwards joined by ſeveral celebrated adventurers in the ſame line. They made ſome valuable prizes; but their principal hope and purſuit was the capture, or at leaſt the attack of the Spaniſh fleet, bound from Lima to Panama. They waited with much impatience for this expected object, which they, at length got ſight of and chaſed, on the 28th of May 1685; but by a dexterous manœuvre, were thrown to leeward by the Spaniards, who, during the enſuing night, ſent one of their ſmall veſſels, with a light, to decoy the Engliſh; and by that means enable them to gain the weather gage. All their hopes of conqueſt were vaniſhed with the dawn; and the promiſed pleaſures of acquired wealth, were totally ſuperſeded by the anxiety of ſelf-preſervation. The Spaniards, who were to windward, and far exceeded the buccaneers both in ſtrength and numbers, became themſelves the aſſailants; and, had they not wanted courage to purſue their advantage properly, they would, in all probability, have captured the greater part of the buccaneers. After this grievous diſappointment, Mr. Dampier and his aſſociates ſtood farther to the northward, and were,

by

by turns, unfortunate and fuccefsful, in a variety of petty enterprifes, which they undertook; and the moft memorable of thefe was, the furprife of the city of Leon, which was facked and burnt. They continued afterwards to cruife on the coaft of Mexico, where they met with very indifferent fortune, till the 31ft of March 1686, when, having parted company with all their former companions, and being now reduced to the number of one hundred and fifty perfons on board one fhip, and a tender, they took their departure from cape Corientes, on the coaft of California, for the Eaft Indies.

They made the ifland of Guam on the 20th of May, and in good time, their provifions being nearly all expended; a friendly intercourfe was foon eftablifhed, and continued to be kept up between the fhips and the Spanifh governor, notwithftanding the latter was well apprized of the profeffion of his vifitors. Neverthelefs, as he was neither able to withftand an attack, nor the fhips inclined to make one, which, though it proved fuccefsful, they well knew would not repay them for the trouble, and lofs they might probably fuftain, it appeared, as if mutually agreed, that hoftilities fhould be confined to the wealthy coafts of Peru, or to fuch encounters as would repay the courage of the victors, and that in every other part of the world, Spaniards, and buccaneers, fhould meet as apparent friends. On the 2d of June, they failed from Guam, for Mindanoa, one of the Philippine iflands, which they reached in fafety on the 22d of the fame month. They continued at this place till the middle of January 1687, when they left the river of Min-

danoa,

danoa, intending to cruife off Manilla. On this ftation they took two prizes of fmall value, one of them
of fo little confequence, that it was immediately releafed. They continued thus occupied, though with the
fame indifferent fuccefs, till the month of May 1688;
when the repeated feuds and difturbances that prevailed
among the crew; their irregular, riotous mode of conducting themfelves, and above all, the difreputable
occupation itfelf, all tended, at this time, to induce
Mr. Dampier to quit them. After a little altercation,
and fubduing a few difficulties, he was at length put
afhore on the ifle of Nicholas, with a Mr. Hall, and
a man named Ambrofe, and having efcaped many
dangers, he at laft arrived at Bençoolen, where he was
well received, and appointed mafter-gunner of the fort
there. Still, however, he continued uneafy, anxioufly
waiting for an opportunity to return to England,
which at laft he happily effected (though much againft
the will of the governor), by creeping through one of
the port-holes of the fort, and getting on board the
Defence, a fhip belonging to the Englifh Eaft India
company, on the 2d of January 1691. The dangers
and difficulties he had fo long encountered, did not,
however, ceafe, with this piece of good fortune; a
dreadful fcurvy broke out among the fhip's company,
occafioned by the unwholefome water that was im-
prudently taken on board at Bencoolen, added to the
condition of their provifions, which were almoft fpoil-
ed, the fhip having been out three years. Such, however, were the exertions of captain Heath, the commander,

mander, that, in spite of these distresses, the ship was brought safe into the Cape in the month of April. The sick being tolerably well recovered, and the place of those who had unhappily died, in some measure, supplied by Dutchmen, who entered at the Cape by stealth, they sailed from thence on the 23d of May, and after touching at St. Helena, arrived in the Downs, without meeting with any remarkable occurrence, on the 16th of September 1691.

Mr. Dampier brought with him to England an Indian chief, curiously tattooed, or, as he styles it, painted. This person he had bought in India, in conjunction with a Mr. Moody, and he was for some time shewn for a sight; but Mr. Dampier being in rather distressed circumstances, was obliged to dispose of a part of this strange property, and by degrees, afterwards, of the whole. He does not himself make any mention of his being engaged in any subsequent voyage for the space of eight years; but having about the year 1698, been recommended by the right honourable Mr. Montague, president of the Royal Society, to the earl of Orford *(admiral Russel)* at that time first lord of the admiralty, he was, on the 26th of July raised to the rank of captain in the royal navy, and appointed to the Roebuck, a small frigate, at that time under equipment, for a voyage of discovery. In this vessel, which mounted only twelve guns, he sailed from the Downs on the 14th of January 1698-9. As the vessel had been purposely victualled, and fitted for a voyage of twenty months duration, he proceeded by

Teneriffe,

Teneriffe, and the Brazils, to the cape of Good Hope; and from thence to New Holland, an immenfe tract of country, little known previous to his time, and in the more extenfive examination of which, he made a very confiderable progrefs. He would, indeed, according to the information which he himfelf has afforded us, have materially extended his inquiries, and voyage, had not the ill quality of the water, which he had been compelled to take on board, not having the good fortune to difcover any better on the coaft, which he was then exploring, dreadfully afflicted his people with the fcurvy, as had been the cafe before, at Bencoolen. He was therefore under the neceffity of bearing away for Timor, from whence, after his people had fufficiently recovered, having again failed, he arrived, for the fecond time, off the coaft of New Holland, on the 1ft of January 1699-1700.

On this voyage he made a confiderable number of new difcoveries, particularly of a large ifland, which he called New Britain, having coafted round it, and found out a paffage, which has ever fince borne his name. The time of the eaftern monfoon approaching, he refolved to fteer for Batavia, where he arrived the beginning of July. He continued in that port till the 17th of October, and met with nothing very remarkable afterwards, during his paffage to the ifland of Afcenfion, which he got in fight of, on the 21ft of February. Between eight and nine o'clock in the morning of the 22d, the fhip fprung a dangerous leak, which quickly increafed to fo violent a degree, that the chain-pump could not keep her clear. Every

poffible

possible method was tried to remedy this disaster : at last, by the assistance of the hand-pump, the ship was freed from water ; and by continuing those exertions, it was kept under. Early on the following morning, captain Dampier stood for the bay, and anchored there, at the distance of about two miles from the shore, about nine o'clock. Every measure, prudence, or ingenuity, could suggest, or contrive, to remedy, or lessen the danger, was immediately carried into execution. These were, unhappily, all fruitless ; for, after clearing the part of the vessel where the defect lay, in order to get at it within board, the plank was discovered to be so rotten, that, to use Mr. Dampier's own words, it broke away like dirt. Nothing remained for him to do in this distressed situation, but to endeavour, if possible, to save the lives of his people. The boats were hoisted out, although it was then dark, that the people might preserve themselves, in case the ship should appear likely to founder at her anchor. As soon as day broke, they got up their anchor, and endeavoured to run in shore, but the land breeze prevented them from effecting this intention so well as they wished, and expected. In the afternoon, on the springing up of the sea breeze, they ran into seven fathom water, and afterwards warped the vessel, by carrying out a small anchor ahead, into three and a half, where they secured her. The greatest exertions were now made to save such articles, as were more immediately necessary for their future existence and preservation. All the seamen's chests and bedding were got safe to land, upon a raft, by eight o'clock at night ; and the next

morning

morning all the sails were unbent, and carried on shore for the purpose of being converted into tents.

It was a considerable relief to their misfortunes, that this island abounded with turtle; and to add still further to their satisfaction, they discovered a few days afterwards, a spring of excellent water, though their joy was somewhat damped, from its being eight miles distant from the bay where they landed, and where the major part of them were obliged to continue, for the purpose of making their distress known to the first vessels that should put in there. To men, however, who have no other employment, than that of satisfying the necessities of nature, difficulties of this kind gradually become less intolerable. After continuing on the island, therefore, in a state by no means so uncomfortable, as that experienced by many other unhappy voyagers, in different parts of the world, the captain and his people were relieved from their anxiety, by the arrival of three English men of war, the Anglesea, Hastings, and Lizard, and the Canterbury East India ship, on the 3d of April. Captain Dampier immediately went on board the Anglesea, with the greater part of his people, the remainder being dispersed into the other ships. He however, with some of his officers, afterwards removed into the Canterbury, for the purpose of getting expeditiously to England, as the ships of war, having missed the island of St. Jago, were obliged to bear away for Barbadoes to procure water. Notwithstanding it was uncandid, and indeed ungenerous in the highest degree, to affix any thing like blame on this gentleman, on account of the already related accident and misfortune;

yet

yet we find there were not wanting thofe, who were by no means fparing of their cenfure : of this captain Dampier feelingly complains in his dedication to the earl of Pembroke, of the third volume of his voyages : " The world (fays he) is apt to judge of every thing by the fuccefs ; and whoever has ill fortune, will hardly be allowed a good name. This, my lord, was my unhappinefs in my late expedition in the Roebuck, which foundered through perfect age near the ifland of Afcenfion. I fuffered extremely in my reputation by that misfortune, though I comfort myfelf with the thoughts, that my enemies could not charge any neglect upon me ; and fince I have the honour to be acquitted by your lordfhip's judgment, I fhould be very humble not to value myfelf upon fo complete a vindication."

A confiderable miftake has moft unaccountably arifen in the ftatements given by all authors, who have furnifhed any biographical memoirs of this gentleman. According to their report, he perifhed with the Roebuck, which veffel was loft on the 24th of February 1700-1. It were difficult to affign the reafon that could have betrayed them into fo ftrange an error ; but the affertion is contradicted not only by the dedication juft alluded to, in which he fays, " As the particular fervice I have now undertaken hinders me from finifhing this volume, fo I hope it will give me an opportunity of paying my refpects to your lordfhip in a new one;" but alfo by the London Gazette, which contains the following notification :

" St. James's, April 18th, 1703. Captain William Dampier being prepared to depart on another voyage to the Weft Indies, had the honour to kifs her ma-

jefty's

jefty's hand on Friday laft, being introduced by his royal highnefs the lord high admiral." It appears, however, that he did not fail on this expedition till the year 1704. In the courfe of it he took the town of Puna in the South Seas; but, putting into Batavia on his return was there imprifoned by the Dutch, who feized on all his effects. He returned to England after his releafe, but is not known to have ever afterwards been employed in the royal navy. There is indeed a report that he was difmiffed, or fufpended from the fervice, by the fentence of a court-martial, for mifbehaviour and ill treatment of his officers and people; but this circumftance is by no means fufficiently eftablifhed, to warrant pofitive affertion of it. He afterwards accompanied the celebrated captain Woodes Rogers in his voyage round the world, in the capacity of mafter, and returned with him to England, where he arrived on the 1ft of October 1711. No particulars are known relative to him after this time. The hiftory of his voyages, particularly his firft, round the world, has been tranflated into moft European languages, while his affiduity, and unremitted perfeverance, have entitled him to a rank among the ableft navigators.

SIR

SIR GEORGE WALTON.

Few men have ever obtained greater celebrity, or
rather publicity as naval officers, than this gentleman;
not merely on account of his services, which, however,
were certainly moft meritorious, and very highly entitling him to public regard and favour, but from a very
extraordinary, and apparently trivial circumftance,
that will be hereafter related, and which from the
oddity and gallantry accompanying it, has caufed him
to be moft honourably noticed by every hiftorian, who
has written the annals of that period, in which he flou-
rifhed.

There is little reafon to fuppofe, but that he was
defcended from a very humble and obfcure ftock, not
that this obfervation ought, or can tend in the fmalleft
degree to his prejudice, fince we find him, in defiance
of all obftacles, raifing himfelf folely by his own merit,
to the higheft pinnacle of popular favour, and public
attention. The firft account given of him as a naval
officer, is, that in the year 1692, he was appointed firft
lieutenant of the Devonfhire, of eighty guns. It is
fuppofed, indeed, that he previoufly obtained that rank,

at

at a much earlier period, although from the uninterefting ftate of his employments, no preceding mention is made of him. In 1695, he ferved as firft lieutenant of the Refolution, a third rate, of feventy guns,
one of the fhips belonging to fir Cloudefly Shovell's
divifion in the main fleet, and on the 19th of January
1697, was promoted to the ftation of captain in the navy,
by commiffion appointing him to the command of the
Seaford frigate. This veffel having been ordered to
be difmantled at the conclufion of the peace at Ryfwic, Mr. Walton entered into the employ of the
merchants, and during one, or two voyages commanded
a Smyrna trader, called the Delaware. This fpecies
of occupation, however, being ill fuited to the natural activity of his mind, he returned to his original
branch of fervice, on the firft profpect of the renewal
of hoftilities in the year 1699, and was appointed to
the Seahorfe, a fmall frigate, at that time employed
on the Mediterranean ftation. The political hemifphere growing ftill more dark, and the idea of war
increafing rapidly in the courfe of the current, and the
fucceeding year, it was confidered neceffary to fend
out an armament of no mean force to the Weft Indies,
under the orders of Mr. Benbow. The command of
one of the fhips which compofed it, the Ruby, a fourth
rate, of forty-eight guns, was beftowed on Mr. Walton. His conduct in that encounter, which took
place between the Englifh fquadron and Du Caffe, and
which proved fo difgraceful to captains Kirby, Wade,
and others, who were engaged in it, was moft highly
honourable ; and owing to the great exertions which

Q 2   he

he perfonally made on that occafion, Mr. Benbow
was principally indebted for his prefervation from
captivity, and his refcue, for 'fo it might be called,
from the fangs of a foe, who acquired every honour
and advantage of a victory, except that of having captured, or annihilated its opponent.

After his return to England in 1704, he was appointed to the Canterbury, the fhip on board which,
fourteen years afterwards, he juftly acquired fo much
renown. He continued in the fame fhip many years,
principally, if not entirely, on the Mediterranean ftation; and in 1707, ferved under fir Thomas Hardy,
who was fent to Lifbon, as commander of a convoy,
to a fleet of two hundred fail, bound thither. The
circumftance of their having fallen in with a French
fquadron, confifting of fix fhips, and not having
brought them to action, expofed fir Thomas to much
cenfure, and, as it appears, very undefervedly fo,
fince, had he acted otherwife than he did, he muft
have left unprotected, at leaft for a confiderable fpace
of time, the valuable charge committed to his care;
and the teftimony of captain Walton on his behalf,
has occafioned the remark fingularly advantageous to
his character, that the fair, and honourable fentiments
he expreffed in regard to his commander in chief's
gallantry, and good conduct in that affair, which drew
on him fo much unmerited obloquy, not only tended
to produce his legal acquittal, but alfo contributed
exceedingly, to reftore him to that degree of popular
favour, which, to fpeak candidly, he never deferved
to have forfeited. How he continued to be employed

from

from the period of the event just mentioned, till the year 1711, does not appear; most probably he was engaged in those annual expeditions which became so extremely uninteresting, from their constant repetition, and want of enterprise, although sent into the Mediterranean, where the principal part of the French naval force had long been concentrated.

At the time, however, that sir Hovenden Walker was sent on the unfortunate expedition against Quebec, captain Walton commanded the Montague, of sixty guns, but though much blame was thrown on many of the officers, employed on that disastrous occasion, it is to be observed, that captain Walton enjoyed at least the negative satisfaction of escaping censure, although he was deprived by fortune, of that reward so truly grateful to all men, possessing a temper, and turn of mind similar to his own, that of augmenting the splendour of his own character. How, or what were the services, and occupations, in which he was engaged after this time, do not appear, till the year 1718, when he was captain of his former ship the Canterbury, one of those sent into the Mediterranean under sir George Byng, on the approach of the rupture, which it was apprehended must inevitably take place between the courts of Great Britain, and Spain. The account given by him to the commander in chief in respect to the conduct of himself and his detachment, when sent in pursuit of the rear-admiral Mari and his division, has occasioned the page of history to relax from its customary gravity, and infused an unusual merriment into the style of the various authors who have recorded that

event.

event. Mr. Corbet, in his account of the expedition
to Sicily, remarks : "The captain was one whofe natural talents were fitter for achieving a gallant action
than defcribing one, yet his letter on this occafion
carries with it fuch a ftrain of military eloquence, that
it is well worth inferting." -It was to the following
purpofe :

"Sir,   *Canterbury, off Syracufe, Aug.* 16, 1718.
"We have taken and deftroyed all the Spanifh fhips
and veffels that were upon the coaft, as per margin.

"I am, &c.

"*To Sir George Byng,*   "GEORGE WALTON."
Commander in Chief, &c."

Generally notorious, however, as this piece of
naval hiftory may be, it would certainly be an act
of injuftice not to give a concife detail of it. On
the 11th of Auguft, the Britifh fleet, which had,
during the preceding day and night, been in clofe
purfuit of the Spaniards, having fo confiderably neared
them, as to render an engagement unavoidable, the
marquis de Mari, one of their rear-admirals, feparated
from the body of their fleet, and ran in for the Sicilian
fhore, with fix fhips of war, and all the galleys, ftorefhips, bomb-ketches, and fire-fhips. Captain Walton
was immediately detached after them, with fix fhips
of the line, by the commander in chief, who himfelf
purfued the remainder, and foon began the attack.
The Argyle, which was the headmoft fhip of captain
Walton's detachment, having got nearly clofe up with
one

one of the Spanish ships of war, fired a shot across her, as is customary, to bring her to. The enemy, taking no notice of it, the Argyle fired a second, which was equally ineffectual; and the Canterbury, which was now approaching very near, firing a third, the engagement commenced with great spirit immediately, by the Spanish ship returning the fire with her stern chace. The result is not only well known, but was, what was so concisely stated in captain Walton's *dispatch.*. His prizes, and the several operations previous to their capture, would, as it is remarked by Campbell, have furnished matter for some pages in a French relation, for from his marginal list referred to, it appeared he had captured four Spanish ships of war, one of them mounting sixty guns, commanded by rear-admiral Mari himself, one of fifty-four, one of forty, and one of twenty-four guns, with a bomb-vessel, and a ship laden with arms; and had burnt one ship of war, mounting fifty-four guns, two of forty, and one of thirty, a fire-ship, and a bomb-ketch.

His gallantry, on the preceding memorable occasion, procured him the honour of knighthood, immediately after his return to England, and many historical, as well as biographical writers, have asserted, that he was raised to the rank of a flag-officer at the same time, as a further remuneration for the same service; but this statement is evidently erroneous; for he was not promoted to be rear-admiral of the blue till the month of February 1702-3, when his advancement became his natural and just right, according to the

regular

regular routine, and 'rules of the fervice. He did not take upon him any command till the year 1726, when he was fent to the Baltic, under the orders of fir Charles Wager, and having early in the enfuing year, been advanced to the rank of rear-admiral of the red, was difpatched in the month of October, with four fhips of the line, to reinforce the fquadron already ftationed at Gibraltar, commanded by the fame admiral, under whom he had ferved the preceding year.

The apparently hoftile intentions of the Spanifh court, had rendered the equipment of thefe armaments not merely prudent, but abfolutely neceffary ; and fir George was detached immediately after having joined fir Charles Wager, to cruife off cape St. Vincent, with a fquadron, confifting of feven fhips of the line, befides frigates, as well for the purpofe of watching the operations of the apprehended enemy, as for that of attacking any fmall afmaments which might attempt, as it was fufpected would be the cafe, any defultory expeditions againft North Britain in favour of the pretender. The whole of the cruife paffed over, however, without affording fir George any opportunity of favouring the world, with a fecond fpecimen of his very concife method of defcribing a naval encounter ; and he returned to England, after a truly uninterefting voyage, in the month of January 1727-8 *. He was not called into feryice again till the year 1729, when

* A few days before his arrival, he was advanced to be vice-admiral of the blue fquadron ; and on the intelligence of vice-admiral Hopfon's death, reaching England in the month of July, fir George was immediately promoted to the fame rank in the white.

he

he was appointed second in command of the fleet, placed under the orders of his old friend and colleague, fir Charles Wager ; but, as its equipment was intended merely as a matter of precaution, that it might be in readinefs for immediate fervice, in cafe the Spaniards fhould manifeft any difpofition of difturbing public tranquillity, the awe in which they were kept, and the confequent quietude which prevailed, prevented it from ever putting to fea. The reft of the commands which he held, during his continuance in the line of active fervice, require only the enumeration of the dates of their feveral appointments, fince in confequence of the amicable arrangement of thofe political difputes, which rendered the equipment of the different fquadrons expedient, it does not appear that any of them quitted the Britifh ports. In 1731, he hoifted his flag as vice-admiral of the white, on board the Sunderland, of fixty guns, at Spithead. On the 29th of June 1732, he was advanced to be vice-admiral of the red ; as he afterwards was, on the 26th of February 1733-4, to be admiral of the blue fquadron. In the month of June following, he was appointed commander in chief of a naval force, confifting of thirteen fhips of the line, which was ordered to rendezvous at the Nore ; and after ftriking his flag, as quickly became the cafe, in confequence of all the veffels being ordered to be difmantled, and laid up, he quitted the line of active fervice altogether, having retired on a penfion, than which, none was ever more juftly beftowed, of fix hundred pounds a year. This reward, more valuable on account of the merit which procured it, than the mere

pecuniary

pecuniary advantage it conferred, he enjoyed for the
fpace of five years, having died fome time in 1740,
leaving behind him a character which his cotemporaries venerated and refpected, and which all fucceeding ages muft contemplate with pleafure, and admiration.

JAMES,

JAMES, EARL OF BERKELEY.

It is heraldically said, that this illustrious nobleman was the representative of the original ancient, and honourable stock, from whence were collaterally descended many noble, and ever to be celebrated naval characters, sir William Berkeley, with Charles and John, lords Berkeley of Stratton. He was the grandson of George, first earl of Berkeley, so created by Charles II. in the year 1679. This George was the lineal descendant, in the twelfth generation, from Maurice Fitzharding, otherwise Berkeley, the son of Robert Fitzharding, who died in the year 1170, in the seventeenth of Henry II. and from whom are descended many noble and great personages who have, in different ages, distinguished themselves, both as statesmen and warriors. Collins, and other heraldic writers give the following account of the origin of this ancient family: " According to the custom of those times, when the English, in imitation of the Normans, began to assume their firnames from the place of their residence, this of Berkeley was then given to

one

one Roger de Berkeley, in the time of William the
Conqueror, whofe defcendants did enjoy the fame for
fome time ; but the male line of that noble family
ceafing, we are to obferve that Robert Fitzharding,
a powerful man in his time, obtaining a grant of the
caftle and honour of Berkeley from Henry, fon of
Maud the emprefs, poffeffed himfelf thereof; whereupon his defcendants affumed the firname, which,
together with the caftle and barony, continues to them
in the male line to this day ; of which Robert, I am
to take notice, that his father is faid to have been the
youngeft fon to one of the kings of Denmark ; or, as
others affirm (which differs but little), to be defcended
from the royal line of thofe kings ; and, that accompanying duke William of Normandy, in that fignal
expedition he made into England, was prefent with
him in the memorable battle where king Harold was
flain."

His lordfhip, for he at that time held by courtefy
the title of lord Durfley, having manifefted a very
early inclination for maritime purfuits, and paffed
regularly with the higheft credit to himfelf through
the fubordinote ftations, according to the eftablifhed
rules of the fervice, was, on the 2d of April 1702,
promoted to be captain of the Sorlings frigate. Almoft immediately after the acceffion of queen Anne,
he was appointed to the Litchfield, a fourth rate, of
fifty guns, and having been detached from the main fleet,
which was then under the orders of fir George Rooke,
to cruife in foundings, he had the good fortune to
fall

fall in with, and capture, after a well-conducted encounter, a French frigate of war, mounting thirty-six
guns, together with a large veffel homeward bound
from Martinique, mounting twenty guns, and valued,
according to fome writers, at no lefs than forty thoufand pounds fterling; both which prizes he brought
with him to Spithead. In the year 1703, he accompanied fir Cloudefly Shovell into the Mediterranean,
and, when on his return homeward, affifted captain
Norris in capturing the Hazard, a French fhip of
war, mounting fifty-two guns, and carrying four hundred men. At the very commencement of the year 1704,
he was appointed to the Boyne, of eighty guns, and
having been on the 7th of March following, called up
to the houfe of lords by writ under his honorary title
of lord Durfley, was foon afterwards fent out under
fir Cloudefly Shovell to reinforce the fleet already in
the Streights under fir George Rooke. At the ever-
memorable battle off Malaga, he was ftationed in the
line, as one of the feconds to fir John Leake, and behaved with the greateft gallantry; the Boyne having
fuffered more than any fhip in the fquadron, except
that of the admiral, fixty-nine of the crew being either
killed, or defperately wounded; among the latter
were the firft lieutenant, the mafter, and the boat-
fwain. Lediard beftows the following pointed, and
particular commendation of his conduct upon this
occafion: " Among the actions of other brave commanders, we muft not forget thofe of the gallant lord
Durfley, commander of the Boyne, an eighty-gun
fhip,

ship, who, though then but about twenty-three years of age, gave many memorable instances of his undaunted courage, steady resolution, and prudent conduct."

In 1706, he commanded the St. George, one of the fleet sent into the Mediterranean, under sir Cloudesly Shovell, with whom he continued to serve during the current, and ensuing year. He distinguished himself very remarkably at the attack and siege of Toulon, for having been ordered to anchor before one of the Hieres islands, on which were three forts of no mean strength, he, with the utmost gallantry, stormed the largest, in consequence of which success, the two smaller immediately surrendered at discretion. Fate had nearly deprived his country of the future services of this great and noble officer, for being on his return to England, in company with sir Cloudesly Shovell, and the fleet, in the month of October following, his ship is reported to have actually struck on the same ridge of rocks, which caused the destruction of the Association, and that the identical wave, which beat over, and destroyed that noble ship, actually proved the preservation of the St. George, by setting her afloat at the same instant. On the 26th of January 1707-8, although he was at that time not more than twenty-seven years old, he was promoted to be vice-admiral of the blue squadron, an advancement extremely singular for two distinct reasons ; it was, in the first instance, contrary to the assertion of Collins, his first appointment as a flag-officer, so that he was not only

advanced

advanced over the heads of every rear-admiral in the
fervice, but was at that time rather young on the lift
of captains, there being many very gallant perfons, his
feniors in that rank, who were not appointed flag-
officers till twenty years afterwards. In order to account for this circumftance, it is elfewhere obferved,
highly to the credit of his lordfhip, that his perfonal
influence and political confequence was greater, we
not only fay than any of his cotemporaries, but had
apparently more weight than that of any fubject, fince
the revolution. · We have in no cafe found the eftablifhed rules of the fervice fo repeatedly broken through,
as they were to make room for his particular promotion. Among other inftances *, when fcarce thirty
years old, he was advanced to the high naval rank of
vice-admiral of the blue, a diftinction and favour the
more extraordinary, fince it has very rarely been practifed, except in the promotion of thofe fons of fovereigns
who have made choice of a naval life. · Let us, however, in juftice to his manifold virtues, his cool determined bravery, and fpirited intrepidity, fo often difplayed, his fkill and knowledge in all concerns relative to the navy, his unqueftioned integrity, and above
all, his firm and fteady attachment to thofe conjunct
principles of liberty and good government, which are
the glory, and conftitute the true happinefs of Britain,

* The lord Berkeley of Stratton (fee p. 92) is alfo an exception againft
the general practice, as though that particular merit and influence, entitling
the poffeffor to extraordinary promotion, had been the peculiar privilege of
this noble family.

confefs

confefs that this exaltation, attended, as it was, with circumftances almoft totally unprecedented, could not have
been more worthily, or happily beftowed.   His merits
filenced even the breath of envy ; and the moft diftinguifhed naval charaĉters were content, without murmur, to ferve under a man, an imitation of whofe conduĉt and gallantry was the certain path to honour,
fame, and national veneration.

Immediately after his elevation to the rank of
admiral, he hoifted his flag on board the Berwick,
being appointed to a command, under fir George
Byng, in the fleet fitted out to oppofe the armament,
equipped by France for the invafion of Scotland, in
favour of the pretender.   The objeĉt of the expedition being completely fruftrated by the capture of part,
and the difperfion of the whole of the enemies' force,
lord Durfley was almoft immediately fubfequent to his
return into port, appointed to command a fmall fquadron fent to cruife in foundings, for the proteĉtion of
the Britifh commerce.   In this fpecies of fervice he
was occupied, without meeting with any occurrence
worth noticing, till the latter end of the month of June,
when he fell in with three large French cruifers,
mounting from forty to fifty guns each ; the latter being
juft out of port, and clean, his lordfhip was not able
to come up with them, or effeĉt any better fervice
than that of driving them back to their own harbours, his own fhips having been long off the ground,
and confequently become extremely foul.   In the enfuing month, he was recalled from the fervice in
which

which he had been fo long employed, and ordered to
put himfelf under the command of fir George Byng,
for the purpofe of carrying into execution an expedition, folely calculated to create an alarm along the
coaft of France, and thereby not only prevent any
troops being detached into Flanders, to moleft and in-
terrupt the duke of Marlborough, who had formed
the fiege of Lifle, but perhaps occafion the recall
of troops from that quarter, to defend the menaced
coafts of France, and confequently render the enterprife undertaken by his grace, lefs arduous and difficult. The alarm was continued uninterruptedly until
the middle of Auguft, and with fuch fuccefs, as completely to produce the hoped-for effect. The object
being obtained, fir George Byng, with the main body
of the fleet, returned into port, and lord Durfley refumed his former occupation, of cruifing in foundings,
with a fquadron confifting of feven fhips of the line,
and a proportionable number of frigates. The foul-
nefs, and ill condition of his fhips, compelled him,
however, to return into port, not long afterwards,
without having met with any better fuccefs, than the
capture of a French merchant-fhip, taken by the
Salifbury. All poffible attention being paid to the re-
equipment of the fhips under his lordfhip's orders, he
was enabled, again, to quit port on the 28th of September, and after continuing to cruife for the fpace of
fix weeks, found it neceffary to return to England with
the larger fhips of his fquadron, having firft taken the
precaution to leave three of the fmalleft, as a protection from the affaults of privateers, to fuch fhips as

fhould

should be either returning to Great Britain, or proceeding from thence, on their outward-bound voyages.

Although the success his lordship met with on this occasion, may at first sight be considered trivial, for it did not exceed the capture of five or six vessels, the most important of which was a privateer, mounting twenty-four guns, his diligence, though apparently unrewarded, and the protection he rendered to the commerce of his country, not only entitled him to the highest encomiums, but actually produced them. Campbell most honourably observes, that the indefatigable diligence of his lordship, though it was not attended with any extraordinary success, gave great satisfaction to the merchants, as it prevented the French privateers from venturing near our coasts, as they had done many years before, to the inexpressible damage of our trade, as well as to the prejudice of our reputation, as a maritime power. He further adds the following eulogium, which appears to be a very just one, by way of note: "What I have here advanced, is on all hands allowed, and even by bishop Burnet himself, who confesses, that much greater care was taken of our trade, and the French privateers were more effectually restrained, than in any year since the war began."

On the 21st of December ensuing, his lordship was advanced to the rank of vice-admiral of the white squadron, and, on that very day, again put to sea, with his force, but was under the necessity of returning into port, after a successless cruise, unattended with any material occurrence, except that of his having fallen in with two French ships of war, one mounting fifty,

and

and the other sixty guns. Owing however to their
being, as in general was the cafe at that day, better
failers than thofe built by Britain, they effected their
efcape, though not without much difficulty, by
lightening their fhips, throwing many of their guns,
together with all their fpars and boats, overboard.
During the enfuing cruife, his lordfhip, though
not much more fuccefsful, than on former occafions, for the principal captures made. by him,
during its continuance, were only two French
privateers, mounting twelve guns each, met with a
confpicuous opportunity, which he by no means neglected, of difplaying his natural gallantry and zeal,
in the fervice of his country. On the 22d of February,
he fell in with eleven French fhips of war, fuppofed
to be a fquadron, commanded by that celebrated officer,
monf. Du Guai Trouin. Although his lordfhip, exclufive of the Kent, of feventy guns, his own flag-fhip,
had only two fhips of fixty, and one of fifty guns,
with him, at the time, he neverthelefs, prepared with
the utmoft fpirit, to attack the enemy; but having loft
fight of them in the night, and the Dartmouth having, in
confequence of fpringing a leak, parted company, his
lordfhip deemed it moft prudent, as it certainly was, to
return into port for the purpofe of procuring a reinforcement. Having obtained this aid, he again immediately put to fea, and not hearing any thing of the
enemy for fome days, detached three of his fhips, to
cruife off Breft, in the hope they might capture fome
veffel, from which he might obtain intelligence. On
the 29th of March, he received orders from the admi-

ralty

ralty board to convoy the outward-bound Lifbon fleet
to a certain latitude. Thefe orders he had fcarcely
fulfilled, when, being on his return to his former ftation, he fell in, on the 9th of April, with the Achilles,
of feventy guns, commanded by monf. Du Guai Trouin
himfelf, and the Glorieux, of forty-four guns, which
véffels had only the day before taken the Briftol, an
Englifh fhip of war, mounting fifty guns. The fignal
for a general chace was immediately made by his
lordfhip, and with fo much fuccefs, that the Briftol was
very foon recovered; but having received a fhot in her
bread-room, foundered almoft immediately afterwards.
All the people, however, on board her, were faved,
twenty men only excepted. The purfuit being continued
with much alacrity, the Glorieux was taken by the
Chefter, captain Thomas Mathews; and the Achilles
alone had the good fortune to effect her efcape, though
very much fhattered. Provifions and water growing
fcarce, his lordfhip was obliged to return to Plymouth, on the 13th of May, with his fquadron, which
then confifted of eight two-decked fhips, and fome
frigates. On his arrival, he received the unwelcome
news, that the Sweepftakes frigate, of thirty-two
guns, one of his fcouts, had been taken, fome days
before, by two large French privateers, each of which
was of greater force than herfelf.

In the month of July (1709), he was ordered to
take upon him the command of a fquadron lying at
the Nore, intended to be fent off Schouwen, on the
coaft of Zealand, for the purpofe of intercepting a
number of fhips, laden with corn, which were ex-

                                    pected

pected from the northward, and were known to be
bound for different ports belonging to the enemy.
The cruife was unfuccefsful, and his lordfhip having
returned into Oofely Bay, on the Yorkfhire coaft, repaired from thence to Plymouth by land, and took
upon him his former command. The enemy deriving
fpirit from his abfence, had pufhed an immenfe flotilla of privateers to fea, eleven of which were faid
to be cruifing in the Irifh channel. His lordfhip therefore, divided his force into three parts; one divifion
confifting of three fourth rates, he fent into the Irifh
fea, for the purpofe of driving away or capturing the
hornets that infefted that quarter. A fecond divifion,
confifting of fix two-decked fhips, was detached by
him, under captain Vincent, on a cruife to the weftward of Scilly, for the protection of a very valuable
fleet, daily expected home from the Weft Indies; and
his lordfhip himfelf having five other two-decked fhips
under him, after keeping for fome days in conftant
motion, and thereby difturbing the cruifing ftations
of the enemy, effectually baffled all the fchemes they
had projected, by joining captain Vincent. The minor
enemies were thus completely difcomfited, and thofe of
fuperior confequence, were prevented from making
their appearance. Having continued to cruife at the
entrance of the Britifh channel, for a few days, after the
defirable end juft mentioned, was accomplifhed, he
had the good fortune to capture a very large and valuable French fhip, homeward-bound from Guadaloupe,
mounting forty guns. He continued occupied in the
fame branch of fervice during the whole of the

R 3   winter,

winter *, and the enfuing fpring ; and, by his extreme
diligence and activity; added, if poffible, to that reputation which he had before acquired by his very ftrict
and fuccefsful attention to the protection of commerce.

Having returned into port early in the month of
May 1710, he ftruck his flag, and appears, after this
time, to have enjoyed a retirement, of feveral years
continuance, from the fatigues of that troublefome and
laborious fervice, in which he had been fo long engaged. By the death of his father, on the 24th of
September 1710, he became earl of Berkeley, and was
immediately conftituted lord lieutenant of the county
of Gloucefter, as well as of the city of Briftol, and
cuftos rotulorum ; he was alfo appointed warden of
the foreft of Dean, and on the 21ft of November
following, high fteward of the city of Gloucefter.
His well-known zeal for the intereft of the houfe of
Hanover, had fo highly recommended him to the notice of king George I. that immediately on the acceffion † of that monarch, he was appointed one of the
lords of the bedchamber, and reftored to the offices of
lord lieutenant of the county of Gloucefter, and city
of Briftol, from which he had, through the influence
of party, been removed in the year 1711. On the 18th
of December, he was alfo reinftated in the office of
cuftos rotulorum of the county above mentioned, from

* On the 14th of November 1709, he was advanced to be vice-admiral
of the red.

† He was appointed by the lords juftices, to command the convoy ordered to attend his majefty to England.

which

which he had, alfo been difplaced. On the 16th of April 1717, he was fworn a member of the privy council, and on the fame day appointed firft lord commiffioner of the admiralty; which high ftation he continued to fill during the whole remainder of the reign of king George I. On the 13th of March 1718-19, in confequence of the rupture with Spain, he was appointed admiral, and commander in chief of the fleet. The author of fir J. Leake's life makes the following obfervation on this appointment; " The earl of Berkeley being then vice-admiral of Great Britain (to which honorary ftation he was appointed on the 21ft of March 1718-19, at a time when fir John Norris was rear-admiral only), and firft lord commiffioner of the admiralty, endeavoured to come as near the lord high admiral as poffible, both in power and ftate; by a particular warrant from the crown, he hoifted the lord high admiral's flag, as it is called (the firft time, I believe, it was ever worn in command at fea), and had three captains appointed under him, as a lord high admiral; Littleton, then vice-admiral of the white, being his firft captain. This appointment was rendered the more extraordinary, from the circumftance of fir John Norris, who was a fenior flag-officer, being at that time employed in the channel, and honoured with no fuch diftinction."

The earl having hoifted his flag on board the Dorfetfhire, at Spithead, failed from St. Helens on the 29th of March, with a fquadron of feven fhips of the line, to join one of the fame force under fir John Norris, which was cruifing between Scilly and the

Lizard.

Lizard. Having stretched as far as Cape Clear, he returned back into the British channel, on the 4th of April ; when coming into Spithead, he struck his flag on the 15th, and repaired to London. After this time, he appears to have retired totally from the line of active service, at least as a naval commander.

Collins, briefly recapitulating the great variety of civil offices, held by this noble lord, gives us the following short account of him, and adds some other interesting heraldic particulars relative to his family. " He was (says he) five times one of the lords justices of Great Britain, whilst his majesty went to Hanover ; and being elected a knight of the most noble order of the garter on March 31st, 1718 ; he was installed on April 30th following, and placed in the fourteenth stall at Windsor. On September 15th, 1727, he was appointed lord lieutenant of Lincolnshire, by his late majesty ; and in November 10th, in that year, was constituted lord lieutenant of the county of Gloucester, and cities and counties of Gloucester and Bristol, as also of the county of Surry, and likewise custos rotulorum of the counties of Gloucester and Surry ; moreover, on the 17th of the same month, he was appointed keeper of the forest of Dean, and constable of St. Briavel's Castle ; also vice-admiral of Great Britain, and lieutenant of the admiralties thereof, and lieutenant of the navies and seas of this kingdom. He departed this life at the castle of Aubigny, a seat of the duke of Richmond, near Rochelle, in France (being there for the recovery of his health), on the 17th of August 1736, and was buried at Berkeley.

" His

"His lordſhip married the lady Louiſa Lenox (eldeſt daughter to Charles, firſt duke of Richmond), who was appointed, on October 30th, 1714, one of the ladies of the bedchamber, to her late majeſty, queen Caroline, then princeſs of Wales, dying of the ſmall-pox on January 15th, 1716-17, in the twenty-third year of her age ; ſhe was buried at Berkeley, leaving iſſue, one ſon, Auguſtus, fourth earl of Berkeley ; and a daughter, lady Elizabeth, married on February 11th, 1727-8, to Anthony Henley, of the Grange, in the county of Southampton, eſquire, elder brother of Robert, earl of Northington ; and died in the month of September 1745."

ADMIRAL

ADMIRAL THOMAS MATHEWS.

THIS brave and unfortunate commander, was the descendant of a very ancient and respectable family, long settled at Llandaff, in the county of Glamorgan, a collateral branch of which stock, soon after the restoration, went over to Ireland, where they have acquired large possessions, and arrived at high honours ; Francis, the representative of that part of the family, being created baron Llandaff, of Thomastown, in the county of Tipperary, on the 12th of October 1783. Archdale, in his account of this noble lord and his ancestors, speaks in the following honourable terms of the family of Mathews : "Edward Mathews, or Ap Mathew, ancestor to this noble lord, resided at Rader, in the county of Glamorgan, about the year 1660, where he inherited a good estate, principally consisting of chiefries, being the remains of an ample fortune possessed by his ancestors, from time immemorial ; he was also possessed of the town of Llandaff, in the same county, whence the present lord, in whom it now vests, takes his title."

Of

Of the earlier services in which Mr. Mathews was engaged, no public mention has ever been made; the first notice taken of him being his appointment, on the 24th of May 1703, to be captain of the Yarmouth. This commission, from the shortnefs of his continuance in the ship juft mentioned, is fuppofed to have been beftowed for the cuftomary purpofe of conferring rank. He removed, quickly afterwards, into a frigate, which being employed merely as a cruiser, and proving unfuccefsful, as has frequently been the misfortune of the moft adroit, and enterprifing commanders, no fubfequent information has been thought worthy of being tranfmitted by hiftorians, and biographers concerning him, till the latter part of the year 1707, at which time he was captain of the Dover, one of the veffels ftationed to cruife in foundings during the winter, under the orders of commodore Evans. While thus occupied, he is noticed as the captor of a French frigate called the Bien Aimé, mounting twenty-fix guns; not long after this fuccefs, he was appointed to the Chefter, a fourth rate, newly launched; and, being one of the officers employed under the command of lord Durfley, in the month of March 1708-9, as related in the life of that nobleman, had the good fortune to capture, after a fhort but fpirited action, the Glorieux, a French ship of war, mounting forty-four guns. He continued in the command of the Chefter during the whole remainder of the war, being employed firft on the Weft Indian, and afterwards on the North American ftation, but without being fortunate enough to meet with any fecond opportunity, either of enriching

riching himfelf, or of procuring additional reputation.
Peace being concluded almoft immediately after his
return to England in 1711, he either continued out
of commiffion, or was fo, unintereftingly. employed
that no mention is made of his occupations, or commands till the year 1718, when he was appointed captain of the Kent, one of the fhips ordered to be
equipped for the Mediterranean fervice, in the fleet fent
thither under the orders of fir George Byng. In the
memorable engagement with the Spanifh fleet off Meffina, he very confpicuoufly diftinguifhed himfelf, having not only captured and taken poffeffion of the St.
Carlos, of fixty guns, commanded by the prince de
Chalay, but afterwards. confiderably affifted captain
Mafter, in the Superb, in capturing the Spanifh admiral
himfelf, who was on board the St. Philip, of feventy-
four guns. In the month of January 1718-19, he was
left, by the commander in chief, with a fmall fquadron,
to cruife off Pontemelia, in order to watch rear-admiral
Cammock, who had taken refuge in Meffina, and
prevent his efcaping to the fouthward. So active and
diligent was he in this fervice, that he drove on fhore,
where fhe was totally deftroyed, one of Mr. Cammock's beft fhips, called the Santa Rofalia, mounting
fixty-four guns; and the rear-admiral himfelf very narrowly efcaped being taken prifoner, in a few days
afterwards, by getting off in his boat, but the veffel in
which he attempted to fly, being a frigate of twenty-
two guns, fell into the hands of his purfuers. It is
remarked, and with truth, that his abilities were held
in fuch high eftimation by the commander in chief,

that

that few measures were adopted in respect to the direction of the British force, during its continuance in the Mediterranean, without Mr. Mathews being previously consulted, and in many instances particularly selected to execute the plans, he had himself advised. After his return to England, he appears, in great measure, to have retired from the line of active service for many years, with the exception, that in 1722, he was sent to the East Indies, as commodore of a small squadron, and returned from thence two years afterwards, without encountering any event sufficiently extraordinary to demand commemoration.

He was certainly a man of high spirit, and endowed with very considerable abilities; and, perhaps, as the greatest men are not exempt from human failings, he might consider it derogatory to those abilities, after having been the friend and counsellor of so great a man as sir George Byng, and acted himself as commander in chief of an armament, that he should again serve in the capacity of a private captain: but all this is mere supposition, for we know nothing decisive, except that he really never did accept of any commission in any of those fleets, which were so repeatedly fitted out, under the apprehensions of ruptures with different powers.

He appeared, in 1736, to have totally relinquished the idea of accepting any subsequent naval command, by receiving, on the 8th of January, the appointment of commissioner of the navy, resident at Chatham. This post he held till the year 1742, when, war with Spain having been for some time carried on with great

fury,

fury, and a rupture with France hourly expected, his high spirit, difdaining to continue ingloriously at home in the enjoyment of a mere civil appointment, while his country needed his affiftance, he folicited a command; which was immediately conferred on him. It was the moft important that could have been beftowed, according to the exifting circumftances of the war which then prevailed, for it was that on the Mediterranean ftation, where it appeared moft probable the combined fleets of France and Spain would be concentrated. Previous to his acceptance of this appointment, he was, on the 12th of March 1741-2, advanced to the rank of vice-admiral of the red, which was the firft he ever held as a flag-officer, and to which he would have attained, according to the regular routine of promotion, from participating in which he had, for a time, difqualified himfelf, by accepting the civil employment already ftated. On his return, therefore, to the fervice, it was confidered as a mere act of juftice, to reftore him to that ftation he would have held, but for the event alluded to. Having hoifted his flag on board the Namur, a fecond rate, of ninety guns, he failed for Gibraltar, with three other fhips of the line under his orders, on the 16th of April; having arrived there, without meeting either with any finifter accident or memorable occurrence, on the 7th of May, he formed a junction with the force already there, under rear-admiral Leftock, and, confequently, took upon himfelf the chief command. It is to be obferved, that, at the time of his arrival, the actual intentions of the French court were ftrongly fufpected,

but

but not openly avowed; a fituation in which they moft probably had it in their power, at that time, to aid their Spanifh friends in fecret, better than could have been done by open hoftility itfelf. To counteract this infidious aid, required the utmoft coolnefs, delicacy, and fpirit; and Mr. Mathews was certainly confidered, by all parties, to have fhewn himfelf in no degree deficient, as to any of the qualities required.

The conveyance of ftores and provifions, under the euftomary and ftale pretence of neutral flags, was immediately reftrained, and, in the end, completely annihilated, by the judgment of the vice-admiral, in ftationing his cruifers, and their diligence in executing his orders: moreover, all attempts to convey naval ftores into the Spanifh ports, through the medium of light veffels and gallies, belonging to that nation, drawing little water, which, by keeping along fhore, pufhed occafionally into neutral ports, when hard preffed, to feek a better opportunity of again efcaping, were alfo totally put an end to, by the attacks made upon them under the orders of the vice-admiral, in the very harbours, whither they had fled for refuge. In few words, the very mention of the Britifh naval power, carried terror with it over the whole Mediterranean. The blockade of the fleet of Spain, which had fheltered itfelf in Toulon, and that of the French fhips alfo, which, with the moft unremitting affiduity had been equipped for the purpofe of reinforcing it, was undertaken by Mr. Mathews himfelf; who, by repairing to Villa-Franca, and keeping conftant crui-

fers

fers off the Hieres-iflands, as well as the harbour of
Toulon, confined the powerful armaments of the
enemy, and prevented the actual declaration of war,
on the part of France, for the fpace of eighteen months.
This circumftance, which is noticed in the plain hiftorical account of the time, pays, in its unadorned, un-
exaggerated ftyle, a higher encomium to the abilities
and conduct of the vice-admiral, than the moft laboured
panegyric could have done. " Admiral Mathews,
when joined by rear-admiral Rowley with a ftrong reinforcement, had a very formidable force with him ;
but it is afferted by fome, that the combined force of
France and Spain, confifted of thirty-fix fhips of the
line, which he confined to the port of Toulon, by de-
taching his two rear-admirals, Rowley and Leftock,
to cruife off the iflands of Hieres, with *twenty-four
fhips.*" By cruifing on the coaft of Provence, and continuing at Villa-Franca, he confiderably impeded the
operations of the Spanifh army, for, a letter from
Florence, dated June 16, 1742, has the following pa-
ragraph: " By letters from Nice, we underftand
that they are making all poffible preparations in
that neighbourhood, for oppofing the paffage of
the Spanifh troops from Provence, and are greatly
affifted therein by the Englifh vice-admiral Mathews,
who continues to lie with part of his fleet at Villa-
Franca."

In the month of Auguft, in confequence of his Sicilian majefty's having fent a body of troops to join the
Spanifh army, the vice-admiral detached commodore
Martin, with five fhips of the line, four bomb-ketches,
and

and their tenders, to Naples. His appearance created much alarm, but his firmnefs, joined to his moderation, effected the purpofe of compelling the recall of the Neapolitan troops, without his being compelled to have recourfe to that dreadful mode of exacting compliance by a bombardment. The towns on the coaft of Catalonia, experienced a feverer fate ; here, the chaftifement which Naples had efcaped, was inflicted with its utmoft horrors. But, though compaffion has prompted many hiftorical, and other writers to condemn this violent manner of carrying on hoftilities, a moment's cool reflection will convince us of the propriety of the meafures adopted by Mr. Mathews, and though, heavy, as well as diftreffing, the mifchief might fall on individuals, the peace of the general community could be reftored by no means more likely, than by fhewing, in the inftance of partial deftruction, what might be expected on a more enlarged fcale, fhould the continuance of hoftilities be much further prolonged.

On the return of commodore Martin to the fleet, he was immediately difpatched to the town of Araffa, in the Genoefe territories, where it was reported confiderable magazines had been formed, for the ufe of the Spanifh army. The intelligence proved true, and the whole contents of the depot were accordingly deftroyed. About the fame time, the vice-admiral, hearing that a Spanifh fhip of the line lay at anchor at Ajaccio, in the ifland of Corfica, he fent thither the Ipfwich, and another fhip of war, to take or deftroy, her. The Spaniards prevented, however, the neceffity

of an attack, by foreftalling the objeƈ of it, and fetting fire to the fhip themfeĮves. The operations of
the year 1743, were entirely of the fame nature with
the preceding. The French and Spanifh fquadrons
ventured not beyond the proteƈion of the batteries
which covered them ; and the Britifh fleet continued
to give law to the commerce of the Mediterranean
fea. The effeƈ produced, was the total prevention
of the Spanifh army in Italy from taking the field ;
the chaftifement of the Genoefe, who were fecretly
and moft dangeroufly attached to the Spanifh caufe ;
and the prefervation of the territories of the king of
Sardinia from infult, and horrors of invafion with
which they were not only threatened, but in all
probability would have been fubjeƈed to, had it not
been for the proteƈion they received from the countenance of Britain, and the exertion of its naval
power.

In the month of Auguft 1743, Mr. Mathews was
advanced to be admiral of the blue fquadron ; and, in
the fucceeding fpring, the court of France, wearied by
the difgrace of having the only armament which it
poffeffed, confined in port, as well as that of their
allies, fent M. De Court to take the command of their
fhips, with orders to put to fea, at all events, and
fupport the Spaniards with the whole of his ftrength, in
cafe they fhould be attacked. The force of the united
fquadrons confifted of twenty-eight fail of the line,
and fix frigates. That under Mr. Mathews was,
indeed, fomewhat fuperior, in point of numbers, but
                                                    had

had the difadvantage of having feveral of its fhips in a very indifferent ftate of equipment, both with refpect to men, and the condition of the fhips themfelves, which had been a long time from England. On the other hand, the French and Spaniards were juft come out of port, and in as good a ftate for fervice as any fleet belonging to them, that ever went to fea. M. De Court arrived at Toulon in the month of January, and, having hoifted his flag on board the Terrible, of feventy-four guns, affumed the command of the combined fleet. Admiral Mathews, about the fame time, returned from Turin, whither he had gone to concert the meafures, neceffary to be purfued in carrying on the war. Having received information that the combined fleet was actually preparing to put to fea, he ftationed a fufficient number of cruifers to look out, and give him the earlieft intelligence of the enemy's motions. On the 8th of February, O. S. * he learned from fome of his fhips, which rejoined him, that the combined fleets would put to fea on the following day. He, accordingly, with all the alacrity becoming a man of high fpirit, made every poffible difpofition to receive, or purfue them. The memorable action which enfued, and which forms fo prominent an event in the naval hiftory of Britain, became long the fubject of political difcuffion and party difpute ; and it is difficult, even at this remote period, to collect the true caufe of the mifcarriage, from thofe various accounts

* On the 18th following, the appointment of admiral Mathews to be rear-admiral of Great Britain, was declared in the Gazette; as was, at the fame time, his promotion to be admiral of the white.

and

and opinions which men of different fentiments have,
from time to time, publifhed as fo many candid ſtate-
ments. The number of fhips in each line was exactly equal, although the French, in their account of
the matter, wifh to imprefs an idea of their having
been manifeſtly inferior : but. Mr. Matthews had a
referve of fix fhips, of fifty guns, which were not put
into the line, and might have fupplied the place of fuch
as were difabled during the action. No perfon can
doubt, but that, owing to fome cauſe or other, an
opportunity was loft of giving the navy of France and
Spain a very fignal and decifive blow. What that
cauſe was, will, perhaps, be afcertained with no little
degree of precifion, by ferioufly and impartially confidering the characters, and referring to the conduct,
both of Mr. Mathews and Mr. Leftock, as well
during the former part of their lives, as their re-
ciprocal behaviour to each other, while they were
thus, unfortunately for the nation, connected in
command.

The admiral, finding all further hopes of bringing
the enemy to a more decifive action, at an end, proceeded to Mahon, where, being much diffatisfied with
the conduct of Mr. Leftock, he propofed certain que-
ries to him, which, not being anfwered to the admiral's
fatisfaction, he thought proper to fufpend the former,
and fend him to England a prifoner, on board the
Salifbury; accompanying this meaſure with the reafons which had occafioned it, and a fpecific charge
againſt Mr. Leftock for mifconduct. The fhips of
the fleet, which had been damaged in the preceding
action,

action, being refitted, Mr. Mathews immediately put
to fea, in the hope of meeting with his former antagonifts, and revenging himfelf on them for his firft
difappointment. Fortune favoured not his endeavours; but, though fuccefslefs in the firft objeft of
his wifhes, he continued to exert the utmoft abilities
of his mind, againft his combined opponents, fo long
as he retained the high truft which had been confided
to him. On the arrival of Mr. Leftock in England,
he retaliated on the admiral, by a charge of recrimination, to the following effect: " That the night before the engagement he brought to, in obedience to
the admiral's night fignal; but, at break of day, by
reafon of the wind's fhifting, and the indraught of the
tides, he found himfelf at a greater diftance from the
main body than he expected; that about eight, he had
an account from the admiral, by Mr. Jafper, his firft
lieutenant, that he would lay by till he could join him
with his divifion, in place whereof the admiral made
more fail, and fent lieutenant Knowles to order him
to do the fame, though he had then crowded all he
could carry; that he did all he poffibly could to get
up with the fternmoft of the Spanifh fquadron, and
even fired a broadfide at the Ifabella, being the hind-
moft, but could not prevent her going ahead of him;
that he did all in his power to affift the admiral, whofe
rafhnefs and *precipitation* in engaging the enemy *before
the line of battle was formed,* contrary to the rules of
war, and the practice of our beft admirals, rendered
his attempts to fuccour and fupport him fruitlefs;
that this conduct in Mr. Mathews was the more in-
excufable.

S 3

excufable, *as he was under no neceffity of hurrying on the action,* fince, by the difpofition of the French and Spanifh admirals, *it plainly appeared they were refolved to fight*; that it was unaccountable the admiral fhould take fuch precautions, not to let the enemy efcape us, when our fleet was not formed in order of battle, and they lay prepared for us before the engagement; and, though we had the advantage of difabling fome of their fhips, and burning another, became of a fudden more cautious, by bringing to in order of battle, at a much greater diftance, without fending out any cruifers to obferve their motions; therefore, the fole mifcarriage was chargeable on the admiral, who, by his imprudence in fighting at firft at fuch a difadvantage, had endangered the whole fleet intrufted to his command, and after, by a quite contrary conduct, fuffered the enemy to efcape out of his hands."

The difappointment excited fo general a national clamour, that it was foon found abfolutely neceffary to inftitute a regular public inquiry into the caufe of it. Mr. Mathews, who had been ordered home from the Mediterranean, being a member of the houfe of commons, as was Mr. Leftock alfo, they were, as is cuftomary in fuch cafes, heard in their places; but, though feveral evidences were examined, it was judged moft proper to refer the whole matter to the confideration of a court-martial, as the fitteft tribunal to determine on the complaint, and the defence againft it. Owing to the abfence of witneffes, and the number of delays unavoidably occafioned by the war, the trial of Mr. Leftock did not commence till the month

of

of January 1746, nor was it concluded till June following. That of Mr. Mathews commenced in the ensuing month, sir Chaloner Ogle being the president. The result was, that Mr. Mathews was declared incapable of holding any subsequent naval command. It is incumbent, however, on us to observe, as an act of common justice to his character, that king George II. himself, is said to have been much dissatisfied at this decision, and, with all that open and generous love for gallantry, which formed so strong a feature in his character, to have for some time actually refused to signify his approbation of a decision, passing so severe a sentence on a man who had acted with so much acknowledged bravery.

The sentence, however it might be intended to calm the stern severe countenance of unrelenting justice, was by no means equally fortunate in appeasing the tumult of popular opinion. The people, especially that part unacquainted with the rules and laws of the service, inquired for the person who had acquitted himself best, in the splendid, brilliant, and ever-favourite character of a gallant man. When they found their commander in chief actively and most spiritedly engaged in the centre of his foes, and when they searched in vain to discover the admiral of a squadron, under that commander, in the same situation; when they were told that, while the first was bravely employed in the manner just mentioned, the latter was not even within gun-shot; when they heard Mr. Mathews himself complain of being unsupported,

of

of being left a sacrifice to the private resentment of an individual ; and, above all, of being deprived, by that conduct, of bringing into a British port, the Spanish admiral Navarro, in a ship mounting one hundred and ten guns, they felt the immediate impulse of a generous indignation ; and, those who were not severe and violent enough to condemn the justice of the court, were obliged to be content with confessing, that the code of naval discipline was what they did not understand.

Confiderable stress has been laid, by those who are adverse to Mr. Mathews, on the former conduct and private behaviour of that gentleman to Mr. Lestock ; and they have endeavoured to find some excuse, for the apparent opposition given by the latter, to the views of the former, by attributing it to resentment, as if such excuse, justifies the smallest breach of public duty. Mr. Mathews is charged with having been austere, haughty, and imperious, when in fact he was nothing worse than a strict disciplinarian, a rigid observer of forms, a man who, when in a subordinate station, had always paid the utmost obedience to command, and for that very reason now justly thought he had every reason to expect, and insist on a similar conduct in those who acted in a similar station under him. His pride was not that of a vain upstart, ridiculously puffed up by an unexpected exaltation to a high national trust, but that of a man, who entertained a proper sense of his own dignity and command ; who, most feelingly alive to every public slight, and insult, which though he might

4   not

not confider merely perfonal to himfelf, he might have forgiven fo far as he himfelf was concerned, but not when he, fuppofed them indignities offered to his ftation, and injuries to the fervice of his country. His gallantry has never been queftioned, even by his bittereft enemies; and the heavieft charge they ever were able to adduce againft him, was, that he under-ftood the practical part of his duty better than the theory of it; or, in plainer Englifh, that he himfelf knew better how to fight, than to command others how to do the fame. Moft hiftorians, in their obfervations on the foregoing tranfaction, remark, that however Mr. Mathews might, on fome accounts, merit cen-fure, the conduct of Mr. Leftock certainly demanded a heavier punifhment. Each perfon may affume to himfelf a privilege, which affuredly is undeniable, of judging for himfelf in all controverfies of this nature, that depend in the fmalleft degree on opinion; but, certainly, all men muft unite in the fame judg-ment, on the conduct of an officer who fuffers pri-vate animofity to influence his public conduct, even for a moment. Thofe who have been ingenious to inveftigate firft caufes, have felicitated themfelves on proclaiming to the world the caufe of this unfor-tunate difagreement. This developement is rather an injury to the character of Mr. Leftock, for it deprives him of every private virtue, as his conduct, in the line of his profeffion had, in the opinion of many, bereft him of every public one. His motives, fuch as they are, which are given us on this occafion, are, with more propriety, transferred to the account

of

of his life. As to Mr. Mathews, he paſſed the ſhort remainder of his days in peaceable retirement, and died, at laſt conſidered, by moſt people, as entitled to their honourable compaſſion, which is the tribute, in degree, next valuable to regret, and public applauſe. The time of his death is not preciſely known, but it is ſaid to have happened ſome time in the year 1751.

ADMIRAL

Harding sc

HON: E:D VERNON ESQ:R

Pub.d 1 Mar. 1800, by Edw.d Harding 98 Pall Mall.

ADMIRAL VERNON.

Is the defcendant of a very ancient and honourable family, of which the following heraldic account is given: "It is defcended from the lords of Vernon, in the dutchy of Normandy: their common anceftor, William de Vernon, affumed his firname from the town and diftrict of Vernon, whereof he was fole proprietor in the year 1052. He founded and richly endowed the collegiate and parochial church of St. Mary, in Vernon, for a dean and fecular canons, and lies interred there under an altar monument, whereon is his effigy. He had two fons, Richard and Walter, who both came into England with William the Conqueror. The younger obtained the lordfhips of Winfleton, Neffe, Ledfam, and Brefton, in Chefhire; Hatwell, Adftock, and Plate-Morton, in Bucks; and had a fhare of his father's poffeffions in Normandy; but, dying without iffue, they defcended to his elder brother, Richard de Vernon, lord of Vernon, who was one of the barons created by Hugh Lupus, to whom William the Conqueror, in the 20th year of his reign,

granted

granted the county palatine of Chefter. It appears
from Doomfday-book, that this Richard de Vernon,
firft baron of Shipbroke, held the lands and manors
of Arton, Picton, Shipbroke, Crew, Hetume, Coche-
fhall, Wice, Malaterne, Waintune, Devenham, Dove-
ftock, Adeline, Boetbury, and others. He was a
benefactor, with Hugh Lupus, to the abbey of St.
Werburgh, in Chefter, and, in temp. William II.
gave tithes of Eafton and Picton to that abbey. He
was fucceeded by his eldeft fon and heir, William de
Vernon, whofe fon, Hugh de Vernon, living in 1119,
was alfo lord of Northwyk, and, with Richard, earl
of Chefter, likewife a great benefactor to the abbey of
Werburgh. He married the daughter and heir of
Richard de Barllot (or Magdiol), lord of Herdewick
and Helgrave, by whom he had iffue, inter alios,
Warine de Vernon, fourth baron of Shipbroke, living temp. Henry III. whofe eldeft fon, Richard de
Vernon, living 37th Henry III. had a grant of the
cuftody of the caftle and manor of the Peeke, and,
dying before his father, left iffue four fons, whereof
William, the third, was chief juftice of Chefter ; and
Warine, the eldeft, married Auda, third daughter
and one of the coheirs of William Malbank, baron
of Wich Malbank, now Namptwich, in the county of
Chefter (defcended from William Malbank, baron of
Wich Malbank, in 20th William I.), with whom he
acquired a great number of manors in that county,
and was the father of Warine de Vernon, baron of
Shipbroke."

Mr.

Mr. Vernon was born at Weftminfter, on the 12th of November 1684: his father, who was fecretary of ftate to king William, and queen Mary, gave him a good education, intending to qualify him for fome civil employment ; but the youth was defirous of entering into the fea fervice, to which his father at laft confented ; and he purfued, with furprifing application and fuccefs, thofe ftudies which were connected with his intended line of profeffion. His firft expedition at fea was under vice-admiral Hopfon, on the expedition againft Cadiz. He afterwards ferved as fecond lieutenant of the Refolution, one of the fhips detached to the Weft Indies, under commodore Walker: in this ftation he is faid to have acquired that complete knowledge of thofe feas, which afterwards became fo ferviceable to himfelf, and to his country. In 1704, he acted in the capacity of lieutenant on board the fleet commanded by fir George Rooke, which convoyed the king of Spain to Lifbon, on which occafion Mr. Vernon had the honour to receive a valuable ring, and a hundred guineas from the monarch's own hand. He was alfo prefent at the battle off Malaga, on the 13th of Auguft the fame year.

After thus previoufly paffing through the feveral fubordinate ftations and ranks in the fervice, he was advanced to be captain of the Dolphin frigate, a fhip, at that time employed in the Mediterranean, being attached to the fleet under the orders of fir John Leake. He was, not long after having received his firft commiffion as captain in the navy, removed into the Rye; and fent to England in the month of Auguft following, as

bearer

bearer of the news that Alicant had furrendered. Having been fent back to the Mediterranean, ftill holding the fame command, he continued there, acting under the orders of fir Cloudefly Shovell, till the end of the year 1707, when he returned to England with that unfortunate admiral, and fuch part of the fleet as was ordered home. Soon after his arrival, he was promoted to the Jerfey, a fourth rate, and difpatched, in the month of May 1708, to the Weft Indies, with captain John Edwards, who carried thither a fmall reinforcement to the fquadron previoufly employed in that quarter, under the command of rear-admiral Wager. The whole occupation in which the Britifh fhips of war could be then engaged in that quarter of the world, was merely the deftruction of the commerce of the enemy, for there was no French fleet on the ftation. As captain of a cruifer, Mr. Vernon was extremely diligent and fuccefsful, feveral valuable merchant-veffels, and fome privateers, having been captured by him, particularly in the month of May 1711 (for he continued in the Weft Indies till the conclufion of the war), when he took a very confiderable prize, mounting thirty guns, bound from Martinique to Breft. From the time of his experiencing this fuccefs, till the ceffation of hoftilities, he was employed by commodore Littleton in watching the motions of a fmall force which the enemy had contrived to collect at Carthagena. When the peace of Utrecht took place, Mr. Vernon quitted the Jerfey, but, in 1714, was appointed to the Affiftance, of fifty guns, one of the fleet ordered to the Baltic under fir John Norris; he continued in this fhip four years,

but

but the fervices on which he was employed have very
little interest to excite our attention, for they extended no further than his ship being one of the fleet
which convoyed king George I. to Holland in 1716,
and having afterwards proceeded to the Mediterranean,
where he continued for the fpace of two years. From
this time during a period of twenty-one years, he took
upon him no other command than that of the Grafton,
a third rate, of feventy guns, fent under the orders of
fir Charles Wager to the northward, for the purpofe
of co-operating with the Danifh fquadron, and counteracting the hoftile defigns of Ruffia againft the peace
of Europe. During a confiderable part of the interval juft alluded to, he ferved as reprefentative in
parliament for the town of Ipfwich, near which he
poffeffed no inconfiderable landed property. Being a
man of great natural abilities, and poffeffed of a fluent
and ftrong, though coarfe, and fometimes improper
mode of delivering his fentiments, he was confidered by
minifters, to whom he was conftantly in oppofition, at
leaft as one of their moft difagreeable antagonifts. It
was natural, therefore, for them to feize, with fome
degree of avidity, the earlieft opportunity of removing him, by any means in their power, from their
immediate prefence. He had a natural impetuofity in
argument, not to be reftrained by prudence, fo that
he was not unfrequently betrayed into affertions men
of greater deliberation would have hefitated to make.
In one of thefe paroxyfms of oratory, after arraigning
moft bitterly the torpid meafures of adminiftration,
againft which there was, in all probability, a ground of-

complaint

complaint too well founded, he·proceeded, in very
,ſtrong terms, to inſiſt on the facility with which the
moſt valuable and formidable of the Spaniſh poſſeſſions
in the Weſt Indies, might be reduced under the dominion, of Britain.   In particular, he aſſerted, not
only that the ·town of Porto-Bello might be taken by
a force not exceeding ſix ſhips of the line, but that he
himſelf was actually ready to hazard his life and reputation, by undertaking ſuch an enterprife, which he
would·anſwer with both, ſhould terminate in ſucceſs. .

· This haſty, and, perhaps, in its origin, far from ſe-
rjous opinion, was inſtantly and eagerly cloſed with by
adminiſtration, and Campbell ſtates, "that the mi-.
niſter embraced this opportunity of acquiring ſome
popularity, and, at the ſame time, of removing a troubleſome opponent in the houſe of commons." He
adds, on· what authority we know not, " that it was
generally imagined the miniſter was not without hopes
that Mr. Vernon might diſgrace himſelf and his party,
by not ſucceeding in ·the· adventure." He was accordingly advanced·to the rank of ·vice-admiral of the
blue, on the 9th of ·July 1739, which, being his firſt
appointment as a flag-officer, it is very evident he was
conſidered as a perſon retired from the ſervice, and
would, in all probability, have continued ſo, had not
the debate, which produced his ſudden propoſal, taken
· place. The whole of the requiſition he had made, was
complied with, as ſoon as he cloſed with the offer of
accepting· the·command.   He accordingly hoiſted his
flag on board the Burford, of ſeventy guns ; and, ſuch
·was the, expedition ıuſed in collecting and equipping
                                                    the

the ships intended to be placed under his orders, that, in eleven days*, from the time of his being appointed a vice-admiral, he was enabled to put to sea. The delays he encountered during his passage, from adverse winds and calms, were extremely severe and distressing; few voyages, perhaps none, either before, or since that time, were ever so tedious: upwards of three months being consumed ere he reached Port Royal, the place of his destination. All possible alacrity, however, was used by the vice-admiral on his arrival, to remedy, as much as might, then, be in his power, the inconvenience to which he had been subjected. The whole squadron being refitted, and revictualled, for the projected expedition, in the short space of thirteen days, he sailed from Jamaica on the 5th of November, with the following ships; the Burford, of seventy guns (the flag-ship), captain Watson; the Hampton Court, of the same force, commodore Brown and captain Dent; the Worcester, of sixty guns, captain Main; the Louisa and Strafford, of the same force, captains Waterhouse and Trevor; and the Norwich, of fifty guns, captain Herbert. Contrary winds retarded his arrival at Porto-Bello till the 20th,

* The force under Mr. Vernon, when he sailed from Spithead on the expedition against Porto-Bello, consisted of four ships of seventy guns, three of sixty, one of fifty, and one of forty. Of these he left three of seventy guns, the Lenox, Elizabeth, and Kent, to cruise off cape Ortugal, for thirty days, in hopes that they might fall in with the azogues ships, which were daily expected in Spain, ordering them to return to England at the expiration of their cruise. He also stationed the Pearl, of forty guns, to cruise for three months, between Lisbon and Oporto, so that the force he carried to the West Indies consisted only of five ships.

and, being apprehenfive of driving too far to the eaftward, fhould he continue under fail during the night,
he came to an anchor about fix leagues from the fhore.
Early in the morning on the 21ft he got under weigh,
and worked into the bay with the fquadron, which was
led by commodore Brown, in the Hampton Court, the
admiral himfelf being in the centre. The attack of
the Iron fort, which particularly defended the entrance, commenced as the fhips could work up, and
was conducted by the feveral commanders with fo
much fpirit, that the Spanifh foldiers, in feveral parts
of the fort, very foon flew from their guns, nor could
they be prevailed upon, by all the rhetoric of their
officers, to return to their duty.

The vice-admiral, obferving this defertion, made the
fignal for the boats of the different fhips to land the
marines and feamen, who were ordered to hold themfelves in readinefs for that purpofe. There was, indeed, much fpirit but little prudence, in the above order, for, as yet, no breach was made, and, if the enemy
had behaved with any degree of refolution, the affailants
would, in all probability, have feverely repented their
temerity. Providence, however, frequently favours the
attempts of the brave, even though they are alloyed by
rafhnefs. The failors having, with that fpirit of impetuous enterprife which is fo much their characteriftic,
fcaled the wall of the lower battery, affifted the foldiers
in afcending after them, and, without further difficulty,
took poffeffion of the fortifications, on which, their
former defenders precipitately taking to flight, they immediately hoifted Englifh colours. There ftill remained

2   an

an interior, and higher work in poſſeſſion of the enemy, but that part of the garriſon, which, at the beginning of the aſſault, conſiſted, in the whole, of about three hundred men, ſeeing the irreſiſtable ardour of the aſſailants, and terrified alſo at the flight of their comrades, hoiſted the white flag, as a ſignal of ſurrendering at diſcretion. The Gloria caſtle, which more immediately defended the town, now began to fire on the Burford, being the ſhip moſt expoſed, as thoſe which had worked in, ahead of the vice-admiral, had fallen to leeward. That ſhip fortunately, however, ſuſtained no other damage than a ſlight injury to its fore-topmaſt, notwithſtanding the fort continued its fire till night. Mr. Vernon returned this cannonade with briſkneſs; and one of his ſhot having paſſed over the fort above-mentioned, and through the houſe of the governor, he was ſo intimidated by that, in addition to the preceding events, that, early on the next morning, he propoſed articles of capitulation, for the town and all its dependencies, which were ſigned and concluded in the courſe of the ſame day.

Thus was this important conqueſt effected with an eaſe, and expedition almoſt unprecedented; and contrary, perhaps, to the expectations of the vice-admiral's friends, or the hopes of thoſe who were of the oppoſite deſcription. Though we muſt, on one hand, pay the higheſt tribute, not only to the admiral himſelf, but the gallantry alſo of thoſe he commanded, yet we cannot but, on the other, confeſs, that the irreſolution and want of ſpirit, on the part of the defenders, contributed, almoſt in an equal proportion, to facilitate

the

the conqueft. The news of this fuccefs was received in England with a degree of ecftacy fcarcely to be defcribed; mothers even taught their children to lifp out the name of Vernon as an hero, whofe deeds ftood far beyond all competition; and, by one fingle action, he acquired an univerfal popularity, which other men, not fo fortunate, have in vain offered the lefs dazzling, but, perhaps, not lefs valuable actions of a long and well-fpent life, without being able to obtain. His conduct to the Spaniards after the above conqueft was effected, although lefs fpoken of by his moft zealous admirers, was not lefs worthy of applaufe than that which had more efpecially attracted their notice. He difplayed a moderation, a tendernefs and humanity for the conquered, truly confonant to the character of a brave man, poffeffing a great and generous mind. Influenced by his authority and example, the conduct, both of the Englifh failors and foldiers, rather refembled that of friends than conquerors; while a ftriking contraft to that behaviour was difplayed by the crews of two large Spanifh guarda-coftas, and a floop of war, which were then lying in the harbour, who fpent the night preceding the furrender in plundering the inhabitants, and committing outrages not exceeded by thofe experienced from an ill-difciplined and ferocious army, on the capture of a town by actual affault. Mr. Vernon was not flow in rewarding the merit of his people, having generoufly diftributed among them ten thoufand dollars in fpecie, which had arrived for the payment of the Spanifh garrifon, a few days before the town was taken.

Another

Another circumſtance, which redounds highly to the vice-admiral's honour, muſt not be omitted. Knowing that ſeveral of the factors, and other perſons employed under the South-Sea company, had been very unjuſtly ſeized, rigorouſly treated and impriſoned, he wrote, immediately after the ſurrender of Porto-Bello, to the reſident of Panama, in whoſe cuſtody they were, inſiſting, in very ſtrong and peremptory terms, on their immediate releaſe; and, the Spaniard, not chooſing to irritate a conqueror, whoſe rapid ſucceſs he had ſo lately beheld with diſmay, endeavoured to pacify him, by immediately cauſing the perſons he demanded to be conducted to Porto-Bello. The joy of the nation had a better foundation on the ſeveral circumſtances attending the conqueſt, than the mere act of wreſting a poſſeſſion, in itſelf little valuable, from the hands of the enemy. The harbour of Porto-Bello was the principal rendezvous of the Spaniſh guarda-coſtas, which had for ſuch a ſeries of years committed depredations, little ſhort of actual piracy; and there was no ſmall degree of ſatisfaction, as well as national juſtice, in cauſing an enemy to feel the firſt exertion of Britiſh reſentment, on the very ſpot from whence Britain had been moſt inſulted. As it never was intended by government to retain poſſeſſion of their new conqueſt, the vice-admiral immediately proceeded to take on board the different ſhips of the ſquadron, all the cannon, ammunition, and ſtores, that were worth removal, and to deſtroy the remainder, together with the fortifications. Theſe different ſervices being completely effected by the 13th of December, Mr. Vernon ſailed on that

T 3   day

day for Jamaica, where having arrived in fafety, he immediately began to refit, and revictual his fhips in preparation for a new expedition.

These duties being accomplished, the vice-admiral failed from Port Royal on the 23d of February 1740, and arriving off Carthagena, bombarded that city for three days, a fpecies of attack in itfelf little calculated to reduce a place, or caufe any other effect than that of infulting and terrifying an enemy. Mr. Vernon failed for Porto-Bello on the 10th of March, and again quitted it on the 22d, having refitted his fmall craft, and completed the water of his fquadron. The next object of his attack was the caftle of St. Lorenzo, fituated at the entrance of the river Chagre, a few leagues diftant from Porto-Bello. The Strafford, which was at that time the admiral's fhip, having fprung her fore-topfail yard when going in, could not come to an anchor till ten o'clock at night, by which time the fire of the fort was confiderably reduced, although it continued to refift till the morning of the 24th. Campbell cenfures rather warmly Mr. Vernon's conduct in not fhifting his flag, and going on board the leading fhip, immediately on the above accident taking place. There does not, however, appear to be any real ground of complaint on the above occafion ; the object of attack was, in itfelf, remarkably infignificant, capable, in all probability, of being reduced, though with more trouble and difficulty, by a fingle fhip of the line ; and the gallantry of the vice-admiral, which muft be admitted by all, to have been moft confpicuous on a former occafion, cannot fuffer any impeachment, by

fo

so trifling a mistake in duty, on one of such inferior consequence. The castle, having, as just mentioned, surrendered on the 24th, the admiral proceeded, as he had done at Porto-Bello, to remove
all the ordnance and stores that were of any value.
These being shipped, together with 4300 bags of Pe-
ruvian bark, and several other articles of merchandise
found in the custom-house, he next began to demolish
the fort. This being laid completely in ruins, the
admiral ordered two guarda-costas, which he found in
the harbour, to be destroyed, and once more returned
to Porto-Bello, where he arrived on the 1st of April.
The remainder of the year was consumed in services
so little important as not to merit notice.

The easy reduction of Porto-Bello, had determined
administration, to send out such a reinforcement to the
West Indies, as should enable Mr. Vernon to attack
the most formidable settlements of the Spaniards in the
new world. An armament, consisting of twenty-five
sail of the line, under the command of sir Chaloner
Ogle, with a proportionate number of frigates, and a
large fleet of transports, having on board upwards of
ten thousand land forces, was accordingly dispatched
from England, to join the vice-admiral. The land forces
were commanded by lord Cathcart, a nobleman of
high character, and great experience in military affairs; but, unfortunately for the expectations of his
country, he died soon after his arrival in the West
Indies, and the command devolved on general Wentworth, an officer without experience, resolution, or
authority; and utterly unqualified for the important

T 4   post

poſt of a commander in chief. The reinforcement
from England joined Mr. Vernon at Jamaica on the 9th
of January 1741, and the fleet under his command
now confiſted of thirty-one ſail of the line. This armament, the moſt powerful which had ever appeared
before that time in the American ſeas, ſailed from
Jamaica, on the 28th of January. The vice-admiral's
firſt objeci was, to proceed off Port Louis, in the iſland
of St. Domingo, in order to aſcertain the ſtrength and
intentions of a French ſquadron, which was ſuppoſed
to be at anchor in that harbour, and againſt which the
admiral thought it 'neceſſary to be on his guard, as
he had good reaſon to believe the diſpoſition of the
French cabinet was unfavourable to the intereſts of
Great Britain. On the 12th of February he arrived
off the iſland of Vache, about two leagues from Port
Louis, when he learnt that the French armament had
ſailed for Europe, being greatly diſtreſſed for want of
proviſions, and by a dreadful mortality raging on board
their ſhips. On this intelligence it was reſolved, in a
council of war, conſiſting of the two admirals, and generals Wentworth and Guiſe, that the fleet, after having
taken in water and wood in the bays of Tiberoon, and
Donna Maria, ſhould proceed from thence, direcily to
Carthagena, which they reſolved to attack vigorouſly
both by ſea, and land.

The fleet anchored on the 4th of March, in Playa
Grande Bay, where the vice-admiral having made the
neceſſary diſpoſitions for landing the troops, and con-
ducìing the attack, iſſued the neceſſary inſtruciions to the
rear-admiral and captains of the ſquadron. On the 9th,
Mr.

Mr. Vernon, with his own division, and that of fir Chaloner
Ogle, followed by all the transports, got under weigh;
and brought to off the fort of Bocca-Chica, which
defended the entrance of the harbour. The first succeſ-
ceſſes of the aſſailants promiſed a ſpeedy, and honourable termination to their enterpriſe. In leſs than an
hour, the enemy was driven by the fire of the ſhipping
from the forts of Chamba, St. Jago, and St. Philip;
which mounted in all forty pieces of cannon, and in
the evening a detachment of grenadiers being landed,
took poſſeſſion of them. The next day, the regiments of Harriſon and Wentworth, and ſix of marines,
were landed without oppoſition, and by the 15th, all
the artillery, and ſtores of the army were brought on
ſhore. The following day, the general having informed the admiral that his camp was much incom-
moded by the enemies' fire, from a faſcine battery on
the weſt ſhore, or Barradera ſide, captains Watſon and
Boſcawen, having under them captains Laws and
Coats, with three hundred ſoldiers, and a detachment
of ſailors, were ordered to deſtroy it. This party was
ſurpriſed at their landing by a maſked battery of five
guns, which immediately began to fire on them, but
which they ſoon got poſſeſſion of. From thence they
proceeded to ſtorm the battery in queſtion, which they
ſoon made themſelves maſters of, with inconſiderable
loſs, notwithſtanding it mounted twenty twenty-four
pounders, and was defended by a proportionate number
of men. Having ſpiked up their cannon, and deſtroyed their platform and carriages, the detachment
returned, with ſome priſoners, to the fleet. On this
occaſion,

occafion, Mr. Vernon was" fo pleafed with the bold-
nefs and fpirit evinced by the feamen, that he rewarded
each of the common men with a dollar. This
fuccefs was an inexpreffible relief to the army, and the
general began to bombard Bocca-Chica, againft which,
on the 22d, he alfo opened a battery of twenty twenty-
four pounders. On the 23d, commodore Leftock was
ordered in, with five fhips, to batter the caftle on the
weft fide ; which fervice he performed with the greateft
bravery, though expofed to a very hot fire, by which
lord Aubrey Beauclerk, commander of the Prince Frederic, was killed. A tolerable breach being made in
the caftle, the general determined to carry it by affault,
and accordingly the neceffary preparations were made
for that purpofe. On the 25th, at midnight, the
troops marched to the attack, and no fooner entered
the breach, than, to their great furprife, the enemy fled
from the caftle without firing a gun. Captain Knowles,
obferving the confufion and difmay of the Spaniards,
immediately concerted the ftorming of Fort St. Jo-
feph, which was deferted with fimilar precipitation.

The enemy, alarmed at thefe fucceffes, prepared to
fink fome of their fhips in the channel, in order to
prevent the nearer approach of the hoftile fleet, which
Mr. Vernon perceiving, ordered the feamen to board,
and take poffeffion of as many of them as they
could. This could not be carried fo fpeedily into
execution, but that the enemy had time to fink the
Africa, and Don Carlos, two feventy gun fhips, and
fet fire to the St. Philip, of fixty guns, which blew up.
The feamen, however, boarded, and took poffeffion of
the

the Gallicia, of eighty guns, the Spanish admiral's ship,
and succeeded in bringing her off. They next proceeded to cut the boom, that was moored acrofs the channel; and on the following day, the admiral, with several
of the ships of war, warped into the inner harbour.
Fortune continued to favour the affailants; and the Spaniards abandoned first the ftrong fort of Caftillo-Grande,
and about the fame time deferted fort Manzanella, on
the oppofite fhore. After furmounting fo many impediments, with fuch facility, after forcing fo narrow
a channel, and of fuch difficult accefs, defended by a
ftrong caftle, three forts, a boom, four fhips of the
line, and two batteries, it need not be wondered that the
befiegers entertained the moft fanguine hopes of their
final fuccefs, and thought that little remained but to
take poffeffion of Carthagena. A fhip was accordingly difpatched to England to that effect, and public
rejoicings took place over the whole kingdom, fcarcely
inferior to what might have been expected, had intelligence been received of the complete reduction of the
place. The vice-admiral undoubtedly was perfuaded,
after the difficulties he had overcome, that Carthagena
muft inevitably fall; but he had formed his opinion
too haftily, and was deftined to experience the mortification of a very ferious reverfe of fortune.

In the early part of April, the troops became fickly,
and died in great numbers, and no good underftanding
fubfifted between the general and the vice-admiral. The
cordiality which, though never very ardent, had hitherto fubfifted between the commanders in chief, was
now totally at an end, and each feemed more eager for
the

the difgrace of his rival, than zealous for the honour
of his country. The only place that remained to
complete the conqueft of Carthagena, was Fort St.
Lazar, and as the enemy were daily throwing up new
works, and making all poffible preparations to defend
themfelves, the general, who was feverely reproached
by the vice-admiral for his inactivity, determined to attempt carrying the place by ftorm. This refolution
was formed, without confulting Mr. Vernon; and generals Blakeney and Wolfe protefted againft it as a
rafh and fruitlefs meafure. As thefe experienced officers had foretold, the enterprife completely failed; and
more than fix hundred men, the flower of the Britifh
army, were killed in the attack. The befiegers now
gave up all hopes of being able to reduce the place;
and the rainy feafon fet in with fuch violence, as rendered it impoffible for the troops to live on fhore.
They were therefore reimbarked, after the vice-admiral
had made an unfuccefsful attempt to bombard the town,
and the armament returned to Jamaica, having loft in
the attack, and by ficknefs, upwards of three thoufand
men. The fortifications which had fallen into the
hands of the Englifh were deftroyed, under the directions of captains Knowles and Bofcawen, and the damage done to the Spaniards was fuppofed to amount to
half a million fterling.

The fleet arrived at Jamaica the 19th of May, and
the re-equipment of the fhips immediately commenced.
The utmoft diligence being exerted, the vice-admiral,
who had received orders from England to retain no
greater force with him, than was abfolutely neceffary

for

for the protection of Jamaica, or to cover such trivial
desultory expeditions as could be undertaken, without
any material hazard, detached commodore Lestock for
Europe, with eleven ships of the line and five frigates,
putting at the same time, under his protection, the
homeward-bound fleet: other ships were ordered out
to different stations, where it was supposed they might
render the most effectual service against the enemy; and
the vice-admiral himself, with sir Chaloner Ogle, put
to sea on the 1st of July, with a force consisting of
eight ships of the line, one of fifty guns, twelve frigates, fire-ships, and small vessels of war, having under their convoy a fleet of forty transports and store-
ships. It had been previously determined, in a general
council of war held at Jamaica on the 26th of May, to
make an attack on St. Jago, in the island of Cuba, as
soon as the fleet and army should be put in a proper
condition to undertake such an expedition. This post,
which was at best of no very great importance, though
considered as a preliminary step to the conquest of the
island itself, was to be first attempted. But, as if success
would have been too certain, if sought for by the means,
on ordinary occasions deemed necessary to ensure it,
it was, as though determined to put as much to the
hazard as possible, resolved to land the troops at a
distance upwards of sixty miles, over land, from
St. Jago, instead of assaulting the place itself, which
being of no very great strength, would, in all probability, have fallen an easy conquest, to the cordially
united abilities of Mr. Vernon, and general Wentworth. The troops were landed on the 18th, and, as

the

the vice-admiral was himself thoroughly satisfied the complete conqueſt of the iſland was as good as effected, by that ſingle effort of hoſtility, he immediately changed the name of the port, which he had thus taken poſſeſſion of, without oppoſition, from Walthenham, to Cumberland Harbour. The news of this ſtep was immediately tranſmitted to Britain, where, with that ardent and ſanguine enthuſiaſm ſo natural to Engliſhmen; it was conſidered as the certain forerunner of the moſt important advantages.

A very ſhort time convinced them of the extreme folly of this deluſion ; general Wentworth, after having continued on ſhore till the 5th of October, totally inactive, except his having ſent out ſmall reconnoitring parties, ſhould be conſidered as one of the greateſt efforts of a warlike mind, on that day informed Mr. Vernon, that he feared it would be impoſſible for him to penetrate by land. This opinion was confirmed by a council of war, compoſed of land officers only, held on the 9th, and after continuing in the ſame camp for ſix weeks longer, equally inactive, the troops reimbarked on the 20th of November, returning diſpirited, and in a condition very unlike that of conquerors, to the ſame port, from whence they had ſailed a few months before, vainly flattering themſelves with the hope of effecting a complete conqueſt of all the Spaniſh Weſt Indies.

Mr. Vernon, after his return, did every thing in his power to render the force, under his particular command, as ſerviceable as poſſible, againſt the enemy.

By

By his prudent difpofition, aided by the activity of
the different commanders, a confiderable number of
prizes were made, both of force and value. On the
15th of January, a long-expected reinforcement of
two thoufand marines arriving at Jamaica, under
convoy of two fhips of fifty guns, and a frigate,
the hopes of obliterating from the memory of their
countrymen, all their former difgraces and difappointments, appeared once more to revive in the
hearts of the few brave furvivors. Before the conclufion of the month, it was refolved, in a council of
war, to land at Porto-Bello, and marching acrofs the
Ifthmus of Darien, to attack Panama, a rich town,
fituated on the South Sea. Two months, however,
unavoidably elapfed, before the fleet was in a condition to fail. At length, every difficulty being overcome, the admiral put to fea about the middle of March,
with eight fhips of the line, five fmaller veffels, and
forty tranfports; having on board a corps confifting
of three thoufand effective men, befides a body of
five hundred negroes, raifed for the expedition, by
governor Trelawny, who himfelf accompanied it.
The armament anchored in the harbour of Porto-
Bello, on the 28th, and the Spanifh governor having
immediately on difcovering the fhips, marched for
Panama, with all the force under his command, which
confifted of only three independent companies of Spanifh troops, and two of mulattoes, the vice-admiral was
fanguine enough to think no obftacle now remained
that could prevent the troops from commencing, and
continuing

continuing their march unmolefted, to the defired object of attack.

It appears that Mr. Vernon, on this occasion, placed greater confidence in the promifes and refolves of a council of war, than they truly feemed to have deferved. He was not yet fufficiently taught by the event of the former expedition, to doubt of fuccefs, where it depended on marching a body of troops, for fo confiderable a diftance in an enemy's country; a country too, remarkably unfavourable, and, indeed, deftructive to European conftitutions. The admiral was a man moft undoubtedly poffeffed of a very ftrong and intrepid mind, of a temper habituated to a contempt of difficulties, thinking that no obftacle was infurmountable, when oppofed by fpirit and activity; but with the nature of the operations of an army, acting at a diftance from his fhips, he certainly could be but little acquainted, and was, perhaps, too apt on fome occafions, to attribute a prudential attention in the general, to the lives of his foldiers, as the effect of timidity. The ill fuccefs which attended every enterprife undertaken during this ill-fated expedition, is a convincing and irrefragable proof, that a want of perfect harmony and good underftanding, is perhaps, more deftructive to public fervice, than any other want that can occur in it.

The fanguine and eager temper of the vice-admiral, received a dreadful fhock from the refolution of a fecond council of war, compofed of land officers only, held immediately after the landing of the troops. The advanced feafon, the force of the army reduced by ficknefs, and the feparation of feveral of the tranfports with troops, added to a report, that the garrison of Panama had received a confiderable reinforcement, independent of the force, which had retired from Porto-Bello, were deemed reafons unanfwerable for not purfuing the expedition any further. Mr. Vernon was far from fatisfied with the conclufion drawn from fuch premifes, but was reluctantly obliged to fubmit to an opinion he held in utter contempt. The army reimbarked, and failed from Porto-Bello early in the month of April, but did not reach Jamaica till the 15th of May, where the whole force remained inactive during the time he continued to command on that ftation. Miniftry were at length convinced of the extreme impropriety, of continuing two men poffeffing fuch jarring tempers, any longer in the fame command. An order of recal, which had been often folicited, in vain, on the part of the vice-admiral, was fent out by captain Fowke, in the Gibraltar frigate; and that veffel arriving at Jamaica on the 23d of September, the vice-admiral failed for England, on the 18th of October, having refigned his command to fir Chaloner Ogle.

Mr. Vernon, after his arrival in England, continued to be unemployed till the year 1745, but in the interim, was, on the 9th of Auguft 1743, advanced to be vice-admiral of the red. His retirement appears to have been compulfive, and borne with a very confiderable degree of impatience, as appears by the following letter written by him to Mr. Corbett, who was at that time fecretary to the board of admiralty.

VOL. II.　　　　U　　　　" SIR,

" Sir,   *Nacton, June 30th, 1744.*

" As, we that live retired in the country, often content ourſelves with the information we derive from
newſpapers on a market-day, I did not ſo early obſerve the advertiſement from your office, of the 23d
of this month, that, in purſuance of his majeſty's pleaſure, the right honourable the lords commiſſioners of
the admiralty, had made the following promotions
therein mentioned, in which I could not but obſerve,
there was no mention of my name among the flag-
officers, though by letters of the 10th inſtant, you
directed to me as vice-admiral of the red, and (by their
lordſhips' orders) deſired my opinion on an affair for
his majeſty's ſervice, which I very honeſtly gave them,
as I judged moſt conducive to his honour, ſo that
their lordſhips could not be uninformed that I was in
the land of the living.

" Though the promotions are ſaid to be made by their
lordſhips' orders, yet we all know the communication
of his majeſty's pleaſure, muſt come from the firſt lord
in commiſſion, from whom principally, his majeſty is
ſuppoſed to receive his information, on which his royal
orders are founded; and as it is a known maxim of our
law, that the king can do no wrong, founded, as I
apprehend, on the perſuaſion, that the crown never
does ſo, but from the information of thoſe, whoſe
reſpective provinces are, to inform his majeſty of the
particular affairs, under his care; the firſt ſuggeſtion,
that naturally occurs to an officer, that has the fulleſt
teſtimonies in his cuſtody, of having happily ſerved
his majeſty in the command he was intruſted with,
                                                       to

to his royal approbation is, that your firſt commiſſioner muſt either have informed his majeſty, that I was dead, or have laid ſomething to my charge, rendering me unfit to riſe in my rank in the royal navy, of which, being inſenſible myſelf, I deſire their lordſhips would be pleaſed to inform me in what it conſiſts, having both in action and advice, always to the beſt of my judgment, endeavoured to ſerve our royal maſter with a zeal and activity becoming a faithful and loyal ſubject, and having hitherto received the public approbation of your board. I confeſs, at my time of life, a retirement from the hurry of buſineſs, to prepare for the general audit, which every Chriſtian ought to have perpetually in his mind, is, what can't be but deſirable, and might rather give me occaſion to rejoice, than any concern, which (I thank God) it does very little; yet, that I might not by any, be thought to be one that would decline the public ſervice, I have thought proper to remind their lordſhips, I am living, and have (I thank God) the ſame honeſt zeal reigning in my breaſt, that has animated me on all occaſions, to approve myſelf a faithful and zealous ſubject and ſervant to my royal maſter. And, if the firſt lord commiſſioner has repreſented me in any other light to my royal maſter, he has acted with a degeneracy unbecoming the deſcendant from a noble father, whoſe memory I reverence and eſteem, though I have no compliments to make to the judgment or conduct of the ſon, &c. &c.

" *To Thomas Corbett, Eſq.* " EDWARD VERNON."
Secretary to the Admiralty."

It

It has been frequently remarked, by the moſt ſaga-
cious obſervers on the economy of the human ſyſtem,
that few better opportunities can occur of procuring
an exact portrait of the mind, than a critical examination of an epiſtolary correſpondence. In no inſtance,
perhaps, was this remark ever more correct than in
the caſe of Mr. Vernon. In the foregoing, as
well as the ſubſequent letters, which will be preſently
inſerted, every mental feature is delineated with as
much correctneſs as that of the viſage could have
been, by the hands of a Gainſborough, or a Reynolds.
While we find, on the obverſe, courage, magnanimity,
and a truly honeſt zeal for the ſervice of his country,
indelibly ſtamped, on the reverſe of the medal, we
lament being obliged to own the lineaments of ungo-
vernable paſſion, ſarcaſm, pride, and improper contempt, traced by an equally bold, and maſterly hand.
Whether the preceding letter, with three or four
others of a ſimilar nature, which Mr. Vernon amuſed
himſelf with writing, were the actual and immediate
cauſes productive of the effect, we cannot pretend to
aſſert, nor whether his conſtant arraignment of the conduct of miniſters, and his daily reprobation of them,
in his capacity of a member of parliament *, induced
them to make terms with him, were ſecrets, known

---

* After having been in 1727, choſen repreſentative for Pearhyn in
Cornwall, and at the commencement of the enſuing parliament for Ipſwich, he was, in 1741, elected member for Portſmouth, though at that time
abſent. This honourable proof of his popularity was conferred on him, in
conſequence of his ſucceſs at Porto-Bello. In the enſuing parliament, he
retuned to the ſtation he before held, of repreſentative for Ipſwich.

only

only to the parties concerned. Minifters, kept their.
own counfel, becaufe they were afhamed, perhaps, of
their own pufillanimity; and Mr. Vernon on his part,.
had too much honour, even in his moft violent mo-
ments, to utter a fingle word, that could lead to the
difclofure of any *private* negotiation. All that is certain is, that he was, on the 23d of April 1745, promoted to be admiral of the white fquadron, and appointed to command the fleet, ordered to be equipped
for the North Sea, in confequence of the impending
invafion of Scotland, in favour of the pretender. It
was at one time in contemplation, to have appointed
him prefident of the court-martial, affembled for the
trials of the admirals Mathews, Leftock, and the reft
of the officers accufed, of being concerned in the mifcarriage off Toulon ; but this idea was prefently abandoned, and we muft confefs, not improperly, when
we confider the impetuous temper of the worthy admiral, which appeared but little calculated for a ftation,
requiring fo much patience, coolnefs, and deliberate
judgment.

In the month of Auguft, he had his flag flying on
board the St. George, in Portfmouth harbour ; but his
fquadron being foon afterwards equipped, he removed
into the Norwich, and failed for the Downs, where
he continued, the intervals of cruifing excepted, during
the greater part of the enfuing winter. This period
of his command was perhaps the moft interefting of
his whole life; and it is but bare juftice to his memory to confefs, no man could have been more diligent,
or more fuccefsful in that particular fervice, to which
the neceffities of his country called him. The prudent

difpofition

difpofition of his cruifers totally prevented the introduction of any important fuccour, and the ferment,
as well as fear of that part of the nation, fartheft removed from the fcene of action, was confiderably
allayed, by the firm confidence all ranks of people
placed in the circumfpection, and diligence of this very
popular character.

This was truly the zenith of his glory, and a continued propriety of conduct might have enfured to him
that lafting fame, which neither the obloquy of party,
nor the envious malice of hiftorians attached to it,
would ever have been able to traduce. It was not,
however, in the nature of Mr. Vernon, to be content
with acquiring honour by the ordinary methods. His
impetuofity had affumed a power of acting, on all occafions, independent of every control or oppofition; and
this principle, which never failed to difplay itfelf in
every tranfaction of his life, was, in all human probability, the bane of that fuccefs, which his own gallantry, had it remained pure, and unalloyed, would
not have failed to have procured, on every occafion
where it was exerted.

The admiral failed from the Downs on a cruife, the
latter end of December, having his flag on board the
Monmouth, of feventy guns, with three fhips of
fifty, two of forty, five frigates, and fifteen tenders,
the greater part of them privateers, which the admiral
had taken upon him to retain in the fervice. The
demon of popularity had infected him, and fome very
new and extraordinary regulations, which, in confequence of that mania, he had taken upon him to make,
being difapproved of by the board of admiralty, produced

duced a remonſtrance on their part, and a paſſionate reply on that of Mr. Vernon. He returned to the Downs in a very few days afterwards, and ſtruck his flag; which he never again re-hoiſted, he himſelf not chooſing to ſubmit to the trammels of rules, regulations, and common uſage, and adminiſtration not being over-anxious, to intruſt a command with a man, whom they found they muſt never preſume to contradict. The admiral, as is cuſtomary in all political diſputes, was extremely violent; he appealed to the public; and, as his laſt reſort, burſt forth into paper attacks on the meaſures of adminiſtration, and the immediate conduct of miniſters to himſelf. The people read; ſome few pitied, and thought him an injured man; a greater part more ſeriouſly judging his caſe, from his own ſtatement, condemned him; but by far the greateſt number turned from the diſpute, as a matter, in which they felt no ſort of concern.

As a proper illuſtration, as well of his gallantry, as his iraſcibility, we ſhall venture to ſubjoin the following letters; we truſt the ſingularity of them will obviate any idea of their being tireſome, and although many parts of them may be reprobated by the cool, and diſpaſſionate claſs of mankind, yet there are others which may be conſidered valuable precedents for the conduct of a man, when the object at ſtake is either the honour of his country, or himſelf.

" SIR, *Norwich, in the Downs, December 30th.*
" As for the intelligence I have procured laſt night, of the enemies having brought away from Dunkirk great numbers of their ſmall embarkations, and many

U of

of them laden with cannon, field-carriages, powder, shot, and other military stores, the Irish troops being marched out of Dunkirk towards Calais, general Lowendahl, and many other officers, being at Dunkirk, with a young person among them they call the Prince, and was said to be the second son of the Pretender; and, as I can't but apprehend they are preparing for a descent from the ports of Calais and Boulogne, and which I suspect may be attempted at Dungeness, where many of my cruisers are in motion for; I have some thoughts of moving to-morrow with part of my ships, if the weather should prove moderate for a descent. I thought it my duty, for his majesty's service, to advise you of it; and I desire you will communicate this, my letter, to the mayor of Deal, and that the neighbouring towns should have advice for assembling for their common defence; and my cruisers signals, for discovering the approach of an enemy, will be their jack flying at their topmasthead, and firing a gun every half hour, and to desire they will forward the alarm.

"I am, Sirs,

"Your humble servant,

"E. VERNON."

"To John Norris, Esq. at Deal Castle,
or to the Mayor of Deal in his absence." —.

Extract of a Letter from Admiral Vernon to the Secretary of the Admiralty.

"I could not but be under some surprise what could be meant by the expression in your letter, of having kept all my great ships in the Downs, and employed only

only my frigates for gaining intelligence, while the
enemy's ships have paffed backward and forward between Oftend, Dunkirk, and Calais, at their leifure,
without hindrance or moleftation. I cannot conceive
where you have picked up fuch intelligence, fo contrary to what is the fact, as my former letters have
related to you, to inform your lordfhips of, viz. That
among other frigates employed on fuch fervices were
the Eagle, York, and Carlifle, which have been, ever
fince the 11th of December, acting under my orders
only, though your letter, Sir, mentions them as privateers, as if they were acting under their own orders. Within that time, I muft repeat it now, five
galliot hoys have been taken coming from Havre de
Grace to Boulognë, and fent into Dover ; and of thofe
coming from Dunkirk going to Calais, a dogger, laden
with five pieces of cannon, feveral field-carriages,
one hundred barrels of gunpowder, and other military
ftores, has been fet on fire, and feen to blow up in
the air, by captain Gregory, who was with them in
a cutter, on that fervice ; two of their fhallop fifhing-
boats funk, twelve others of them chafed on fhore,
and three, with cannon and military ftores, brought
into Dover. A Calais dogger privateer has been
taken, of fix guns and fifty men, thirty-one of which
I have on board the Princefs Louifa, and have defired
vice-admiral Martin to give himfelf the trouble of ex-
amining fome of them, to try if better intelligence cannot be procured from them, than what captain Hill
has been able to gather from them, which you had
enclofed in my yefterday's letters, as you have had of
the

the twelve fail of ſhips chaſed.from within two leagues
of Calais back into Dunkirk road, by the Sapphire and
Folkſtone, one of which they chaſed on ſhore upon
the ſands, and the pilot would not venture ſo near as
the captain took upon himſelf to do.   Surely theſe are
inſtances of the enemy's having been watched much
cloſer than could have been expected in this winter
ſeaſon; and what are the large ſhips I have kept in
the Downs? the Norwich and Ruby, two fifty-gun
ſhips; for, till the arrival of the Monmouth and Falkland, I have had no other.   I thank God, by a prudent
conduct, the enemy have been prevented from ſailing,
either from Dunkirk or Oſtend, for this month paſt,
and none of his majeſty's ſhips have been ſhipwrecked
by any imprudent diſpoſition of them ; ſo that I think
I have acted prudently and ſuccefsfully to his majeſty's
ſervice, though in many of your letters I have been
treated as if I had done neither.   As to my reaſons for
mentioning the counties of Kent and Suſſex to be my
province, I have ſome letters of yours that mention it
to me as ſuch, in which it appears to me pretty fully
expreſſed.   I ſhall always ſerve my royal maſter with
a ſincere zeal for his ſervice, and with the utmoſt diligence, reſolution, and capacity that I am capable of ;
and, while my ſervices are approved of, I ſhall always
continue them with pleaſure ; but, if I am judged not
to have a capacity for it, as, by the ſtyle of your letter,
ſeems to be inſinuated, ſure it is the fault of a ſincere
zeal to ſay, that if you have thought of any one you
judge more proper for it, all that I deſire is, that
                                                  his

his majesty may be most effectually served, and I shall with pleasure resign my command I have to him.

"Captain Knowles has brought another letter of yours of the 23d; he is come to serve with me as a volunteer, and, as I, well know captain Knowles's zeal and activity for his majesty's service, his coming gives me a particular pleasure, as I shall be glad to advise with him for his majesty's service, and, at all times, ready to furnish him with any opportunity that he can suggest to me, for our royal master's service, and defeating the enemy's intention for invading his majesty's dominions. Their lordships will see my orders to vice-admiral Martin; I have strengthened his command with all the force their lordships have ordered, for watching the enemy's motions from Ostend and Dunkirk; and, as to the four ships lately arrived from Cape Breton, which, by their lordships' orders of the 23d, I am to take under my command, those I hope to meet withal in their passage here, and shall incorporate into my division upon my meeting with them, or detach a part of them to join vice-admiral Martin, as subsequent intelligence shall make necessary. Nothing either has, or shall be omitted for his majesty's service, that I can think of, or any one can suggest to me, to be most expedient for it, and you have always had copies of the orders I have issued for that purpose sent for their lordships' approbation.

"I am, Sir, &c.

Dec. 25th.   "E. VERNON."

Extract

Extract of a second Letter from the same to the same.

"This morning, captain Scot, of the Badger, came on board me, with a letter from vice-admiral Martin; and, though the vice-admiral has, as he says, sent you copies of them, yet, as the advice was sent to me, I choose to do the same.

"It could not but give me great pleasure to find the gentleman's letters from Holland entirely confirm the intelligence I have given their lordships, and to find that he thinks with me likewise, that my diligent exertion of my duty has even been said there to have frustrated their intentions of invading this part of the kingdom, this last full moon, of which nothing could give me greater pleasure than having rendered such effectual service to his majesty and my country, though I have been treated in that contemptuous manner in your letters. I have given captain Hill the orders you have enclosed a copy of, for his weighing with the first of the flood, for making a fresh inspection at Calais, this evening or to-morrow morning. As soon as the windward tide makes, I shall weigh with the squadron, and keep plying and exercising my ships in line of battle, and for being ready at hand on any advice of the enemy's motions, till I have but barely time for anchoring in the Downs before night, when I shall obey their lordships' commands, consign the command of the fleet to vice-admiral Martin, then strike my flag, and go on shore, pursuant to their lordships' orders.

"I am, &c.

Jan. 1*st.*   "E. VERNON."

Extract

Extract of a Letter from the same to his Grace the Duke of Bedford, First Lord of the Admiralty.

" As I am conscious I have done nothing ever justly to forfeit that good opinion, that engaged your grace to honour me with your patronage and friendship, I entertain too good an opinion of your grace to think I have not the continuance of it, notwithstanding the late incident of my being hunted out of my command, by the operative malice of some malicious and industrious agent, that is too well screened over for my being able particularly to discover him, and point out who it is, so that must remain to me a secret, till some happy providence, in course of time, may more easily discover it, not being, nevertheless, in my own mind doubtful but I can trace the original cause of it, and guess pretty nearly at who may be the concealed director of it. As the pen of the secretary of the admiralty conveyed these bitter shafts that were levelled at me, I thought it right to suggest that his pen might be tinged with a gall-flowing from his own mind, beyond the direction he might receive from it; from which I thought it my duty to acquit him, on a gentlemanlike apology, in regard to his office, which I was no stranger to its being his duty to obey, and on an assurance of a good will he had always professed, and I well know I had never given him occasion to alter the sentiments of a professed friendship for me.

" One of the occasions taken to justify this conduct towards me, has been, that I had, within the channel of England, on a ship's service being immediately

.. **wanted**

wanted for proceeding to fea, and being without a
gunner (certainly a neceffary officer for her defence),
and which I could not think myfelf juftified in permitting to go to fea without, prefumed, as it is called,
to warrant a gunner to her, for to proceed to fea in her,
as I judged it to be abfolutely neceffary for his majefty's fervice, and the defence of the fhip.

"Having now ftated the fact, my fentiments are,
that to fupport the neceffary command of the officer
the king had appointed, it was the government's intereft that the commander in chief fhould name all
officers that fell vacant, and has not been denied while
the depending fervice was effential ; but pretences have
been made from the admiralty, that the fhips were not
affembled, or not under orders, and as checks are in
their power, they have contradicted it, though always
to the prejudice of the crown's fervice; for, when the
people of the fleet fee their commander in chief can
neither fupport their pretenfions of merit, nor his own
authority over them; they muft naturally look after
thofe who are no judges of their fervice, and renders
the commander contemptible to the fleet. This power
is known to have been abfolute in the commanders in
chief in the Channel; and in one who has added honours to your grace's family ; and when that power
has been wanting, it has, I believe, been always found
prejudicial to the fervice of the crown, and profperity
of the kingdom.

"I fhall now only add, that I am at prefent detained
here; for having my baggage embarked for proceeding
to Harwich in one of the armed veffels vice-admiral

Martin

Martin has been so obliging as to affign me to carry it to my houfe on the Ipfwich river.

"I propofe, at prefent, being in London by Tuef-day or Wednefday night; whenever it is, I fhall be at your grace's door the next morning after my arrival, in order to pay my duty to your grace; and, after-wards, before I fet out for Suffolk (if it has your grace's approbation), to be prefented by you to pay my duty to his majefty. And the favour I fhall now defire of your grace is, that your porter may have orders from you, to let me in, if fuch a vifit be agreeable to your grace; and, if not, that I may be told fo, not to give an unneceffary trouble to you or myfelf.

"E. VERNON."

The reafon affigned by moft perfons for his fudden difmiffion from the fervice, and at fo critical a time, is, that it was in confequence of his majefty's fpecial command, becaufe he had written two pamphlets, in which he had inferted the letters of the fecretary of ftate, as well as thofe he had received from the board of admiralty. This we believe to have been the true caufe of his being ftruck off the lift of admirals, which was done on the 11th of April; but he himfelf volun-tarily, and, indeed, wilfully quitted his command three months before. From this time he lived almoft to-tally in retirement, troubling himfelf but little with public affairs. After a temperature of mind, for eleven years, which he would never have experienced had he continued a public character, he died in an

advanced

advanced age, at his feat at Nacton, in Suffolk, on the 30th of October 1757.

Of all men who have been fortunate enough to obtain celebrity as naval commanders, few appear to have taken greater pains to fully their public fame, by giving full scope to all their private feelings; yet, probably, owing to this, not very uncommon reason, he rose the greater favourite of fortune in the minds of the people, to that pinnacle of popularity, the height of which was indeed, great enough to dazzle, and distract the firmest minds; so that to the infirmity of human nature, may, in some measure, be ascribed that extravagance of conduct, which might otherwise be more condemned. To say he was a brave, a gallant man, would be a needless repetition of what no person has ever presumed to deny him. His judgment, his abilities as a seaman, are unquestioned; and his character, as a man of strict integrity and honour, perfectly unsullied. How must we lament then, that points so brilliant, should have their lustre dimmed by the dark shade of obstinacy, vanity, and intemperate folly! yet, when we really find these several heterogeneous qualities strangely mingled in one person, we should, thinking humanely of his failings, consider them as foils used to increase the lustre of the virtues which are set on them, and lament, that the brightest jewels which can adorn the human mind, should need such extraneous aid to render them most conspicuous.

VICE-

VICE-ADMIRAL RICHARD LESTOCK

WAS the son of captain Richard Lestock, who
served in the royal navy during the reigns of Charles
and James II. William III. and queen Anne. He
was promoted to be captain of the Fowey, which
was the first commission he ever held in that rank,
on the 29th of April 1706. He remained constantly
employed during the whole of the war, and, on
two different occasions distinguished himself most conspicuously; the first of these occurrences took place
in the month of December 1706, and the following
account of it is given by Campbell, Lediard, and other
historians of reputation: "On the 26th of December, captain Coney, of the Romney, having the Milford and Fowey in company, chased, and came up
with a French ship, called the Content, that carried
sixty-four guns; the captain of her, instead of attempting to fight the English ships, got, as soon as he could,
under the cannon of a little castle, about eight leagues
west of Almeria, where he kept as close as possible to
the shore. Captain Coney anchored before him, and

ordered the Milford, captain Stanhope, and Fowey, captain Leftock, to do the fame, the one ahead, the other aftern.   They plied their guns for about three hours very brifkly, and then the French fhip took fire, blew up, and was entirely deftroyed, with moft of her men."   The fecond opportunity took place in the year 1711, at which time he was captain of the Weymouth, one of the fhips employed on the Weft India ftation, under the orders of commodore Littleton, and among the prizes captured by him, while in that quarter of the world, was the Thetis, a French fhip of war, mounting forty-four guns, together with feveral others of inferior note, and fome armed veffels, equipped as cruifers, by private adventurers.

No mention is made of this gentleman's having held any command after the conclufion of the war, till the year 1717, when, being captain of the Panther, one of the fleet fent into the Baltic, for the purpofe of overawing the machinations of that ever-reftlefs character Charles XII. king of Sweden, he diftinguifhed himfelf extremely by the activity and diligence he difplayed in a cruife off Gottenburgh, and the capture of feveral veffels, equipped as privateers, which, had they not been thus prevented, might have effected confiderable mifchief againft the commerce of Great Britain.   The commander in chief particularly noticed his conduct upon this occafion, and ever afterwards continued to promote his intereft, as well as to fhew him every poffible mark of attention.   When, in the enfuing year, fir George Byng was fent into the Mediterranean, he recommended Mr. Leftock to the command

of

of the Barfleur, the ship on board which he himself hoisted his flag; and it is remarked, that his conduct most fully justified the good opinion entertained of him, by so able a commander. After his return to the Mediterranean, he was appointed successively, though not till after the accession of king George II. to the Princess Amelia, of eighty guns, and the Royal Oak, of seventy; the latter of which was, for two, or three years, employed as a guard-ship. After his quitting the latter command, it is supposed, though on what account is not distinctly known, that he withdrew himself from the service, for a time; several officers, among whom were the admirals Haddock and Ogle, having been promoted to flags, who were his juniors on the list of captains, while he himself experienced no such advancement. It is not improbable, say writers, that the remembrance of this circumstance, continually sharpened by the very violent impetuosity of temper he was known to possess, might have contributed to increase many extravagant points in his conduct, which his enemies may have represented, in rather too glaring colours, but which his warmest friends have never been able to refute, or defend.

Early in the year 1740, whether the idea of his having retired from the service be true, or false, he was appointed to the Boyne, of eighty guns, one of the fleet ordered on the expedition against Carthagena, under the command of sir Chaloner Ogle, who was sent to reinforce vice-admiral Vernon, to whose charge the supreme direction of the whole armament was confided; Mr. Lestock, soon after he was commissioned

to

to this ship, was promoted to be an established commodore, and to command one of the divisions. Common justice, indeed, required this advancement, which,
to speak the truth, was not adequate to the just claims
of promotion Mr. Lestock possessed. As a captain,
he was only three months junior, in respect to the date
of his first commission, to Mr. Vernon, the commander in chief, and he was two years senior to sir
Chaloner Ogle, under whose orders he sailed from
England; so that we rather apprehend, though such
fact is not sufficiently known to warrant the assertion
of it, that he had suffered some former suspension of
rank, either on account of an impetuous sally of
temper, or other complaint, preferred against him; on
the subject of which both historians, and biographers
have been silent. After the fleet had arrived at the
West Indies, and the necessary previous arrangements
were made, it proceeded, without delay, to the destined point of attack, and came to an anchor in the
bay of Playa Grande, on the 4th of March; but no
show of attack was made till the 9th. The commodore, with his division, was left at anchor, while the
other two squadrons, under Mr. Vernon, and sir Chaloner, proceeded to attack the several forts, and batteries, which defended the entrance of the harbour of
Carthagena. On the 23d, Mr. Lestock, with five ships
of his squadron, was ordered to get under weigh, and
attack the sea-front of the castle of Bocca-Chica, the
most formidable of all the defences the Spaniards possessed, the fort of St. Lazar, which was the citadel of
Carthagena, excepted. The commodore executed the
service

service allotted to him with the greateft activity and fpirit, but, apparently, with little other fuccefs, than that of having created a temporary diverfion, and thereby, in fome degree, facilitated the affault from the land fide. The attack was renewed on the following day, and with the fame kind of fecondary fuccefs, for the land batteries effected a breach during thefe combinations of affaults, which, having encouraged the Britifh to make the neceffary difpofitions to ftorm the fort, the Spaniards avoided the fhock, by evacuating their works, at the inftant the affailants were prepared to enter the breach. After the conclufion of this unfortunate expedition, in which Mr. Leftock does not appear to have been any otherwife concerned than as already related, he was ordered to return to England, with fuch fhips as it was confidered neceffary fhould be fent home, their affiftance being no longer wanted. He accordingly fhifted his broad pendant to the Princefs Carolina, of eighty guns, and having failed from Port Royal on the 20th of June, with a very valuable fleet of merchant-fhips under his convoy, conducted them in fafety to Europe, and arrived at Portfmouth the latter end of Auguft.

He was almoft immediately afterwards appointed to command a fquadron fent into the Mediterranean, where he arrived early in the month of February 1741-2, and ferved for a fhort time under Mr. Haddock. During this period, he is faid to have exhibited fome proofs of that impatient temper, and improper profeffional pride, which afterwards becoming infinitely more apparent, cannot but be condemned, even by thofe who

are

are fo warmly attached to him, as to infift no part of his conduct was ever injurious, or prejudicial to the caufe and interefts of his native country.

On the 13th of March following, he was promoted to be rear-admiral of the white, as he was, moreover, in fucceffion, on the 9th of Auguft, to be rear-admiral of the red; and, thirdly, on the 7th of December, to be vice-admiral of the white fquadron. A very curious circumftance is related, relative to the latter promotions, and may be depended upon as authentic: owing to fome delay, or accident, in fending out the official information of the firft, that of the fecond followed it fo foon, Mr. Leftock had his flag flying one day only as rear-admiral of the red; on the fucceeding morning he hoifted that of vice-admiral of the white: he was, at that time, on board the Neptune, in which fhip he continued while he remained in the Mediterranean. The health of Mr. Haddock rendering him unfit to fulfil the duties of his ftation, he was under the neceffity of foliciting his recall; and, having failed for England feveral weeks previous to the arrival of Mr. Mathews, who was appointed his fucceffor, the chief command of the fleet neceffarily refted with Mr. Leftock during that interval. Short as was this opportunity of difplaying the arrogant features of his mind, in colours more ftriking than he perhaps had ever before been able, he failed not to avail himfelf of it, in its utmoft extent. It is a ftrong indication, and, indeed, proof, of that too common human frailty, which, influencing the minds of men not poffeffed of principles moft truly noble, induces them to exact obedience in terms which politenefs, or, perhaps, decency can hardly excufe; although, if again they fhould themfelves be reduced to a fubordinate ftation, they know but ill how to bend, and conform themfelves, on any terms, to that behaviour their country's welfare, and the well-known principles of military regulation, unequivocally demand. Mr. Mathews, having arrived in the Mediterranean in the month of May 1742, affumed the chief command of the fleet, a circumftance which highly offended Mr. Leftock, who felt himfelf, according to report, much hurt at being fuperfeded. At their firft meeting, fay authors, a cloud of mutual difagreement appeared to lour inaufpicioufly on all fervices, which thefe gentlemen might hereafter be deftined to carry on in concert together. The firft caufe of this mutual diflike was noticed by Mr. Leftock in the fpeech delivered by him at the bar of the houfe of commons, in the month of April 1745: " When vice-admiral Mathews," faid he, " arrived from England, I not only faluted him myfelf, but I ordered all the fhips in the fleet to do it, and went in my boat out of the port of Villa-Franca, to meet him before he got in. Had he been of the royal blood I could not have paid him more refpect, or fubmiffion; in return to which, immediately on feeing me, before monf. Corbeau, the commandant of the county of Nice, and fome field-officers in the king of Sardinia's fervice, as well as a great many captains of the fleet, who were then on board of him, without any regard to decency, or good manners, my rank and reputation as an officer, he began with reprimanding me, telling me he was furprifed that, as I had been fo long in his majefty's fervice, I had not, yet learned to comply with his inftructions, in writing to him, and fending a frigate down to Gibraltar to him. I anfwered, that I had done both, and, if he had not received my letters, nor met with the frigate, it was not my fault." Notwithftanding this ominous appearance, the regular duties of the fervice continued to be carried on between thefe two gentlemen, without either reprehenfion, or recrimination on either fide, till the fatal encounter with the combined fleets in the month of February 1743-4, when, in confequence of the difapprobation of his conduct, entertained by Mr. Mathews, he was fufpended by that gentleman from his command, and fent home to England, under arreft, on board the Salifbury, a charge, of which tho following is the fubftance, being, at the fame time, preferred againft him by the admiral: " That he, not obeying his fignals, and falling too far aftern the night before the action, was incapable of affifting, by which the enemy efcaped : that he might have ftopped the rearmoft fhips of don Navarro's divifion, but neglected attacking them ; which fhips, coming up to attack the admiral, he was obliged to quit the Real, which he had difabled, and would otherwife have taken : that the vice-admiral had, on this occafion, vifibly facrificed the honour of his country, to gratify his private refentment : that while he nicely pretended to obferve the rules of difcipline, he fhamefully fet an example of defertion and cowardice; the neceffity of circumftances arifing from unforefeen events, is a fuperior

direction

direction to any standing rules: that it was the duty of a good officer, when he saw his admiral in danger, and so ill supported by his own division, to crowd all the sail he could carry to his assistance: that no possible plea can be offered for a man; who sees his commander exposed at a distance, without stirring to his relief: that the admiral was under the necessity of engaging as he did, otherwise he would have lost the opportunity of engaging at all, as the enemy's squadron were all clean, and could sail three feet to our one; and, though the admiral did his duty, by attacking the Spanish squadron (the only part of the enemy's fleet he could come up with), he had the mortification neither to be seconded by his own division, nor that of Mr. Lestock's, who was therefore justly chargeable with the disgrace of the day."

To the foregoing charge the vice-admiral presented a long detail, in the form of a journal, to the house of commons, on the 12th of March 1744-5, in which, among other circumstances, he stated the following, which appear particularly intended in exculpation of himself: "Sunday, February the 12th; about half an hour past one o'clock, the centre of our fleet being abreast of the enemy's rear, the Spanish squadron, our van was near abreast with their centre, while I and my division were left a great way astern, with little wind, a great swell, and a great probability of a calm; the rear-admiral, instead of being far enough ahead to attack the enemy's van, was, where the admiral should have been; the admiral, instead of being far enough ahead to attack the enemy's centre, was, where I should

have

have been; and I, inftead of being far enough ahead
to attack the enemy's rear, was left a great diftance
aftern.   In this difpofition, contrary to the fignal for
the line of battle then abroad, admiral Mathews, without hinting to me the leaft information of his defign,
bore down with the Marlborough upon the Spanifh
admiral, and began the engagement.   The admiral
was not long engaged before he left the Marlborough,
in the heat of action againft the Real, and her fecond
aftern, that lay upon her quarter.   The Norfolk engaged the Real's fecond ahead of her, which fhip foon
bore away out of their line.   The three headmoft fhips
of the Spanifh fquadron exchanged a broadfide in
paffing, at the headmoft fhips of the admiral's divifion,
but continued their courfe to the fouthward with the
French fquadron, making in all nineteen fhips.   The
Somerfet, Princeffa, Dragon, Bedford, Kingfton,
Guernfey, and Salifbury, engaged at too great a diftance the Poder, a Spanifh fhip, next to the Spanifh
admiral's fecond ahead, until the Berwick bore down
and gave her battle, to which fhip fhe afterwards
ftruck, being difmafted.   About two o'clock, the rear-
admiral Rowley, and the Princefs Caroline, got along-
fide of M. de Court, the French admiral and his fecond, and engaged them for fome time.   The Boyne
and Chichefter alfo fired at the French, but at too great
a diftance.   The three other foremoft fhips, the Naffau, Warwick, and Stirling Caftle, though there was
no fignal of direction to the contrary, did not engage
according to the fignal abroad, but kept their wind,
endeavouring to prevent the French (who had fo great
                                    a fuperiority

a superiority as nineteen against seven), from tacking and doubling upon them.

" Between two and three o'clock, the Marlborough's main and mizen masts were shot by the board; nevertheless she continued to make good fires upon the enemy, although she had no assistance from her neighbours in the line, that continued lying to windward, and firing at the ships in the enemy's rear, not within gun-shot. At four o'clock, the Dunkirk and Cambridge, being to windward of me, I fired a shot to windward of them, and made the Dunkirk's signal. A half-past four o'clock I tried to reach the sternmost ship of the enemy, and fired a broadside at her, but could not stop her from going ahead: she was before my beam, top-gallant sails lowered, only under her main and fore-topsails, with her mizen-topsail aback ; notwithstanding which she drew ahead of me, though there was very little wind, with so high a southern swell, that it was all that I could do to keep the ports open to fire the lower tier of guns. As soon as I fired, she returned it, then hoisted her top-gallant-sails, filled her mizen-topsail, and let fall her foresail, and bore away from me; I kept going down after her, until I found I should only be able to fetch into her wake. At this very time I observed the Anne galley fire-ship, with all her sail abroad, going down upon the Spanish admiral, who lay disabled with his stern to the Marlborough. The enemy, in the rear of the Spanish admiral, fired at the fire-ship, excepting the two sternmost ships, but their shot seemed to fall short of her. About five o'clock, the Anne galley fire-ship, without

being

being properly affifted, appearing to be very near the
Real, which fhip had fired feven or eight guns at her,
was prefently fet on fire, and blew up, without doing
execution. A great launch, full of men, was fent from
the Real, to take her, but fhe blew up before the
launch boarded her. At the fame time, faw rear-admiral Rowley, and his divifion, ftanding to the northward towards us, with the fignal out, for the fhips of
his divifion to bear down into his wake; and the
French fquadron, on the other tack, fo clofe after
them, that, their heads being turned towards us, we
could hardly diftinguifh them from one another.

"In this difpofition, when the fire-fhip had mif-
carried, and our van were making what hafte they
could to join our centre, with the French clofe after
them, in good order of battle, admiral Mathews hauled
down the fignal to engage the enemy, and the fignal
for the line of battle, and hoifted the white flag at the
flag-ftaff, on the fore-topmaft head, the fignal to give
over chafe; upon which I hauled down the fignal for
the line of battle, repeated the fignal to give over
chafe, and fhortened fail: when the French tacked
upon our van, they had it in their power, by their
great fuperiority, to deftroy it; but, though they ranged
within piftol-fhot of four, or five of our fhips, where
they could have raked them fore and aft, they did not
fire one fhot, but bore away to the affiftance of the
Spanifh fquadron. At half-paft five o'clock, the admiral made the fignal for the fleet to draw into the line
of battle ahead, which fignal I repeated. There was,
at this time, very little wind, and fo great a fwell, that,

with

with the loss of a good deal of room, it was all that the ships would wear. The admiral wore, and formed the line of battle on the other tack (the starboard, the same the rear-admiral was upon); leaving the Poder, the ship that struck, to be retaken by the French squadron, with the Berwick's lieutenant, and twenty-three of her men : so precipitate was our flight from the French, that there was not time to save the people." After other immaterial remarks, the vice-admiral continues, "At daybreak saw the enemy in the S. W. quarter, little wind about N. E. and one of our ships (which proved to be the Somerset), distant three or four miles, exchanging some shot with one of the enemy's ships, that was separated from their fleet. It received a letter from admiral Mathews, directing me, when he made the signal for the line of battle ahead of each other, to lead with my division, let it be with the starboard, or larboard tacks on board... At the same time sent my compliments to the admiral, by captain Long, with my opinion, that we should do nothing unless we engaged the enemy in a proper disposition of battle." To the narrative he subjoined the following observations:

"The account I have now given, is, to the best of my knowledge, judgment, observation, and belief, a faithful and true account of the disposition and proceedings of his majesty's fleet, and of the combined fleets (so far as my situation would allow), previous to, and after the engagement ; and, if in the delivery of it, I appear too minute, I must beg leave to inform this honourable house, that, in the course of this

inquiry,

inquiry, many incidents and accidents, small in themselves (and to gentlemen not properly well acquainted
with maritime affairs, appearing perhaps trivial), may
be attended with great, very great consequences, particularly in regard to myself, whose behaviour upon
that important occasion, must in some measure be justified, or condemned from them ; and although it has
been my misfortune, not my fault, to receive, what
I must humbly presume to call, a severe and undeserved censure of my conduct, in the engagement, yet
I am not without hopes, that when this inquiry is perfected, the gentleman, whose authority laid the present
suspension on me, will have reason to think, I did
not deserve it ; and I flatter myself no less, that when
all circumstances shall be laid before this house relating
thereto, with such evidences, as in a short time, I shall
be able to produce in support of them, that my conduct shall appear in a light, very different from what
my enemies have placed it, and not unworthy the
trust, the post, and duty of an admiral. My honour,
my experience, and long service, make an inquiry most
welcome to me, either here, or in any other place. It
is what I have long solicited for, and as the result of
it will give public satisfaction, I eagerly, and earnestly
attend to it, as the only means of having justice done
to myself, and to every other object of it."

To say the court-martial assembled to decide on the
case of Mr. Lestock, employed nearly six months in
the investigation of it ; in hopes that the length of the
deliberation might palliate the disappointment, it was
apprehended the public would feel, in consequence of
the

the decision not tallying with popular opinion, would perhaps be assuming too much. Certain it is, however, that the indignation which had been at first raised in the minds of the people, against the supposed authors of the miscarriage, had in no small degree subsided, ere the verdict of acquittal was given; so that the dying embers of general clamour, did not retain sufficient force to produce those flames, which had burst forth at the earlier stage of the business. In fine, the court-martial published their decision of honourable acquittal on the 3d day of June 1746, and in two days afterwards, Mr. Lestock was restored to his rank, promoted to be admiral of the blue squadron, and appointed to command a strong armament, which had been fitted out a short time before, with the intent of attempting the reduction of Canada. Such a variety of delays had, however, taken place in its equipment, that the French were enabled to send a force into the same quarter, infinitely superior to that of Britain, and completely competent to counteract any attempt, that might be made by her. The direction of the impending blow was immediately changed, it was aimed at a place, considered to be vulnerable, and the destruction of which would most materially have injured the dearest interests of France. L'Orient, the grand depot of its East India company, became the threatened spot; and the force of the armament sent against it, was considered fully adequate to the magnitude of the undertaking; it amounted to no less than sixteen ships of the line, eight frigates, and two bomb-ketches, together with a fleet of transports, sufficient for the con-

veyance

veyance of a land-force, amounting to nearly six thousand men, with their camp-equipage, artillery, and
different stores, required for the formation of the siege.
Although the attempt had been projected for a long
time, such a variety of delays took place in carrying
it into execution, that even those who had augured most
favourably of it in the beginning, entertained doubts
of its successful termination. At length, on the 14th
of September, the fleet sailed from Plymouth, and in
four days afterwards, came safe to an anchor, in Quim-
perley Bay, on the coast of Brittany; here too, as if
those to whom the execution of the design was intrusted, considered it had not even yet, been sufficiently
procrastinated, a delay of four days longer took place
ere any operations commenced, although it had been
evident to every person possessing the least discernment,
that the chief hope of success was founded on the effect
of a coup de main. _____
Late, however, as the season was, the wretched state
of the fortifications, and the insufficiency of the garrison, afforded the zealous, no slight ground of hope
that, although that mode of attack, which, if adopted
in the first instance, would, in all probability, have produced the instantaneous surrender of the place, had
been neglected, yet still the place would not be capable
of a long resistance, against so fine a body of men
as were prepared to attack it, if a serious assault should
once commence. Soon, however, did all these hopes
vanish, and a resolution was most unaccountably taken
of re-embarking the troops employed, at the very moment, when it is reported, the governor was engaged

in

in arranging the terms of capitulation, which he meant to propose, to the affailants, for himfelf, his troops, and the fortrefs they were placed to defend. Authors have fatirically remarked, that the troops re-embarked on the 28th, unmolefted by the enemy; but as if it was intended to make them fome recompenfe for having caufed fo vain an alarm, four pieces of cannon, a mortar, and no inconfiderable ftock of ammunition were left behind. Various attempts have been made to account for, and explain the caufe of this retreat; a retreat almoft unprecedented, when we take into confideration the feveral circumftances that accompany it. Moft people, but they are not friends of Mr. Leftock, infift that the general was induced to take this difgraceful ftep, in confequence of the want of co-operation from the fleet, it being a part of the plan of attack, that the admiral fhould force his way into the harbour, which fome have been bold enough to infift he never attempted.

Mr. Leftock is faid to have alledged in his defence, that the enemy had blocked up the entrance in fuch manner, as to render it impoffible for him to get in. To do the admiral proper juftice, it does not appear that his conduct really was the caufe of his failure, for if the operations of the army had been conducted with any energy, all extraneous affiftance would have been needlefs. The principal, and indeed only lofs fuftained by the enemy, in this expedition, was the deftruction of the Ardent, a fhip of fixty-four guns, driven on fhore, and burnt by the Exeter, on her paffage home, after a very defperate encounter. The fleet having

taken

taken on board the troops, and fuch ftores as the Englifh thought proper to preferve from falling into the hands of the enemy, quitted the coaft of France on the 8th of October, and arrived fafe, without having fuftained any lofs during the expedition. The miniftry was diffatisfied; the people murmured, but both were content, with reciprocally cherifhing their griefs, by relating them to each other, without taking any fatisfaction on the authors of them.

This was the laft command ever intrufted to Mr. Leftock, who did not long furvive the mifcarriage, dying on the 13th of December 1746, as fome fay, of mere chagrin at the above failure, or what is more probable, of rage, occafioned by that neglect and indifference, with which he found himfelf treated, and which his haughty fpirit was little able to brook. Of all men, who have been unfortunate enough in their conduct to render it the fubject of party controverfy, none appears to have been lefs qualified for fuch an undertaking than this gentleman; unconciliating in his manners, auftere when in command, reftlefs when in a fubordinate ftation, he had fewer friends than fell to the lot of moft men, and that number, which was gradually diminifhing, his behaviour never appeared capable of recruiting. His perfonal courage, we believe, to have been undoubted, even by his enemies; and his abilities were of a clafs, if properly directed, that might have raifed him to the pinnacle of fame, and effentially benefited his country. Confiding too much in them, and demanding both from his equals and fuperiors in command, a deference, which all men are

ready

ready gratuitoufly to offer, but pay moft reluctantly on compulfion, he found himfelf, on many occafions, in the irkfome ftate of being neither loved, nor feared. His life, however, affords this ufeful leffon to mankind, that neither abilities, nor gallantry, even when connected together, are fufficient to form a good, and revered commander, unlefs true benevolence of heart accompanies them.

ADMIRAL

ADMIRAL NICHOLAS HADDOCK

WAS the third, and youngeſt ſon of ſir Richard
Haddock*, knight, comptroller of the navy, and ſome-
time joint admiral of the fleet, in the reign of king
William III. Having, after the example of his parent, made choice of a maritime life, and entered into
the royal navy at a very early age, he was, after previouſly paſſing through the ſubordinate ſtations, with
the higheſt credit and reputation, when little more
than twenty years old, promoted to be captain of the
Ludlow Caſtle. This veſſel was one of thoſe ſtationed
to cruiſe in the North Sea ; and Mr. Haddock is ſuppoſed to have held no other command, or ſerved in
any other ſtation during the remainder of the war.
On the 30th of December, ſubſequent to his promotion, he had the fortune to fall in with two veſſels,
which had formerly been Britiſh frigates, called the
Squirrel and Nightingale ; but which at the time alluded to, were fitted out from the port of Dunkirk,
as privateers. Notwithſtanding the great ſuperiority

* See his life, vol. ii. page 3.

of

of their force to his own, captain Haddock hesitated not a moment in giving them chace; and having got up with the Nightingale, about eleven o'clock at night, compelled her to surrender, after a short action. The Squirrel, witnessing the fate of her comrade, while Mr. Haddock was necessarily engaged in securing the prize he had already made, was fortunate enough to effect her escape. After the conclusion of the war, this gentleman appears to have held no commission till the year 1717, when he was appointed to the Shrewsbury, of eighty guns, one of the fleet sent to the Baltic, under sir George Byng; and having removed from that ship into the Grafton, of seventy guns, immediately after his return to England, proceeded to the Mediterranean, in the ensuing spring, under the same admiral. He distinguished himself most conspicuously in the memorable action with the Spanish fleet off Sicily. His ship, together with the Orford, being excellent sailers, led the van of the British fleet into action. After having, for a considerable time, engaged the Prince of Asturias, of seventy guns, in which was rear-admiral Chacon, disdaining to waste longer time in securing a vessel so completely disabled, that it was very evident she must fall a prey to the next assailant, captain Haddock left her to the next ship that came up, and pursued one of sixty guns, which, during his preceding engagement with the Prince of Asturias, had kept up a very warm fire on his starboard bow. Historians have been unanimous in their praises conferred on the conduct of Mr. Haddock, and in the relation given of the encounter,

Y 3 the

the following very honourable mention is made of him : " The ship which fuffered moft with us, was the Grafton, the captain of which, though he had not the fortune to take any particular ship, yet was engaged with feveral. He behaved himfelf very much like an officer and a feaman ; and bade fair for ftopping the way of thofe four ships he purfued, which efcaped, not through his fault, but failure of wind, and his own fails and rigging being much fhattered." He continued in the Mediterranean, during the remainder of the war ; and, in conjunction with captain Winder, in the Rochefter, funk a Spanifh ship of war, mounting feventy guns, and alfo drove another, mounting fixty, afhore, in the bay of Catania. He alfo took feveral other prizes of confequence, in particular two tranfports, with fix hundred Swifs recruits on board for the Spanifh army.

Soon after the return of the fleet to England, captain Haddock was appointed in 1721, to the Torbay, of eighty guns, and retained the fame command, almoft without interruption, during the fpace of feven years next enfuing. He had acquired the higheft clafs of reputation, in refpect to diligence, nautical knowledge, and thofe peculiar qualifications, which are more particularly requifite to an officer, filling the ftation of captain to a commander in chief ; and on that account, moft probably, in preference to any other reafon, we find him feldom acting in any other capacity, from the time of his appointment to the Torbay, as juft related, until he himfelf became advanced to the rank of a flag-officer. No ftation can certainly

certainly reflect more honour on the character of a captain in the navy, than having received such a re-iterated species of appointment, even in the time of profound peace. It affords an indubitable proof that while the more active scenes of war on one hand, had established his character for gallantry, the poffeffion of every other, lefs brilliant, perhaps, though not lefs valuable qualifications, was confeffed by thofe great perfons, whofe names will ever be revered, as among the firft of Britifh heroes.

Almoft immediately after he had received his commiffion for the Torbay, fir Charles Wager hoifted his flag on board that fhip, as commander in chief of the armament, intended to be fent to Lifbon, to chaftife the infolence of the Portuguefe, who in breach of public faith, and the law of nations, had imprifoned and otherwife injurioufly treated two Britifh fubjects, Mr. Wingfield, and Mr. Roberts. The fubmiffion, however, of that impotent nation, obviated the neceffity of the fleet ever putting to fea. In 1726, as well as the two fucceeding years, the Torbay again bore the flag of fir Charles Wager, firft, when fent into the Baltic, as already related in the life of that admiral, to crufh the confederacy entered into againft the peace of Europe, between Spain and Ruffia, and afterwards, to Gibraltar and the Mediterranean, to punifh the infolence, and reprefs thofe hoftilities which the former of thofe powers had actually commenced. On the return of the fleet to England in the month of April 1728, the Torbay, being found unfit for further fervice, without undergoing a thorough repair, captain Haddock removed into his old fhip, the Grafton, one of thofe, which the

Y 4

apparently

apparently unfettled ftate of the political hemifphere,
rendered it prudent, fhould be kept in a conftant ftate
of equipment, againft any fudden emergency, but
which, during the two fucceeding years, never quitted
the fhores of Britain. In 1731, however, he accompanied fir Charles Wager to the Mediterranean, for
the purpofe of accommodating the difference between
the Emperor and Spain, and putting the infant Don
Carlos, in poffeffion of the territory bequeathed him,
by the duke of Parma. After his return from this
fervice, the Grafton was put out of commiffion, and
Mr. Haddock appears to have had no other appointment, during the time he continued merely a private
captain. On the 4th of May 1734, he was promoted
to be rear-admiral of the blue fquadron, and immediately afterwards hoifted his flag, on board the Namur
of ninety guns, being appointed third in command of
the armament, collected under the orders of fir John
Norris, at Spithead. No neceffity, however, occurred,
of ordering it to fea, during the courfe of the current
year; and, as a matter, which may be confidered as
one of courfe, no interefting event took place, with
refpect to Mr. Haddock, except his having been, on
the 16th of December 1734, appointed rear-admiral
of the white, and being, moreover, on the 2d of March
enfuing, advanced to the fame rank, in the red fquadron. Immediately after his latter promotion, the
fleet, which had been equipped during the preceding
year, failed for Lifbon, to protect the Portuguefe, from
a threatened invafion and attack, expected from Spain.
Its very appearance, however, terminated the difpute,

and

and the Britifh force returned home, after continuing fome time in the Tagus, with the pleafant reflection of having preferved public tranquillity, by the terror of its power, without being compelled to the actual exertion of it.

In 1738, the depredations of the Spaniards continuing, in fpite of every mild and pacific remonftrance, the Britifh miniftry were induced to require fatisfaction for fuch repeated infults and injuries; and, in order to give the greater weight to fuch an unpleafant demand, it was determined to difpatch Mr. Haddock, on the 22d of May, to the Mediterranean, with a fquadron of nine fhips of the line. The appearance of the Britifh fleet produced the fame effect on this occafion, that it frequently had done on others. The Spaniards immediately profeffed the warmeft difpofition to negotiate; but their piratical infults in the diftant parts of the world were not, as yet, in any degree reftrained. It was therefore judged neceffary to give ftill greater weight to the juft reprefentations of Britain, by ordering out a fquadron of four fhips of war, and three bomb-ketches, well provided with fhells, and other warlike ftores, to reinforce Mr. Haddock, who, by thefe, and other intermediate aids, which he had received, now commanded a fquadron, confifting of twenty-one fhips.

This powerful armament, together with the profpect of its continuing during the winter at Port-Mahon, as the Spaniards were given to underftand would be the cafe, produced no fmall effect upon their counfels.

counfels. The king of Spain ratified the preliminary articles of the treaty, but had artfully and furreptitioufly added fuch a number of reftrictions relative to trade, and the right of Britifh fhips to board, or vifit Spanifh veffels of any defcription, that the people of England, when informed of this piece of chicanery, contrived merely for the purpofe of gaining time, were unanimoufly clamorous, calling aloud for war, as the juft, and only means of obtaining true fatisfaction from thofe, who had aggravated infult, by impofition. To this end, Mr. Haddock was, among other commanders, in different parts of the world, ordered in the year 1739, to make reprifals on the Spaniards. In this fpecies of warfare, which, even confidered in a national point of view, affected them moft ferioufly, and fenfibly, he was remarkably fortunate. Among his prizes, were two fhips from the Caraccas, fuppofed to be worth two millions of dollars, befides feveral others of very great, though inferior value to the foregoing, and a confiderable number of privateers. In fhort, it is remarked by many hiftorians, that "no fquadron had for many years been fo fuccefsful." He continued on the fame ftation, during the year 1740, experiencing an uninterrupted repetition of the fame fpecies of good fortune. The Spaniards, not having it in their power, during that time to collect a naval force, fufficient to meet the Britifh fquadron in fair conteft, were compelled to confine their larger fhips, within the limits of their own harbours, and permit the ruin of their commerce to pafs on unmolefted,

and

and unrevenged, except, indeed, by the paltry casual captures made by their privateers, or some of their smaller ships of war, who were hardy enough to venture out. Mr. Haddock was not, however, totally occupied in this predatory kind of war, during the whole of the year 1740. His success had raised him to such a degree of reputation, and caused the people at large to enter into the war, with so much spirit, that the Spaniards exerted every nerve to raise a force sufficient to face him. By making a feint to recover the island of Minorca, they succeeded in drawing off Mr. Haddock, from before the port of Cadiz, and embraced that opportunity of slipping out, with nine ships of the line, and two frigates, which got into Ferrol, where other ships were ready to join them. Intelligence of these measures being received by the British ministry, Mr. Balchen was ordered out to reinforce him, with a squadron of six ships of the line. One of the principal objects of the expedition was, to intercept the assogue ships, as already related in the life of Mr. Balchen, which were daily expected from Vera-Cruz at Cadiz. This having failed, through the extreme caution of the Spaniards, and other ships being sent out to Mr. Haddock, so that he had a force sufficient to block up the enemies' fleet in the harbour of Cadiz, Mr. Balchen returned to England, leaving him again commander in chief on the Mediterranean station.

The events of the year 1741 were, towards the conclusion of it, in some degree more interesting, than those of the preceding had been. Mr. Haddock, who on the

11th of March, was promoted to be vice-admiral of
the blue, continued during the fummer, to block up the
port of Cadiz, and prevent the junction of the Spanifh
fhips there, with the Toulon fquadron, and a large
fleet of tranfports collected at Barcelona, for the purpofe of convoying a formidable army into Italy, intended for the attack of the queen of Hungary's dominions. So highly was the admiral efteemed, and
fo complete was the fatisfaction afforded by his conduct
in every department, that the Italian merchants, early
in the year 1741, addreffed the lords of the admiralty,
thanking them in the warmeft and handfomeft terms,
for the extraordinary protection afforded to their commerce, by the fquadron under Mr. Haddock; and they
paffed alfo a vote of thanks to the admiral himfelf,
prefenting him, as a more fubftantial proof of their
efteem, with a magnificent gold cup. Mr. Haddock
continued to keep the fea, cruifing between Cape
St. Mary, and Cadiz, till the beginning of the month
of November, when the tempeftuous weather compelled
pelled him to put into Gibraltar, to refit. The Spaniards had completed the embarkation of their troops
at Barcelona, to the number of fifteen thoufand men;
and on the 24th of November, the fquadron, commanded by Don Navarro, taking advantage of the
darknefs of the night, put to fea from Cadiz, in hopes
of getting through the Streights of Gibraltar, unob-
ferved; in this, however, they were difappointed. A
ftrong eafterly wind arifing on the morning of the 25th,
drove them back in fight of Gibraltar, and detained
them two days in that fituation; a favourable breeze
                                          then

then fpringing up, enabled them to effect a junction, off Malaga, with De Court's fquadron, from Toulon: Admiral Haddock was, in the interim, ufing every endeavour to refit his fquadron, which having, by almoft incredible exertions, effected by the 2d of December, he quitted the bay of Gibraltar, in queft of the enemy. In a few days he got fight of the combined fquadrons, which were drawn up in a regular line to receive him ; but, as he was bearing down on the Spaniards, and almoft on the point of attacking them, the French admiral, De Court, fent a flag of truce, with a meffage, to inform Mr. Haddock, " that as the Spaniards and French were at that time engaged in a joint expedition, he muft obey his orders, and protect his mafter's allies." Mr. Haddock immediately deemed it neceffary, on this extraordinary event, to call a council of war, as well on account of the nature of his inftructions, and the extreme delicacy of his fituation, as the great fuperiority of the combined fquadron, which confifted of near fifiy veffels of different defcriptions, while his own force amounted not to thirty. It was unanimoufly decided, that the fquadron fhould repair to Mahon, and wait there for the reinforcement which was expected from England, under the command of commodore Leftock. Before, however, this could arrive, the French and Spanifh fleets had repaired to Barcelona, and on the 24th of December, proceeded from thence to Italy, with a fecond embaikation of troops.

The vice-admiral was joined by Mr. Leftock on the 1ft of February, and made all poffible difpatch in

getting

getting ready for fea, in order to fcour the coafts of Italy, and prevent the introduction of any fupplies and reinforcements, for the Spanifh army, under the duke of Montemar. Before, however, the fleet was in a condition to fail, the vice-admiral was unhappily attacked by fo fevere an indifpofition, that he was, very reluctantly, compelled to refign the command of the fleet to Mr. Leftock, and return in the Roebuck, a forty-gun fhip, to England, where he arrived on the 26th of May. This illnefs of the worthy admiral's, is faid to have been of the moft melancholy and affecting nature, an extreme dejection of fpirits, occafioned, as fome infift, by mere chagrin, at not having had it in his power to ftrike fome fignal blow, which might eventually lead to the termination of the war. He never took upon him any command, after his return to England, but was, neverthelefs, moft defervedly promoted, on the 9th of Auguft 1743, to be vice-admiral of the white, and on the 7th of December following, to be vice-admiral of the red; and on the 19th of June 1744, he was farther advanced to be admiral of the blue. After having attained this very elevated rank in the fervice, and lived univerfally refpected, and efteemed by all men, he paid the debt to nature on the 26th of September 1746, being then in the 60th year of his age. His death being lamented by all, his memory has been traduced by none.

KENNETH,

KENNETH, LORD DUFFUS.

KENNETH Sutherland, lord Duffus, was the eldeſt ſon of James, ſecond lord Duffus, and the lady Margaret Mackenzie, daughter of Kenneth, third earl of Seaforth. The common, though honourable proverb, of Fortes creantur fortibus, et bonis, was never, perhaps, more fully exemplified, than in the hiſtory of this noble perſon. The great and illuſtrious family from which he was deſcended, yields to none in the whole kingdom of Scotland for antiquity; hiſtorians, making mention of thanes and earls of Sutherland, as ſoon as thoſe dignities were known there. The Sutherlands are ſaid to be ſprung from a warlike people, called the Moravii, who came from Germany in the reign of king Corbed I. and afforded him great aſſiſtance againſt the Romans. That monarch rewarded them nobly; and gave them large poſſeſſions in the northern parts, where they ſettled. From them the county of Murray had its name; and their poſterity became proprietors of all that large tract of country, now called Murray, Roſs, Sutherland, Caithneſs, &c.

The

The firſt immediate anceſtor of this family, noticed
by ſir Robert Gordon, of Gordonſtown, who has
written its hiſtory, is Allan, thane of Sutherland, a
man of high rank and conſiderable authority, who
flouriſhed in the reigns of Duncan, and Macbeth the
uſurper.   His eldeſt ſon, Walter, was created earl of
Sutherland by king Malcolm III. in the year 1067,
ſoon after he had obtained poſſeſſion of his throne, and
is mentioned among the firſt perſons in the kingdom,
who ever obtained that dignity.   The lord Duffus
was lineally deſcended from Nicholas, ſecond ſon of
Kenneth, ſixth earl of Sutherland, who, in the year
1360, obtained a grant from his brother William,
ſeventh earl of Sutherland, of certain lands; which
grant was afterwards confirmed by a charter under the
great ſeal, from king David Bruce, the ſaid lands being
erected into a free barony.   This Nicholas married
Mary, daughter and heireſs of Reynald de Cheyne,
with whom he received the lands and barony of Duffus,
which afterwards became the family title.   Douglas,
in his heraldic account of his lordſhip, ſtates briefly,
but at the ſame time ſomewhat incorrectly, " that the
genius of Kenneth, third lord Duffus, leading him to
a ſea-faring life, he ſoon acquired ſuch great ſkill and
knowledge in maritime affairs, that her majeſty, queen
Anne, gave him the command of the Advice, a fifty-
gun ſhip of war; in which ſtation, he ſo remarkably
diſtinguiſhed himſelf in ſeveral expeditions, that he
did honour to himſelf and his country by his conduct,
undaunted courage, and reſolution."   The fact is,
that having regularly paſſed through with the utmoſt

' honour,

honour, the feveral fubordinate ranks according to
the cuftomary routine of the fervice, he was, on the
7th of April 1707, promoted to be captain of the
Portfmouth frigate, and in confideration of that well-
earned reputation, which he had then gained, was
very quickly afterwards appointed to the Advice, a
fourth rate. His lordfhip's naval life was peculiarly
fhort, for he does not appear ever to have held any
command after he had quitted the Advice. Short,
however, as it was, it was marked with one of the
moft glorious actions that has adorned the page of
Britifh naval hiftory. In the month of June 1711,
he had the misfortune to fall in with a complete fquadron of French privateers, amounting to no lefs than
eight in number. The fyftem of warfare had, of late
years, become confiderably changed on the part of
France. The navy of Louis the fourteenth, had been for
a long time, and with very few exceptions, confined to
its own ports, by the vigilance of thofe commanders,
to whom the direction of the Britifh fleet was confided.
Private adventurers endeavoured, as much as poffible, to
remedy this misfortune, by fitting out veffels, not
merely intended to act againft the defencelefs fhips,
generally employed for commercial purpofes, but even
capable of attacking fuch lighter fhips of war, as
were in general appointed to protect them. Of that
clafs, were many in the fquadron, which attacked
the Advice, who mounting herfelf only forty-fix guns,
was actually inferior in apparent force, to many
individual veffels among thofe which affailed her.

VOL. II. Z The

The encounter took place off Yarmouth, and commenced, on one of the beſt ſailers coming nearly cloſe up to the Advice, but the enemy not thinking it ſufficiently ſafe, to engage her ſingly, ſhortened ſail, till the reſt of the ſquadron came up alſo. About half an hour paſt ten, five of them came cloſe alongſide, and hoiſted French colours ; about eleven; they engaged, moſt of them lying always upon the quarters of the Advice, relieving each other, while the reſt kept aſtern, ſo that they maintained a continual fire. In half an hour, the ſails of the Advice were torn to pieces, and not a brace, or bowline left. Her maſts were alſo much wounded, and the greater part of the ſhrouds cut ; however, lord Duffus continued the engagement, ſtill keeping his ſhip under way ; but the enemy plied their guns and ſmall ſhot ſo warmly, and overpowered him ſo much by their numbers and ſtrength, that he was, after a very vigorous defence, in which he himſelf received five balls in his body, and had two thirds of his people killed, or wounded, obliged to ſurrender. He was carried, according to report, with great triumph, into Dunkirk, where the captors moſt inhumanly ſtripped both the officers and private men, of their wearing apparel, and, had it not been for the kindneſs of the inhabitants, had left them in a great meaſure naked.

His lordſhip does not appear, after his return from captivity, to have been re-appointed to any other ſhip. In all probability, he retired into his native country, Scotland ; where, in the year 1715, he was ſo imprudent as to engage in the rebellion, but made

his

his escape beyond seas, and was attainted by parliament. He was, shortly afterwards, apprehended at Hamburgh, and committed prisoner to the Tower. An act of grace being passed in the following year, his lordship was included in it; nevertheless, having by his offence, not only forfeited his title and estate, but all hopes and pretensions to any future employment, in the line of his profession, he withdrew immediately after his release to Russia. He was received there a very welcome visitor, as might naturally be expected, when we consider the enthusiastic attachment of the Czar Peter to his navy, and his eagerness to entertain in his service all foreigners, whose judgment and experience he deemed likely to promote, or improve the darling object of his reign. He was, almost immediately after his arrival, honoured with the rank of a flag-officer, and was always held in the highest esteem. The particulars, and time of his death, are, on account of his having estranged himself from his native country, unknown.

A curious political circumstance has been remarked, arising out of the conduct of this nobleman, and that of his noble relative, the earl of Sutherland. The latter, as well as all his descendants, have constantly distinguished themselves in a most remarkable manner, by their steady attachment to the house of Brunswick, while lord Duffus appears as a misguided alien to the principles of his family, and relinquished fame, title, and fortune, in support of a visionary project, too shallow for any, but those men, who unfortunately

laboured

laboured under an infatuation, bordering on frenzy, to hope fuccefs from, and which, had it proved fuccefsful, would have been productive of the ruin, and downfall of their native country. The braveft, the wifeft, the beft of men, have, at different periods, fallen victims to political madnefs.

SIR CHALONER OGLE

WAS the descendant of a very ancient, and respectable Northumbrian family: of the earlier part of his services no mention is made, but we find him promoted on the 14th of March 1708, from being commander of the Wolfe sloop of war, to the rank of post-captain in the navy, by appointment to the Tartar frigate. He continued in the same vessel, which was principally, if not entirely, employed as a cruiser on the Mediterranean station, during the remainder of the war. In the occupation just mentioned, he met with some considerable success, having made prizes of two or three very valuable vessels; but, after the cessation of hostilities, is no otherwise noticed, than as having, in the year 1717, commanded the Worcester, a fourth rate, of fifty guns, sent, that season, with the fleet into the Baltic.

He very particularly distinguished himself, by the capture of Roberts, the pirate, and his whole squadron, in the month of April 1722, being, at that time, captain of the Swallow, a fourth rate, and cruising off the

coast

coaft of Africa, in fearch of the marauders, when he
received intelligence they were in a bay clofe to Cape,
Lopez. He immediately took every method poffible
to difguife the Swallow, fo that it might pafs on his
defperate antagonifts for a merchant-veffel. On ftanding in for the fhore, he difcovered the fhips he was in
queft of, the largeft being that commanded by Roberts himfelf, mounting forty guns, and the fmalleft
carrying twenty-four, were lying high up in the bay,
on their heel, cleaning their bottoms. Captain Ogle's
ftratagem was fo completely executed, that the pirates
were deceived into a belief, that the Swallow was an
unarmed fhip, or, at moft, a veffel of inconfiderable
force. Roberts, the commander in chief, made a
fignal for the only fhip which was in a condition for
immediate fervice, to flip his cable, and run out after
the Swallow. This mounted thirty-two guns, and
was commanded by one Skyrm, a man of much refolution and intrepidity. Captain Ogle pretended to fly,
and, in fhort, conducted himfelf through the whole of
this difficult bufinefs with fo much fpecious timidity,
that he decoyed the pirate to a diftance, at which the
report of the guns could not be heard by his comrades.
He then tacked upon his antagonift, and brought him
quickly to action ; but, although Skyrm himfelf was
wounded by the firft broadfide, fuch was the defpe-
ration with which his people fought, well knowing
the ignominious death, which awaited them if taken,
that they did not furrender till after an action of an
hour and a half's continuance. Captain Ogle, after
having taken poffeffion of his prize, hoifted the piratical

ratical colours over thofe of the king, and returned
to the bay, where he had left Roberts and his companion. Thefe having, in the interim, righted their
fhips, and being deceived by the plaufible appearance
of fuccefs, which Mr. Ogle's precaution had flattered
them with the hope of, immediately ftood out of the
bay, thinking to congratulate their companion on his
conqueft. Their joy, however, was of fhort duration,
for the Swallow, bringing their fhips to action, captured them both, after a conteft of two hours continuance, in which Roberts himfelf was killed. The
three prizes were carried into St. Thomas's, and the
prifoners to Cape Coaft Caftle, where they were tried.
Seventy-four received fentence of death, of which
number fifty-two were executed; the greater part of
them being afterwards hanged in chains along the coaft,
as a terror to future depredators of the fame clafs.

The conduct of captain Ogle, and the fuccefs which
attended it, was confidered fo highly redounding to
his honour, that, immediately after his return to England, that of knighthood was conferred on him; but
he does not appear to have accepted any fubfequent
command till the year 1729, when he was appointed
to the Burford, a third rate, one of the fleet collected
at Spithead, under the orders of fir Charles Wager.
With the fame admiral he again ferved in 1731, on
his expedition to the Mediterranean and Leghorn, being, at that time, captain of the Edinburgh, a fhip of
the fame force as the former. Except in the inftances
juft mentioned, he does not appear to have held any
other commiffion, previous to his advancement to the

rank

rank of a flag-officer. On the 11th of July 1739, he was appointed rear-admiral of the blue; and, having immediately hoisted his flag on board the Augusta, was, in consequence of the rupture daily expected to take place with Spain, ordered to proceed to the Mediterranean, as commander of a squadron, confisting of twelve ships of the line, fent thither for the purpose of reinforcing Mr. Haddock, who already commanded there, though with a force inadequate to the importance of the station. Nothing material took place during his abfence on this fervice, and, immediately after his return to England, he was fent out on a fummer-cruife, into the Atlantic, as third in command of the fleet under the orders of fir John Norris; an occupation equally unchequered with incident, as the former had been. On his return into port, on the approach of winter, and the confequent termination of the fummer cruife, he was ordered to take upon him the command of a confiderable armament, fitted out to reinforce Mr. Vernon, preparatory to the attack of the most confiderable of the Spanish fettlements in the West Indies. Having, accordingly, shifted his flag from the Shrewsbury, of eighty guns, to the Ruffel, of the fame force, he failed from Spithead on the 26th of October, at the head of a fleet, confifting of twenty-four ships of the line, one of fifty guns, feveral ftore and fire ships, and upwards of one hundred and fifty transports. They had fcarcely cleared the Land's End, when they were overtaken by a dreadful gale of wind; a circumstance which alarmed the whole nation for their fafety; but, though they did not perfectly

escape

efcape without injury; they fuftained much lefs damage than might reafonably have been expected, one
of the fhips of war being the only veffel forced back,
the tranfports, though fome of them were in a crippled
ftate, purfuing their voyage to Jamaica, where, after
having watered at the neutral ifland of Dominica, they
arrived, without farther accident, on the 9th of January 1741-2.

The feveral operations during the fiege of Carthagena,
have been already related at fufficient length; in the memoirs of Mr. Vernon; nor, indeed, does fir Chaloner appear to have been engaged, either in that, or any fubfequent expedition that took place, while he continued
to act under the orders of Mr. Vernon, more particularly than in carrying on the regular routine of fervice.
After the return of the vice-admiral to Europe, fir
Chaloner, who, on the 9th of Auguft 1743, had been
raifed to the rank of vice-admiral of the blue, and, fecondly, on the 7th of December following, to the
fame ftation in the white fquadron, was left commander in chief on the Jamaica ftation ; and, government being fenfible of the difadvantages, which had
attended a divifion of command between land, and fea
officers, endeavoured to remedy the inconvenience in
future, by giving the admiral an abfolute authority
over the marines, or any other foldiers that might be
embarked on board the fleet. His conduct gave the
moft univerfal fatisfaction, for a private letter, dated
at Port Royal, April 29th, 1744, beftows the following encomium on him : " The inhabitants of this
ifland begin to recover their fpirits ; the lofs of admiral
Vernon

Vernon is in a great measure compensated for, by the
vigilance and good conduct of sir Chaloner Ogle."
On the 19th of June 1744, he was advanced to be
admiral of the blue. He remained in the West Indies
till the following year, but neither the Spaniards nor
the French having any naval force for him to contend
with, and he himself having neither a land force sufficient to support, nor instructions to undertake any
enterprise against their settlements, the whole of the
period, during which he was commander in chief of
the above station, was consumed, merely in cruising
for the protection of commerce, except in the attacks
made on La Guira and Porto-Cavallo, in neither of
which sir Chaloner was personally engaged, they having been confided to a detachment of the fleet put
under the orders of commodore Knowles. Having
shifted his flag on board the Cumberland, he returned
to Europe, and arrived at Spithead, with three other
ships of the line, and a small convoy of merchant-
vessels, early in the month of June 1744. In the
month of September he was appointed president of
the court-martial assembled on board the London, in
the river Medway, for the trials of the admirals Mathews and Lestock, with the captains and other officers,
against whom different charges were made, relative to
the miscarriage in the action off Toulon. He continued to hold this station only till the conclusion of the
trials of the lieutenants, and captains. The court was
afterwards removed to Deptford, and sir Chaloner
Ogle was succeeded by rear-admiral Mayne.

After

After this time he does not appear either to have accepted any naval command, or to have appeared in any public station whatever. He was, on July 15th, 1747, advanced to be admiral of the white squadron; and, to the still higher rank of admiral of the fleet, on the 10th of July 1749. The latter advancement he did not long enjoy, dying some time in the year 1750.

If the services and expeditions on which this gentleman was employed, were not crowned with that brilliant success, which is not unfrequently the sole title that can be exhibited as a claim to popular favour, and to public distinction, (although that success may not have been earned, or absolutely acquired by the individual who arrogates it to himself), his merit is by no means to be depreciated on that account. On all occasions, where any personal exertion of gallantry became requisite, he was active, spirited, and brave. In situations where prudence, coolness, and circumspection were necessary, he was wary, diligent, and sagacious. If the applause he received was faint, censure, on the other hand, was totally silent; so that it might be truly said of him,

"'Tis not in mortals to command success,
But we'll do more, Sempronius, we'll deserve it."

COMMODORE

COMMODORE BROWN.

———————————

THIS gentleman is faid to have embraced a maritime life, and to have been introduced into the navy by the fpecial recommendation, and under the immediate patronage of fir George Byng, afterwards lord vifcount Torrington. This circumftance is related merely on the traditional report of his relatives; for, in refpect to the actual occurrences of his early life, the materials are fo extremely deficient, that even thofe, who, in the line of defcent, ftand neareft allied to him in blood, are totally unacquainted with his fervices and occupations, previous to his promotion, on the 18th of March 1709, to be captain of the Strombolo.

Neither during the remainder of the war, nor at any fubfequent period, previous to the year 1717, is any further mention made of him. Indeed, this dearth of intereft will appear by no means wonderful, when it is recollected, that for feveral years preceding the treaty at Utrecht, little, or no opportunity whatever was afforded to the moft enterprifing characters, of particularly diftinguifhing themfelves, otherwife than by the ftricteft attention to the very tame and languid

fervices,

fervices, on which they were feverally employed, and
after the ceffation of hoftilities, the want of intereft
confeffedly became increafed. During the long
fucceeding period that public tranquillity, with the
feweft exceptions, continued undifturbed, little other
information can be expected, than the mere detail of
the feveral commands that were, at different times,
beftowed on him. In 1717, he was captain of the
York, a large fourth rate, one of the fleet fent into
the Baltic, under the command of his friend and patron
fir George Byng. From this time till the year 1726,
there is a perfect chafm in the life of this gentleman;
but, at the time juft mentioned, he is known to have
commanded the Advice, one of the fleet ordered to the
northward, under fir Charles Wager, as he afterwards
did in the fucceeding year, the Oxford, of fixty guns,
under the fame admiral, who was fent into the
Streights, for the protection of Gibraltar, which had
been for fome months threatened, and was afterwards
actually befieged by the Spaniards. In 1731, he was
captain of the Buckingham, a third rate, one of the
fhips which it was deemed neceffary to keep in conftant readinefs for immediate fervice, and in which
Mr. Brown actually proceeded to the Mediterranean,
in that year, under the fame admiral as before (fir
Charles Wager).

No mention is made of this very worthy, and truly
brave man, after his return, till his appointment, about
the year 1738, to be commander of the Hampton
Court, in which fhip he was ordered, immediately
for Jamaica, where he commanded as fenior officer,

with

with a small squadron, till the arrival of Mr. Vernon, at the latter end of the year 1739. Previous, however, to this taking place, the Spaniards, having manifested strong and frequent indications of an hostile disposition, Mr. Brown resolved at last to retaliate on them, for insults so frequently repeated, and battered down a fort, which they were then erecting between the Matterfees, and the Havannah. Left it may be thought he acted with too much precipitation on the foregoing occasion; it may not be improper to observe, he acted not merely in conformity to his own feelings, but in strict obedience to instructions he received from England: for, as soon as it was foreseen a war was unavoidable, the British ministry took the proper measures for attacking the enemy in the West Indies, the South Seas, and every other part of the world, where they were thought to be most vulnerable. Orders were specially sent out to Mr. Brown, to make every possible reprisal, and neglect no opportunity of distressing the enemy, to the utmost of his power. Mr. Brown having joined the vice-admiral at Port Royal, on the 28th of October, the attack, and conquest of Porto Bello took place immediately afterwards. This having been already generally related, and at some length, it is needless to take notice of that event, otherwise than in such parts, as the commodore was more particularly engaged in.

"The attack of the Iron fort was led by the commodore, it being generally customary, in small squadrons, to assign that post of honour to the second in command. Unfortunately, when the ship came within

a cable's

a cable's length of the object of affault, it was fuddenly
becalmed by the high land to windward, and, before
the guns could be brought to bear on the enemy, was
expofed to a very fmart cannonade. As foon, however, as the fhip could get to its proper ftation, and
was brought to an anchor, it feemed, in an inftant, as
Campbell expreffes himfelf, a cloud of perpetual
thunder, and appeared to the reft of the fleet to be all
on fire. This may eafily be credited, if we believe,
and, as we have no reafon to doubt the affertion of the
fame author, that four hundred cannon fhot were fired
from that fhip in the fpace of twenty-five minutes.
All hiftorians are unanimous in beftowing the higheft
commendations on this very brave, and experienced
officer ; and there are not wanting thofe, who, with
much appearance of reafon on their fide, affert, without the fmalleft wifh of taking away from the merit
of the renowned, and popular Vernon, that the commodore contributed, in at leaft an equal fhare with
him, to this very fpeedy, and important conqueft.

After the reduction of the place, the demolition of
the Gloria caftle, and St. Jeronimo fort, were particularly committed to the commodore's fuperintendance
by the vice-admiral. After the fquadron returned to
Jamaica, and was refitted, and Mr. Vernon proceeded
to fea, with the intent of bombarding Carthagena,
and attacking fort Chagre, he left Mr. Brown to command at Jamaica, with two fhips of the line and two
frigates, a force confidered fully competent for the
protection of that ifland, from any cafual infult that
could be committed by cruifers, or effected by any
trivial

trivial operations in the line of *petite. guerre.* Mr.
Brown did not long continue in the Weſt Indies, having returned, in the courſe of the ſummer to England,
in the Diamond frigate, on board which ſhip he hoiſted
his broad pendant, as commander of the convoy to the
homeward-bound fleet. Almoſt immediately on his
arrival in England, he was appointed to act in his former ſtation of commodore, and accordingly hoiſted his
broad pendant on board the Duke, but was not fortunate enough to meet with any opportunity of adding to
his former laurels. On the promotion of Mr. Mathews to the Mediterranean command, in the month
of March 1741-2, the office of commiſſioner of the
navy, reſident at Chatham, which he had previouſly
enjoyed, became vacant. Mr. Brown was appointed
his ſucceſſor, and continued, till his death, which happened on the 23d of March 1753-4, to fill that ſtation,
with the ſame unblemiſhed reputation which had, in
the more active line of ſervice, attended all the former
employments he had ever received.

CAPTAIN

CAPTAIN ST. LOE.

We have been induced to give fome account of this gentleman, in confequence of a whimfical and entertaining anecdote in his life, which, at once, exemplifies both his fpirit, and ingenious turn of mind. He was appointed captain of the Valeur frigate, in the year 1713, and afterwards received feveral commiffions to veffels of the fame clafs, fo as to have remained, according to report, almoft conftantly employed, though in what particular fhips is unknown. In the year 1727, however, he was captain of the Ludlow Caftle, one of the veffels employed on the American, and Newfoundland ftation, and is mentioned as having prefented an addrefs to his majefty king George II. on his acceffion to the throne, from the inhabitants of Placentia, and other Britifh fettlements on the fouthern coaft of Newfoundland. Having repaired to Bofton, during the winter of the year 1728, for the purpofe of avoiding thofe difficulties, and dangers, which frequently attend veffels compelled to keep the fea in fuch inhofpitable latitudes, pending that inclement feafon, the ridiculous anecdote, already alluded to, took place. Hav-

A a ing

ing put into that port on a Sunday, and his wife, who
had refided, for fome time before, at that place, in the
eagernefs to fhew her affection, haftening to the fhore
to meet his boat, captain St. Loe, forgetful of the fanc-
tity of the place and day, moft *irreligioufly* prefumed
to falute her. He was immediately apprehended by
the conftables, and, after being confined all night,
was carried on Monday before the mayor; he was
fined, but refufing to pay it, was, for his contumacy and contempt of authority, fentenced to fit on
the gallows, a cuftomary punifhment .in that part
of the world for fuch delinquents, for the fpace of one
hour, during the time of change. This fentence was
put in execution, without the leaft mitigation. While
the captain fat in durance, the grave magiftrates admo-
nifhed him, to refpect in future the wholefome laws of
the province; and reverend divines exhorted him, ever
after to reverence and keep holy, the Sabbath day.
At length the hour expired, and Mr. St. Loe was fet
at liberty. As foon as he was freed, he, with great
feeming earneftnefs, thanked the magiftrates for their
correction, and the clergy for their fpiritual advice, and
confolation; declaring, that he was afhamed of.his paft
life, that he was refolved to put off the old man of fin,
and to put on the new man of righteoufnefs; that he
fhould ever pray for them, as inftruments in the hands
of God, of faving his finful foul.

. This' fudden converfion rejoiced the faints; after
clafping their hands, and cafting up, their eyes to
heaven, they embraced their new convert, and returned
thanks for being made the humble means of fnatching
.:. a foul

a foul from perdition. Proud of their fuccefs, they fell to exhorting him afrefh, and the moft zealous invited him to dinner, that they might have full time to complete their work. The captain fucked in the milk of exhortation, as a new-born babe does the milk of the breaft. He was as ready to liften, as they were to exhort : never was a convert more affiduous, while his ftation in Bofton harbour lafted; he attended every Sabbath day their moft fanctified meeting-houfe ; never miffed a weekly lecture ; at every private conventicle he was moft fervent and loud in prayer; he flattered, and made prefents to the wives, and daughters of the godly : in fhort, all the time he could fpare from the duties of his ftation, was fpent in entertaining them on board his fhip, or in vifiting and praying at their houfes. The faints were delighted with him beyond meafure, they compared the punifhment they had inflicted on him, to the voice from heaven, and their naval convert to St. Paul, who, from their enemy, had become their doctor.

Amidft their mutual happinefs, the mournful time of parting arrived. The captain received his recall : on this he went round among the godly, he wept and prayed, affuring them he would return, and end his days among his friends in the Lord. Till the day of his departure the time was fpent in regrets, profeffions, entertainments, and prayer. On that day, about a dozen of the principal magiftrates, including the felect men, accompanied the captain to Nantafket road, where the fhip lay, every thing being ready for failing. An elegant dinner was provided for them on board, after which many bottles and bowls were drained. As the blood of the faints waxed warm, the cruft of their hypocrify melted away; their moral fee-faws, and fcripture texts, gave way to double-entendres, and wanton fongs. The captain encouraged their gaiety, and the whole fhip refounded with the roar of their merriment. Previous to the arrival of the company, captain St. Loe had inftructed the firft lieutenant to get the anchor up without any noife or buftle, and fuffer the fhip to drop down quietly with the tide.

Proper care was taken to prevent the crew of the boat which had conveyed the faints on board, from noticing the alteration of pofition, by entertaining them very liberally between decks, while that inattention, which generally accompanies conviviality, prevented alfo the guefts in the great cabin from obferving it. In the midft, however, of their mirth, though not until the Ludlow Caftle had fallen down with the tide to a fufficient diftance for captain St. Loe's purpofe, it was difcovered, by one of the company, that the fhip was actually under weigh. Captain St. Loe was not without a plaufible excufe at hand, for not having, till that time, acquainted them with the circumftance. After a parting glafs had been recommended, and taken with the utmoft warmth of friendfhip by all parties prefent, the captain addreffed the mayor with great ceremony, telling him, that as he had never had the honour of introducing him to one of the moft worthy men, and able officers in his majefty's fervice, who then ferved under his command, he would, if his worfhip thought proper, do him that pleafure, as the laft he

fhould

fhould be able to confer for a confiderable time. The offer was accepted, and the introduction of the boat-fwain to the mayor, took place on the quarter-deck, with the greateft ceremony. After a recapitulation on the part of Mr. St. Loe, of the eminent fervices that had been conferred on him, and the obligations he owed to his worfhip, for having reclaimed his mind from wickednefs, by the punifhment of the gallows ; he concluded with faying, it was his intention to repay them with gratitude, if not fully, at leaft as well as his circumftances would permit ; and defired his friend, the boatfwain, to adminifter all the fpiritual comfort in his power, by beftowing on him thirty-nine lafhes, laid on with his beft art and force. Mr. St. Loe then bowed refpectfully, and took his leave. His worfhip's new acquaintance, immediately and moft ftrictly com-plied with the orders of his commander. In like manner each of the guefts were ferved, till the punifh-ment had been inflicted on the whole affembly ; Mr. St. Loe, in fucceffion, taking a very polite leave, and earneftly entreating the felect men to remember him in their prayers. They were then let down into the boat that was waiting for them ; the crew faluted them with three cheers, and the Ludlow Caftle failed for England.

Captain St. Loe, immediately on his arrival, per-fectly aware of the violence he had committed, related the tranfaction to fome powerful friends, connected with the admiralty, and requefted their advice. The confe-quence was, he was put out of commiffion, and his pen-dant ftruck ; from which moment the admiralty board,

A a 3   ceafing

ceafing to hold any civil control over him, the whole
of the affair was no longer cognizable, otherwife than
in a court of common law. This Mr. St. Loe eafily
contrived to avoid, by retiring, for a fhort time, into a
diftant part of the kingdom, until the faints and their
agents, incapable of difcovering his haunts, and finding themfelves held up to ridicule by all the reft of the
world, who were informed of the circumftance, gave
up all further purfuit, and fat down contented, refolved
to bear the ignominy, and the fmarts they had undergone, with all the ftoicifm of ancient philofophers.

In refpect to Mr. St. Loe, in the year 1731, he was
appointed to the Experiment, a fhip of twenty guns,
ordered to be equipped for the Weft Indies, to protect
the commerce of that part of the world, from the infults and depredations daily committed on it by the
Spanifh guarda-coftas. We find no mention made of
him after this time till the year 1745, when he commanded the Princefs Royal, a fecond rate. On the
15th of July 1747, he was put on the fuperannuated
lift, with the rank and half-pay of a rear-admiral, a
comfortable and honourable remuneration for his paft
fervices, which he enjoyed till his death, on the 28th
of December 1757.

HON^{BLE} WILL^M ROWLEY ESQ^R

Pub. Jan 1, 1800, by Edw. Harding 84. Pall Mall.

SIR WILLIAM ROWLEY.

ALTHOUGH few, or no perfons, can ever attain fo high a rank, as the fubject of the prefent memoir, and no one ever poffeffed a ftronger claim to popular notice and diftinction than himfelf, yet few have, on the other hand, been lefs fortunate in opportunities of raifing themfelves into celebrity. As a fingular, and, perhaps, unparalleled proof of this affertion, no public mention whatever is made of him from his firft appointment to be captain of the Bideford, on the 26th of June 1716, till his advancement to the rank of commodore, in the year 1742-3. This extraordinary circumftance is only to be accounted for, by fuppofing fome ftrange coincidence of events, which prevented his being appointed to any of the fhips included in the various armaments, fitted out during the period alluded to. This dearth of intereft, however, was merely accidental; it was his misfortune, and not his crime. The firft particular mention made of him, is, that in the month of December 1743, being then rear-admiral of the white fquadron, which was the firft flag he ever hoifted, he was ordered to the Mediterranean, as the

A a 4 commander

commander of a reinforcement to the armament previoufly employed on that ftation, under the orders of
Mr. Mathews. During the ever-memorable and difreputable encounter, between the Britifh fleet and the
combined force of France and Spain, in the month of
February 1744-5, he commanded the van divifion ;
but not the fmalleft particle of the difgrace then incurred, was ever imputed to Mr. Rowley, he having,
in the opinion of all perfons, as well prior to the commencement of the action, as during the continuance
of it, exerted himfelf, in every refpect, confonant to
the character of a gallant, and able officer. The
French divifion, under monf. De Court, which led the
enemy's van, manifefted the ftrongeft difpofition of
wifhing to avoid a clofe action. Their admiral would,
for a fhort time, lie to, with much apparent refolution ; but, whenever Mr. Rowley and his fquadron
approached him, he fet all his fails, and, from the
advantage of having his fhips juft out of port, and
clean, was enabled, for fome hours, to prevent the
Britifh fquadron from clofing with, and bringing him
to action. Thefe wavering and unfteady manœuvres,
were at laft, indeed, productive of the very confequence they were intended to avoid. The Spanifh
fhips, being heavy failers, M. De Court was obliged
to bring to for them, or they would otherwife have
fallen an eafy prey to the fuperior force of Mr.
Mathews.

Mr. Rowley, therefore, in confequence of the above
circumftance, clofed with, and began to engage the
French admiral and his fecond aftern, about two
o'clock.

o'clock. The encounter continued with the greateſt vigour and reſolution for near two hours; during which, he was very ably ſupported by captain Oſborne, in the Princeſs Caroline. M. De Court, finding, between three and four o'clock, that he had decidedly the worſt of the action, ſet his foreſail, and made off, leaving his two ſeconds to ſecure the retreat in the beſt manner they could. The conteſt with theſe ſhips did not continue longer than twenty minutes; when they alſo followed the example of their commander in chief. Theſe three were the only ſhips of the French diviſion which were engaged, the remainder keeping their wind, with intention to tack upon and weather, Mr. Rowley; a manœuvre they were prevented from carrying into execution by the leading ſhips of the van, which dexterouſly and attentively purſued the ſame meaſure. In the above action Mr. Rowley had eighteen men killed, and thirty wounded; a loſs which, conſidering its ſhort duration, very ſufficiently proves the vigour and ſpirit of the conteſting parties. Mr. Rowley continued in the Mediterranean after the above encounter, but, as it is well known, no ſubſequent engagement took place. On the 19th of June 1744, he was advanced to be vice-admiral of the blue; and admiral Mathews, having, on the 21ſt of Auguſt following, ſtruck his flag in Vado bay, reſigned the chief command of the fleet to him. The ſubſequent naval operations of that part of the world, appear, indeed, to have been principally confined to perpetual cruiſes, for the purpoſe of protecting the Britiſh commerce, by confining the enemies' fleets in port.

Nothing,

Nothing, indeed, can more ſtrongly prove the vice-admiral's ſuperiority, and ſpirited conduct, than his having, with numbers far inferior to the fleet, which France and Spain had it in their power to collect in that part of the world, ſailed from Mahon, in queſt of the enemy, who were timid enough to ſhrink from the conteſt, by continuing in port.

Mr. Rowley remained on the ſame ſtation till the year 1746, during the whole of which time the Britiſh flag continued completely triumphant in thoſe ſeas. The fleets of its enemies remained inactive; their commerce was annihilated; the petty Italian republics, who, under the maſk of neutrality, were baſe enough to afford all the inſidious aſſiſtance in their power, to the cauſe of France and Spain, not only trembled at his approach, but ſmarted under the juſtice of his puniſhment. Even the vain-glorious boaſt of thoſe ſtates, on whom it was inflicted, that the damage they ſuſtained was of trivial conſequence, reflected honour on his conduct, for it ſtood as a ſelf-evident truth to the whole world, that the complete deſtruction of the offending parties, was not owing to the want of power on the part of Mr. Rowley, but to his lenity in not exerting it. On the 23d of April 1745, he was advanced to be vice-admiral of the white ſquadron; but, after his return to England, as before ſtated, he never accepted of any naval command.

On the 15th of July 1747, he was advanced to be admiral of the blue, as he was, on the 12th of May in the following year, to be admiral of the white. On the 12th of June 1749, he received the honorary ap-

                                        pointment

pointment of rear-admiral of Great Britain; and, on the 22d of June 1751, was made one of the commiſſioners for executing the office of lord high-admiral. In 1753, he was elected one of the knights of the moſt honourable order of the Bath, and continued to hold the office of commiſſioner of the admiralty, through three commiſſions, till the 20th of November 1756. He returned again to the ſame ſtation on the 7th of April 1757, but remained in it only till the 2d of July following.

The intereſt, and political conſequence derived by lord Anſon from his wealth, his ſucceſs over the French fleet in 1747, together with the honours beſtowed on him as a reward for his conduct on that occaſion, procured that nobleman, although junior in rank to ſir William, the offices of vice-admiral of England, and admiral of the fleet, in preference to the latter; but, on the death of his lordſhip, in 1762, ſir William, as a matter of courſe, ſucceeded to the ſtation of admiral of the fleet, and, on that occaſion, reſigned the office of rear-admiral of Great Britain. Having thus, with much honour, and the moſt unblemiſhed reputation, attained the higheſt rank in the ſervice, he continued to live ever afterwards in retirement; and died, as may naturally be ſuppoſed from the length of his ſervice, in an advanced age, on the 1ſt of January 1768.

GEORGE,

GEORGE, LORD ANSON,

THE defcendant of a Staffordfhire family, both ancient and highly refpectable, was the fecond and youngeft fon of William Anfon, efquire, of Shugborough, in that county, and his wife, Elizabeth Lane, one of the daughters and co-heirs of Ralph Lane, efquire, and fifter to Mary, countefs of Macclesfield. Having very early in life difcovered the ftrongeft propenfity to the naval fervice, he received the neceffary education for fuch a purfuit; and, paffing through the fubordinate ftations of midfhipman and lieutenant, with much credit and reputation, was, in 1722, advanced to the rank of commander of the Weazle floop. He was, on the 1ft of February 1723-4, promoted to that of captain, and appointed to the Scarborough frigate. No mention is made either of the fervices, or ftations on which he was employed, or even the fhips he commanded, till the year 1731, at which time he was captain of the Diamond, a fifth rate, of forty guns. This veffel was one of thofe originally intended to have been fent to the Mediterranean, under fir Charles Wager, but never proceeded thither. In 1737, till

which

Pub. May 1 1801 by E. Harding 98 Pall Mall

GEORGE LORD ANSON

which time we have no further account of him, he
was appointed to the Centurion, of fixty guns, and
fent as commanding officer, with a diftinguifhing pendant, to the coaft of Africa, from whence he paffed
to Carolina, and returned to Europe in the enfuing
year.

For a number of years, during the pacific adminiftration of fir Robert Walpole, Spain had beheld, with
an evil eye, the growing commerce and increafing
naval confequence of Great Britain, particularly in the
neighbourhood of that part of her dominions (her
poffeffions in South America), where fhe was moft
vulnerable, and entertained the greateft jealoufy of
intrufion. Defirous of monopolizing to herfelf, the
whole commerce and wealth of Mexico and Peru, the
veffels of foreign powers were forbid, under fevere
penalties, to approach within a certain diftance of her
American poffeffions; and, to enforce this regulation,
the American feas were filled with Spanifh cruifers,
whofe enormities at length attracted the attention of
the Britifh parliament. After fruitlefs reprefentations
to the court of Madrid for redrefs, the Britifh miniftry
at length determined on hoftilities; and, to the great
joy of the nation, whom the atrocities of the Spaniards
had bitterly incenfed, war was formally declared againft
Spain on the 23d of October 1739.

On this event taking place, it was immediately determined by the miniftry, that captain Anfon, who had
for fome time commanded the Centurion, of fixty
guns, fhould be employed in an expedition againft the
Spanifh poffeffions in the South Seas. It was at firft

propofed

propofed that he fhould proceed to attack Manilla, the capital of the Philippine iflands, and a depot of immenfe wealth; but this plan, though well imagined, was laid afide. The moft unaccountable delay, and many difagreeable circumftances attended the equipment of his fquadron, fo that, though he received his commiflion on the 10th of January 1740, he was not able to put to fea till the 18th of September, by which means the Spanifh court, which was informed of his deftination, had full time to warn the governors of their provinces in America, of the intended expedition. His fquadron confifted of the Centurion, his own fhip, the Severn and Gloucefter, of fifty guns, the Pearl, of forty, the Wager ftore-fhip, an old Indiaman, mounting twenty guns, purchafed into the fervice, and very unfit to be fent on fo dangerous a voyage; and the Trial, a fnow, carrying eight guns; to thefe were added two vićtuallers, one of four, the other of two hundred tons burthen. The land forces, that is to fay, the invalids and marines, amounting together to four hundred and feventy men, were commanded by colonel Crachcrode. From what we have premifed, it may be concluded, that all unprejudiced perfons could entertain but very flender hopes of fuccefs. The force was in itfelf by no means adequate to the magnitude of the undertaking; and the extraordinary delay, from the month of January, when the extent of the expedition was firft arranged, to the month of September, when it proceeded to fea, not only enabled, as it was well known, the Spaniards to equip and fend to fea, a fquadron of fuperior force, to counterać its operations,

but

but expofed Mr. Anfon, and his fhips, to the extreme
danger of making their paffage round Cape Horn, and
paffing through thofe very inclement feas, at the moft
inhofpitable and improper feafon, a circumftance that
contributed more to the fubfequent fafety of the
enemy's fettlements, than their ability of refiftance,
the ftrength of their fortifications, or the protection
afforded them by Mr. Pizarro's fquadron.

Mr. Anfon, being at length at liberty to purfue his
voyage, fteered for the ifland of Madeira ; but, as if
Providence had leagued with the authors of his former
delay, and united to effect the utter ruin of this apparently devoted fquadron, he was thirty-feven days on
his paffage thither, a run which is moft frequently
made, if the wind prove favourable, or moderate, in
ten or twelve. On his arrival there, on the 25th of
October, he had intelligence that a fquadron, confifting of feven or eight Spanifh fhips of the line, and a
patache, had been feen cruifing to the weftward of that
ifland for feveral days ; this was, in truth, the very
fquadron under admiral don Pizarro, of which we
have already made mention. The commodore immediately difpatched a fmall veffel to reconnoitre, but
fhe having returned without affording him any information, and the water of the fquadron being completed, he failed, on the 3d of November, fteering for
the coaft of Brazil. On the 28th he croffed the line,
and, on the 21ft of December, came to an anchor at
the ifland of St. Catharine's.

The ficklinefs of the different crews rendered it expedient to put into this port, in the hope that the fup-

pofed

pofed falubrity of. the air, and a conftant fupply of frefh provifions, would fufficiently and fpeedily re-eftablifh the health of the fick.· In both thefe expect-ations, however, the commodore found himfelf mi-ferably difappointed ; the inhofpitable, unfriendly con-duct of the Portuguefe, in fcantily furnifhing the re-quired refrefhments, and the natural climate, which proved extremely deleterious, not merely to the con-dition of the fick and valetudinarians, but to thofe who had previoufly enjoyed a good ftate of health, aug-mented, rather than diminifhed, the ficknefs in the -fquadron, and Mr. Anfon could only lament the ad-ditional inconvenience he had incurred by delay, without having experienced any palliating advantage from it.

The fquadron failed from St. Catharine on the 18th of January, and, during its paffage along the fouth-eaft coaft of America, was fo near the Spanifh arma-ment, under the orders of don Pizarro, that one of the fhips, the Pearl, having feparated from the reft in the night, very narrowly efcaped falling into the hands of the enemy, who ufed every imitative deception, the moft accurate information could fuggeft the adoption of. The fquadron arrived at Port St. Julian, not far diftant from the fouthern extremity of South America, on the 18th of February ; and, as if fate had predeftined a reiteration of delays, the continuance of the Britifh fhips at that place was unavoidably lengthened to nine days, in confequence of the Trial floop having loft her mainmaft on the paffage, and the time confumed in replacing the fame. This operation being per-formed,

formed, the squadron once more put to sea, and passed
the streights Le Maire, without experiencing further
inconvenience, on the 7th of March. The ships were
now supposed to have passed the boundary of all difficulties, and to have entered the Pacific Ocean, where
their crews would have no storms to encounter, nor any
other occupation but that of distressing the enemies of their
country, and enriching themselves. The different vessels,
taking all circumstances together, were far from being in
a bad condition for service, their crews not remarkably
unhealthy, and those, who were oppressed with disease,
would, as it was hoped, soon recover, under the benign
influence of a milder climate, and those repeated
opportunities which were expected, of procuring fresh
provisions, from their foes, or otherwise. These
pleasing ideas were, however, scarcely raised, ere they
vanished; for the sternmost ships of the squadron had
not cleared the narrow passage, ere a most tremendous
hurricane nearly caused their immediate destruction;
and the horrors of instant demolition being, with the
utmost difficulty avoided, by the skill and diligence of
the commodore, with the rest of the officers on board
the squadron, their fate constantly impending, appeared
deferred, not avoided, for the space of the two succeeding months. During the whole of this period,
the ships were constantly exposed, to the contending
violence of the most furious tempest, and of a dreadfully agitated sea. Separation became unavoidable;
two of the ships, the Severn and the Pearl, put back
to the Brazils; the Wager, store-ship, was wrecked;

and the remaining veffels, after, fuftaining the utmoft extremity of diftrefs, reached the fecond rendezvous (the ifland of Juan Fernandez) fingly, with emaciated crews, and in a condition, that feemed to afford no hope whatever, of their ever being able to act against the enemies of Britain.

The commodore himfelf, after having, with the moft incredible difficulty, fucceeded in making his paffage round Cape Horn, notwithftanding it was the opinion of every man in the fhip, that none had furvived the tempeft but themfelves, proceeded for the firft appointed rendezvous, where, having cruifed in vain for upwards of a fortnight, in hopes of meeting with fome fhips of the fquadron, and being difappointed, he was confequently, together with his people, ftrengthened in the firft opinion. Still did he hold it his indifpenfable duty, to perfevere, while the poffibility of fulfilling his firft inftructions exifted. He accordingly fteered for the ifland of Juan Fernandez, and on the 28th of May actually arrived in fight of it; but from its appearance, in confequence of the ftate of the atmofphere at that time, it was deemed only a cloud. The fhip accordingly altered her courfe, and on the 30th of May, the crew were convinced of their former error, by a perfect fight of the high land of Chili. Their ftate was now become truly deplorable, water was grown very fhort, and the people fo fickly, that it was no uncommon difafter, for fix, or feven of them to die in the courfe of twenty-four hours. Thofe who furvived, were fo enfeebled, that

they

they almoſt deſpaired of reaching the fertile and ſalubrious ſpot, where their health might again be renovated. The Centurion was, however, fortunate enough to reach this objeĉt of general wiſh on the 9th of June. So reduced were her crew by the ſcurvy, and fatigue, that of four hundred and fifty men, who three months before paſſed the ſtreights of Le Maire, in what might be called good health and vigour, ſcarcely half that number were alive; and ſo many of the ſurvivors were confined to their hammocks, that, although the manual aſſiſtance of all the officers, without exception, was afforded, it was with the utmoſt difficulty, they could muſter ſufficient ſtrength, to bring the ſhip, to anchor on the following day.

The firſt buſineſs entered upon was, as might be reaſonably ſuppoſed, the landing of the ſick; from the ſpeedy recovery of whom, the commodore found the report of the ſalubrity of the climate, and the efficacy of the vegetable produĉtions of the iſland, in caſes of perſons affliĉted with the ſcurvy, by no means exaggerated; for though a very great number might be conſidered, in the laſt ſtage of that diſtemper, yet, after the two firſt days, ſcarcely ten perſons died during the time of their continuance on the iſland, a period of three months. The commodore was, ſome time afterwards, joined by the Glouceſter, Trial ſloop, and Anna pink, viĉtualler; the two former, if poſſible, in a worſe condition than the Centurion had been. The health of the ſurvivors was, however, reſtored, and the ſhips refitted as well as circumſtances would ad-

B b 2   mit.

mit. Such was the state of affairs, when a strange ship was discovered in the offing. The Centurion being in the most forward state of equipment, the commodore immediately slipped his cable, and ran out to sea in pursuit. The vessel he had seen escaped for the night ; but to make him amends for this temporary disappointment, he fell in with, and captured her on the following day. She proved to be a Spanish merchant-ship of considerable value, having some specie on board, bound coastwise. Finding, by letters taken in the prize, as well as by the information of the people, that some considerable captures might probably be made, before the coast was completely alarmed, and a voluntary embargo laid on the merchant-vessels, the commodore, on his return to Juan Fernandez, made every possible dispatch in getting the Gloucester and Trial ready for sea; the victualler having been condemned and broke up. They accordingly, as well as himself, made every possible dispatch, in getting ready for their final departure, from the hospitable spot, where they had derived so much succour.

. Several other ships and vessels were captured by the commodore and his companions, during the subsequent cruise, the cargoes of which were of considerable value, particularly to the enemy. The Trial sloop having sustained much damage, became so leaky and defective, that it was resolved to scuttle her ; and intelligence having been received from one of the prizes, taken by the Centurion, that a considerable treasure had been landed just before at Paita, from some ships which had put in there, in consequence of having

having received intelligence that the commodore was on the coaft, he immediately refolved to attempt it by a coup de main ; and in this enterprife he was completely fuccefsful. Thirty thoufand pounds in fpecie were carried off, and in confequence of the refufal on the part of the Spaniards to ranfom the town, with the commodities it contained, the whole was fet fire to, and deftroyed, to the amount of a million and an half of dollars. All the veffels that remained in the port, except one, being fcuttled and funk, as confidered of no value, the fquadron quitted the bay, with a newly acquired prize the Solidad. The commodore failed on the 16th of November, and was, two days afterwards, joined by the Gloucefter, who had only taken two fmall veffels. The grand object, and point of their future operations, was the capture of the galleon, which, according to the common courfe of events, was expected to arrive from Manilla, at Acapulco, in the month of January following. It was only the middle of November, and it was therefore reafonably expected, that the fquadron would be able to get into the neceffary latitude, in proper time. The force under the commodore, including prizes, amounted to eight fhips ; but two of them were found fuch indifferent failers, that, to prevent delay, they were ordered to be cleared of the moft valuable part of their cargoes, and then fet on fire, as was a third immediately afterwards. In the beginning of December, the fquadron arrived at the ifland of Quibo, near the bay of Panama. The commodore, while at Juan Fer-

nandez, had formed to himſelf, hopes of procuring, at
this place, a reinforcement of men, acroſs the iſthmus
of Darien, from Mr. Vernon, who he knew was ſent
on the expedition againſt Carthagena ; but theſe expectations were annihilated, by letters found on board
one of the prizes, from which he learnt that the enterpriſe had failed ; ſo that after a ſtay of eight days, the
ſquadron left Quibo, ſteering its courſe for the coaſt
of Mexico.   Previous to its departure, the commodore diſtributed to the captains, and commanders of
the different ſhips, orders for them, in caſe of ſepara-
tion, to uſe their utmoſt endeavours to get a little
northward to the harbour of Acapulco, that being the
track of the expected prize.   But though the ſhips
never loſt ſight of each other, they were ſo much retarded by calms, contrary winds, and other cauſes,
that they did not fall in with the coaſt of Mexico till
the 29th of January.

Now were the hopes of every individual in the
ſquadron, raiſed to the higheſt pitch ; each flattering
himſelf, with the pleaſing golden dream, of returning back to his native country ſufficiently enriched,
according to his ſtation, to make him amends for
labour, fatigue, and complicated miſery, induced by
diſeaſe, all which, by far the greater part of them, had
felt in their moſt ſevere ſhape.   This happy deluſion
was ſoon fruſtrated, or at leaſt, the poſſeſſion of the
expected riches was for ſome time poſtponed ; for
the commodore learnt from three negroes, who were
ſurpriſed in a canoe by the crew of his barge, off the
                                                    harbour

harbour of Acapulco, that the galleon had arrived
there on the 9th of January, twenty days before he
himself had made the coast. As a palliative, however,
to this disappointment, he learnt, through the same
channel, that her sailing from Acapulco, on her return
to Manilla, was fixed for the 3d of March; so that both
himself and his people, comforted themselves with the
reflection, that her cargo having, on her arrival at
Acapulco, been exchanged for silver, she would be a
much more advantageous capture, than she would have
been, if taken on her passage thither. The interval
passed somewhat slowly, as might naturally be expected,
in the minds of men raised to the very tiptoe of expectation.
Their principal employment was anticipating their future greatness, and considering the most likely measures
to ensure its completion. The arrangements made by
the commodore, were, in every respect, the most judi-
cious, that could have been conceived. He formed a
line of twenty leagues, by stationing the several ships
of his squadron, as well as the cutters of the Centurion and Gloucester, at equal distances from each
other, all, at such an offing from the shore, that they
could not be observed. The cutters had orders to
stand nearer the shore every night, and work off again
on the approach of day, so that it was actually impossible for any vessel to pass in, or out of the harbour
unobserved. On the expected day, every eye was
eagerly turned towards the quarter, from whence the
treasure was expected to approach, and strained in
fruitless gazing. A second, and a third day succeeded,

and

and, were equally unproductive, of fuccefs. Every
cloud was converted by the credulous eye of fancy,
into a fail ; and a fire on the fhore was chafed with
the utmoft eagernefs, during one whole night, in which
time, the moft pofitive affertions were made, by different perfons on board, of circumftances and appearances,
which, all proving fantaftic, fufficiently demonftrate
how much a mind, blinded by prejudice, may be inclined to embrace and affert, as an incontrovertible
truth, the vifion of fancy, and of vain credulity.

Nearly a month was fpent in this torment of expectation, and hope ; and it was at laft generally believed,
what afterwards proved to be really the cafe, that the
barge, when firft fent to difcover the harbour of Acapulco, at the fame time when the canoe with the negroes was feized, had been defcried from the fhore, and
that the failing of the galleon was of courfe deferred till
the enfuing feafon. A multitude of fchemes were fug-
gefted for poffeffing themfelves of the hoped-for prize ;
but from the impoffibility of carrying them into execution, were abandoned, as foon as framed. One of
thefe was ftarted by the commodore himfelf ; who propofed to attack the town of Acapulco, by landing two
hundred of his people, under the fire of the fhips of
war, which were to have run in clofe for the purpofe ;
but this alfo was given up, as the numbers remaining
behind, were by no means adequate to the intended
fervice. Having, however, continued on their ftation,
as long as ever their ftock of wood and water would
permit, the fquadron, unfuccefsful as it was, was obliged

to

to make for the harbour of Chequetan, about thirty leagues to the weftward of Acapulco, where it arrived on the 7th of April. All hope of further fuccefs on the coaft of ·America being now totally at an end, nothing remained but to put their fhips in the beft poffible condition to crofs the Pacific Ocean, and patiently wait for the enfuing feafon, in the hope of intercépting the long-fought-for prize on its paffage to Manilla. The united crews of the whole fquadron amounted not to more than three hundred and thirty perfons, a number far inferior to the complement of the Centurion alone, and totally inadequate to the tafk of navigating five fhips, over the immenfe ocean which intervened between America and China, the next land, where they could, with certainty, rely on receiving fuccour, after they quitted the former continent. The moft active meafures were immediately taken, to clear the prizes of all thofe goods which were moft portable, and valuable ; which being performed, they were immediately towed to a proper diftance from fhore, where they were· fcuttled and funk. The crews of the Centurion, and her companion, the Gloucefter, having been by thefe means confiderably reinforced, and the impediments to expedition naturally attendant on the company of fluggifh-failing fhips, removed, the commodore flattered himfelf with the hope of making a favourable paffage acrofs the Pacific Ocean, and procuring in other feas, fome recompenfe for thofe difappointments, which, with very few exceptions, appeared to have conftantly attended him, while on the ·American coaft.

The

The web of his ill fortune, seemed not even yet to have been completed. Calms, contrary winds, and tempestuous weather, conspired so violently together to impede his progress, that ten days were in the first instance consumed, from the time of his putting to sea, ere he lost sight of the American coast, and at the end of nearly four months, he was still at some distance from the Ladrone islands, the first place, where he could receive any relief for his crews, reduced by disease and mortality, to the most distressed and melancholy state. At length, on the 15th of August, the absolute inability of working both the ships, with the very scanty numbers of people which then remained alive or fit for duty, added to the injury the Gloucester had sustained in her masts, together with her leaky condition, compelled Mr. Anson to have recourse to that mortifying expedient of destroying her, after removing such part of the valuable commodities she had on board, as time and circumstances would permit. Freed, therefore, from every other cause of delay, but what might arise out of her own misfortunes, the course of the Centurion was immediately shaped for the island of Tinian ; since by the quickness of the passage to that supposed salubrious spot, their only remaining hopes were centred, of restoring to health, those, whom disease had not absolutely reduced to an irrecoverable state, and preserving the lives of the miserable remnant, which had still been fortunate enough to prolong their existence, through such an accumulation of misery, misfortune, and disease. The hour of disaster, however, was not even yet, at an end ; the Centurion was scarcely freed

from

from her confort, ere fhe herfelf fprung a leak; but
by the exertions of thofe few, who ftill remained able
to do their duty, no further inconvenience arofe from
it, than that naturally attendant on the fmalleft additional labour, exacted from fo debilitated a crew. At
length, on the 15th day after the deftruction of the
Gloucefter, the Centurion was fortunate enough to
come to an anchor in the road of Tinian. The firft
occupation was that of landing the fick, to the number
of one hundred and twenty-eight perfons; ahd though
many of them were fuppofed to be in the laft ftage of
that dreadful, and deftructive difeafe, the fcurvy, yet
the effect produced on them by the fruits and vege-
tables, added to the air of the ifland, was almoft inftantaneous. Mortality in a very few days totally
ceafed, and the remainder rapidly recovered their
health and vigour.

The crew were in a tolerable ftate of convalefcence,
when a very alarming accident took place. A violent
tempeft arofe, and drove the Centurion to fea, the
commodore, and one hundred and thirteen of his
people remaining on fhore. All agreed in opinion,
that the Centurion muft have been inevitably loft;
and their firft care was, confequently, to provide fome
means of efcape to China, as the neareft place of refuge. When they firft took poffeffion, as it may be
faid, of Tinian, they found there a Spanifh bark of
fifteen tons burden, fent thither to procure a lading
of falt, which is produced naturally in ponds, by the
exhalation of the fun. This veffel was immediately
hauled on fhore; and fuch fpeedy means were ufed

to

to lengthen and fit it for fea, that, on the return of
the Centurion, after an abfence of nineteen days, fo
confiderable a progrefs was made, that in a very.fhort
time longer, it would have been actually completed.
When the fhip came again to an anchor, the commodore, and the greater number of his people, went
immediately on board, leaving only about forty perfons on fhore, to finifh.the neceffary duties of wooding,
watering, and collecting different articles for their fea
ftore: A fecond tremendous gale drove the Centurion
once more to fea. It was inferior in violence, as well
as fhorter in duration than the former; and the crew
being not only: much ftronger, but alfo animated by
the prefence of their commander, the fhip returned to
its former anchorage, after a much fhorter abfence
than the preceding. The Spanifh veffel had, in this
painful interval, undergone a fecond transformation;
thofe who remained on fhore, defpairing of the Centurion's return, and thinking it an ufelefs wafte of
labour and time, to attempt carrying the firft project into execution, when the veffel, in its original
ftate, would have been fufficient to tranfport them to
China, they immediately began to fit it for that expedition, and had actually fo far proceeded, as to bring
together again the two ends of the veffel, which had,
on the former occafion, been cut afunder for the purpofe
of lengthening it. A very.fhort time would have enabled
them to complete their defign, when the fecond happy
return of the Centurion into the bay rendered it ufelefs.
The health of the whole crew being completely re-eftablifhed, and the fhip refitted, as well as the fituation

and exifting circumftances would permit, every trivial
duty remaining, was haftened with the greateft fpirit,
as experience had taught the commodore, the danger
of continuing any longer, at that feafon of the year,
in fo unfafe an anchorage. Every thing being ready
for departure, the Spanifh bark, and all the materials
collected for its equipment, that were not worth removal, were fet on fire; and the commodore took
his final leave of the enchanting fpot, where not only
the health of his crew, but of himfelf alfo, which, on
his arrival, was in a very precarious ftate, had been
completely re-eftablifhed. The Centurion failed from
Tinian, on the 21ft of October, fteering directly for
Macao, a Portuguefe fettlement, near the entrance of
the river Canton, in China, where it was intended to
refit the fhip more completely. They made the coaft
of China on the 5th of November, and without any
intervening accident, or extraordinary occurrence, anchored in the road of Macao on the 12th.

The repair, and refitment of the fhattered veffel, was
the firft object that occupied the mind of the commodore; it was neceffary for a twofold reafon, firft, for
the fimple conveyance of himfelf and his people back
to Europe, but, fecondly, for the accomplifhment of
an intervening project he had formed, and which
acted no lefs forcibly on his mind. Difappointed in
his views of capturing the galleon the preceding feafon, off the coaft of America, he refolved to try his
fortune a fecond time, by cruifing for her in the Chinefe feas. Doubly encouraged to the attempt, were
both himfelf and his people, by the hope, that in con-

fequence

fequence of the valuable veffel in queftion having been fruftrated in its intended voyage, on the former oc- cafion, there would now be two of equal value, in- ftead of the fingle prize, which they had before flat- tered themfelves with the ideal poffeffion of. The commodore having at length, and not without the extremeft difficulty, fuccefsfully combated with, and overcome the prejudices, the rapacity, and treachery of the Chinefe, was enabled to put to fea from Macao, on the 19th of April 1743; his fhip, being in no in- different ftate of equipment, and his crew, in fome degree ftrengthened, by the addition of twenty-three Lafcars, or Indian feamen, whom he enlifted during his continuance in port. He immediately proceeded for cape Efpiritu Santo, a point of land, known to be always made by the galleon on her paffage; and arrived on his ftation, with the fmall remains of his people, all in the higheft health and fpirits, on the 20th of May. Nothing, it is obferved, can more thoroughly prove the ardour of the Britifh nation, than this cir- cumftance; a crew reduced by difeafe to very little more than half its complement, fo far from defiring to avoid an enemy, who fingly would have nearly tri- pled its numbers, wifhed for nothing fo eagerly as to meet with two galleons, in full confidence that it pof- feffed fufficient fpirit, and ability, to effect a conqueft of both. The hopes of the commodore and the gallant adventurers, whom he commanded, began to lofe ground confiderably, when, on the 20th of June, being the thirty-fecond day of their cruife, the long-fought-

for

for object of purfuit, was difcovered from the maft-
head of the Centurion at fun-rife. One only, indeed,
appeared; but hopes of meeting a fecond at a future
hour, were entertained, from the circumftance of the
galleon's firing a gun, and hoifting a flag at the fore-
topmaft head, as foon as fhe became vifible from the
Centurion's deck. The commodore reafonably concluded, that was a fignal to her confort, for whom fhe
had miftaken the Centurion, and by way of continuing
the delufion, ordered a gun to be fired to leeward.
The fuppofition of the miftake made by the commander
of the galleon, was, in great meafure, ftrengthened in
the minds of Mr. Anfon and his crew, from the circumftance of that veffel's bearing down with the greateft
coolnefs, and apparent unconcern, to the Centurion;
for the Englifh were yet ignorant of the real caufe of
this conduct; that the Spaniards, well acquainted
with the enfeebled ftate, and diminifhed numbers of
their foes, had determined to attack them, in no degree
defpairing of becoming themfelves the conquerors.

The enemy had the misfortune, however, to find
themfelves difappointed in their expectations. The
galleon, though defended with the utmoft bravery by
her commander, was compelled to yield to the fuperior abilities of Mr. Anfon and his people. The account given of it by himfelf is almoft as concife, as
that detailed by fir George Walton, relative to the deftruction of the Spanifh fquadron. "When fhe came,"
fays Mr. Anfon, "within two miles, fhe brought to,
to fight me; and after an engagement of an hour
and an half, within lefs than piftol-fhot, the admiral
struck

ſtruck his flag at the main-topmaſt-head. She was called the Neuſtra Senora del Caba Donga, don Geronimo Montero, admiral; had forty-two guns, ſeventeen of which were braſs, and twenty-eight braſs pedereroes; five hundred and fifty men, fifty-eight of which were ſlain, and eighty-three wounded; her maſts and rigging were ſhot to pieces; and one hundred and fifty ſhot paſſed through her hull, many of which were between wind and water, which occaſioned her to be very leaky. The greateſt damage I ſuſtained was, by having my foremaſt, mainmaſt, and bowſprit wounded, and my rigging ſhot to pieces. I received only fifteen ſhot through my hull, which killed me two men, and wounded fifteen. Being under great difficulty in navigating two ſuch large ſhips, in a dangerous and unknown ſea, and guarding four hundred and ninety-two priſoners, I was apprehenſive of loſing company, and thought proper, for the ſecurity of the galleon, and the great treaſure in her, which could not be removed (the weather being very tempeſtuous), to give my firſt lieutenant a commiſſion to command her, with other proper officers under him."

The Centurion, with her prize, got into the river of Canton, on the 14th day of July, and having diſpoſed of the latter, through compulſion, as being unable to navigate her to a Britiſh port, for one tenth of her real value, he quitted China, after a continuance of five months, and reached England on the 15th of June 1744; without having been oppoſed by any accident, or even met with any material occurrence during his voyage. Yet it is obſerved, that as if that Providence,

vidence, which had before so remarkably manifested itself in the protection of this ship, and the poor remains of her once formidable crew, was resolved to continue, and make known its exertions to the world, even to the last moment of the voyage, it was found, on the arrival of the commodore at Spithead, that he had passed through the centre of a French squadron, which was then cruising at the entrance of the British channel, for the express purpose of intercepting him; that he had been enveloped, as it were, in a cloud, and obscured from their sight by a mist, so thick, as to excite the astonishment of every person on board; but which, during its continuance, little sensible of their impending danger, they had considered as an event, of the most inconvenient, and not improbably, unfortunate kind.

Thus ended an expedition, which though attended by more disasters, than perhaps ever fell to the lot of any that preceded, or have since followed it; yet, if we except the loss of those brave but unfortunate men, who unavoidably fell victims to disease, when the prevention of its peculiarly fatal effects was less known than at the present hour, and whose fate humanity must ever lament, it proved in its consequences, by no means unproductive of national advantages. The capture, or destruction, no matter by what means it may be effected, of an enemy's squadron, is the first and leading feature of hope, in all expeditions whatever. Of the armament, equipped by Spain under Pizarro, consisting of five ships of the line, to counteract that under Mr. Anson, one only returned to Europe; and

without

without having acquired the fmalleft advantage to
counterbalance its difafter. The lofs of England
was, on the other hand, only one fhip of fifty
guns, an old Indiaman, converted into a ftore-fhip,
together with a fmall fnow floop of war. As a coun-
terpoife to this, the country acquired an influx of de-
terminate and pofitive wealth, amounting to one million fterling, an advantage, confidered in a public
light, little inferior to that, derived by the fortunate
individuals, who were more particularly, and immediately enriched by it.

In eight days after Mr. Anfon's arrival in England,
he was promoted to be rear-admiral of the blue fquadron ; but though advanced to that rank, he not only
remained unemployed, but is actually faid to have declined accepting of it, owing, according to report, to
a mifunderftanding which arofe between himfelf and
the admiralty board, relative to the appointment of fir
Piercy Brett to the rank of poft-captain. A complete
change, however, in adminiftration, having taken place
in the month of December following, his former
ground of complaint was not only obviated, but he
himfelf was appointed one of the commiffioners for executing the office of lord high admiral, and advanced to
be rear-admiral of the white. He did not, however,
take upon himfelf any naval command till the month
of July 1746, when he was raifed to the rank of vice-
admiral of the blue, and commander in chief of the
fleet employed on the Channel fervice. No material
occurrence took place during the current year,
owing to the duke d'Anville, who was on his return

from

from America, with a shattered squadron, having accidentally received information of Mr. Anson's position, and, consequently, altered his course in sufficient time to allow his avoiding him; but intelligence having been received, early in the year 1747, that two formidable squadrons, equipped in the port of Brest, were on the point of sailing, one for the West, the other for the East Indies, having a considerable number of transports, store-ships, and other vessels under their convoy, Mr. Anson was chosen to command the armament intended to intercept them: that under monf. de Jonquiere, destined for the East Indies, being ready for sea, and the other by no means in a forward state of equipment, the impatience of the French court could no longer restrain itself, but sent a positive order to the chef d'escadre, to proceed on his voyage, without waiting for the West India squadron.

Mr. Anson sailed, on the 9th of April, from Plymouth, for his station, being directed to cruise between Ushant and cape Finisterre. He remained off Ushant and Brest, till the 20th, and then stood to the south-west, in order to make cape Finisterre. He cruised off that place till the 2d of May, when, the cape bearing S. W. distant twenty-four leagues, he fell in with his object of pursuit, the French squadron, and their convoy. Jonquiere immediately drew together his ships of war, which were nine, or ten in number, five of which were of two decks, and appeared, prepared to make the best defence in their power; while the ships under their protection, amounting to near thirty in number, including six small frigates,

C c 2 gates,

gates, or armed veſſels, which remained with them as
their convoy, crowded all the ſail they could, in hopes
of being able to effect their eſcape. Mr. Anſon at
firſt made the ſignal for his ſquadron to form the line of
battle ; but, finding the French ſquadron ſo inferior in
force, and that it was uſing every poſſible means to
get off, intending only to divert the attention, by a
ſhow of reſolution, till the convoy was out of reach,
he ſoon ſtruck his ſignal for the line, and hoiſted one
for a general chaſe ; and that each ſhip ſhould engage,
as ſhe could get up, and cloſe with the enemy. About
four o'clock in the afternoon, the Centurion began to
attack the ſternmoſt of the enemy's ſhips, and was
ſoon afterwards ſupported by the Namur, Defiance,
and Windſor, which veſſels were very warmly engaged
with the reſt of the French ſquadron. The enemy
defended themſelves with uncommon ſpirit, and, notwithſtanding their very unequal numbers, maintained
a conteſt for three hours, when the commodore himſelf
having ſtruck to rear-admiral Warren, the Invincible,
which was the moſt powerful ſhip of the ſquadron,
being diſmaſted, and Mr. Anſon himſelf up with the
remainder of his fleet, the reſt of the ſhips, very much
damaged, all ſurrendered about ſeven o'clock in the
evening ; the Diamant being the laſt that ſubmitted,
after having been in cloſe action with the Briſtol for
nearly three hours.

Mr. Anſon immediately brought to with his ſquadron and the prizes, having ſoon after ſeven o'clock
diſpatched the Monmouth, Yarmouth, and Nottingham, which ſhips had ſuſtained no damage in the preceding

ceding action, to pursue the convoy, which then bore
weft by fouth, at the diftance of between four and five
leagues. The Falcon had been ordered to follow them
from the commencement of the preceding action, and
that veffel continued, during the night, to make fignals
to the fhips that were detached, by burning falfe fires.
The purfuers were, in confequence enabled, on the
morrow, to capture the Vigilant and Modefte, of
twenty-two guns each, and fix other fhips of inferior
note; the remainder unfortunately made their efcape.
This blow was moft feverely felt by France, who had
vainly flattered herfelf, that by means of that armament, fhe fhould render herfelf miftrefs of the Indian
feas, and, by that fuperiority, be enabled to wreft
from the hands of the Britifh, their moft valuable poffeffions in that part of the world. The admiral returned immediately to England, bringing the captive
fquadron with him to Spithead; and fo high an opinion
was entertained of the addrefs with which he had conducted himfelf, that, on the 13th of June, he was
created a peer of Great Britain, by the title of lord
Anfon, baron of Soberton, in the county of Southampton. On the 17th of July he was advanced to be
vice-admiral of the red; and, on the 12th of May
1748, to be admiral of the blue. Immediately after
this, he was appointed to command the fquadron that
convoyed king George II. to, and from Holland; but
was not engaged in any other material fervice till the
year 1758, fome time after the recommencement of
the war with France. In the month of April 1748,
his lordfhip married the lady Elizabeth Yorke, eldeft

daughter

daughter of Philip, firft earl of Hardwick, and Mary
his wife, daughter of Charles Cocks, of the city of
Worcefter, efquire. Lady Anfon died on the firft of
June 1761, leaving no iffue.

The fubfequent commands held by his lordfhip,
though important and honourable, were, neverthelefs,
unmarked by any interefting occurrence. On the death
of fir John Norris, in the month of July 1749, he
was appointed vice-admiral of Great Britain; and, on
the 22d of June 1751, on the refignation of the earl
of Sandwich, was promoted to be firft commiffioner
of the admiralty, a ftation in which he continued, with
a very fhort intermiffion, till his death. In 1752 he
was named one of the lords juftices for the adminiftration and direction of public affairs, during the abfence of his majefty in Germany, as he was again in
1754, on a repetition of the fame occafion. About
this time, the conduct of the French court became
extremely fufpicious; and, though it, perhaps, might
be fomewhat unfair to attribute exclufively to his lordfhip's neglect, the lofs of the ifland of Minorca, yet
that unfortunate event excited fo general a clamour,
that he confidered it prudent to refign his office as firft
commiffioner of the admiralty, on the 28th of November 1756. But a fubfequent change of adminiftration
caufed him to be reftored to his former high office, on
the 2d of July in the enfuing year. He was a fhort
time before advanced to be admiral of the white, and,
in the enfuing year, hoifted his flag on board the Royal
George, as commander in chief of the Channel fleet,
fir Edward Hawke being his fecond in command, an

appointment

appointment than which none could have been more politic, as it entirely obviated the rifk that might have attended an encounter, in the event of his lordfhip having been deftitute of fo able a fupporter.

The enemy, however, confined themfelves to their own ports ; and, after the return of the fleet to England, on the approach of winter, his lordfhip ftruck his flag, and never took upon him any fubfequent command till the year 1761. About that time, a fingular inftance took place, of the unjuft partiality which is fometimes difcoverable, even in the wifeft adminiftrations, when they wifh to reward, to flatter, or to bribe the individual, who, by his accumulated wealth, or extenfive influence, has rendered himfelf either ufeful, or terrible. On the death of admiral Clinton, lord Anfon was appointed admiral of the fleet, a mark of royal or public favour very unprecedented, as fir William Rowley who was a fenior officer to his lord-fhip, was alive, and was indeed, as has been obferved in his life, himfelf advanced to that very ftation after his lordfhip's deceafe, which he ought, according to the rules of the fervice, to have received in the firft inftance.

Soon after the acceffion of his prefent majefty, on the conclufion of a treaty of marriage between himfelf and the princefs Charlotte of Mecklenberg Strelitz, his lordfhip was chofen to command the fquadron def-tined to convoy the queen elect from Germany. He accordingly failed from Harwich, on the 17th of Auguft 1761, and, after a very long and tempeftuous paffage from Germany, happily landed his royal paf-

C c 4   fenger,

senger, at the same port, on the 17th of September, having been just one month absent on that service. After this period his lordship never went to sea: his health had for a long time been in a very languishing state, and he was advised by his physicians to drink the Bath waters, from which he was thought to have received considerable benefit; but, soon after his return, he was seized with a very sudden indisposition, having just before been walking in his garden, apparently in as good health as he had been for some time past. He died, in consequence of that stroke, at his seat at Moor Park, in Hertfordshire, on the 6th of June 1762. By his will he bequeathed the bulk of his fortune to his sister's son, George Adams, esquire, member for Saltash, in Cornwall, who immediately assumed the name of Anson, in pursuance of his lordship's direction.

Notwithstanding the fair delineation of his lordship's character, which we shall hazard, may be thought by some persons most ridiculously paradoxical, yet we trust there are others, who, judging coolly and reflectingly on the various transactions of his life, will admit the following opinion to be neither intemperate, exaggerated, nor foolish. Although a stream of misfortune appeared almost incessantly pursuing him for a long period of time, he was, perhaps, the most fortunate man who ever had, previous to that time, held the rank of a naval commander. Although the energies of his mind were undoubtedly of the strongest quality, yet, on the only occasion where the greatness of it met with a brilliant opportunity of becoming manifest, it completely failed; for, had Jonquiere been opposed to the

abilities

abilities of his lordship only, it is a matter of much doubt whether he would not have reached his destined port in safety. In short, he appears to have possessed patience, assiduity, and perseverance, in a more than ordinary extent, as a retribution afforded by nature for the scantiness of her gifts in all other respects. Some have sarcastically observed, though, perhaps, with some truth on their side, that, had the Manilla ship escaped the vigilance of the English commodore, he would, in all probability, have been laid aside on his return to England, as a superannuated captain, and died in obscurity; but his great wealth created considerable influence, and threw a new lustre on those talents, which would otherwise have passed unnoticed.

CAPTAIN

CAPTAIN CORNWALL.

———

THE obfervation, made in refpect to fir William Rowley, will ftrictly apply to this gentleman. Although few more deferving officers, as well on the fcore of bravery, as the perfect knowledge of every branch of his profeffion, have ever contributed to raife the fplendour of the Britifh naval character, he neverthelefs glided fo quietly through life, that the greater part of his countrymen were unacquainted with his deferts, till they were compelled to regret the lofs of them. He was the defcendant of a very refpectable Herefordfhire family, and after a regular fervice, in the different fubordinate ftations, was promoted on the 3d of April 1724, to be captain of the Sheernefs frigate. No mention whatever is made, as to the intervening commiffions he held, from that time till the year 1733, when he was made captain of the Greyhound, a twenty-gun fhip, in which he was fent, with two others of the fame force, to exact a reparation from the Salletines, for the outrage committed by one of their corfairs, in capturing a Britifh mer-

chant-

chant-veffel. Mr. Cornwall was the commanding officer of this little fquadron, and although the truft might
at the firft view, be confidered trivial, yet a moment's
reflection will be fufficient to imprefs the conviction,
that it was far from unimportant. He executed the
truft with the fpirit of an hero, and the diplomatic
prudence of an ambaffador. This little armament
failed from Portfmouth, on the 3d of March, and
arrived, after a very quick paffage, at Gibraltar, on
the 11th. It failed the next day for Tetuan, the
bafhaw of which place was fo much the friend of
peace, that he difpatched a fpecial meffenger to Me-
quinez, to intercede with the emperor, and induce
him to comply with the juft demands of the Britifh
court. The matter would, in all probability, have
been amicably, and fpeedily fettled, had not a confiderable number of Portuguefe been taken, a little time
before, by fome of their corfairs, and carried into
flavery. Thefe, his imperial majefty would not con-
fent to the releafement of, and, in confequence of his
refufal, the Britifh fhips, together with fome of the
Dutch nation, took their ftations off Tetuan, and
blocked up the port fo completely, that none of the
corfairs could put to fea. It is fcarcely neceffary to
detail the effect produced by thefe determined, though
quiet meafures. The pride and infolence of the Salletines fhrunk under the terror of a pointed attack.
The neceffary reparation was made, and tranquillity
reftored, without the neceffity of fpilling one drop of
blood.

Mr.

Mr. Cornwall does not appear to have been engaged in any subsequent memorable service, during the continuance of peace; but immediately after the commencement of hostilities with Spain, he was pitched upon to command a squadron, intended to be sent into the South Seas, round Cape Horn. A second armament of equal force, was to have been sent to the East Indies, under Mr. Anson, who was to be joined by Mr. Cornwall. This plan, which in all probability, would have been of the highest consequence and utility, was afterwards most strangely abandoned, and, as we have already shewn in the life of Mr. Anson, one part only of the intended armament was dispatched. This was put under that gentleman's command, who proceeded to the South Seas, instead of Mr. Cornwall. In 1741, he commanded the Bedford, a third rate, of seventy guns, one of the fleet employed in the Atlantic, under the orders of sir John Norris, as well for the purpose of protecting the British commerce from the insults of cruisers, as the prevention either of single ships of war, or of small armaments, from slipping out of the ports of Spain, in the hope of carrying into execution, without chastisement, some predatory expedition in a distant quarter of the world. He was not long afterwards, however, ordered to the Mediterranean, where he was, on the resignation of captain Graves, appointed to succeed him in the command of the Marlborough. He served with the most distinguished reputation in the unfortunate encounter with the French and Spanish fleets off Toulon, being stationed as one of the seconds to Mr. Mathews, the commander in chief, whom he moſt nobly and gallantly ſupported, till the fatal moment that deprived him of life, and his admiral of ſo brave a ſupporter.

The following extract from a letter, written by an impartial perſon, on board the Marlborough, will ſufficiently explain the ſhare that unfortunate ſhip held in the encounter: " The firſt intention of the admiral, was, to attack the French commander in chief in the Terrible, of ſeventy-four guns; our ſhip and the Norfolk, were to have been his ſeconds; and accordingly paſſed by within muſket-ſhot of the Real, without firing at her; but finding the French admiral ſtretched away with all the ſail he could, in order to get to windward, the admiral thought he might intercept ſome of the Spaniſh ſhips, and ordered us to tack, and engage the Real. He likewiſe tacked, and fired at, receiving one broadſide from the Real himſelf, which wounded his main-maſt, and hurt his rigging very much, ſo that he fell off, and could not come up again, till we were diſabled. We were within leſs than piſtol-ſhot alongſide of the Real, who had for her ſecond, a ſeventy-gun ſhip, that lay upon our quarter. We fired our firſt broadſide at one o'clock, and continued engaged with both theſe ſhips, without any aſſiſtance, till thirty-five minutes after four; ſometimes ſo near, that our yard-arm touched that of the Real, and were never farther diſtant than piſtol-ſhot; at laſt, all the Real's guns were ſilenced, and ſhe went off; her ſecond followed her,

her, and gave us a broadside at parting. The Real
had her main-yard and fore-topmaſt ſhot through
in ſeveral places; two port-holes beat into one.
We likewiſe were diſabled; our main-maſt, and
mizen-maſt were ſhot away; our captain, Cornwall, was killed, having both his legs ſhot off. Captain Godfrey, of Read's regiment, part of which were
on board our ſhip, was killed; our firſt lieutenant,
Frederic Cornwall, had his right arm ſhot off; our
maſter, Caton, both his legs, and is ſince dead; fifty
men were killed, one hundred and forty wounded.
Dalrymple, enſign in Read's, had all his clothes torn,
his back raſed, and himſelf ſtunned by a cannon-ball;
he was carried down as dangerouſly wounded, to the
ſurgeon; but as ſoon as he recovered himſelf, finding
his wound but ſlight, he returned with great courage to
his poſt. Thus diſabled, we ſaw five large ſhips of
the enemy coming down upon us; we were in no
condition either to fight, or make off, but ſent to
acquaint the admiral with our ſtate. He had made a
ſignal to the Anne Galley, fire-ſhip, Macky, to endeavour to burn the Real; but the Spaniſh admiral
having perceived his intention, ſent his launch full
of men, to take the fire-ſhip. In the ſcuffle, both
launch and fire-ſhip were burnt, and all in them.
Our admiral then bore down upon the Real, which
being perceived by the ſhips, which were going to
attack us, they left us to aſſiſt their admiral. This
was followed by a very ſmart engagement between
ſome of our ſhips and theirs, which laſted about an
hour, when the night parted them."

The

The parliament, in gratitude to the bravery of this great, though unfortunate commander, voted a considerable sum of money for the erection of a splendid monument in Westminster Abbey, to his memory.

SIR

SIR PETER WARREN.

THIS gallant officer, whofe merit raifed him to the higheft eminence in his profeffion, was the defcendant of an ancient and refpectable family in Ireland. He was born about the year 1703. With his earlier profeffional fervices we are unacquainted; but learn, that having entered into the navy, at an early period of life, and having paffed through the regular gradations of rank, he was, on the 19th of June 1727, appointed poft-captain of the Grafton. This event happened four days after his late majefty king George II. had been proclaimed king of Great Britain. The Grafton, to which captain Warren was appointed, was one of four fhips of the line, which were fent out under fir George Walton, to join fir Charles Wager in the Mediterranean. Early in the year 1728, the court of Madrid acceded to the preliminary articles of a general peace, which had been a long time in difcuffion; in confequence of which, foon after his arrival at Gibraltar, captain Warren removed into the Solebay frigate, for the purpofe of carrying out to the Weft Indies, the king of Spain's orders for execut-

ing

Harding sc.

S.ʳ PETER WARREN

Pub.ᵈ 1 May 1800. by Edw.ᵈ Harding 98 Pall Mall.

ing there the preliminaries alluded to. He proceeded on this service on the 5th of May, and, having executed his commission, as far as related to the West Indies, sailed, in compliance with his instructions, to Carolina.

Captain Warren returned to England in 1729, and immediately on his arrival, was appointed to the Leopard, of fifty guns. In this year, the Spaniards, not having conformed to the articles of the treaty, which had been agreed on, a fleet of twenty sail of the line, and five frigates, was ordered to be got ready ; and on the 30th of June, it assembled at Spithead, where it was joined by a squadron of Dutch ships, under the command of rear-admiral the baron de Sommeldyke. The court of Spain, alarmed at the assemblage of so strong a naval force, was induced to agree to terms proposed for a general pacification. The fleet remained three months at Spithead, when the Dutch returned home, and twelve sail of the line were ordered to be paid off. The Leopard, however, with the remainder of the fleet, continued at Spithead, under the command of sir Charles Wager, during the two succeeding years. In 1735, captain Warren, who still continued to command the Leopard, accompanied sir John Norris, who was ordered to Lisbon, with a powerful fleet. They sailed from Spithead on the 27th of May, and arrived in the Tagus on the 29th of June, where they were received by the Portuguese as their deliverers. The appearance of such a formidable fleet in the neighbourhood of the Spanish coast, created so great an alarm at the court of Madrid, that it soon lis-

tened to an accommodation with the Portuguefe. No
mention is made of any fubfequent commiffion held
by this gentleman, from the time of his quitting the
Leopard, till the fecond year after the commencement
of hoftilities with Spain; when, that is to fay, in
1741, he was captain of the Squirrel, a twenty-gun
fhip, on the American ftation. In 1742, he commanded the Launcefton, of forty guns; but the only
memorable mention we find made of him is, his having
captured the Peregrina privateer, mounting fourteen
carriage, and four fwivel guns, in company with captain Edward Aylmer, of the Port Mahon. He was
fometime afterwards promoted to the Superbe, of fixty
guns; and being ordered to the Weft Indies, was left
by fir Chaloner Ogle, commodore of a fmall fquadron,
on the Antigua ftation. He very much diftinguifhed
himfelf by his extraordinary exertions while employed
in this fervice, and having taken a ftation off Martinique, his fquadron captured between the 12th of
February, and the 24th of June 1744, twenty-four
valuable prizes; carrying two hundred and two guns,
eight hundred and thirty-two men, and amounting in
burthen to four thoufand three hundred and thirty-two
tons. One of the prizes was a regifter fhip, taken by
the Woolwich, valued at two hundred and fifty thoufand pounds.

In 1745, a project was formed in the general affembly at Maffachufett, in New England, to furprife the
city of Louifbourg, the capital of Cape Breton, and
to drive the French entirely from that ifland. Government, having been well informed of the importance

ance of the enterprife, commodore Warren was ordered to quit his ftation, at the Leeward Iflands, and
to join the Amerian expedition. This armament was
raifed with fo much fecrecy and difpatch, that an army
of three thoufand eight hundred and fifty volunteers,
under the command of William Pepperel, efq. was
ready to embark at Bofton, before the French government was apprifed of the intention. The naval
force under Mr. Warren confifted, exclufive of his
fhip, the Superbe, only of the Launcefton, and Eltham,
of forty guns each, which were, foon after his arrival
on the coaft, joined by the Mermaid, of the fame
force. He arrived at Canfo, in Nova Scotia, on the
25th of April, and found the troops encamped, they
having reached the place of rendezvous, upwards of
three weeks before, under convoy of ten private
armed veffels. On the 29th, the troops reimbarked,
and the whole of the armament came to an anchor in
Gabarus Bay, about a league diftant from Louifbourg,
on the 30th. Nothing could exceed the confternation,
into which the inhabitants and garrifon were thrown,
by this very unexpected vifit. The governor feebly
endeavoured to prevent the landing of the troops, by
fending out a detachment of one hundred men for that
purpofe; but the fpirit with which the invaders attacked them, compelled them to retire, almoft without
a blow. The debarkation was effected without lofs,
and the city formally invefted on the land fide. While
the troops were fuccefsfully employed on both fides
of the harbour on fhore, commodore Warren was
equally vigilant and fortunate in his own proper ele-

D d 2

ment.

ment. He fo fecurely blocked up the mouth of the
harbour, that during the whole continuance of the
fiege, only one veffel got in to the relief of the city,
and even that effected her paffage with the greateft difficulty. The commodore, who paid the utmoft attention to providing a proper convoy for their protection,
was joined by feven tranfports, having on board military ftores, and fix months provifions, for the land
forces, which, on the 17th of May, arrived in Gabarus Bay, from Bofton. The Britifh fleet was afterwards reinforced by the Canterbury, and Sunderland, of fixty guns each, and by the Chefter, of fifty
guns. Thefe were fo properly ftationed, that on the
20th of May, two French fhips, and a fnow, were
taken, and fent into Gabaru's Bay. In the mean time
the commodore, with the Mermaid, commanded by captain Douglas, and the Shirley galley, captain Rous,
went out in chafe of a large fhip, which proved to be the
Vigilante *, a new French man of war, of fixty-four
guns, and five hundred and fixty men, commanded
by the marquis de Fort Maifon, which was taken on
the 21ft, after the lofs of fixty French and five Englifh. The Vigilante was laden with ftores, a great
number of heavy cannon, and a thoufand half-barrels
of gunpowder for the city of Louifbourg; independent of articles for the equipment of a feventy-gun
fhip then building in Canada. Her whole cargo was
valued at fixty thoufand pounds. On the fame

* Among the important prizes made by the fquadron, when ftationed
off Louifbourg, were two very valuable French Eaft Indiamen, and a fhip
from Lima, having on board upwards of three hundred thoufand pounds in
fpecie, befides a very valuable cargo.

day,

day, the commodore took a large brigantine from France, laden with brandy and stores. By these fortunate acquisitions, the French were deprived of all their expected succour by sea, and the city was reduced to the utmost necessity.

About the commencement of June, from the circumstance of their powder running short, the besiegers were beginning to slacken their fire. This misfortune, however, was speedily remedied, by the arrival of some vessels from Boston, with six hundred barrels of powder, and additional stores for the army. These ships brought intelligence that one thousand men had been voluntarily raised in New England, to reinforce the troops, and also, that the French fleet, destined for the relief of Cape Breton, was detained at Brest by the British squadron. This diffused a general joy through the army, inspiring new life, spirits, and indefatigable strength, which were further augmented by the capture of a French ship, of fourteen carriage guns, and about three hundred tons burden, laden with stores and provisions for the city. This loss was the more to be regretted by the French, as they subsisted entirely on salt fish, bread, and peas. The besiegers also learned, from some deserters, that there were not above one hundred barrels of powder left in the city; and, in addition to this distress, the governor had the mortification to hear of the capture of three other vessels, laden with stores and provisions for the garrison. Owing to the extraordinary dispatch of the orders from the British government for naval assistance, the commodore, on the 11th of June, was further reinforced by the Princess Mary, of sixty guns, with the Hector and

Lark,

Lark, of forty guns each; so that the whole squadron
consisted of four ships of sixty guns, one of fifty, and
five of forty guns, besides the French man of war,
that had been captured, several privateers, and other
vessels of force.

On the 14th of June, every thing was prepared
for a general assault, both by land and water; but, on
the 15th, at four P. M. a flag of truce came to the
British camp, with proposals from the governor to surrender the city; commodore Warren and general Pepperel directed the bearer to attend on the following
morning, at eight o'clock, for their determination. At
the appointed hour the flag of truce attended, and carried back the terms of capitulation, which were proposed by commodore Warren and the general. Under
these terms, which were agreed to by monf. Chambon,
the governor of Louisbourg, the French were permitted to enjoy all their personal effects, and to be
conveyed to France at the expense of the besiegers.
The French flag was struck on the 17th, and the British flag was hoisted in its place, at the island battery, of which the besiegers took possession early in the
morning. At two o'clock in the afternoon, Mr.
Warren, with all the men of war, privateers, store-
ships, and transports, made a fine appearance on their
entrance into Louisbourg harbour; and, when all were
safely moored, they fired a grand feu de joie on the occasion. On the 4th of July, the garrison, and a
great number of the inhabitants, were embarked on
board fourteen cartel ships, which were convoyed by
the Launceston man of war, to Rochefort. In this
manner, after a continued siege of forty-seven days,

the

the Britifh forces caufed the reduction of the city of
Louifbourg, and the fubjection of the whole ifland of
Cape Breton, to his Britannic majefty. As foon as
the news of the fuccefs reached England, Mr. Warren, to whofe gallant exertions fo much praife was
due, was promoted to the rank of rear-admiral of the
blue fquadron, his commiffion bearing date Auguft the
8th, 1745.

After his return to England, he appears to have enjoyed a fhort repofe from the fatigue of public bufinefs, during the enfuing year; in the courfe of which
he was, neverthelefs, on the 14th of July, advanced to
be rear-admiral of the white. In the beginning of the
year 1747, he was appointed fecond in command of
the fquadron fent out under Mr. Anfon and himfelf,
for the purpofe of intercepting the united French fquadrons bound to America and the Eaft Indies, which
were reported to be on the point of failing from Breft.
The latter of thefe armaments was referved for a future victory; that bound to America, under the command of monf. De Jonquiere, being the only one that
put to fea. Its deftination was the re-conqueft of
Louifbourg, fo that its difcomfiture and capture muft,
on that ground, have been particularly grateful to Mr.
Warren. The operations of the Britifh armament
have been already related, in general terms, in the account of Mr. Anfon; fuffice it therefore to fay, on
the prefent occafion, that Mr. Warren had, happily,
an opportunity of fignalizing himfelf very remarkably
in the courfe of the action alluded to. The circumftance
we particularly refer to is not generally known, but, in

juftice

juftice to the memory of rear-admiral Warren, cannot be made too public. When the French fleet, amounting in the whole to thirty-eight fail, was firft difcovered, Mr. Anfon, the commander in chief, who was in the rear, made the fignal for the fhips under his command to form the line of battle; but Mr. Warren, who was in the van, judicioufly obferving, that confiderable time would be loft by purfuing this meafure; confequently, affected to take no notice of Mr. Anfon's fignal, but, in defiance of all the rules and regulations of the fervice, made that for a general chafe, fetting his topgallant-fails at the fame inftant. Mr. Anfon faw the propriety of Mr. Warren's meafures, and, inftead of enforcing his own, repeated Mr. Warren's fignal: the refult was, that the headmoft fhip foon clofed with the enemy, and brought them to action; while, on the other hand, had the cold nautically pedantic method of purfuit in a regular line of battle been adopted, it is highly probable the greater part, if not the whole of the French force, would have made their efcape.

The conduct of Mr. Warren, on this occafion, was entitled to the greater praife, becaufe, by acting in the manner he did, he endangered not only his reputation, but his life. If Mr. Anfon had been petulant, and had adhered ftrictly to the purfuit of his own firft intentions, he might not only have fubjected Mr. Warren to the heavieft cenfure, for the difobedience of his orders, but it is impoffible to fay to what extent the fentence of a court-martial might have reached, had the failure been attributed, as it might have been, to the

non-

non-compliance of Mr. Warren with the orders of his
commander in chief. Of this circumstance, Mr. West,
his captain, was perfectly aware, and entreated him,
almost with tears in his eyes, not to incur so dreadful
a risk. Mr. Warren spiritedly replied, " Sir, I am
obliged to you for your advice; but if I obey the signal
that is just made, the enemy will get off; I am determined, if they do, nothing shall lie on my conscience, as not having done the utmost in my power
to prevent them ; make the signal, and loose the top-
gallant-sails." The Devonshire, of sixty-six guns, on
board which ship he had hoisted his flag, got up with
monf. De Jonquiere himself, on board the Serieux ;
and, after receiving his fire, which was well directed,
closed within pistol-shot, and continued to engage till
the Serieux struck. Mr. Warren, having silenced this
antagonist, proceeded to attack the Invincible, commanded by the commodore de St. George, the second
officer in the French squadron ; and, after a short
time, had the satisfaction of seeing himself so well seconded by the Bristol, captain Montague, that their
opponent was quickly dismasted. The issue of this
memorable encounter was glorious, and may be comprised in very few words : the whole of the French
squadron, consisting of six ships of two decks, including the Gloire, of forty-four guns, besides four frigates, were taken. Mr. Warren was not forgotten on
this occasion ; his gallantry was rewarded with the order of the Bath, a remuneration for his services, which
being honorary only, was, in all probability, more
grateful to a man of his well-known generous turn

of

of mind, than one of a more fubftantial and lucrative nature would have been.   In the month of July following, fir Peter, being ftationed with a fquadron to cruife
off cape Finifterre, fell in with, on the 21ft of that
month, four valuable merchant-fhips, convoyed by two
French fhips of war, which ran into a bay on the
ifland of Sifargo.   Sir Peter, purfuing them, the whole
ran afhore ; one of the fhips of war, mounting forty-
four guns, was fired by the crew, and blew up, before
the boats of the fquadron could get on board ; but the
merchant-fhips were got off the next day, and carried
into Plymouth.   On the following day, fir Peter was
informed, by the captain of a privateer, that he had,
on the 17th and 18th of the fame month, chafed a large
fleet of coafters into Sediere bay, a fmall port to the
weftward of cape Ortegal ; he, therefore, by the advice of captain Harrifon, of the Monmouth, difpatched
captain Roddam, in the Viper floop, of fourteen guns,
with the Hunter dogger, and the privateer, to endeavour to take or deftroy them.   Captain Roddam accordingly ftood into the bay, and, with great refolution, attacked a fmall battery, which he foon filenced.
He then landed, fpiked up the guns, and deftroyed the
battery, after which he burnt twenty-eight fail of
fmall veffels, and, two days afterwards, rejoined the
admiral, with five others, and a Spanifh privateer.
Sir Peter, to teftify his approbation of captain Roddam's
fpirited conduct, recommended him fo ftrongly to the
admiralty, that he was immediately made poft captain,
in the Greyhound frigate.   On the 8th of July, fir
Peter's fquadron chafed and drove on fhore another
                                         French

French frigate of thirty-fix guns, about eight leagues weftward to cape Pinas ; and on the 15th of the fame month he was advanced to the rank of vice-admiral of the white fquadron.

Sir Peter failed again from Spithead, on a cruife, on the 2d of September, but, falling fick, was compelled to quit his command, and retire to his country feat, at Weftbury, in Hampfhire. This was the laft fervice he ever lived to perform ; for peace being concluded in the enfuing year, the fleet was of courfe difmantled ; and he lived not to fee a renewal of thofe times, when fervices like his own were needed. Few men ever attained, or better deferved a greater fhare of popularity. He had not only the fingular happinefs of being univerfally courted, efteemed, and beloved ; but had the additional confolation of having paffed through life without making, as far as we can inveftigate, a fingle enemy. At the general election in 1747, fir Peter was chofen reprefentative in parliament for the city of Weftminfter ; and, on the 12th of May 1748, was promoted to be vice-admiral of the red. In 1752, an occurrence moft highly honourable, though, perhaps, fomewhat laughable, took place with refpect to fir Peter Warren : the death of the lord mayor (Thomas Winterbottom, efq.) of London, producing a vacancy of alderman for Billingfgate ward, the citizens, who had, at a previous meeting, to fhew their refpect for fir Peter Warren, prefented him with the freedom of the city, and of the Goldfmiths' company, on account of his gallant behaviour at fea, nominated him for their alderman.

As

As foon as fir Peter was informed of their intentions, he very politely begged leave to decline accepting their offer, urging, that his character in life muft undoubtedly prevent his being able to difcharge, with propriety, the duties of that important office. In confequence of this, the deputy and common council fent him the following letter, dated Billingfgate ward, June 9th, 1752:

"HONOURED SIR,

" You have given us the utmoft concern, in telling us that it is inconfiftent with your duty, and other avocations, to honour us in being our alderman. Ourfelves in particular, and the inhabitants in general of the whole ward, are fo truly fenfible of the greatnefs of your character and true worth, that unanimity in your election would have expreffed how highly we thought ourfelves honoured by your acceptance of our choice; and it is with the greateft reluctance that this difappointment fhould occafion us, fo early as to-day, to return you our fincereft thanks for the great civilities you have fhewn us, and for the further affurance you have been pleafed to give us of the honour of your friendfhip; on which reliance we beg leave to make this application to you, moft earneftly defiring you to reconfider this matter, hoping fome lucky incident may ftill induce your acceptance, that we may have a more joyful caufe for the expreffion of the zeal we have for your high abilities and diftinguifhed merit, and to affure you that we fhall ever retain the higheft fenfe of the obligation you will thereby confer on,

" SIR," &c. &c.

Sir

Sir Peter, in return to this, immediately fent the deputy and common council the following anfwer: ...

" To the Deputy and Common Council-men of the Ward of Billingfgate.

"*Cavendifh Square, June 9th,* 1752.

"GENTLEMEN,

" I am extremely obliged to my worthy friends, the inhabitants of your ward, for the diftinguifhed mark of your favour, and to you, for the warm expreffions of regard contained in your letter of this date. But, as the acceptance of a civil office would interfere with the military one, that I have the honour to hold, in which I fhall ever be ready to ferve my king and country, I hope I fhall ftand excufed in declining the fingular honour fo unanimoufly and obligingly conferred on,

"GENTLEMEN, &c. &c.

(Signed) " P. WARREN."

With this letter the admiral fent the common council of Billingfgate ward two hundred pounds; one moiety to be diftributed among the poor of the faid ward, and the other to be difpofed of at their difcretion. The deputy and common council, not fatisfied with this anfwer, waited on fir Peter in perfon, hoping they might prevail on him to accept the office. He received them with great politenefs, but ftill refufed complying with their requeft, faying, it was incompatible with the duty he owed to his king and country, as a naval officer. Notwithftanding this, he was chofen alderman of Billingfgate ward, but, on the 23d of June,

fent

sent a message to the court of aldermen, desiring to be excused from serving the office to which he had been elected, and paid the fine of five hundred pounds for that purpose.   Immediately after the above event, sir Peter repaired to his native country, Ireland, where he was unhappily seized with a violent inflammatory fever, which put a period to his existence on the 29th of July 1752.   He was uniformly lamented by all persons, who have joined in agreeing, there could not exist a better and honester man, or a more gallant officer.

ADMIRAL BYNG

Publiſhd 1 May. 1800. by Edw.ᵈ Harding 98 Pall Mall.

ADMIRAL BYNG.

THIS unfortunate man was the fourth son of that eminent naval character fir George Byng, afterwards created lord vifcount Torrington, and Margaret, his wife, daughter of James Mafter, of Eaft Langdon, in the county of Kent, efquire. He was born at South-hill, in the year 1704, and entered into the fea fervice under the aufpices of his father, at the age of thirteen years. On the 8th of Auguft 1727, he was appointed captain of the Gibraltar frigate, and employed on the Mediterranean ftation. No mention is made of the commiffions he held fubfequent to this time, till the year 1741, when he commanded the Sunderland, a fourth rate, of fixty guns; in which fhip he foon afterwards proceeded to Newfoundland, as governor and commander in chief on that ftation. On his return to England, he removed into the Winchefter, one of the fleet ftationed in the Channel, and, on the 8th of Auguft 1745, was promoted to the rank of rear-ad-miral of the blue. In a few days after he had expe-rienced this promotion, he was fent commander in

chief

chief of a squadron stationed off the coast of Scotland,
for the purpose of preventing the introduction of any
supplies from France into that country, for the support
of the Pretender and his army.   In this occupation he
was extremely diligent and successful; and, when the
rebellion was quelled, was ordered to the Mediterranean.   While thus employed he was, on the 15th
of August 1747, advanced to the rank of vice-admiral
of the blue ; and, almost immediately subsequent to
the promotion just mentioned, succeeded admiral Med-
ley as commander in chief on that station.   After his
return from thence, at the conclusion of the war, he took
upon him no naval command, till the restless temper
of the French court began again to manifest itself in
the year 1755; Mr. Byng was then appointed to command a squadron equipped for the purpose of cruising
in the bay of Biscay, and off cape Finisterre.

Information having been received, at the very commencement of the ensuing year, that a very formidable
armament was in a forward state of equipment at
Toulon, intended, as was supposed, for the invasion
of the island of Minorca; Mr. Byng was chosen to
command the British squadron, intended to be sent into
the Mediterranean, for the purpose of counteracting
its efforts; and he was, previous to his putting to sea,
advanced to be admiral of the blue. A variety of delays,
disappointments, and contradictory orders, the constant
attendants of a weak, timid, half-measured administration, took place on this occasion.   Mr. Byng was detained in port many weeks longer than would have
been the case, under an able and zealous minister;

even

even when at length the armament did put to sea, the ships were ill manned, many of them, ill equipped, much out of repair, and completely unequal to the task of meeting so formidable an opponent as they had to encounter; an opponent whose ships were fresh out of port, in the highest condition, and evidently superior in point of actual strength to those under Mr. Byng. The experiment has once been tried, and with success, of rendering the commander in chief the innocent victim for the blunders and the infamy of a wretched administration: but, let the honest indignation which all ranks of people felt, and expressed, at the cruel fate which attended this unfortunate gentleman, stand as a warning to those, who are intrusted with the future management of public affairs, in any country in the universe, not again to repeat it; they may live to make it, but no honest men would wish they should survive it. In few words, he proceeded to the Mediterranean, met the French ships, enjoyed the empty honour of seeing them use every possible precaution, notwithstanding their superiority, of avoiding a close action, while he himself did not possess that peculiar skill, capable of preventing it.

Little doubt can be entertained, from every complexion of the measures pursued by the enemy, but that, if Mr. Byng had failed when he ought to have done, and with the force he might have done, instead of keeping a number of ships, in a better state of equipment than those he commanded, inactive in the British, ports, the island of Minorca would not have been wrested from the crown of Great Britain; but, cir-

cumstanced

cumftanced as the admiral was, the event might have
been confidered completely natural ; and yet, for a
defect in the abilities of the mind, and, as a cover for
the blunders of thofe, who muft have been aware of
that defect, Mr. Byng was ordered to England, conducted as a criminal, and treated, after his arrival, with
a rigour not exceeded by any which could have been practifed towards the worft of murderers, or traitors. Thofe
who were hardy enough to doubt his guilt, were proclaimed enemies to their country ; the recommendations
of his judges for mercy, were at leaft difregarded, if not
treated with contempt ; and, as if thofe who had employed him, confidered there was no fafety for themfelves, while he continued in exiftence, the unfortunate
admiral was configned to a fate, which would have
been ignominious, had it not been unmerited. He
was fhot on board the Monarch, on the 14th of
March 1757. Such, it is elfewhere obferved, was the
unhappy end of the unfortunate John Byng, who, as
it has been frequently remarked, feems to have been
rafhly condemned, meanly given up, and cruelly facrificed to the fafety, or popularity of men, who had
not the fmalleft claim to either.

ADMIRAL

ADMIRAL OSBORNE.

THIS gentleman was the defcendant of a family, fuppofed by heralds to have been originally of northern extraction, and, in later days, to have fettled in Effex. Peter Ofborne is found to have been fituate at Purleigh, in that county, in 1442, temp. Hen. VI. who, befides feveral other children (of which one was a prieft, another a nun at Malden) left Richard Ofborne, his heir. Henry Ofborne, of whom we are fpeaking, was the third fon of fir John Ofborne, bart. the fecond who bore the title, and was in the feventh defcent from the Peter Ofborne firft mentioned.

The fervices, in which he was engaged as a private captain, were, as is too often the cafe, extremely unimportant. On the 4th of January 1727-8, he was appointed to the Squirrel frigate ; in 1734, he commanded the Portland ; in 1739, the Prince of Orange, one of the fhips ordered to the Mediterranean, and after his return from thence, where he continued but a very fhort time, was appointed to the Litchfield, from whence he removed back into his former fhip, as foon as it was re-equipped for fervice. He after-

wards

wards proceeded to the Weſt Indies, and was very
unintereſtingly employed, under the orders of Mr.
Vernon, for he was not even preſent at the attack of
Carthagena, which was the only memorable event
that took place, while he continued in that quarter of
the world. After his return to England, he was appointed to the Princeſs Caroline, of eighty guns, in
which ſhip, having been ordered to the Mediterranean,
he very conſpicuouſly and gallantly diſtinguiſhed himſelf, in the encounter with the combined fleets of France
and Spain off Toulon, having been ſtationed in the
line as one of the ſeconds to Mr. Rowley. Towards
the cloſe of the year, he was advanced to the rank of
an eſtabliſhed commodore; and having hoiſted his broad
pendant on board the Eſſex, was employed in cruiſing
off the coaſt of Italy; and afterwards, in the enſuing
ſpring, was ſtationed to watch the motions of the
Spaniſh ſhips at Cadiz; but the Spaniards made no
attempt to put to ſea. About this time he was advanced to be rear-admiral of the blue, and having
returned to England in the month of June following,
on board the Barfleur, did not again take upon him
any naval command, till the year 1757 *. He was
then appointed to the Mediterranean ſtation. His
outſet was rather unfortunate, for he was driven back
by ſtreſs of weather, and obliged to put into Plymouth; but ſailing a ſhort time afterwards, he made

* On the 15th of July 1747, he was promoted to be rear-admiral of
the red. On the 12th of May following, to be vice of the white. In the
month of May 1757, to be vice-admiral of the red, and very ſoon afterwards to be adm lof the blue.

his paffage without any further inconvenience. The object of this armament was the attack, or blockade of fome of the fmall French fquadrons, which were faid to be ready for fea, at Toulon, or different parts of that coaft, intending to fail feparately for America, Breft, and other places of their deftination, in the hope, that by thus dividing their force, they might produce the fame effect on that of Britain, and probably have an opportunity of eluding the vigilance of its commanders.

Early in the year 1758, Mr. Ofborne, who then lay off Carthagena, where he had for fome time kept M. de la Clue, and his fquadron, impounded, received information that a fmall detachment, confifting of three fhips of two decks, and a frigate, were on the point of failing from Toulon, under the marquis du Quefne, in the hope of joining de la Clue, whofe force would, in cafe that junction was accomplifhed, have become fufficient to have enabled him to have conтefted the point, with fome appearance, or hope of fuccefs. The neceffary arrangements were accordingly made to prevent it ; and fo judicioufly and happily, that the fhips juft mentioned, falling in with the Britifh fquadron on the 28th of February, two of them, the Foudroyant, of eighty guns, and Orphee, of fixty-four, were purfued, and captured by different fhips. The Oriflamme, of fifty guns, was driven on fhore under the caftle of Aiglos, on the coaft of Spain, by the captains Rowley and Montague, who were prevented from effecting any further injury to the enemy, by the refpect always paid to a neutral port. The

Pleiade

Pleiade frigate alone, made her efcape by outfailing her purfuers. Mr. Ofborne having difpatched the feveral fhips in chace, ftood in for Carthagena, with the remainder of his fquadron to watch the motions of de la Clue, who continued quietly at anchor, without making the fmalleft attempt to refcue his companions, by pufhing out and engaging Mr. Ofborne. This was the laft important fervice he was able to perform. In a very fhort time afterwards he was obliged to re-fign his command to fir Charles Saunders, in confe-quence of a dreadful and fudden paralytic ftroke. Al-though the ftrength of his conftitution, enabled the admiral to efcape the immediate effects of an attack fo violent, yet he found his health fo much impaired, that he requefted permiffion to refign his command. He did this in the month of July, arriving at Spithead on the 21ft, in the St. George, of ninety guns, accom-panied by the Montague. Notwithftanding he, in fome degree, recovered his ftrength, he never was again ap-pointed to any active, or actual command afterwards ; but, as a convincing proof of the high fenfe retained of his paft fervices, he was, on the 4th of January 1763, on the death of lord Anfon, appointed his fuc-ceffor, as vice-admiral of England, and admiral of the white fquadron. His former appointment he refigned in 1765, and had a penfion granted him, on the Irifh eftablifhment, of twelve hundred a year, which he re-tained to his death, on the 4th of February 1771.

It is obferved, that in refpect to his character, we find in it much to praife, and alas (it is not in human nature to be void of blame) fome things to cenfure.

His

His bravery, his attachment to the caufe of his country, and his diligence, while employed in its actual fervice, have never been even queftioned ; but thofe who
were his warmeft friends, could not deny him to have
been, of a cold faturnine difpofition, ill habituated to
the warmth of fincere friendfhip, or even to thofe
attachments, which men are generally, from their
very nature, prone to form. Having fcarcely ever
made a friend, though poffeffed of habits not actively
inclined to create enemies, it is little to be wondered
at, that his public virtues fhould not have had fufficient
weight, to annihilate what were thought, private de-
formities. On the other hand, it is certainly no flender
proof of his worth, confidering him as a profeffional
man, that thofe admitted it, who feelingly felt the cold-
nefs of his difpofition, they themfelves, perhaps, poffeffing hearts overflowing with benignity ; that others
did not deny it, who fmarted under his aufterity, which
fcarcely knew how to diftinguifh between tyranny,
and the exaction of due obedience, from perfons who
were fubordinate to him ; and laftly, that perfons fhould
not refufe to acknowledge the merit of him, who was
himfelf, probably, as little attentive to that of others,
as any man who ever had the honour of holding a
naval command.

VICF

VICE-ADMIRAL LEE.

THE honourable Fitzroy Henry Lee, was the ninth son of fir Edward Henry Lee, of Ditchly, in the county of Oxford, baronet, created earl of Litchfield, by king Charles II. on his marriage with lady Catharine Fitzroy, one of the natural daughters of the aforefaid king, and Barbara Villiers, dutchefs of Cleveland. This family of Lee, which hath been very ancient in the county palatine of Chefter, took its firname, as it is prefumed, from the lordfhip of Lee, in the parifh of Wibonbury, in the faid county; of which family was fir Walter, at Lee, knight, who lived about the latter end of the reign of Edward III. and left iffue fir John, at Lee, of Lee-hall, knight, to whom fucceeded another, John, and to him Thomas, father of John Lee, of Lee-hall, efquire, who by Margery his wife, daughter of fir Ralph Hocknell, in the county of Chefter, had iffue, Thomas Lee, of Lee-hall, from whom the Lees, now of Lee-hall, are defcended. Another fon of the faid John, and Margery, his wife, was Benedict Lee, who about the beginning of the

reign

reign of Edward IV. came out of Cheshire, and settled at Quarendon, in the county of Bucks, and by Elizabeth his wife, daughter and heir to John Wood, of the county of Warwick, esquire, had issue Richard Lee, of Quarendon; which Richard altered his arms to argent a fess, between three crescents sable, and had issue by Elizabeth his wife, one of the daughters and coheirs of William Sanders, of the county of Oxford, esquire, four sons, viz. sir Robert Lee, of Burton, in the county of Bucks, knight, Benedict Lee, of Hulcotte, esquire, Roger Lee, of Pickthorn, and John, from whom the Lees of Binfield, in Berkshire, derive their descent.

Mr. Lee, after having regularly passed through the different subordinate stations, was appointed on the 25th of October 1728, to be captain of the Loo, a forty-gun ship. No mention is made of his having held any naval employments subsequent to this time, till the year 1735, when he was promoted to the rank of commodore, and accordingly hoisted his broad pendant on board the Falkland, of fifty guns, as governor, and commander in chief, on the Newfoundland station. He held this distinguished command during the current, and two succeeding years, being the period usually allotted to such commands. On the commencement of the war with Spain, in 1739, he was appointed to the Pembroke, of sixty guns, and ordered to the Mediterranean, where he served in succession, under the admirals, Haddock, and Mathews. He returned to England at the close of the year 1742, or the commencement of the ensuing spring. In 1744, he

he was captain of the Edinburgh, but how, or where
he was employed, does not appear. In the month
of March 1745-6, having hoifted his broad pendant,
on board the Suffolk, a third rate, he proceeded to
the Weft Indies, though with the rank of commodore
only, being appointed commander in chief of his majefty's fhips and veffels, on that ftation. Some mif-
underftanding having arifen (a circumftance by no
means wonderful, confidering his ftrange whimfical
temper) between the inhabitants of that part of the
world and himfelf, a variety of petty complaints, were
tranfmitted home to England againft him; among
thefe was one, which, had it been true, would have
borne exceedingly hard on his character. For it was
no lefs than that of having permitted a fleet and convoy
belonging to the enemy, to pafs by unmolefted.

His promotion to the rank of a flag-officer, was
accordingly fufpended, till the matter had been properly inveftigated; but his arrival foon filenced the
ill-founded clamour; and the charge, being even without the ceremony of a legal inquiry, difcovered to be
totally groundlefs, Mr. Lee was, on the 15th of July
1747, promoted to be rear-admiral of the red, which
owing to the circumftance already ftated, was his firft
flag. On the 12th of May 1748, he was advanced
to be vice-admiral of the white, which was the higheft
rank he ever attained. He had been an imprudent,
or what is generally called a free liver. Though far
from having reached an advanced age, his conftitution became fo much impaired, that he received a
fevere ftroke of the palfy, of which he died on the

18th

18th of April 1751. As to his character, he was among the seamen, far from being popular. This disgust had arisen from his supposed too great severity, and appears to have been in a great measure improperly conceived, for we are told, and from good authority, that an intimate friend mentioning this dislike with a good deal of surprise, the admiral answered, very seriously, he himself was as much astonished, as any person could be, for, though he totally disregarded and despised the calumny, he could boldly defy the world to prove, he had ever committed an ungenerous, or an ill-natured action.

A variety of trivial anecdotes are told of this gentleman, which prove him to have been a man, possessed of infinite humour, though of very coarse manners. In service he was a rigid disciplinarian, a trait of character, which became the chief cause of his being unpopular. Mr. Mostyn and Mr. Byng were equally eminent for pursuing the same line of conduct, and consequently equally disliked. Some forecastle wit, accordingly, composed the following distich on these gentlemen :

> " From Mostyn, Byng, and Lee,
> " Good Lord, deliver me."

When this was reported to the admiral, and the very person of the poet pointed out, so far from expressing any anger, he sent for the poor fellow, who expected nothing less, than a very heavy punishment, and agreeably surprised him, by giving him a dollar, and saying, with the greatest good humour, " I did not
think

think you had been fo clever a fellow, but you certainly put my name in only for the fake of the rhyme." This fame gentleman was once lying at anchor in a line of battle fhip, during a violent gale of wind. The cables, both of the fmall and beft bower parted, the fheet anchor was let go, which held the fhip for a fhort time ; but afterwards dragging, the firft lieutenant ran down below, in the utmoft hafte and agitation, to inform the captain, who was laid up in the gout with both feet ; "Sir," faid the lieutenant, "the fheet-anchor is come home."—"Upon my foul," faid his commander, "the fheet-anchor is very much in the right of it, I don't know who the devil would ftay abroad in fuch weather as this is, if he could help it."

COMMODORE BARNET.

It is not precisely known, under whose protection and patronage, this brave and worthy officer first went to sea; but in 1726, he is known to have served in the rank of lieutenant, under sir Charles Wager, the commander in chief of the fleet, sent during that year into the Baltic; and to have been specially intrusted by the admiral, on many important occasions, as a confidential person, on whose courage and prudence he could implicitly rely. In particular, he was sent to Cronslot, in the Port Mahon frigate, as the bearer of dispatches to the empress, and admiral Apraxin, and to confer with them, touching particular points, on which the event of the expedition depended. So well did he establish the good opinion, which sir Charles most deservedly entertained of him, that he continued ever afterwards through life, to manifest towards him on all occasions, the most cordial friendship and esteem.

On the 26th of January 1731, he was promoted to the rank of post-captain, and appointed to the Bideford frigate; in 1734-5, he commanded the Notting-

ham,

ham, a guard-ship, mounting sixty guns; and after the commencement of hostilities with Spain in 1739, being then captain of the Dragon, also a sixty-gun ship, he served under the orders of Mr. Haddock, in the Mediterranean. He had there the good fortune to distinguish himself extremely, and receive the highest complimentary honour from the admiral, in reward of his conduct, on the occasion which we shall briefly describe. Being detached soon after his arrival in the Mediterranean, on a cruise, in company with another British ship of the line, they fell in with three French ships of war, off Cadiz, which they imagined were register-ships, laden with treasure from the Spanish West Indies. Mr. Barnet accordingly hailed them, but received no sort of answer, till after a third repetition of that mode of inquiry. Even then it was so dissatisfactory, and equivocating, that he was still the more confirmed in his original opinion; he accordingly fired a single shot ahead of the French ships, which the chevalier de Caylus, who commanded, returned with a broadside. A sharp contest ensued; and, after a continuance of two hours, the French, who had lost one of their captains, and a considerable number of men, besides having upwards of seventy wounded, thought proper to desist, and come to a proper explanation. They were so severely handled as to be obliged to put into Malaga to refit. Mr. Barnet, and his companion, on their parts, sustained considerable injury in their masts and rigging; but had only four men killed, and fourteen wounded, several of them very slightly.

Mr.

Mr. Haddock was, not long afterwards, under the neceffity of returning to England, on account of the ill ftate of his health, and refigning the command to Mr. Leftock, who, during the very fhort time he held it, ingenioufly and wantonly contrived an altercation with Mr. Barnet. It is not, we hope, affuming too much in praife of that gentleman, nor will it, on the other hand, we truft, be confidered as depreciating from the merits of other worthy officers, that the conduct of no perfon employed in his majefty's fervice, was ever more correct than that of Mr. Barnet. On the prefent occafion, therefore, as no man could be more undeferving of cenfure, fo could no one repel the infolence of a fuperior, ridiculoufly proud of his elevated fituation, with more firmnefs, decency, and fpirit: obferving, at the time he defended his own character, the greateft decorum towards the commanding officer, who had moft illiberally and wantonly attacked him.

It is not a little fingular, that the points of controverfy were immaterially diffimilar to thofe, which foon afterwards became the fubject of difpute, between Mr. Mathews, and Mr. Leftock. An advocate for the exiftence of the fpirit of prophecy, might almoft perfuade himfelf, that Mr. Barnet had an intuitive knowledge of what was hereafter to happen, and had actually ftudied a proper rebuke for the future conduct of his admiral, to whom he farcaftically replied, in the courfe of their epiftolary conteft, " I prefume there are inftances both of whole divifions going down to the enemy too foon, and of coming in fo late as to

have

have no part in the action." Mr. Leftock defisted on finding Mr. Barnet a man of too much firmnefs to endure the fhadow of an infult, and poffeffing too good an underftanding to fuffer himfelf to be impofed upon, or betrayed into a confeffion of having been in the wrong, when he knew not only the integrity of his own heart, but was, in every refpect, a competent judge, as well of the duties of a private captain, as of thofe of the admiral, under whofe orders he then acted.

Mr. Barnet returned to England very foon afterwards, and was almoft immediately appointed commodore of a fmall fquadron, ordered to the Eaft Indies, for the protection of the Britifh fettlements in that quarter. The force put under his command, confifted of the Deptford (his own fhip), and Medway, of fixty guns each, the Prefton, of fifty, and the Diamond frigate, of twenty. He failed from Portfmouth on the 25th of May 1744, and, in the courfe of his paffage, rendered a fingular piece of juftice to a number of perfons, whofe veffels had been captured, in defiance of the laws of nations, in different ports of the cape de Verd iflands, by a Spanifh privateer, which he found on his arrival lying at Porto Praya, together with a prize fhe had juft before taken. Refpecting the neutrality of the place, he at firft offered no difturbance whatever to the enemy; but being prefently afterwards informed of the illegal manner in which the Spaniard had conducted himfelf, with regard to the rights of neutral powers, he civilly informed the governor, that he fhould no longer confider the neutrality of the port a protection to the foe, who had fo fcandaloufly con-

ducted

ducted himself. The privateer and her prize were immediately taken poffeffion of, together with a brigantine, which had alfo been captured, but was retaken by the boats in the offing. The Britifh veffels were reftored immediately to their owners, without falvage, and all poffible reftitution was made to them, as well as to the crews of two other inferior veffels, that had been burnt by the fame enemy, of all the articles and commodities they could claim, which were found on board the privateer. This piece of juftice having been performed, the commodore proceeded on his voyage.

Soon after quitting Madagafcar, where he procured a much-needed fupply of water and provifions, he divided his little fquadron into two parts; his own fhip and the Prefton paffing through the ftreights of Sunda, and from thence to Banca; while the Medway and Diamond fteered for the ftreights of Malacca. Mr. Barnet took every poffible precaution to difguife both his own fhip and his confort, by painting and adorning them after the Dutch fafhion. After having remained for fome time ftationary in the ftreights of Banca, on the 25th of January 1744, he got fight of three large French-built fhips, of which he fuppofed two to be merchant-veffels from China, and the third a French fhip of war, mounting fifty guns, from Pondicherry, which he had received information was in thofe feas. Mr. Barnet immediately got under fail, accompanied by the Prefton, in order to attack them; and fo perfect was the deception, that the enemy had no doubt of their being Dutch fhips, till they were within mufket-fhot

of them, when, striking their Dutch, they hoisted English colours. The French ships were not, however, surprised, though deceived; for they were all completely
ready for immediate action. Mr. Barnet was mistaken
in the first opinion he had formed of them, for the ship
of fifty guns was not in company; and the vessels he attacked were the Dauphin, Jason, and Hercules, large
ships, all of them of seven hundred tons burden, each
mounting thirty guns, and carrying one hundred and
fifty men, deeply and richly laden with cargoes of tea,
china-ware and silk. Mr. Barnet ordered lord North-
esk, in the Preston, to board one of the ships, while
he himself prepared to act in the same manner against
that which was, apparently, of the most force, and
which he accordingly supposed to be the commodore.
While, however, they were both endeavouring to carry
this measure into execution, an unlucky shot from one
of the enemy's ships cut both the tiller ropes, when they
were on the point of sheering on board them. This
unfortunate accident delayed the capture for some
time; but, being repaired with all possible expedition,
the enemy's ships were all secured, after a very stout,
and, indeed, more determined resistance than could
have been expected, of two hours continuance. They
were all prizes of considerable value, the cargoes being
valued at upwards of three hundred thousand pounds,
had they arrived safe in Europe. The prizes were
sent to Batavia, and the commodore himself, with his
consort, pursued his voyage to the British settlements
in India.

During

During the enfuing year, he was fingularly fortunate, not only in affording the moft complete protection to the commerce of Britain, but in foiling the attempts of the enemy by land, and alfo in capturing every veffel they poffeffed. Three of thefe confifting of two fhips of fix hundred, and one of four hundred tons burden, fully laden, and completely armed for defence, fell into the hands of the Prefton and Lively, which fhips the commodore had prudently ftationed off cape Palmiras, for the purpofe of intercepting any of the enemy's veffels that might endeavour to enter the Ganges. In the month of January following, the Medway and Lively joined the commodore, having completed the fuccefs of the fhips under his orders, by capturing the Expedition, of fourteen guns, the only cruifer which, at that time, remained to the French. Nor was this the only line of fervice in which he was employed: in the month of January he repaired to Pondicherry, where his prefence completely baffled a project formed by the French for the attack of Fort St. David. They had marched out of Pondicherry, with a corps of one thoufand infantry, four hundred of which were Europeans, together with forty horfe, and a fufficient number of cannon. They encamped within a mile of Fort St. David; but, on Mr. Barnet's arrival, and his making apparent difpofitions for landing, by fending his boats to found, and practifing every other oftenfible manœuvre preparatory to that intent, the enemy decamped with the utmoft expedition from Fort St. David, thinking it a happinefs to get, by forced marches, once more into Pondicherry, which they

F f 2 felicitated

felicitated themfelves in having been the caufe of preferving from the deftructive arms of the Englifh.

This was, unfortunately, the laft exploit in which
Mr. Barnet had it in his power to be ufeful to his
country, a premature indifpofition having put a period
to his exiftence, when in the very prime of life, on
the 29th of April 1746.

Harding sc

THE HON.BLE S.R EDW.D HAWKE

Pub. Feb.1.1800 by Edw.d Harding 98 Pall Mall.

LORD HAWKE

―――――

Was the only fon of Edward Hawke, of Lincoln's Inn, efquire, barrifter at law, and Elizabeth, his wife, relict of colonel Ruthven, and daughter of Nathaniel Bladen, efquire, alfo of Lincoln's Inn, and of the fame honourable profeffion as his fon-in-law. After a regular progreffion through the feveral fubordinate fituations, he was, in 1733, appointed commander of the Wolfe floop of war; and was from thence promoted, on the 30th of March 1733-4, to be captain of the Flamborough frigate. In 1739 he was ordered to the Weft Indies, being then, according to the reports of fome perfons, captain of the Lark, a forty-gun fhip; this circumftance appears, however, doubtful; be that as it may, in 1741, he is known to have commanded, on the fame ftation, the Portland, of fifty guns. Soon after this time, he was appointed to the Berwick, a third rate, one of the fhips ordered, at the fame time, to the Mediterranean, for the purpofe of reinforcing Mr. Mathews. The encounter off Toulon was the firft event that fortune afforded him of diftinguifhing himfelf in any particular manner; for, continuing to

command

command the Berwick, he bore a moſt conſpicuous
ſhare in that well-known encounter, and it has been,
with great truth remarked, that if every officer in the
fleet had exerted himſelf as ſpiritedly as Mr. Hawke, the
combined fleets of France and Spain would either have
been captured or annihilated. The greateſt injury inflicted on the enemy, was effected by himſelf; the
Poder, a Spaniſh ſhip of the line, the only one taken
or deſtroyed in the encounter, having been captured
by the Berwick ſingly. On the enſuing day, captain
Hawke experienced the dreadful mortification of being
compelled to deſtroy his newly-acquired prize, in
conſequence of her diſabled ſtate, and the very near
approach of ſeveral ſhips belonging to the enemy's
fleet, which had ſuſtained little or no damage in the
preceding action.

There is a nautical legend, which has for many
years been in common circulation, though ſuppoſed
completely deſtitute of foundation, that, in order to
enable him to take poſſeſſion of the Poder, he was
under the neceſſity of breaking the line, for which
breach of maritime law, he was tried by a court-
martial, and, in compliance with the very ſtrict ar-
ticle under which he fell, and which admitted of no
palliation, was ſentenced to be diſmiſſed the ſervice.
This puniſhment, it is ſaid, was actually inflicted;
and that he was reſtored (a circumſtance which completely effaced all ſhadow of diſgrace) to his rank on
the enſuing day, by the ſpecial command of king
George II. Be that as it may, nothing further is related of this very renowned and worthy character, till
the

the year 1747, when he was, on the 15th of July, promoted to be rear-admiral of the white. He was immediately afterwards appointed to command a ſtrong ſquadron, ordered to ſea, in the hope of intercepting a numerous fleet of merchant-ſhips, collected at the iſle of Aix, and intended to be convoyed to America by a very formidable force, under the command of M. de l'Etendiere, chef d'eſcadre.

Mr. Hawke, having hoiſted his flag on board the Devonſhire, of ſixty-ſix guns, ſailed from Plymouth on the 9th of Auguſt, having five ſmall fourth rates, and nine third rates, under his orders. A very dull and unimportant cruiſe, of long continuance, was at length repaid by a ſight of the French ſquadron, on the 14th of October, at ſeven in the morning. The force of the enemy was ſoon diſcovered to conſiſt of eleven or twelve large ſhips of war, having a numerous fleet of merchant-veſſels under its convoy. One or two ſhips of war, together with ſeveral large frigates, having been ordered by the French commodore to make all poſſible ſail with the charge committed to his protection, he drew the remainder, conſiſting of eight ſail, ſeven of which were very large, and capital ſhips, into a line, for the purpoſe of favouring the eſcape of his friends. The action commenced about half paſt eleven, between the leading ſhips of the Engliſh, and the rear of the enemy; nor did the encounter cloſe, owing to the very ſcattered ſtate in which it was unavoidably maintained, till ſeven in the evening, when the Terrible, of ſeventy-four guns, the laſt of ſix ſhips of the line, which ſurrendered on that oc-

F f 4

caſion,

cafion, having ftruck to the rear-admiral, he deemed
it prudent and neceffary to make the fignal to bring to,
in order to colled his fhips, and their feveral prizes ;
two only, out of that force which engaged the Britifh
fquadron, having, with the utmoft difficulty, made
their efcape in a very fhattered ftate.   On the enfuing
morning, the Weazel floop was detached to the Weft
Indies, whither the enemies fhips were bound, to ap-
prife the commander in chief, on that ftation, of the
event which had taken place ; and, owing to this diligent meafure, a very confiderable number of them were
captured by the Britifh cruifers in that quarter.   Mr.
Hawke having, in confequence of the very difabled
ftate of the prizes, been compelled to lie to fome days,
for the purpofe of ereding jury-mafts and otherwife
refitting them, did not arrive at Portfmouth till the
31ft of Odober, and, as a juft reward for his bravery, and very excellent condud on the preceding
occafion, was, in the enfuing month, eleded one of
the knights companions of the moft honourable order
of the Bath.   In the month of January 1747, he was
appointed to command a fquadron ftationed to cruife
in foundings, and, in a very few days afterwards, two
of his fhips had the good fortune to meet with and
capture a very fine French third rate, of feventy-four
guns, called the Magnanime.   Peace fucceeded in a
very few months afterwards, and no further memorable incident contributed to render the fervices of this
gallant gentleman more fplendid than they had already
been.

Although

Although his employments, during the time of peace, neceſſarily became leſs intereſting than before it, they continued to be of a nature that could not fail to reflect on him the higheſt honour. In 1749 he commanded the convoy ſent to North America, with the intended ſettlers of Nova Scotia, and his character and conduct cannot, perhaps, be more juſtly and candidly delineated than in the words of Collins, who ſtates, that "he performed this duty with all that integrity and care that could be expected from a perſon of his honour and veracity:" the ſame author adds, "that having, after the commencement of peace, acted as preſident of ſeveral naval courts-martial *, he always took the greateſt care to diſtribute juſtice without any regard to rank or connexions: the innocent were ſure to meet with his protection, and the guilty to feel the rod of puniſhment." In 1750, he was appointed to the Portſmouth command, and, on the 15th of Auguſt, entertained on board the Monarch, his flag-ſhip, then lying at Spithead, their royal highneſſes the prince and princeſs of Wales, with ſeveral of their children, an honour no admiral had, at that time, ever before received. The conduct of the French court becoming extremely ſuſpicious, in the year 1755, ſir Edward, who had, many years before, that is to ſay, on the

---

* In the month of July, 1749, he preſided on the trial of lieutenant Couchman, and others, for piratically running away with his majeſty's ſhip the Cheſterfield; and, very ſoon afterwards, on the trial of an officer of rank, on the charge of diſobedience of orders. In the month of December 1749, he ſat on the court-martial held at Deptford, for the trial of rear-admiral Knowles; and, in the month of February following, on a fourth, held for the trials of captains Holmes and Powlett.

12th of May 1748, been raifed to the rank of vice-admiral of the blue, was advanced to the fame ftation in the white fquadron, and appointed to command one of thofe fmall fleets, that it was deemed prudent fhould be kept conftantly at fea, at the entrance of the channel, for the purpofe of parrying any fudden attacks of an infidious, and fubtile enemy. He returned into port in the month of September, being relieved by Mr. Byng, with an armament of nearly the fame force with his own. In the month of May, in the enfuing year, he was fent out to Gibraltar, in the Antelope, of fifty guns, with orders to fuperfede, and fend home the officer juft mentioned, whofe conduct, as may be feen in the memoirs given of him, had afforded the higheft diffatisfaction to the Britifh minifter. Fort St. Philip having, however, furrendered before his arrival, and the whole ifland of Minorca, confequently, become fubject to the enemy, the French admiral fhrunk from all further conteft, and to enfure his better fafety, returned to Toulon.

In 1757, fir Edward was felected to command an expedition equipped for the attack of Rochefort: his force confifted of no lefs than fixteen fhips of the line, two bomb-ketches, two fire-fhips, two buffes, one ftore-fhip, and fifty-five tranfports, exclufive of the Jafon, of forty guns, employed as a tranfport; and the Chefterfield, as a repeating frigate. The land forces confifted of ten regiments of infantry, two of marines, a fquadron of light horfe, and a proportionate train of artillery. Formidable, as was the force of this armament, the delays and hefitation of the general, and

other

other land officers, rendered the whole of the project abortive. The smallest blame, however, on account of the failure, was by no means imputable to sir Edward, to whose conduct the immortal Wolfe himself paid the profoundest tribute, in the evidence given by him on the trial of general sir John Mordaunt, who commanded the land forces; and Collins concludes his remarks on the expedition in the following handsome terms: " Sir Edward Hawke engaged to do every thing in his power to assist the land forces in their attempt against Rochefort; but nothing was done, except taking the small isle of Aix, though the gallant admiral exerted himself to the utmost, to answer the intention of the expedition." Having returned to Portsmouth with the transports, and troops, on the 6th of October, he repaired again to his station off the coast of France, on the 22d of the same month, for the purpose of blocking up their several ports, and preventing any smaller armaments from putting to sea. He was almost uninterruptedly occupied in this particular line of service, without meeting with any memorable incident, till the 3d of April following. He had then the fortune to discover a numerous convoy belonging to the enemy off the isle of Rhee, but was not happy enough to prevent their making their escape into St. Martins, together with the three frigates which escorted them. After this disappointment, he, in the afternoon of the same day, got sight of a squadron, and convoy belonging to the enemy, off the isle of Aix; its force consisted of seven ships of the line, as many frigates, and forty merchant-vessels, or transports, under

their

their protection. It is almoſt needleſs to ſay, the enemy immediately fled, preferring their ſhips ſhould take the ground, with all its conſequences, to their falling into the hands of the Britiſh admiral. The meaſure certainly diminiſhed the diſaſter of the enemy, which, however, notwithſtanding all their care, fell extremely heavy; by throwing the guns, ſtores, ammunition, proviſions, and even their ballaſt overboard from the men of war, together with part of the cargoes from the merchant-veſſels, they ſucceeded in dragging their ſhips through the mud, into the harbour of Rochefort, and thus was the whole of their expedition completely put an end to. Sir Edward gave a finiſhing ſtroke to their loſs, by ſending the boats of his ſquadron on the following morning, to cut away the numerous buoys which they had laid on their cannon, and other unperiſhable articles.

Having, through indiſpoſition, been compelled to a temporary retirement from ſervice, in the month of June following, he did not take upon himſelf any ſubſequent command, till the month of May 1759; he was then appointed admiral in chief of the very powerful fleet, equipped, to oppoſe an equally formidable force, which the French were then very buſily employed in equipping, at Breſt, and other ports, for the avowed purpoſe of invading Britain. The prudence and caution of the enemy, however, prevented the exertion of ſir Edward's gallantry, for the ſpace of nearly ſix months, till having been driven from his ſtation, in the month of October, and compelled to take refuge in Plymouth-ſound, in ſpite of every attempt he could

make,

make, to keep the fea, on the 8th of the enfuing month, the enemy feized the glorious opportunity of his abfence, and quitted the harbour of Breft fix days afterwards. Sir Edward, foon as the gale moderated, loft not a moment in attempting to regain his ftation, and, on the 19th of November, had the good fortune to fall in with the marquis de Conflans, at the head of twenty-one fail of the line, befides fmaller veffels, at the very inftant he was attempting, like a kite; to pounce on a fmall look-out fquadron of Britifh fhips, ftationed in Quiberon bay, under the orders of commodore Duff. A moft fpirited, though irregular conteft, neceffarily occafioned by the inclemency of the wea-ther, and the rocky coaft, on which the action took place, immediately commenced; and ended in the deftruction, or capture of a confiderable part of the French force * : the injury fuftained by the remainder

which

* The Soleil Royal, the marquis de Conflans's own fhip, ran on fhore, and was afterwards burnt. The fame fate attended the Hero, of feventy-four guns. The Thefee and Superbe were funk in the action; and the Formidable, of eighty guns, bearing the rear-admiral's flag, was captured. Sir Edward, in his official difpatches, affigns the following modeft annexed excufe, for the lofs of his antagonifts not having been much greater than it proved : " In attacking a flying enemy, it was impoffible, in a fhort win-ter's day, that all our fhips fhould be able to get into action ; or all thofe of the enemy brought to it. The commanders and companies of fuch as did come up with the rear of the French, on the 20th, behaved with the greateft intrepidity, and gave the ftrongeft proofs of a true Britifh fpirit. In the fame manner, I am fatisfied, thofe would have acquitted themfelves, whofe bad going fhips, or the diftance they were at in the morning, pre-vented from getting up. Our lofs by the enemy is not confiderable, for in the fhips, which are now with me, I find only one lieutenant, and thirty-nine feamen, and marines killed, and about two hundred and two wounded.

When

which efcaped being captured was moreover fo great, that very few of them were ever again fit for fervice.

Sir Edward, crowned with the laurels of victory, did not return to Plymouth till the 17th of January in the enfuing year; the whole of the intermediate time being employed, in attempting to deftroy the fugitives, feveral of which had, with the greateft difficulty, and in the utmoft diftrefs, made their efcape into the river Villaine. A penfion of two thoufand pounds a year, was immediately beftowed on the admiral, with a reverfion to his fons, and the furvivor of them, by his majefty. On the 28th of January following, being the firft day of his attendance in the houfe of commons, as member for the town of Portfmouth, which place he had unceafingly reprefented for thirteen years, he received the thanks of that houfe from the fpeaker. In fhort, the juft tribute moft defervedly rendered to his gallantry, had fcarcely ever before been equalled, and never exceeded. The foregoing event might fairly be confidered, as having given a decifive blow to the French naval power, during the continuance of the war, however long it might be protracted. The fequel proved the truth of the fact, for no French fleet ever

When I confidered the feafon of the year, the hard gales on the day of action, a flying enemy, the fhortnefs of the day, and the coaft we were on, I can boldly affirm, that all that could poffibly be done, has been done. As to the lofs we have fuftained, let it be placed to the account of the neceffity I was under of running all rifks, to break this ftrong force of the enemy. Had we had but two hours more day-light, the whole had been totally deftroyed, or taken, for we were almoft up with the van, when night overtook us."

again

again appeared at fea. In the month of Auguft 1760, he refumed the command of the fleet, ftationed in Quiberon bay, for the purpofe of watching the few fhips of war, that ftill remained to that country. He was employed in the fame uninterefting line of fervice, till the conclufion of the war ; and perhaps it may be confidered, as the beft eulogium that can be beftowed upon him, that he met with no fecond opportunity of diftinguifhing himfelf, merely becaufe he could find no enemy hardy enough to contend with him. On the 22d of April 1761, he was elected one of the elder brethren of the Trinity-houfe, and on the 4th of January following, the very honourable civil appointment of rear-admiral of England was beftowed upon him ; from whence he was further advanced, on the refignation of Mr. Ofborne, on the 5th of November 1765, to be vice-admiral thereof. On the 2d of the enfuing month, he was appointed firft commiffioner for executing the office of lord high admiral, a ftation which he continued to fill with the higheft honour, till the 10th of January 1771, when he voluntarily refigned it.

This brave, and truly worthy man, for no one ever poffeffed more true gallantry, or unfullied integrity, retired, in a great meafure, after this time, from what might be called public life ; intermixing no farther with the adminiftration of affairs than what belonged to him, firft, as a member of parliament, and afterwards as a peer of the realm. In confideration of the very great and eminent fervices he had rendered his country,

country, he was advanced, by letters patent, bearing date May 20th, 1776, to the dignity of a peer of Great Britain, by the ftyle and title of baron Hawke, of Towton, in the county of York. Purfuing the fame line of conduct to the laft moment of his life, he died univerfally refpected, and truly lamented, on the 17th of October 1781, at Sunbury, in Middlefex. He was buried at Swaithling, near Botley, in the county of Hants.

His lordfhip married Catharine, daughter of Walter Brooke, of Barton-hall, in the county of York, efquire, and by that lady, who died on the 28th of October 1756, had iffue three fons, and one daughter.

It becomes an intrufion, almoft impertinent, to attempt any delineation of a character fo well known, and fo highly revered, as that of his lordfhip. To fay he was prudent, circumfpect, and brave; able, as a naval commander, and honeft, whether confidered as a private gentleman, or a fenator, would be only a faint outline of thofe high merits, all men muft allow him to have poffeffed, and at the fame time, would affert nothing neceffary to be made known to thofe who are in any degree acquainted, either with the general hiftory of their native country, or thofe particular tranfactions, intimately connected with the life of this great and noble perfon; but, if any fhould exift, who are really uninformed of that tribute of gratitude, they juftly owe to their renowned countryman, to fuch we fhall beg leave to fay, briefly, that to the moft confummate courage, and moft active

tive

tive spirit, he joined a cool, deliberate temper, not to be ruffled by accident, or shaken by any unforeseen, and sudden misfortune. In service, he was always a steady enforcer of discipline, but at the same time the constant friend, and patron of merit. If those who were remiss in their duty, met an implacable foe, those of a contrary description, always found a warm, and most zealous friend; so that to sum up his character in very few words, bad men feared him, good men loved him, and the natural enemies of his native country, stood in awe of him.

ADMIRAL BOSCAWEN

―――

WAS the third fon of Hugh, firft lord vifcount Falmouth, and Charlotte, eldeft of two daughters and co-
heirs of Charles Godfrey, efq. by Arabella Churchill,
his wife, fifter to John, duke of Marlborough. He
was born on the 19th of Auguft 1711; and, having
betaken himfelf to a naval life, was, after paffing
through the feveral fubordinate ftations with the higheft
credit, promoted, on the 12th of March 1737, to be
captain of the Leopard, a fourth rate, of fifty guns.
In 1739 he commanded the Shoreham frigate, on the
Jamaica ftation, and that fhip needing fome repairs
when Mr. Vernon failed to attack Porto Bello, captain
Bofcawen requefted permiffion to attend him as a volunteer, and was one of the officers employed, after the
reduction of the fortrefs, in fuperintending its demolition. He diftinguifhed himfelf very confpicuoufly
at the attack of Carthagena, having been appointed
to command a detachment of three hundred failors,
ordered to attack fome batteries erected by the
Spaniards, that confiderably impeded the operations
of the befieging army. The moft complete fuccefs
crowned

Harding sc

THE HON^{BLE} EDW^D BOSCAWEN

Pub^d April 1, 1800. by Edw. Harding 98 Pall Mall.

crowned the attempt. On the death of lord Aubrey
Beauclerk, who unhappily was killed in the attack of
Bocca-Chica, Mr. Boscawen was appointed his successor as captain of the Prince Frederic of seventy
guns. He returned to England in this ship in the
month of May 1742, and was principally, if not entirely, employed during the three succeeding years, in
cruising in the British channel, or the neighbourhood
of it. In the latter part of the year 1755, he commanded the Dreadnought, of sixty guns, in which
ship he captured the French frigate, called the Medea.
At the conclusion of the year, he was appointed to
the Royal Sovereign, a first rate, stationed at the Nore,
and was, moreover, invested with a species of civil
office, as superintendant of all the vessels, purchased,
or hired for his majesty's service, and fitted in the river
Thames, during that important crisis, the continuance
of the rebellion in Scotland.

He held the office just mentioned, however, but a
very few weeks, for in the month of January 1746,
he was appointed to the Namur, a ship then for the
first time fitted for sea, after having been reduced from
a second to a third rate. During a great part of the
ensuing summer, he was senior officer of a small squadron, stationed at the entrance of the channel; in
which occupation he had the good fortune to make
two important prizes, one of them being an advice-
boat, sent to Europe by the French chef d'escadre,
on the American station, with an account of the death
of the duke d'Anville, and the total failure of the expedition intrusted to his care. In 1747, he served

G g 2   as

as captain of the Namur, in the fleet fent out under the orders of the admirals Anfon and Warren, and diftinguifhed himfelf in the moft gallant manner during the encounter with a French fquadron under De Jonquiere, in which he was very feverely wounded in the fhoulder by a mufket-ball. His bravery was rewarded on the 15th of July following, not only by his advancement to the rank of a flag-officer, as rear-admiral of the blue fquadron, but by the very fingular appointment of commander in chief of all his majefty's forces by fea and land, employed in the Eaft Indies. The naval force under his orders, confifted of fix fhips of the line, and the troops of three battalions of infantry, with a due proportion of artillery. The fquadron failed from St. Helen's, on the 4th of November 1747, and after landing the troops for refrefhment at the Cape of Good Hope, during a fhort time, made the ifland of Mauritius, which was the firft object of attack, on the 23d of June in the following year. The fituation of the enemy was, however, found fo ftrong and impregnable, and the natural protection afforded by rocks, had been fo formidably increafed by the erection of numerous heavy batteries, that it was thought prudent to defift from the attempt ; which, even fhould it prove fuccefsful, might be expected to be deftructive of any further operations.

The fleet accordingly proceeded to Fort St. David, where it arrived on the 29th of July; the fiege of Pondicherry was immediately refolved on ; and admiral Bofcawen, having left the command of the fquadron to captain Lifle, of the Vigilant, with proper

per

per inftructions, went on fhore, and affumed the command of the army. Notwithftanding every poffible exertion was made, in the commencement, and profecution of the fiege, the ftrength of the French garrifon, which amounted to nearly two thoufand Europeans, while Mr. Bofcawen's whole force did not reach two thoufand feven hundred men, delayed confiderably the approaches of the affailants, till the rainy feafon commenced, which neceffarily compelled an abandonment of the whole defign. Although the intelligence of the peace concluded at Aix la Chapelle, reached the Eaft Indies very foon after the difappointment juft mentioned, yet the arrangements called for by the treaty itfelf, added to others attendant on it, which the intereft of Britain required fhould be properly executed, caufed the continuance of Mr. Bofcawen in that quarter of the world, fome time longer. Having fortunately for him, been on fhore, when the violent ftorm took place on the 13th of April 1749, he, in all probability, efcaped deftruction, with his flag-fhip, which foundered off Fort St. David, fifty of her people only, officers included, being faved, out of fix hundred. Fort St. George having been delivered up to the admiral, according to the ftipulations in the treaty of peace, he failed from Fort St. David's, on the 19th of Auguft 1749, and arrived at Portfmouth on the 14th of April following, without having met with any occurrence more unfortunate, than that of having been feparated a few days before his arrival, from fome of the fhips under his orders, all of which reached port in perfect fafety, a few days afterwards.

G g 3 Notwithftanding

Notwithſtanding he had accepted a command in ſo diſtant a quarter of the world, he continued to retain the ſtation of repreſentative in parliament for the borough of Truro, for which place he had been returned in the month of June 1741, and very ſoon after his return to Europe, his well-known abilities in the line of his profeſſion were too attractive, not to excite the attention of miniſters, and cauſe an earneſt deſire of having a man for their colleague, who was capable of adviſing, and, indeed, directing all particulars relative to the naval branch of adminiſtration : he was accordingly, on the 22d of June 1751, appointed one of the commiſſioners for executing the office of lord high admiral, a ſtation he continued to hold during life. He was about the ſame time elected one of the elder brethren of the Trinity Houſe ; and on the 4th of February 1755, was advanced to be vice-admiral of the blue. Intelligence having been received, not only that the court of France had countenanced a variety of aggreſſions againſt the Britiſh ſubjects, and poſſeſſions in North America, but that a very formidable fleet was in a forward ſtate of equipment, intended to be ſent thither, for the purpoſe of promoting its hoſtile views, Mr. Boſcawen was nominated commander in chief of a ſquadron, conſiſting of eleven ſhips of the line and a frigate, which were ſent to cruiſe off the banks of Newfoundland, in the hopes of intercepting the French armament, and preventing its entering the river St. Lawrence. The commandant, however, aware perhaps that he was purſued, divided his force into two parts ; one diviſion

made

made for the river St. Lawrence by the ordinary route,
while the other went round, and entered it by paffing through the ftreights of Belleifle, a courfe never
before attempted by any fhips of the line. Mr. Bofcawen lay with his fleet off cape Ray, or Wrath,
the moft fouthern part of Newfoundland, which was
deemed the propereft ftation for intercepting the enemy, be their courfe to Quebec what it might. They
however effected their efcape, two fhips only of the
fquadron excepted: thefe were the Alcide and Lys,
the former of fixty-four guns, and four hundred and
eighty men, the latter armed *en flute*, being pierced
for fixty-four guns as well as her companion, but
mounting, when taken, only twenty-two, fhe being
then ufed as a temporary tranfport, and having on
board eight companies of foldiers. Thefe fhips, which
had feparated from their companions on the 9th of
June in a fog, fell in, on the next day with the Dunkirk and Defiance, both of them fourth rates of fixty
guns, to which fhips they furrendered after a very
brave, and obftinate defence.

In 1756, Mr. Bofcawen was advanced to the rank
of vice-admiral of the white, and very foon afterwards
to the fame ftation in the red fquadron; but did not
take upon himfelf any naval command till 1758, when,
after having been on the 8th of February raifed to the
rank of admiral of the blue, he was appointed commander in chief of the formidable fleet, deftined for the
attack of Louifbourg. It confifted of no lefs than
twenty-three fhips of two and three decks, together
with eighteen frigates, firefhips, and other veffels. On
the arrival of the fleet at Halifax, the admiral was

joined

joined by general Amherft and the army; and having proceeded towards the place of its deftination on the 20th of May, the armament, which confifted of no lefs than one hundred and fifty-feven veffels, including tranfports, came to anchor in Gabarus bay on the 2d of June; from which time the operations were imme- diately preffed with fo much vigour, that on the 26th of July the chevalier Drucour, who commanded in the for- trefs, propofed to furrender. The terms of capitulation were, without much difficulty, fettled with the Britifh commanders in chief; and the garrifon, confifting of near fix thoufand men, became prifoners of war.

On the return of Mr. Bofcawen to England, he had the honour of receiving the thanks of the houfe of commons; and having, by his conduct and fuccefs on the foregoing occafion, completely eftablifhed that re- putation which he had before fo defervedly acquired, and convinced the world that his judgment was as folid, and well adapted to cool deliberation, as his abilities in the heat of action were dazzling, and fplendid, he was, by his majefty's command, fworn a member of the privy council on the 2d of February 1759, and took his feat at the board. He was immediately afterwards invefted with the command of a fquadron, confifting of fourteen fhips of the line and two frigates, ordered for the Mediterranean. He failed from St. Helen's on the 14th of April, and inftantly after his arrival on his ftation, repaired to Toulon, off which port he cruifed for fome days, in hopes of provoking M. de la Clue, who lay there with a fquadron confifting of twelve large fhips and three frigates, to come out

and

and engage him." The deſtruction of this fleet, was
the principal object which caufed the equipment of
that, Mr. Boſcawen commanded; it was a point of the
moſt ſerious and important national concern ; M. de
la Clue being under orders to repair to Breſt, and put
himſelf under the command of the marquis de Conflans, whoſe operations were extremely diſconceited by
the demolition of this formidable reinforcement. Every
inſult that could be offered to a blockaded enemy not
having produced the effect of drawing M. de la Clue
from his place of ſecurity, Mr. Boſcawen was at length
under the neceſſity of proceeding to Gibraltar with his
fleet, for the purpoſe of repairing damages, which ſome
of the ſhips had ſuſtained in a variety of attacks on the
batteries of the enemy. This was conſidered by the
French chef d'eſcadre, as the happy moment in which
his eſcape might be effected, and he accordingly put
to ſea with his whole force; but not having had the
good fortune to eſcape the vigilance of Mr. Boſcawen
on his paſſage through the Streights, his ſhips ſeparated,
and the larger diviſion, in which was the admiral himſelf, were followed, overtaken, and completely defeated.
The Ocean of eighty guns, the flag-ſhip, and the Re-
doubtable of ſeventy-four, were burnt; the Centaur
and Temeraire, of ſeventy-four guns each, with the
Modeſte of ſixty-four, were taken; and the whole of
the enemy's project completely diſconcerted. The
object of the expedition being thus glorioufly accom-
pliſhed, Mr. Boſcawen returned to England, and
arrived ſafe at Portſmouth with part of his prizes on
the 1ſt of September. It is almoſt needleſs to ſay, on

this

this occasion, that he was received in the most flattering manner by his majesty; and, as a proper reward
for those services we have just recorded, he was on the
9th of December following declared general of marines, with a salary of three thousand pounds a year.
The magistrates of Edinburgh, about the same time,
wishing to shew the high sense, they, in common with
the rest of the people, entertained of his great merit
and deserts, presented him with the freedom of their
city.

In the month of January following, he was appointed
to command a small fleet, kept constantly stationed off
the coast of France, alternately with another of equal
force, under the orders of sir Edward Hawke, for the
purpose of confining in port the miserable remnant of
that armament, which had been defeated by the latter
in the month of November preceding. The enemy
made no attempt, however, to put to sea; and this
brave and truly worthy character was, on the 10th of
January 1761, prevented by a premature death from
displaying any longer, those virtues, and those qualities,
which had contributed alike to the ornament, and to
the defence of his country.

SIR

Sr GEORGE POCOCK K^{n.t}

Pub.^d Cliff.^t 1. Sept. 1800 by Edwd Harding 93. Pall Mall.

SIR GEORGE POCOCK, K. B.

WAS the fon of the reverend Thomas Pocock, A.M. chaplain to Greenwich Hofpital, and fellow of the Royal Society, by ——, his wife, daughter of James Mafter, efquire, and Joyce his wife, only daughter of fir Chriftopher Turner, knight, one of the barons of the exchequer in the reign of Charles II. He was born on the 6th of May 1706; and having betaken himfelf to a naval life, when only twelve years of age ferved under fir George Byng, who was his uncle, during his very memorable expedition to the Mediterranean in 1718. He continued to be employed in the fubordinate ranks of his profeffion for the fpace of twenty years, not having been advanced to the rank of captain in the navy till the 1ft of Auguft 1738, when he was appointed captain of the Aldborough frigate. After a variety of uninterefting, though highly honourable commands, he was, in 1748, ordered to the Weft Indies as commodore of the fmall fquadron employed in that quarter. His diligence and activity were fortunately rewarded with a variety of very valuable prizes, among

which

which were nearly forty veffels which had been under
the convoy of M. de l'Etendiere, who had been attacked by rear-admiral Hawke with the greateft fuccefs,
almoft immediately on his quitting the French coaft.
In 1754, Mr. Pocock, who was then captain of the
Cumberland, was ordered to the Eaft Indies with rear-
admiral Watfon; and having been on the 4th February 1755 advanced to be rear-admiral of the white
fquadron, hoifted his flag on board the fame fhip,
and continued to ferve as fecond in command of the
armament.   The reduction of Chandernagore was the
firft enterprife which graced the annals of naval hiftory
in that quarter of the world; and on the death of vice-
admiral Watfon, which took place on the 16th of
Auguft 1757, the chief command of the fleet devolved on Mr. Pocock *.   He remained commander
in chief in the fame quarter of the world during
the two fucceeding years; and though oppofed by
a fuperior naval force, commanded by one of the
ableft officers in the French fervice, and on fome
occafions was not fupported with that fpirit he ought
to have been, by fome of the officers under his command, he effectually prevented the French from
making any impreffion on our territorial poffeffions,
or injuring the Britifh commerce throughout the whole
of that extenfive fea, which he was appointed to guard.
The compliment paid him by Campbell in refpect to
his conduct is extremely concife and perfectly juft.

* On the 4th of June 1756 he was promoted to be rear-admiral of
the red, and on the 31ft of January 1758, to be vice admiral of the
fame fquadron.

" Admiral

"Admiral Pocock (he obferves) had, during the whole time he held the chief command in the Indian feas, feconded, with the greateft fkill and activity, every effort made by the army. He had more than once compelled M. d'Aché to take fhelter under the walls of Pondicherry, having reduced the French fhips to a very fhattered condition, and killed a great number of men;" he might have added, too, with a force infinitely inferior. "But what is the moft extraordinary, and fhews the fingular talents of both admirals, they had fought three pitched battles in the courfe of eighteen months, without the lofs of a fhip on either fide." Mr. Pocock having returned to Europe in 1761, enjoyed a temporary relaxation from thofe long fatigues of fervice, which he had endured for fo many years in a climate, highly injurious to European conftitutions, not being appointed to any fubfequent command till the year 1762.

In 1761 he was, as a juftly-earned reward for his fervices in India, honoured with the order of the Bath, and in the courfe of the fame year was promoted to be admiral of the blue. The rupture which had taken place with Spain, having engaged miniftry to turn their thoughts to the reduction of the diftant, which were on many accounts, at the fame time, the moft valuable poffeffions belonging to that nation, among other expeditions which it was refolved fhould be immediately fet on foot, was one againft the Havannah. The force of the armament, when collected together, was extremely formidable; it confifted of nineteen fhips of the line, eighteen frigates, and a fleet of tranf-

ports

ports containing ten thoufand foldiers. (which were to
be joined when landed on. Cuba, by 'four thoufand
more expected·from New York), with all the imple-
ments neceffary to offenfive operations.   The admiral,
reflecting that the feafon was far advanced, and that.in
a fhort time the commencement of the periodical rains
would totally put a ftop to all offenfive operations,
refolved to attempt paffing through the ftreights of.
Bahama. This meafure confiderably. fhortened the
voyage, but was confidered extremely hazardous, that
track being unfrequented, efpecially by the Britifh, and
almoft unknown to them. Mingling the moft careful
prudence and precaution, with the greateft fpirit, he
took every means human forefight could fuggeft, to
fecure the paffage of fo numerous a fleet in fafety :
fuccefs, in the moft extenfive fenfe, crowned his exertions ; fo that by the 5th of June the whole armament had made its paffage through the ftreights, without encountering the fmalleft finifter accident. During
the whole of the fiege, the admiral moft warmly co-
operated in every enterprife and attack, where the
affiftance of the fleet was deemed in the remoteft degree neceffary, and certainly contributed very eminently to the fuccefsful termination of the expedition.
On the furrender of the place, he became the friend
and protector of the vanquifhed, fhielding them by
every poffible means in his power, from thofe acts, of
intemperance, which, in defiance' of the beft regulations, fometimes take place on fuch occafions... After
his return to England, he never accepted any fubfequent command ; but, in 1766, refigned even his flag;
                                                  and

and retired completely from the fervice, apparently in difguft. Variety of reafons have been affigned for this conduct, fome of them too ridiculous for repetition. The moft probable caufe of offence that has been given, appears to have been the appoinment of fir Charles Saunders, who was his junior officer in the fervice, to the high ftation of firft commiffioner at the admiralty board, in preference to himfelf. Having continued ever afterwards to live a private life, he died on the 3d of April 1792, at his houfe in Curzon Street, May Fair, being then in the eighty-feventh year of his age.

It has been elfewhere remarked, and apparently with the greateft truth, that his hiftory, both in public and private life, was of fo exemplary a nature, as to demand a tribute of the higheft refpect, a refpect moft juftly due to the memory of a worthy, and excellent man; he was admired, he was revered, even by his enemies; he was efteemed and beloved by all the officers who had ferved with him, and held almoft in adoration by every feaman, who had ever been under his command. Nor were his private virtues lefs the fubject of regard and honour, than thofe, of greater and more public notoriety: as a parent, he was with the greateft truth, unexcelled; as a brother, moft exemplarily benevolent; and, as a relative, affectionate in the higheft degree to all his connexions. To a confummate modefty, which rendered him unconfcious of his own high merits, he added an humanity improved by an extenfive generofity, which raifed him up as a bleffing to all his neighbours, whofe indigence called

forth

forth his ever attentive bounty. It is faid of him, that, unlike the generality of naval officers, he was *never* known to fwear, even on board his fhip ; and that as he certainly poffeffed the moft undoubted courage, fo did he unite with it the greateft refolution and moft ferene temper : a circumftance which rendered his retirement, in the manner it took place, the more extraordinary to all who knew him. All acquainted with his character muft bear teftimony to the truth of thefe affertions, and join lamenting the death of fo great, fo good a man.

SIR CHA.ˢ SAUNDERS

Publish'd July 1, 1800, by Edw. Harding 98 Pall Mall.

SIR CHARLES SAUNDERS.

THIS truly worthy and brave officer is not known in the naval fervice till he obtained the rank of lieutenant, foon after which he was, under the fpecial recommendation of commodore Anfon, appointed to ferve in that capacity on board the Centurion, the fhip which bore the broad pendant of that gentleman, during his well-known voyage round the world. On the death of captain Kidd of the Pearl, and the confequent promotion of Mr. Cheap, who had commanded the Trial, to be captain of the Wager, Mr. Saunders was, on the 31ft of January 1741, advanced to be his fucceffor in the Trial; but was at that time, however, fo dangeroufly ill of a fever on board the Centurion, that he did not remove to his new command for feveral days afterwards. During the difaftrous paffage made by the fquadron round cape Horn, the ftricteft attention and energy, added to the moft confummate nautical fkill, became repeatedly neceffary for the prefervation of the Trial; it was, indeed, a veffel extremely ill calculated for the navigation of thofe tempeftuous feas,

VOL. II.   H h   and

and the selection of it to form a part of the squadron in
question, must ever be considered an act of absurdity,
not to say, heinous misconduct. When captain Saunders was, after surmounting so many disasters, at length
fortunate enough to reach Juan Fernandez, he had
buried considerably more than half his people; the remainder were so extremely diseased, and debilitated,
that himself, with his lieutenant and three men only,
formed the whole that could be considered properly
capable of doing their duty.

The Trial being refitted as well as circumstances
would permit, and her distressed crew recovered, captain
Saunders was detached on a cruise in the month of September, and on the 18th of the same month had the good
fortune to fall in with and capture, a large merchant-
frigate of six hundred tons burden, having on board a
very valuable cargo. Owing, however, to one of the
masts of the Trial being sprung during the chase, and
the other in a squall a few days afterwards, the commodore was under the necessity of ordering that vessel
to be destroyed, after giving Mr. Saunders a commission to command that, which he had captured, as a
post ship, mounting twenty guns, in the British
service. Mr. Saunders was consequently present at
all the different operations in which the squadron was
concerned, till the 27th of April following, when the
crews of the different ships becoming much more reduced by deaths and disease, it was considered expedient to destroy all the vessels which had been captured,
for the purpose of reinforcing by their crews, the Centurion and the Gloucester. In the month of Novem-

ber

ber following, which was immediately after the Centurion reached China, captain Saunders, being charged with difpatches from the commodore, took his paffage to England on board a Swedifh fhip, in which he arrived in the Downs, after a profperous paffage, in the month of May 1743. He was, not long afterwards, appointed captain of the Sapphire, of forty-four guns, in which fhip he continued till the month of March 1745, when he was promoted to the Sandwich guardfhip, of ninety guns. In 1747, he was captain of the Yarmouth, one of the fhips under the orders of fir Edward Hawke, which fell in with, defeated, and captured nearly the whole of M. d'Etendiere's fquadron. Captain Saunders very eminently diftinguifhed himfelf on this occafion; two of the enemy's fhips of feventy-four guns each, the Monarch and Neptune, having, as is reported, ftruck to the Yarmouth; nor, in all probability, would his fuccefs have ended here, had not the unfortunate death of the brave captain Saumarez, who commanded the Nottingham, put a ftop to the further purfuit of the Tonant of eighty guns, and the Intrepide of feventy-four, which were followed with the utmoft avidity by the Yarmouth, fupported by the Eagle, and the Nottingham juft mentioned. In the month of January 1751, he was appointed commodore of a fquadron ordered to the Streights, but never proceeded thither, having in the month of May following been nominated governor and commander in chief on the Newfoundland ftation. In the month of April 1754, he was made treafurer of Greenwich Hofpital, an office he held twelve

years,

years, and then refigned on being promoted to the very
elevated ftation of firft commiffioner of the admiralty＊.

On the apprehenfion of a rupture with France in
the month of March 1755, he received a commiffion to
command the Prince, a fecond rate, of ninety guns;
but refigned that fhip in the month of. December following, on being appointed comptroller of the navy.
Soon as the firft intelligence reached England of the
fuppofed mifconduct of Mr. Byng, in the action with
the French fquadron off Minorca, Mr. Saunders was
promoted to be rear-admiral of the blue, and proceeded
to the Mediterranean as a paffenger on board the Antelope with fir Edward Hawke, on whom the chief
command was beftowed: Mr. Saunders being appointed the fucceffor to Mr. Weft, who was ordered
home. On the return of fir Edward to England in
the month of January 1757, Mr. Saunders was left
commander in chief on that ftation.

He met, however, with no occurrence in the
fmalleft degree remarkable, except that, of having
in the month of April fallen in with a fmall French
fquadron bound to Louifbourg, which, aided by a
ftrong Levant wind, was fortunate enough to effect its
efcape after a very flight fkirmifh †. In 1758, Mr.

Saunders

＊ In the month of April 1750, he was elected reprefentative in parliament
for the borough of Plymouth, as fucceffor to the lord Vere Beauclerk, then
created a peer of Great Britain; and in the parliament which met in 1754,
was returned for the borough of Heydon, in Yorkfhire.

† The difcontented caricaturifts of the day feized that opportunity of
venting their ridiculous fpleen on Mr. Saunders, but their impotent malice
was treated with the contempt it deferved. The features of Mr. Saunders

were

Saunders was advanced to be rear-admiral of the white, and having been in the enfuing year further promoted to be vice-admiral of the blue, was appointed commander in chief of the expedition fent againft Quebec; and after having moft eminently contributed to fecond all the operations of the army, and provided, as well as circumftances would permit, for the prefervation and future fafety, of the newly-conquered city, was on his paffage to Europe, when he received information that the Breft fleet was actually at fea. Difdaining, therefore, to return when there was the fmalleft chance of fignalizing himfelf againft the enemies of his country, he altered his courfe, in the hope of falling in with fir Edward Hawke, having firft difpatched one of his light veffels for England, with intelligence of the meafures he had taken, together with his reafons, and requefting the approval thereof by the admiralty board. Having, however, heard, foon after, that Conflans was totally defeated, he again changed his route, and landed at Cork, from whence he proceeded by land to Dublin, and afterwards paffed over to England. His reception in London, both by his fovereign, and the people, was equally honourable to him. Some days previous to his arrival, he was appointed lieutenant-general of marines: and on taking his feat in the houfe

vere extremely ftrong; his nofe exceeded the fize generally allowed by nature to that feature; and the witticifm confifted in a pretended portrait of the admiral ftanding on the hill of Gibraltar, his nofe reaching over, like a bridge of one arch, to the Barbary fhore: the print being entitled, "A Britifh Admiral fuffering a French Fleet to pafs under his Nofe."

of commons, on the 23d of January 1760, the thanks of
the houfe were given him by the fpeaker.

In the enfuing fpring he was appointed commander
in chief in the Mediterranean ; but no occurrence took
place in that quarter of the world, for the naval power
of France was annihilated in thofe feas. In 1761 he was
chofen one of the knights companions of the moft honourable order of the Bath ; and having continued at
Gibraltar till the conclufion of the war, was raifed during his abfence to the rank of vice-admiral of the white.
On the 30th of Auguft 1765 he was appointed one of
the commiffioners for executing the office of lord high
admiral ; and on the 16th of September 1766, being
advanced to be firft commiffioner, was fworn in one
of the members of his majefty's privy council. He
retained his high office only till the 13th of December
following, and then refigning, never, fubfequent to
this time, returned to any public ftation. In the funeral proceffion of the duke of York, on the 3d of
November 1767, he was one of the admirals who fupported the canopy. In the month of October 1770,
he was advanced to be admiral of the blue ; and in the
new parliament convened in 1774, after having been
an unfuccefsful candidate for the borough of Yarmouth, was, for the fourth time, re-elected for Heydon. He did not long furvive this event, having died,
truly lamented by all who knew him, of the gout in
his ftomach, on the 7th of December 1775.

SIR

Sᴿ CHARLES HARDY

Pub. Aug 1 1800 by Edw. Harding 98 Pall Mall.

SIR CHARLES HARDY

WAS the fon of a very worthy flag-officer, bearing the fame name; and having followed the example of his parent, in attaching himfelf to the fea-fervice, was, on the 10th of Auguft 1741, appointed captain of the Rye, of twenty-four guns. In this veffel he proceeded to North America, where he was for a confiderable time employed in cruifing off the coafts of Carolina and Georgia, on the latter of which provinces the Spaniards had effected a defcent. In 1744, having been appointed to the Jerfey, of fixty guns, he was made governor and commander in chief of the ifland of Newfoundland, and its dependencies; a ftation, which he filled with the higheft credit to himfelf, notwithftanding the ill-founded clamours of fome difcontented perfons, who preferred a formal complaint againft him, on account of the capture of fome fhips that were under his protection, by the enemy. While captain of the Jerfey, he diftinguifhed himfelf extremely in a very gallant action with a French fhip of war called the St. Efprit, of feventy-four guns. The action

took

place near the Streights' mouth, and after a conteſt of
two hours and an half's continuance, the beaten anta-
goniſt fled for ſafety into Cadiz, having ſuſtained
conſiderable damage.

In 1755 he was advanced to the very important
ſtation of governor of New York, and at the ſame
time received the honour of knighthood. In 1756,
being raiſed to the rank of rear-admiral of the blue,
he hoiſted his flag on board the Nightingale in that
harbour; and from thence ſoon removing into the
Sutherland, of fifty guns, he, after having collected
together all the naval force in that quarter, ſailed for
Halifax from Sandy Hook on the 20th of June, with a
fleet of tranſports with ſtores and troops on board under
his convoy, which, he was inſtructed to put, together
with himſelf, under the orders of Mr. Holbourne. The
expedition againſt Louiſbourg, which had been projected, was not however carried into effect during that
year; and having, not long after his return to New
York, reſigned the government of that city and province, he returned to England, where he was, on the 7th
of February 1758, advanced to be rear-admiral of the
white. After hoiſting his flag on board the Captain,
of ſixty-eight guns, he immediately proceeded back to
New York, for the purpoſe of forwarding the necef-
ſary arrangements, previous to the then meditated renewal of an attack on the enemy, in the ſame quarter,
where it had the preceding year proved unſuccefsful,
Mr. Boſcawen followed not long afterwards, and ſir
Charles joined him off Louiſbourg on the 14th of
June. He immediately removed his flag on board the

Royal

Royal William, and was occupied during the whole of the fiege in blockading the harbour, a fervice which he very diligently and effectually performed. After the furrender of the place, he was employed to convoy fome tranfports with troops to Gafpée, in the river St. Lawrence; and after firft rejoining Mr. Bofcawen, proceeded immediately to England, where he arrived in perfect fafety on the 1ft of November, without having met with any more material occurrence, than that, of an inconfiderable fkirmifh with a fuperior fquadron of French fhips of war, which availed themfelves of the approaching night for the purpofe of declining any farther conteft. In 1759 he was promoted to the rank of vice-admiral of the blue, and ferved under fir Edward Hawke, as fecond in command in the Channel fleet: his conduct in the memorable engagement with the French fleet under Conflans, reflected on him the higheft honour, and has been particularly noticed by hiftorians, and others. He continued to be employed on the home, or Channel fervice, during the whole remainder of the war, which, in confequence of the crippled ftate of the French marine, paffed on without encounter. After its conclufion, the occurrences of his public life became neceffarily confined to his promotions * and honourable appointments; nor did he again take upon himfelf any active command till the year 1779, when, on the re-

* In October 1762, he was promoted to be vice-admiral of the white; on the 28th of October 1770, to be admiral of the blue; and, in 1778, to the fame rank in the white fquadron. In the month of November 1767, he was one of the fupporters of the canopy at the funeral of his royal highnefs the duke of York; in 1771, was appointed governor of Greenwich Hofpital; and, in 1774, became member for the borough of Plymouth.

tirement

tirement of admiral Keppel, he was appointed commander in chief of the main, or Channel fleet.

The junction of the Spanish armament with that of France, forming an accumulation of force amounting to one hundred sail, nearly seventy of which were of the line; while that of Britain did not exceed forty, several of which were but in an indifferent state for service, it became expedient that instructions should be sent to sir Charles, ordering him to act merely on the defensive. The measure was strictly prudential, and the event glorious; for the confederated enemies of Britain, after having enjoyed the empty triumph of parading the British channel for a few days unmolested, returned back into their own ports without having obtained the slightest other advantage than that of capturing a single British ship of war, the Ardent, which casually fell into their hands. The same honourable post, was intended to have been continued to him during the ensuing year; but when the fleet was nearly equipped, and ready to sail, death put a sudden and immediate stop to his services. He died at Portsmouth on the 18th of May 1780, in an apoplectic fit, having very deservedly obtained the character of a brave, prudent, gallant, and enterprising officer. Without making any ostentatious display of his noble qualities; he was generous, mild, affable, and intelligent; his virtues commanded the most profound respect; they enabled him to pass through days, when the rage and prejudice of frensied party blazed with a fury, that has rarely been equalled. In such dangerous times he lived without exciting calumny, or reproach, and died, without having furnished to the most captious partizan, the slightest ground of complaint, or reprehension.

LORD

Harding sc

S.ᴿ GEO.ˢ BRIDGES RODNEY BAR.ᵀ

Pub.ᵈ June 1. 1800. by Edw. Harding 98 Pall Mall

LORD RODNEY.

THIS nobleman was the second son to Henry Rodney, of Walton upon Thames, in the county of Surrey, esquire, and Mary, eldest daughter and coheir to sir Henry Newton, knight, envoy extraordinary to Genoa, Tuscany, &c. L. L. D. judge of the high court of admiralty, and chancellor of the diocese of London. After a regular service in the subordinate stations, he was taken early in the year 1742, by Mr. Mathews, to be one of his lieutenants on board the Namur; and was, on the 9th of November in the same year, promoted by the same admiral to be captain of the Plymouth, of sixty guns: he afterwards commanded the Sheerness, of twenty-four, and the Ludlow Castle, of forty-four guns; but met with no opportunity of acquiring either renown, or fortune, till the year 1746, when he became captain of the Eagle, a new fourth rate, stationed as a cruiser off the coast of Ireland. While thus occupied, he had the good fortune to capture two very fine privateers; one of them a Spaniard, called the Esperance; the other, a

French

French ship, which had formerly been the Shoreham British frigate. In 1747, the Eagle was one of the ships placed under the orders of rear-admiral Hawke, and was consequently present at the defeat and capture, of the greater part of monf. de L'Etendiere's squadron, on which occasion Mr. Rodney distinguished himself very conspicuously.

After the cessation of hostilities, he was, in the month of March 1749, commissioned to the Rainbow, of forty-four guns; and on the 9th of May following was nominated governor and commander in chief of the isle of Newfoundland * and its dependencies. In 1753, he was appointed to the Kent, of seventy guns, one of the guardships stationed at Portsmouth, and afterwards became progressively captain of the Prince George, of ninety guns, and the Dublin, of seventy-four; in which latter ship he served first in 1757, under sir Edward Hawke, during the expedition undertaken against Rochfort, and afterwards in the ensuing year accompanied Mr. Boscawen on his voyage to Louisbourg; but was not engaged in any of the operations of the siege, the Dublin, in consequence of her becoming extremely sickly, having been under the necessity of bearing away for Halifax. On the 14th of February 1759, he was raised to the rank of rear-admiral of the blue, and was immediately invested with the command of a small squadron, consisting of the lighter class of ships of

---

* In the month of May he was chosen representative in parliament for the borough of Saltash, and after the period of his government expired, married, on the 2d of February 1753, miss Jane Compton, daughter to Charles Compton, esquire, and sister to the earl of Northampton.

war,

war, with feveral bomb-ketches, fitted out for the
attack of Havre de Grace, where, as it was faid, a
large quantity of flat boats were built, or collected, and
a variety of other preparations, ftill more formidable
and expenfive, were making in aid of the armament
equipping, by order of the French government, for
the invafion of Great Britain, or Ireland. This fervice
he moft expeditioufly and effectually performed; and
Collins very juftly remarks, that on this occafion Mr.
Rodney had the happinefs of totally fruftrating the defigns of the French court, and fo completely ruined
not only the preparations, but the port itfelf, as a
naval arfenal, that it was no longer in a ftate to
annoy Great Britain, during the continuance of the
war. He was afterwards employed in a variety of little
defultory attacks of the fame nature, in which he was
almoft, without exception, fuccefsful. In the new
parliament, convened in 1761, he was chofen reprefentative for the borough of Penryn, in Cornwall;
and in the month of September following, was appointed commander in chief of the armament then
under equipment, deftined for the attack of the French
ifland of Martinique. The moft vigorous meafures
were purfued, as well by the army as the navy, and
Mr. Rodney very diligently, and effectually co-operated
in every meafure, that appeared likely to promote fuccefs; fo that in lefs than five weeks from the commencement of the attack, not only the firft object of
the enterprife furrendered; but the iflands of Grenada,
St. Vincents, St. Lucia, and, in fhort, all the French
poffeffions in that quarter of the world, awed as it were

by

by the fate of what might be confidered their capital, furrendered to the arms of Britain almoft immediately afterwards. So highly were his fervices eftimated on the preceding occafion, that towards the conclufion of the fame year, he was advanced to the rank of vice-admiral of the blue, and was not long afterwards created a baronet of Great Britain *. In the year 1768, on the diffolution of parliament, he offered himfelf a candidate for the town of Northampton: his election for which place he carried againft Mr. Howe, by a poll of fix hundred and eleven to five hundred and thirty-eight, after a ftrong and very expenfive conteft, by which he moft materially impaired his fortune. In the month of October 1770, he was progreffively advanced to be vice-admiral of the white and red fquadrons; and, in the month of Auguft 1771, to be rear-admiral of Great Britain. In confequence of his having been appointed commander in chief on the Jamaica ftation, he refigned in the early part of the year laft mentioned, the government of Greenwich Hofpital; and having hoifted his flag on board the Princefs Amelia, of eighty guns, proceeded to the Weft Indies not long afterwards. It has been reported, and we believe with truth, that the command in India, which was much more valuable, was offered him; but declined, under the hope of fucceeding to the government of Jamaica, in the event of the death of fir William Trelawney, who then held that poft, and whofe health was

* In the month of November 1765, he was appointed governor of Greenwich Hofpital; and, in 1767, was one of the vice-admirals who fupported the canopy at the funeral of his royal highnefs the duke of York.

in a very precarious ftate. Difappointed, however, in this view, he returned to England at the expiration of the period usually allotted to fuch commands, and being in rather diftreffed circumftances, retired to France, where he lived in obfcurity, till after the recommencement of hoftilities with that power. We muft not, on this occafion, omit mentioning the conduct of a French nobleman of high rank, towards this unfortunate man. Knowing him to be neceffitous, and fuppofing him, moft probably on that account only, to be prevented from returning to his country, and offering his fervices, he waited on him, and preffed on him a fum fufficient to anfwer his purpofes: a loan, which fir George, with the utmoft promptitude, took care to repay after his return to England.

He had, during his abfence, on the 29th of January 1778, been promoted to the rank of admiral of the white; and at the conclufion of the enfuing year, was appointed commander in chief in the Weft Indies. The fleet already employed on that ftation confifted of no lefs than feventeen, or eighteen fhips of the line, under the orders of rear-admiral Parker; fo that the force which he was ordered to take with him, confifted only of his own flag-fhip, the Sandwich, of ninety guns, and three others, the Ajax, Terrible, and Montague, of feventy-four guns each. It being, however, indifpenfably neceffary a reinforcement of troops, and provifions fhould be fent to Gibraltar, which was to be convoyed by rear-admirals Digby and Rofs, with fixteen or feventeen fhips of the line, fir George was ordered to join them with his little fquadron, and proceed with

them

them firſt, to the objeƈt of their deſtination, as commander in chief of the whole.   On his paſſage to the
Streights he was ſingularly fortunate, having not only
fallen in with a valuable convoy belonging to the Caracca
company, the whole of which he captured *, but in addition thereto having met with don Juan de Langara, a
Spaniſh admiral, with a ſquadron conſiſting of eleven
ſhips of the line and two frigates, off cape St. Vincent's.
Of theſe, the Phœnix, of eighty guns, the flag-ſhip, the
Monarca, Princeſſa, and Diligente, of ſeventy guns
each, were captured after a very ſpirited defence ; two
others alſo, of ſeventy guns each, ſurrendered, but
were afterwards driven on ſhore by ſtreſs of weather,
and are reported to have been loſt : added to theſe, the
St. Domingo, of ſeventy guns, blew up, ſoon after the
commencement of the encounter †.

---

* On this occaſion the Guipuſcoana, of ſixty-four guns, four frigates,
and two corvettes, belonging to the royal company of the Caraccas, together with ſixteen ſail of merchant-veſſels, laden with proviſions and ſtores,
fell into his hands.

† On the 29th of February the thanks of the houſe of commons were
unanimouſly voted to ſir George Rodney for this great and important ſervice,
and the ſame teſtimony of gratitude was on the next day offered by the houſe
of lords alſo : on the 6th of March the freedom of the city of London was
voted in common council, to be preſented to him in a gold box of an hundred
guineas value ; a ſimilar compliment of the freedom of the city of Edinburgh
having been previouſly paid to him.

Sir George had now acquired the very zenith of popularity : the praiſes
univerſally laviſhed on him amounted almoſt to idolatry.   At the general
election which took place in the month of September, in the current year,
he was, though abſent, elected member for the city of Weſtminſter without
his ſolicitation, and merely on the ground of that high eſtimation in which
he was then held, particularly by that which called itſelf the patriotic party :
how ſtrangely and rapidly he afterwards fell in their eſteem, will be preſently
ſhewn.

Gibraltar

Gibraltar being revictualled, and the garrison re-inforced, sir George quitted the bay, on the 13th of Fe-bruary, with the whole fleet; and having, five days after-wards, parted company from the rear-admirals Digby and Rofs, proceeded to the Weft Indies, where he ar-rived without meeting with any finifter accident, or oc-currence worthy notice, in the enfuing month. He imme-diately, after taking upon himfelf the chief command of the fleet, proceeded off Fort Royal, where he for two days offered battle to the enemy, who were far fuperior to him in force, but who thought proper to decline the challenge. He left therefore a fquadron of his beft failing fhips to watch the motions of the enemy, and repaired with the remainder, to St. Lucia, where he came to an anchor, ready to put to fea at a moment's notice, on the firft motion of the enemy. The count de Guichen, who commanded the French fleet, failed on the 15th of April in the middle of the night, with his whole force, confifting of twenty-three fhips of the line, one of fifty guns, with five frigates, or fmaller veffels; hoping thereby to elude the vigilance of fir George, whofe force confifted only of twenty fhips of the line, together with one of fifty guns, many of which were in fo crazy and fhattered a condition, as to be fcaicely fit for fervice.

The vigilance of the Britifh admiral prevented, how-ever, the efcape of his antagonift: the French were brought to action on the 17th, and after a fevere con-teft of feveral hours, in which many of the Britifh fhips received confiderable damage, fuffered all the ignominy of a total defeat, without experiencing that

lofs

lofs in refpect to fhips, which is confidered the indifpenfable requifite to a great victory. As foon as the
difabled veffels were put in as good a condition for
fervice as circumftances would admit, fir George loft
not a moment's time in purfuing the fugitives; and,
on the 29th of the fame month, had the good fortune
to meet once more with the much fought for enemy. In
vain did he ufe every poffible endeavour, during the fpace
of three days, to force them to a fecond action, while
the French admiral, on his part, took equal pains to
avoid one; and at length, when a temporary alteration of the wind enabled fir George to cut off his return to Martinique, he immediately ran to leeward,
and took fhelter under Guadaloupe, rather than hazard
the repetition of an encounter. Two other partial and
indecifive fkirmifhes, took place on the 15th and 19th
of May following; but further purfuit then becoming
fruitlefs, on account of the ftudied caution of the enemy, fir George was induced to defift, and return to
Barbadoes, where he arrived on the 22d. Scarcely
had he refitted and watered his fhips, ere he received
the important intelligence that a Spanifh fquadron,
confifting of twelve fail of the line, was on its paffage
from Europe. He accordingly made, with the utmoft
promptitude, the beft difpofitions in his power, in the
hope of intercepting them, ere the count de Guichen
fhould have got his fleet again refitted, and fit for fervice. The prudence and caution of the Spanifh admiral rendered this project abortive: inftead of purfuing
the regular and accuftomed track, he fteered direct for
Guadaloupe, from whence having difpatched a frigate

to

to inform the count de Guichen of his arrival, and
folicit a union of their force, he was accordingly
joined very foon afterwards by eighteen ſhips of the
line, which had been leaſt damaged, and had been
again put in a good condition for ſervice. The ſtrength
of the combined armaments, being conſequently rendered nearly double that of the fleet under the orders of
ſir George, the latter was under the painful neceſſity
of continuing inactive, or acting merely on the defen-
ſive, till his reinforcements, expected from Europe,
ſhould arrive : theſe, however, did not reach the Weſt
Indies till towards the cloſe of the year, and when the
feaſon for naval operations in that quarter of the world
was over ; ſo that ſir George was not enabled to do
more, than make ſuch detachments as he conſidered
neceſſary for the protection of the different colonies,
and the convoy of the feveral fleets of merchant-veſſels
which were ready to ſail for Europe. Having executed this neceſſary duty, he proceeded to America
during the hurricane months with the remainder of
his force, conſiſting of eleven ſhips of the line, and
four-frigates.

No occurrence in any degree intereſting took place
during his abfence in the Weſt Indies, where on his
return, he witneſſed the effects of that dreadful deſola-
tion which had been cauſed by a terrible hurricane, which
laid waſte the greater part of thoſe unfortunate iſlands.
Intelligence having been received that the fortifications erected, and in poſſeſſion of the French, on the
iſland of St. Vincents, were materially injured by the
convulſion of nature, juſt mentioned, an attempt was

made

made by the British admiral, in conjunction with general Vaughan of the army, on that place. Reports,
however, proved the hopes of success more chimerical
than had been apprehended, and the enterprise was
suspended without the smallest loss or injury. Soon
after this event, the British fleet were joined by a reinforcement under the orders of rear-admiral Hood,
consisting of seven ships of the line.

Hostilities having commenced between Great Britain
and the United Provinces, immediate information of the
circumstance was accordingly dispatched to the British
admiral, and was accompanied by orders to possess himself of all the Dutch colonies and settlements, in that
quarter of the world. He accordingly proceeded with
his fleet to St. Eustatia, which surrendered at the first
summons, and every other of the Dutch possessions
followed the same example. The property, public
and private, found in the different colonies, particularly in St. Eustatia, was immense; the latter island
had long been the sole mart for provisions and naval
stores, in that quarter of the world; and the joint commanders in chief, under the pretext of the inhabitants
having acted contrary to the true faith of a neutral
power, and given a decided preference to the enemies
of Great Britain, by furnishing them with naval
stores, when they were refused to purchasers on the
part of Great Britain itself, declared the whole of the
property, stores, and merchandise, forfeited to the
crown. This conduct drew down a wonderful deal of
obloquy on the character of sir George, and his former
popularity vanished like a mist from before the eyes of
those

thofe who cenfured him. An unfortunate circumftance contributed to ftrengthen the virulence of his
enemies. He had received information that a French
fquadron of fome force was daily expected at Martinique, under the orders of count de Graffe; and for
the purpofe of intercepting him, he detached rear-
admirals Hood and Drake, with eighteen fhips of the
line belonging to his fleet; a force he confidered fully
adequate to the magnitude of the undertaking. The
intelligence unhappily proved erroneous; the force of
the French fquadron was infinitely fuperior to what
had been reprefented, for it amounted to twenty-one
capital fhips of the line; and being affifted by the
co-operative conduct of the French chef d'efcadre
at Martinique, who put to fea with all the fhips
previoufly in Fort Royal harbour, forced its way
into the deftined port, in fpite of every oppofition that
could be made by fir Samuel Hood and his colleague.
The circumftance of fir George having continued at
St. Euftatia, with two or three fhips only, was feized
with the utmoft avidity by his enemies, as affording a
frefh ground of attack on him: he was charged openly
in the houfe of commons, with having degraded the
character of a Britifh admiral; and debafed himfelf,
as well as difgraced the fervice, by acting in the capacity of a broker, and an auctioneer. The virulence of
party, however, has long affumed a fpecies of prefcrip-
tive right, to carry on its attacks by the aid of fcurrility
and abufe; the actual exiftence of facts being by no
means neceffary to the foundation of a political charge,
of their having taken place.

The

The caution of the enemy, and their superiority in respect to numbers, prevented any encounter ; but the island of Tobago having fallen into their hands, in spite of every exertion on the part of the British admiral to protect it from them, appears to have completed the catalogue of his alledged delinquencies : little suspected by his enemies was it, that the ensuing year would again raise him to his former proudly-establithed throne of popularity.

When the approach of the hurricane months, and the departure of the French admiral for America, made it again necessary for the British naval force to proceed thither, sir George resigned the command of the fleet to sir Samuel Hood, and shifting his flag to the Gibraltar, which ship needed some considerable repairs, sailed for England, where he arrived at the close of the year, though in a very indifferent state of health, for the recovery of which he had returned home. Immediately on his arrival, his conduct became the subject of parliamentary attack ; but he defended himself with so much spirit and apparent truth, that his enemies obtained no advantage over him. On the 6th of November he was advanced, on the death of the late lord Hawke, to be vice-admiral of Great Britain, and lieutenant of the navies and seas thereof, and was in a few days afterwards reinstated in his West Indian command. Having hoisted his flag on board the Arrogant, from which ship he very soon afterwards removed into the Formidable, of ninety guns, he proceeded to the West Indies, with a squadron consisting of twelve ships of the line ; and being joined by other reinforcements,

ments, as well as having formed a junction with fir
Samuel Hood, he found himfelf at the head of the
moft powerful Britifh armament, that had ever been
feen in thofe feas.. That of France was not inferior;
and after an immaterial fkirmifh, which took place on
the 9th of April, the conteft for the naval fuperiority
in the weftern world, was effectually decided in favour
of Britain, by the total difcomfiture of the compte de
Graffe on the 12th. The admiral himfelf in the Ville de
Paris, of one hundred and ten guns, together with the
Glorieux, Cæfar, and Hector, of feventy-four guns
each, and alfo the Ardent, of fixty-four, having been
captured; and one of feventy-four, fuppofed to be the
Diadem, funk in the action. Nor did the tide of fuccefs ftop here; for in a few days afterwards, fir Samuel
Hood, who had been detached in purfuit of the flying
enemy, with fuch fhips as had received leaft injury,
having fallen in with them, captured the Jafon and
Caton, of fixty-four guns each, together with a frigate and corvette. Sir George purfuing his courfe to
Jamaica, arrived in fafety with his prizes at Port
Royal on the 29th of the fame month; and it is almoft
needlefs to add, that the difcomfiture of the French prevented any renewal of r val encounter, during the remainder of the year. A complete change of the Britifh
miniftry having taken place at home, immediate orders
were difpatched for the recall of fir George, and admiral
Pigot was appointed his fucceffor. At this critical moment, the news of the victory obtained by the Britifh
fleet reached England, and the new minifters were
extremely anxious to revoke their own act; but admiral Pigot had abfolutely failed, ere the exprefs contain-

ing

ing the revokement of his commiffion reached Plymouth. With refpect to fir George, it has been obferved that fuccefs, as is almoft invariably the cafe,
raifed him from that indifferent rank in the public
opinion, in which he had been held for fome time,
through the clamour of thofe who condemned his
chaftifement of the Dutch, and he became exalted
once more, to the higheft pinnacle of popularity. The
people adored him; minifters careffed him; and the
fovereign ennobled him: for he was advanced by patent, bearing date June 19th, 1782, to the rank of a
peer of Great Britain, by the title of baron Rodney,
of Rodney Stoke, in the county of Somerfet. For
the better fupport of this dignity, and as a more fubftantial remuneration for the fervices juft ftated, the
houfe of commons, on the 1ft of July following, voted
him a penfion of two thoufand a-year, fettling it not
only on his lordfhip, but on fuch as fhould afterwards
fucceed to, and enjoy the title.

Nothing occurred material enough to demand our
particular notice, during the time of his lordfhip's continuance in the Weft Indies, from whence he returned,
foon after Mr. Pigot's arrival. Having fhifted his
flag on board the Montague, of feventy-four guns, he
failed from Port Royal on the 23d July, and arrived
without meeting with any extraordinary occurrence,
at the cove of Cork, on the 7th of September. After
this time, his lordfhip never took upon himfelf any
command, or interfered in public bufinefs, farther than
by his occafional attendance to his duty, as a peer in
parliament. He died in London, the 24th of May,
1792.

REAR.

Harding sc

RICH.ᵈ TYRELL ESQ.ᵉ

Pub May 1 1800 by Edwᵈ Harding 98 Pall Mall.

REAR-ADMIRAL TYRREL.

THIS gentleman, who was nephew to that brave and excellent officer, fir Peter Warren, was introduced into the naval fervice under the honourable aufpices of that admiral. After the regular, and neceffary probationary years of fervice in the different fubordinate ftations, he was at the clofe of the year 1743, raifed to the rank of poft captain, and appointed to the Launcefton. He does not appear to have been fortunate enough, to have found any opportunity of diftinguifhing himfelf during the remainder of the war; but his conduct after the conclufion of it, has entitled him to the higheft praife from hiftorians and others. It appears that the French governor-general of Martinique, had not only invited fettlers to eftablifh themfelves on the ifland of Tobago, but had actually landed a force of three hundred men, and erected batteries for their protection ; the governor of Barbadoes being informed of this circumftance, difpatched captain Tyrrel, in a frigate, to afcertain the fact. Finding the intelligence correct, he made fo fpirited a reprefentation to the French commanding officer, that

he

he immediately took advantage of the night, reimbarked his troops, and returned to Martinique. In 1755, this gentleman commanded the Ipfwich; but is not again noticed, until his appointment in the year 1758, to be captain of the Buckingham, of fixty-fix guns, in which he was prefently afterwards ordered to the Weft Indies. Almoft immediately fubfequent to his arrival, the Buckingham was detached, in company with the Cambridge, to attack a fort in the ifland of Martinique, under which a number of fmall privateers were accuftomed to take fhelter; and at the very hour of the attack, there were four veffels of that defcription anchored under its guns. The fort, however, was very foon deftroyed, together with three of the veffels, and the fourth was carried out as a prize by the conquerors. In the month of November following, he moft pre-eminently diftinguifhed himfelf, in a defperate, and ever-memorable encounter with the Floriffant, a large French fhip of war, of feventy-four guns, and two frigates. After a long conteft * the Floriffant ftruck, and the two frigates immediately fled; but the Buckingham herfelf had been fo dreadfully difabled in the very unequal encounter, that it was not poffible to take poffeffion of the prize with the neceffary expedition; and the enemy, deriving advantage from that circumftance, and aided by the approach of night, contrived to fet their tattered fails, and were fortunate enough to effect their efcape.

* Mr. Tyrrel received feveral wounds in the action, and loft three of the fingers of his right hand.

No

No further particular mention is made of Mr. Tyrrel during the time he continued in the West Indies, from whence he returned in the month of March, with the dispatches from commodore Moore, containing an account of the attack made in the month of January preceding, on the island of Martinique; and that more successful one, which succeeded it, on Guadaloupe. It is almost needless to add, he was most graciously and affectionately received by his majesty, to whom he was introduced, immediately on his arrival, by lord Anson. In a few months afterwards he was appointed to the Foudroyant, of eighty guns, a ship recently captured from the French, and esteemed at that time the finest of her class in the world. This appears to have been the last command he ever held as a private captain, and he is not known to have met with any second opportunity, of adding to that celebrity which he had already gained. In the month of October 1762, he was raised to the rank of rear-admiral of the white; but was not employed till after the conclusion of the war, when he was appointed commander in chief on the Antigua station. By his vigilance and attention, which were ever conspicuous, he frustrated a scheme which the French had in contemplation, of forming a settlement on some of the islands adjacent to Cayenne. This is the only mention we find made of him during the time he held the command, which he quitted in the following year. Unhappily, dying on board the Princess Louisa, his flag-ship, when on his return to England, on the 27th of June 1766, his corpse was, at his own desire, thrown into the sea.

LORD

LORD VISCOUNT KEPPEL.

───────

THIS nobleman was the second son to William Anne, second earl of Albemarle, and the lady Anne Lenox, daughter of Charles Lenox, first duke of Richmond. He was born on the 2d of April 1725; and having attached himself to the naval service, was sent at a very early age to sea, under the protection and care of commodore Anson, when that gentleman was ordered to the South Seas. Of the few hostile encounters in which this armament was concerned, the attack of Paita may be remembered among the most important; and Mr. Keppel is recorded as having experienced in the trifling defence made by the enemy, a very narrow and singular escape. He accompanied Mr. afterwards sir Percy Brett, who commanded; and one of the few random shot fired at the boats, shaved, as is expressed in the account of commodore Anson's voyage, the peak of a jockey-cap he then wore, close to his temple. Mr. Keppel was, on the capture of the Spanish galleon, promoted to the rank of lieutenant; and almost immediately after his return to England,

was,

Pubd. June 1 1801 by E Harding 98 Pall Mall

THE HON^{BLE} AUGUSTUS KEPPEL

was, in the month of September 1744, appointed commander of a floop of war, from whence he was, in the month of December, ftill further advanced to be captain of the Sapphire frigate. He retained this command two years, and being conftantly employed as a cruifer, his diligence and activity were rewarded with a confiderable number of important prizes. In 1746, he became captain of the Maidftone, of fifty guns, in which he had the misfortune to be wrecked off the coaft of France, in confequence of running too near the fhore in purfuit of a French privateer. Being moft honourably acquitted of all blame, in refpect to the misfortune juft mentioned, he was appointed to the Anfon, a new fhip, of fixty-four guns; but the war then drawing near to a clofe, no further mention is made of him till his appointment to command with the rank of commodore, on the Mediterranean ftation, whither he immediately repaired, having hoifted his broad pendant on board the Centurion, of fifty guns. He very confpicuoufly diftinguifhed himfelf, while thus employed, by the firmnefs of his conduct towards divers of the piratical ftates on the coaft of Barbary; feveral petty depredations which they had committed, received every poffible recompenfe, and the fubmiffive conduct of the deys themfelves, appeared fully to promife a greater propriety of behaviour in future. He returned from the Streights in the month of Auguft 1753, and in the enfuing year again hoifted his broad pendant on board the Centurion, as commanding officer of the fhips of war fent to North America, for the purpofe of protecting thither a fleet of tranfports, having on board

general

general Braddock, with a confiderable body of regular troops. The unfortunate general was repeatedly loud in his praifes of Mr. Keppel's conduct, and moft gratefully acknowledged the affiftance he received from him, on all occafions, where his aid was neceffary; particularly his having furnifhed him with cannon from his fhips, the artillery which was fent with the army, being by no means adequate to the exigencies of the fervice *.

After the defeat of Mr. Braddock, the commodore returned to Europe, as a paffenger on board the Sea-horfe; and a number of fhips of war being at that time ordered for equipment, in confequence of an appre-hended rupture with France, he was almoft immedi-ately appointed to the Swiftfure, from which fhip he prefently removed into the Torbay. In the fhip laft mentioned he continued five years, always moft actively employed, but without being placed in any fituation where he could particularly diftinguifh him-felf, till the year 1758, when he was appointed com-mander in chief of the expedition fent againft the French fettlement at Goree, on the coaft of Africa. The force placed under his orders confifted of three fhips of the line, exclufive of the Torbay, two fmaller fhips of two decks, a floop of war, two bomb-ketches, and a fire-fhip; together with a fufficient number of tranfports, having on board two regiments of foldiers.

* In 1755, he was chofen reprefentative in parliament for the city of Chichefter; and at the general election he was returned for Windfor, which place he continued to reprefent through every fucceeding parliament till 1780, when his great popularity procured his return for the county of Surrey.

He

He failed from England on the 19th of October, and experienced a variety of misfortunes, having been overtaken by the most dreadfully tempestuous weather, when on his paffage. One of the ships under his command, the Litchfield, of fifty guns, together with a transport, were wrecked on the coast of Barbary; but with the remainder of his force he came to anchor off the island of Goree, on the 24th of December. The neceffary difpofitions being made for the attack, the whole of the fquadron proceeded to the pofts allotted them on the 28th, and fo tremendous was their fire, that in a very short time every one of the batteries being filenced, the fort, which was extremely well fortified, together with the whole of the diftrict, which it had been erected to protect, furrendered to the Britifh arms. On his return from this fervice, in the enfuing fpring, he ftruck his broad pendant, and continued to ferve during the whole of the year, as a private captain in the fleet commanded by fir Edward Hawke, and held a very diftinguifhed fhare in the defeat of the French fleet, under the marquis de Conflans: the Thefée, of feventy-four guns, having, as is currently reported, been funk by the fire of the Torbay. In 1760*, Mr. Keppel removed into the Valiant; and after ferving during the fummer, as a private captain under fir Edward Hawke, and occafionally commanding one of the fmall armaments, at that time employed in cruifing off the coaft of France, he was, towards its

* In the month of February he was appointed colonel of the Plymouth divifion of marines.

conclufion,

conclusion, chosen to command a squadron consisting of ten ships of the line, besides frigates and smaller vessels, destined for some expedition, the real object of which has never yet been clearly known, and which the death of his late majesty, an event which took place a few days before it would have been ready to have put to sea, prevented from sailing. Early in the ensuing year, it was determined by the British minister that it should proceed against Belleisle; and although the expedition met with some of those occasional checks, to which all naval and military enterprises are liable, yet it ultimately proved completely successful. The citadel of Palais capitulated on the 7th of June, and after the reduction of the place, Mr. Keppel continued on the same station to cover, and protect it from any attempt that might be made on the part of France, to wrest it back from the arms of Britain.

In the month of January following, Mr. Keppel, with the whole of his squadron, was driven from their station in a violent gale of wind, and did not again resume his former occupation, being appointed to command one of the divisions of the fleet then collecting under the orders of sir George Pocock, and destined for the expedition against the Havannah. On the arrival of the armament off that place, Mr. Keppel was appointed to cover the landing with a detachment of six ships of the line, a service he very happily and diligently performed. On the 22d of October 1762, he was promoted to the rank of rear-admiral of the blue squadron; and having continued commander in chief at the Havannah, after the return of the greater part

of

of the fleet to England, captured, owing to the able
difpofition of his cruifers, a number of very valuable
fhips, both from the French, and the Spaniards.   He
held no command after his return to Europe, till the
month of September 1766*, when he had the honour
of convoying and attending the queen of Denmark to
Holland.   In the month of October 1770, he was
appointed to command a fquadron ordered to be fitted
out with the utmoft expedition, in confequence of an
apprehended rupture with Spain, relative to the Falkland iflands. The difpute was, however, amicably
adjufted, and the armament ordered to be difmantled,
without having ever put to fea.

At the commencement of the year 1778, it being
forefeen that a rupture with France was become, as it
were, inevitable, Mr. Keppel was promoted to be
admiral of the blue fquadron, and was appointed commander in chief of the fleet, intended in the actual
event of a war, for home, or channel fervice. Having
hoifted his flag, in the month of March, on board the
Prince George, of ninety guns, from whence he afterwards removed it on board the Victory, he failed from
St. Helen's on the 8th of June, at the head of a fleet

* In 1763, he was appointed one of the grooms of his majefty's bedchamber, and on the 31ft of July 1765, a commiffioner for executing the
office of lord high admiral; both of which honourable employments he refigned in the month of December 1766. On the 18th of October 1770, he
was advanced to be rear-admiral of the red; and on the 24th of the fame
month to be vice-admiral of the blue; on the 31ft of March 1775, he
was ftill further promoted to be vice-admiral of the white, as he was moreover to the fame rank in the red fquadron on the 3d of February 1776.

confiſting of twenty-one ſhips of two and three decks, three frigates, and as many ſmaller veſſels. On the 27th of the ſame month, the look-out ſhips having diſcovered two French frigates, together with their tenders, apparently employed in reconnoitring the fleet; the frigates and men of war neareſt them were ordered, by ſignal from the commander in chief, to bring them under his ſtern; a command which their captains not thinking proper to comply with, one of them was detained, the other, which was a frigate of the largeſt claſs, called the Belle Poule, was purſued to a conſiderable diſtance, and even till they came in ſight of the French coaſt, by an Engliſh frigate called the Arethuſa, of very inferior force; when, after a ſmart conteſt, both ſhips being completely diſabled, the Frenchman effected his eſcape. This apparently determined hoſtile conduct, induced the admiral to detain a ſecond frigate, which he caſually fell in with a few days afterwards; and having procured intelligence from papers found on board the two veſſels juſt mentioned, that the force of the French fleet was much ſuperior to his own, he deemed it prudent to return back to port, for the purpoſe of procuring a reinforcement. Being accordingly joined by all the ſhips that were ready, he again put to ſea on the 10th of July, and very ſoon diſcovered the fleet of the enemy. Several days were ſpent, according to the practice of French naval tactics at that time, in manœuvring; but at length the whole of their fleet was brought to a general action on the 27th of July.

This encounter, when compared with others bearing the ſame denomination, namely, that of a

general

general action between two powerful fleets, certainly deserved no more dignified appellation than that of an indecisive skirmish: the event, however, proved the source of one of the greatest political convulsions, in respect to opinion, that has perhaps ever occurred in the annals of Britain. It is elsewhere observed, and we consider with the strictest truth, that the political contest, the diversity of opinions, the private as well as public animosities which this remarkable event gave birth to, are still too recent in the minds of all, to make it proper or decent for us to enter into any animadversions, or remarks on the subject; we shall therefore confine ourselves strictly to the relation of mere facts; for, when men present at the encounter, and of the highest reputation in the service, have entertained, and publicly declared sentiments the most opposite from each other, we shall not presume to enter either into exculpation, or censure. We cannot, however, refrain from inserting a declaration, as made by the count d'Orvilliers himself, given us by a friend, who, soon after the action, was a prisoner at Brest: the cool dispassionate opinion of an honourable enemy is, perhaps, among the best evidence that can ever be adduced on any occasion whatever. The count said, " That during the action itself the English had, as he conceived, the advantage; but that, after the firing ceased, he had *out-manœuvred* Mr. Keppel." On canvassing his declaration a little closer, it appeared the count imagined he had completely misled and deceived the British admiral, by impressing on him an idea, that he (the count) intended to renew the action

K k 2

on

on the morrow. This Mr. Keppel himfelf, in great meafure, admits to be true, when he fays in his difpatches, " I allowed their doing it" (forming their line without moleftation), " thinking they meant handfomely to try their force with us next day."

Mr. Keppel returned into port, for the purpofe of refitting thofe fhips of the fleet which had received any material damage, and failed from Plymouth on the 23d of Auguft to join the divifions of fir Robert Harland and fir Hugh Pallifer, which had put to fea on the preceding day. Nothing, however, fufficiently material to merit notice took place, during the remainder of the naval campaign, which was finally clofed by the return of Mr. Keppel into port on the 28th of October. The fecret murmurs occafioned by the indecifive action in the month of July, though fmothered for a confiderable time, at length began to manifeft themfelves fufficiently to fhew that the fire of difcontent exifted, though latent, and concealed; the friends of Keppel were partial enough to him, to caft the whole blame of the mifcarriage on fir Hugh Pallifer; and it could not be expected that the latter, with his party, would endure the obloquy patiently, while there appeared any poffible means of getting rid of it: invective begot recrimination, and the houfes of parliament rang with the clamours of the different parties. Sir Hugh Pallifer at length preferred a fpecific charge againft Mr. Keppel at the admiralty board, and demanded a court martial, which, notwithftanding moderate men unanimoufly conceived it improper and impolitic fhould be inftituted, after fo long an interval, and a memorial

rial

rial figned by feveral of thofe who had been, and were then confidered among the leading and moft diftinguifhed characters in the Britifh navy, was prefented to his majefty, befeeching him to ftop all further proceedings, was, neverthelefs, commanded to be profecuted in the regular manner. An order was accordingly iffued to fir Thomas Pye, admiral of the white, to hold a court martial for the trial of Mr. Keppel, on the 7th of January: it confequently met on that day on board the Britannia. After going through the neceffary forms of fwearing in the members, it adjourned to the governor's houfe; a particular act of parliament having, for the accommodation of Mr. Keppel, who was extremely indifpofed, been paffed for the purpofe of authorizing a meafure, till then unprecedented. It is not within our limits to give even an abridged detail of the trial, which continued, through feveral fhort intervening adjournments, till the 11th of February: fuffice it, that we briefly ftate, Mr. Keppel was acquitted. Were we even competent to fo arduous an undertaking, delicacy to both perfons, forbids our making the fmalleft comment on an event fo recent, except that the demon of party appears, in many inftances, on both fides of the queftion, to have taken full poffeffion of many; who, both as officers and men, ftood very defervedly in the higheft rank of public opinion. Mr. Keppel having, through reafons already given, poffeffed confiderably the greateft fhare of what is called popularity, was congratulated on his acquittal by his private friends and his public partifans, with a warmth certainly never yet exceeded, and we fancy but feldom equalled.

The

The admiral, however, ceafed to be employed, a circumftance rather naturally to be expected than wondered at, confidering not only the extraordinary political fchifm which his cafe and conduct had created, but alfo the very fevere animadverfions made by his friends, on the behaviour of minifters towards him. He continued, however, conftantly to attend in parliament, where his mere prefence on fome occafions, and the fevere remarks which fometimes fell from him, in the courfe of debate, ferved to fan the ftill unextinguifhed embers of rancour, till at length a political revolution put a period to their exiftence. The complete overthrow of the miniftry then exifting, in the month of March 1782, ferved to introduce Mr. Keppel to his country once more, in a public character, and indeed a more elevated one, than any in which he had been hitherto feen: he was conftituted firft commiffioner of the admiralty, and fworn in one of the members of the privy council; an advancement attended immediately afterwards by profeffional promotion, and his exaltation to the rank of vifcount. On the 8th of April he was made admiral of the white, and on the 29th of the fame month was created vifcount Keppel, of Elvedon, in the county of Suffolk.

His ftation of firft commiffioner of the admiralty he quitted for a few weeks, on the 28th of January 1783, but refumed it again on the 8th of April enfuing; the celebrated coalition then taking place between a felect number of his lordfhip's party, and feveral of the leading perfons of the former ex-miniftry, who had, in the preceding year, been ranked among the moft

violent

violent of his enemies. He retained his high ftation only till the 30th of December following, when a political convulfion, equal in extent to that which firft introduced him into it, caufed him finally to quit this public charaƈter of firft minifter of marine. He furvived but a very few years, dying on the 2d of Oƈtober 1786, having been long affliƈted with the gout, and other grievous bodily infirmities, in the fixty-third year of his age.

It has been obferved, that with many excellent qualities poffeffed by this noble lord, were certainly mingled fome failings, a confequence naturally attendant on the imperfeƈtion of human nature; and thofe who wifh to imprefs on pofterity an idea of perfeƈt charaƈter in any individual, are certainly guilty of premeditated falfehood and flattery.

EARL

EARL OF BRISTOL.

THIS nobleman was the fecond fon of John, lord Hervey, and Mary, daughter of brigadier-general Nicholas Le Pell, at the time of her marriage one of the maids of honour to her royal highnefs Caroline, then princefs of Wales: he was, confequently, grand-fon to John, firft earl of Briftol. He was born on the 19th of May 1724, and being advanced to the rank of lieutenant in the navy, ere he had attained the age of twenty years, and ferved in that capacity on board the Cornwall, under vice-admiral Davers, on the Jamaica ftation. In the month of September 1746, he was promoted to be commander of the Porcupine floop. In this veffel, which was employed as a cruifer, he had the fingular good fortune to fall in with and capture a French privateer, belonging to Cherbourg, which had been, for many years, the continued depredator on the commerce of Britain, and was remarked for having captured a greater number of prizes, than any three cruifers the enemy poffeffed. In the month of January 1747, he was advanced to be captain of the Princeffa,

of

Harding sc

THE HON^{BLE} AUGUSTUS HERVEY.

Pub. Apr. 1.1800. by Edwd Harding N° 98 Pall Mall.

of feventy guns; and having removed in the enfuing year on board the Phœnix, a fmall frigate, was difpatched to the Mediterranean with information that hoftilities had ceafed between Great Britain, France, and Spain. He returned back to England in a fhort time, but was reappointed to the fame fhip in 1751, and again ordered to the Streights, where he continued and retained the fame command, till after the recommencement of hoftilities with France, in 1756. On the arrival of Mr. Byng, whofe fquadron was deftitute of a fire-fhip, captain Hervey very fpiritedly offered that the Phœnix fhould be converted to that ufe; and propofed a plan for doing it, without depriving the admiral of her fervices as a frigate, till the fignal fhould be made for him to prime. The fuggeftion was received with much thankfulnefs by the unfortunate Mr. Byng; but the circumftances attendant on the action, did not render the ufe of a fire-fhip neceffary, though the Phœnix had been properly prepared for that purpofe.

After the termination of the indecifive engagement which took place, captain Hervey was appointed to the Defiance, as fucceffor to captain Andrews, who had fallen in the fhort encounter; and being afterwards ordered home as a witnefs on the impending trial of his admiral, was immediately after its conclufion promoted to the Hampton Court, of feventy-four guns, and fent back to his former ftation. While in this fhip, he was fortunate enough to make feveral important prizes, and to deftroy a very large French frigate, which ran herfelf on fhore on the ifland of Majorca, in the hope of efcaping. The expectation of

the

the enemy, was founded on the exertions they made in landing several of the ship's guns, and forming a battery on shore for their protection; but captain Hervey, despising the natural and artificial impediments thrown in his way, and having run the Hampton Court as close in, as the depth of water would permit, soon compelled his antagonists to abandon both their vessel and their battery, after having set the former on fire. In 1758, he removed into the Monmouth, of sixty-four guns; and in the month of July distinguished himself, for a second time, in the destruction of another French man of war, called the Rose, which he drove on shore on the island of Malta, and set on fire. In 1759, he returned to England, and still continuing in the Monmouth, was employed on the home, or channel service. In the month of July in this year, he behaved with extraordinary gallantry, having attacked four French ships, which attempted to get into the port of Brest, in despite of him, through the passage De Tour. Captain Hervey, who had the Pallas frigate in company, immediately on discovering them, got under way, and accompanied by the frigate, worked up to the enemies' ships, which anchoring under some batteries, cannonaded and threw shells at the assailants as they went in. The latter were not in the least intimidated by so spirited a resistance; the boats, setting all opposition at defiance, boarded, cut the cables, and brought off all the four ships, which had hoisted Swedish colours, and were laden with cannon and warlike stores for the use of the enemies' fleet.

The

The Monmouth and Pallas, by a conftant and well-directed fire, drove the people in the forts and batteries from their pofts, and the prizes were carried off by the frigate, having received very little damage. The Monmouth maintained her ftation till they were all in fafety, and then followed herfelf, having fuftained no injury, or, at moft, what was very trivial; being un-oppofed by any part of the enemies' naval force, though they had at that very time no lefs than four flags flying in full view of the whole tranfaction, and twenty fail of the line completely ready for fea. He is not otherwife particularly noticed till his appointment in the enfuing fpring to be captain of the Dragon, on board which fhip he ferved in 1761, under the command of Mr. Keppel, in the expedition againft Belleifle; and having in the autumn of the fame year proceeded to the Weft Indies with commodore Barton, was ordered by rear-admiral Rodney, who commanded at the attack of Martinique, to filence a battery at Grand Ance, preparatory to the landing of the troops: this fervice he very fpiritedly and expeditioufly performed. He afterwards commanded the left divifion of the boats which landed the troops; and on the conqueft of Martinique being effected, was fent with a detachment againft St. Lucia, of which ifland he took poffeffion without meeting with any refiftance.

In 1762, he ferved under fir George Pocock in the attack upon the Havannah, and was one of the firft officers employed in active fervice when the fleet approached the ifland of Cuba, being ordered to attack the caftle, which defended the river Coximar. This

fervice

fervice he effected without difficulty, and thereby opened an unmolefted paffage for the earl of Albemarle and the army, to the ground which it was deftined to occupy during the meditated fiege. He was afterwards fent, together with the captains Gooftry and Barnet, in the Cambridge and Marlborough, to attack the Moro caftle from the feaward, and thereby to create a diverfion in favour of the land batteries. This fervice was performed with much coolnefs and intrepidity, but not without confiderable lofs; the Dragon alone, though lefs damaged than the Cambridge, having had fifty-three men killed and wounded: fhe had the mif- fortune almoft to touch the ground on the falling of the tide, but got off without damage, after having ftaved her water-cafks. Captain Hervey was fent home by the admiral, with the welcome intelligence of the Havannah having furrendered; and on his paffage to England, had the good fortune to fall in with, and capture a large French frigate, laden with military ftores for Newfoundland; and peace very foon follow- ing his arrival in England, Mr. Hervey quitted the Dragon, and was appointed to command the Centu- rion, of fifty guns, the fhip on board which his royal highnefs the duke of York had hoifted his flag, as vice- admiral of the blue. This was the laft naval com- mand he ever held.

At the general election in 1761, he was returned one of the reprefentatives for St. Edmondfbury; but vacated his feat in the month of April 1763, on being appointed colonel of the Plymouth divifion of marines. In the month of November following, he was nomi-

nated

nated one of the grooms of his majesty's bedchamber; and was soon after returned to parliament, as member for the borough of Saltash. In 1767, he rendered himself very popular in the navy, by a motion, made by him in parliament, for an augmentation of one shilling per day in the pay of lieutenants. This highly commendable augmentation, and measure he promoted and pursued, with unabated perseverance, till success at last crowned his very laudable, endeavours; endeavours certainly meriting the highest praise, as their object was the relief of a brave and oppressed body of officers, many of whom, on account of the very scanty pittance allowed them, suffered every extremity of want and distress. At the general election in 1768, he was again returned for the same place he before represented, St. Edmondsbury, as he was moreover for the third time, at the general election which took place at the end of the year 1774. On the 26th of January 1771, he was appointed one of the commissioners for executing the office of lord high admiral. This station, together with the office of groom of the bedchamber, and his command in the marines, he retained, till by the death of George William, the second earl of Bristol, he succeeded to the peerage, on the 18th of March 1775. He immediately resigned all his appointments, and was, on the 31st of the same month, promoted to be rear-admiral of the blue: on the 28th of April 1777, he was further advanced to be rear-admiral of the white, as he moreover was on the 23d of January 1778, to be rear of the red; and on the 19th of March 1779, to be vice-admiral of the blue.

He

He did not long furvive this his laft advancement, dying at his houfe in St. James's Square on the 23d of December 1779, in the fifty-fixth year of his age.

On the 4th of Auguft 1744, being then fcarcely twenty years old, and a lieutenant only in the navy, he was privately married to Mifs Chudleigh, at that time one of the maids of honour to her royal highnefs the princefs of Wales: they afterwards lived together privately in London for a fhort time, till his lordfhip was ordered on fervice to the Mediterranean. When he returned, after an abfence of nearly a year and a half, their intercourfe was again renewed; but a mif-underftanding prefently fucceeding, a mutual indifference arofe, which ended firft in a feparation, and fecondly, in an ecclefiaftical divorce. The lady, under the idea of this fentence, having totally, and in a legal fenfe, annulled the marriage, efpoufed his grace the duke of Kingfton. The event is too recent to be forgotten, or to require any further account. His lordfhip, how-ever, entered into no other matrimonial contract; and the child, which was the iffue of this marriage, having died when an infant, the title defcended, on his lord-fhip's deceafe, to his brother, the right reverend Frederic, lord bifhop of Derry, in the kingdom of Ireland.

COMMODORE

COMMODORE GRIFFITH

From an Original Miniature in the Possession of Capt. Walter Booth

Pub.ᵈ Aug. 1, 1800, by Edw. Harding 98 Pall Mall

COMMODORE WALTER GRIFFITH.

THIS gentleman was the defcendant of a very ancient and refpectable Welfh family, and he himfelf
poffeffed a landed property, far from inconfiderable, in
the county of Merioneth. He was promoted to the
rank of lieutenant on the 7th of May 1755, and continued to act in the fame ftation for the fpace of
four years. During the latter part of his fervice in
the capacity juft mentioned, he was lieutenant of the
Royal George, the flag-fhip of admiral lord Anfon.
He was promoted, after holding the intermediate rank
of commander, during a few days only, for mere
form's fake, and to comply with the cuftomary eti-
quette of the naval fervice, to be captain of the Gibraltar, a poft-fhip, of twenty guns, by commiffion
bearing date the 11th of December 1759. That fhip
was then employed on the Mediterranean ftation,
where captain Griffith remained, ftill retaining the
fame command, till after the ceffation of hoftilities;
and after his return to England continued captain of
the Gibraltar, it being one of the fhips retained on the

peace

peace eſtabliſhment, for the cuſtomary period of three years. From this time till the year 1770, he is not known to have held any commiſſion, but was then appointed to the Namur, a ſecond rate, one of the ſhips ordered to be equipped on the apprehenſion of a rupture with Spain; but, which preſently ſubſiding, put a period to captain Griffith's command. In 1776, he was appointed to the Nonſuch, of ſixty-four guns, one of the ſhips employed in cruiſing in ſoundings, and off the coaſt of France, for the purpoſe of reſtraining the American commerce; an occupation in which he appears to have been ſo ill rewarded, that he is not known to have taken more than one, or two inconſiderable prizes. Early in the year 1778, he was ordered to America; and having ſailed at the ſame time with a convoy of tranſports, having on board a reinforcement of troops and recruits for the army, he arrived at New York on the 25th of May, three days before his companions, which all got in ſafe. He was afterwards employed, and much diſtinguiſhed himſelf, in a variety of little deſultory expeditions, which, notwithſtanding the conduct of this gentleman, on thoſe occaſions, reflected on him much honour, are ſcarcely of ſufficient conſequence to require any particular detail. The moſt material operation in which he was engaged, during the year 1778, appears to have been that of attending lord Howe, when he put to ſea in the month of Auguſt, hoping, though with a force ſo much inferior, ſome opportunity might preſent itſelf that might enable him to attack the French fleet to advantage. At the cloſe of the year, captain Griffith

proceeded

proceeded to the Weſt Indies, with the ſquadron and convoy under commodore Hotham. He continued to ſerve in the Nonſuch during the greater part of the ſummer, and was preſent at the encounter off Grenada; but does not appear to have been materially engaged, as the name of the Nonſuch is totally omitted by the admiral in the return of the killed and wounded. When Mr. Byron ſailed for Europe, he left rear-admiral Parker commander in chief on the Weſt India ſtation, and that gentleman removed his flag into the Princeſs Royal. Captain Griffith ſucceeded him in the Conqueror; but unhappily did not long ſurvive, being killed in a trivial ſkirmiſh with the French ſquadron in Port Royal bay, on the 18th of December following.

No greater eulogium need, or indeed can be paid to the memory of this brave and good man, than the conciſe, but at the ſame time elegant ſentence, which concludes the official account, given by the commander in chief, of the action in which he fell. After moſt honourably expatiating on his merits, and pathetically lamenting his death, he adds, " *The ſervice cannot loſe a better officer or a better man.*"

GENERAL INDEX

TO THE NAMES OF THOSE WHOSE MEMOIRS ARE
GIVEN IN THE FIRST AND SECOND VOLUME.

——————

N. B. *Afterisks are affixed to the Names of those whose Portraits are given.—The Letters* L. H. A. *mean Lord High Admiral.*

——————

	Vol.	Page
*ALBEMARLE, George Monk, duke of	i.	386
Allen, fir Thomas	i.	461
Anfon, George, lord	ii.	380
Arundel, fir John	i.	103
Arundel, Richard Fitz Alan, earl of	i.	106
Afhby, fir John	ii.	35
Ayfcough, fir George	i.	434
Balchen, fir John	ii.	219
Barnet, commodore	ii.	445
Bedford, John de Lancafter, duke of	i.	142
Bedford, John, lord Ruffell, duke of, L. H. A.	i.	212
Benbow, John, vice-admiral	ii.	127
Berkeley, fir William	i.	456
Berkeley, of Stratton, John, lord	ii.	91
Berkeley, James, earl of	ii.	251

INDEX.

Vol. Page

*Blake, admiral .... i. 365
*Boscawen, hon. Edward .... ii. 466
 Botetourt, John de .... i. 53
*Bristol, Augustus Hervey, earl of ...... ii. 520
 Brown, commodore .... ii. 364
*Buckingham, Villiers, duke of, L. H. A. ...... i. 357
*Byng, admiral, hon. George .... ii. 431

 Cabot, Sebastian .... i. 162
 Cavendish, Thomas, esq. .... i. 299
 Cornwall, captain .... ii. 410
 Cumberland, George Clifford, earl of .... i. 332

 Dampier, captain William .... ii. 228
 Delaval, sir Ralph .... ii. 272
*Drake, sir Francis .... i. 265
 Dudley, sir Robert .... i. 306
 Duffus, Kenneth, lord .... ii. 351

 Effingham, William Howard, lord of .... i. 230
 Effingham, Charles Howard, baron of, afterwards
     earl of Nottingham, L. H. A. .... i. 238

 Fenton, captain Edward .... i. 302
 Frobisher, sir Martin .... i. 283

 Gilbert, sir Humphrey .... i. 286
*Grenville, sir Richard .... i. 281
*Griffith, commodore .... ii. 527

*Haddock, sir Richard .... ii. 3
 Haddock, admiral Nicholas .... ii. 340
*Hardy, sir Charles .... ii. 487
 Harman, sir John .... i. 464

Hawke,

INDEX.

	Vol.	Page
*Hawke, lord	ii.	453
*Hawkins, sir John	i.	255
Hawkins, sir Richard	i.	296
*Holles, sir Tretswell	i.	454
Holmes, sir Robert	i.	458
*Howard, sir Edward, L. H. A.	i.	178
Howard, sir Thomas, afterward earl of Surrey and duke of Norfolk, L. H. A.	i.	183
Hosier, sir Francis	ii.	211
Huntingdon, William de Clinton, earl of	i.	72
Huntingdon, William, lord Clinton and Say, earl of	i.	138
*Jennings, sir John, knight	ii.	147
*Jordan, sir Joseph	i.	440
Jumper, sir William, knight	ii.	182
Kempthone, sir John	i.	430
Kent, Hubert de Burgh, earl of	i.	23
*Keppel, lord	ii.	508
Knevet, sir Thomas	i.	176
Lawson, sir John	i.	425
*Leake, sir John	ii.	97
Lee, vice-admiral, hon. Fitzroy Henry	ii.	440
Leibourne, William de	i.	51
Lestock, admiral Richard	ii.	321
Lincoln, William, lord Clinton and Say, earl of, L. H. A.	i.	226
Mansel, sir Robert	i.	347
Mathews, admiral Thomas	ii.	266
*Mingh, sir Christopher	i.	451
Monson, sir William	i.	350
Morley, Robert de	i.	58

Narborough,

INDEX.

	Vol.	Page
Narborough, fir John	ii.	11
Norreys, fir John	i.	262
Norris, fir John	ii.	161
Northumberland, John Dudley, vifcount Lifle, duke of	i.	198
*Northumberland, Henry Percy, earl of	i.	291
Ogle, fir Chaloner	ii.	357
*Orford, Edward Ruffel, earl of	ii.	39
Ofborne, admiral Henry	ii.	435
Pembroke, John de Haftings, earl of	i.	82
*Pembroke, Thomas, earl of, L. H. A.	ii.	157
Pendergaft, fir John	i.	136
Penn, fir William	i.	468
*Pennington, fir John	i.	354
Philpot, John	i.	99
*Pocock, fir George	ii.	475
Poynings, fir Edward	i.	169
*Rawleigh, fir Walter	i.	315
Reeves, fir William	i.	470
*Rodney, lord	ii.	491
*Rooke, fir George	ii.	51
*Rowley, fir William	ii.	375
*Rupert, prince	i.	416
Salifbury, William, earl of	i.	23
St. Loe, captain	ii.	369
*Sandwich, Edward Montague, earl of	i.	402
*Saunders, fir Charles	ii.	481
*Seymour, of Sudleigh, Thomas, lord, L. H. A.	i.	206
Shovell, fir Cloudefly	ii.	79
Southampton, William Fitzwilliams, earl of	i.	192

INDEX.

	Vol.	Page
*Spragge, fir Edward	i.	441
Stayner, fir Richard	i.	413
*Terne, captain Henry	i.	453
Tiptoff, Robert	i.	44
Torrington, Arthur Herbert, earl of	ii.	18
*Torrington, George Byng, lord vifcount	ii.	111
*Tyrrel, rear-admiral Richard	ii.	505
*Vernon, admiral Edward	ii.	283
*Wager, fir Charles	ii.	192
Walton, fir George	ii.	242
*Warren, fir Peter	ii.	416
Warwick, Ambrofe Dudley, earl of	i.	236
Willoughby, fir Hugh	i.	220
Winter, fir William	i.	223
Worcefter, fir Thomas Percy, earl of	i.	120
*York, James, duke of, L. H. A.	i.	473

END OF VOL. II.

S. GOSWELL, Printer, Little Queen Street, Holborn.

Lightning Source UK Ltd.
Milton Keynes UK
UKOW011851270112

186201UK00006B/276/P